Logic and Contemporary Rhetoric

Logic and Contemporary Rhetoric

The Use of Reason in Everyday Life

Fifth Edition

Howard Kahane

University of Maryland
Baltimore County

Wadsworth Publishing Company
A Division of Wadsworth, Inc.
Belmont, California

Philosophy Editor: *Kenneth King*
Production Editor: *Hal Lockwood, Bookman*
                 Productions
Print Buyer: *Randy Hurst*
Designer: *Paula Shuhert*
Copy Editor: *Sylvia Stein*
Compositor: *Carlisle Communications*
Signing Representative: *Robert Gormley*

Printed in the United States of America
1 2 3 4 5 6 7 8 9 10—92 91 90 89 88

ISBN 0-534-09018-4

Library of Congress Cataloging in Publication Data

Kahane, Howard, 1928–
  Logic and contemporary rhetoric.

  Bibliography: p.
  Includes index.
  1. Fallacies (Logic) 2. Reasoning. 3. Judgment
(Logic) I. Title.
BC175.K25 1988   160   87-31719
ISBN 0-534-09018-4

For Bonny sweet Robin . . .

Ignorance is preferable to error; and he is less remote from the truth who believes nothing, than he who believes what is wrong.
— Thomas Jefferson

It ain't so much the things we don't know that get us in trouble. It's the things we know that ain't so.
— Artemus Ward

Nothing is so firmly believed as what we least know.
— Montaigne

Contents

*I do not pretend to know what
many ignorant men are sure of.*
　　　　　　—Clarence Darrow

*To know that we know what we
know, and that we do not know
what we do not know, that is true
knowledge.*
　　　　　　—Henry David Thoreau

We have met the enemy and he is us.
　　　　　　—Walt Kelly's "Pogo"

*Many people would sooner die than
think. In fact, they do.*
　　　　　　—Bertrand Russell

Preface

The purpose of this fifth edition of *Logic and Contemporary Rhetoric,* as of the previous four editions, is to help students improve their ability to reason well about everyday problems and issues. The intent is not to move students to the right or left on the social/political spectrum but to help them move *up* on the scale of rational sophistication.

The text contains examples and exercise items drawn from a broad range of sources—advertisements, political speeches, newspaper columns, and so on. It quotes testimony by Lt. Col. Oliver North before the Iran-Contra Congressional hearings, *Time* magazine on responses to the AIDS epidemic, disputed passages from recently censored public school textbooks, and canned letters sent by members of Congress in response to queries from constituents. Drawings by David Levine, Edward Sorel, Garry Trudeau, Hank Ketchum, Jules Feiffer, and others illustrate significant points in a lively and interesting manner. The strong point of *Logic and Contemporary Rhetoric* has always been, and still is, its ease of comprehension and its up-to-date and interesting material for students. Textbooks need not be dull!

Although the general subject matter covered by this new edition has not changed, a great deal of the text has been rewritten with dated items replaced by more current material and with improved organization, style, and flow. The book is now comprised of seven parts:

1. Chapter 1 introduces students to some basic ideas about cogent reasoning, including introductory material on deduction and induction, the importance of background information in the evaluation of arguments, and so on.

2. Chapters 2, 3, and 4 deal with fallacious reasoning, concentrating on how to avoid fallacies by becoming familiar with the types most frequently encountered.

3. Chapter 5 deals with psychological impediments to cogent reasoning such as self-deception, wishful thinking, rationalization, and prejudice.

4. Chapter 6 discusses the ways in which language itself can be used to manipulate thinking—for instance, via double-talk or long-winded locutions—and contains a section on sexism in language that is unique in critical thinking texts.

5. Chapter 7 deals with the analysis of more extended passages—argumentative essays, editorials, political speeches, and so on. It also contains a section on the construction of cogent, argumentative essays.

6. Chapters 8, 9, and 10 discuss three important sources of information that determine so many of our background beliefs—namely, advertising (singling out political ads for special scrutiny), the media (television, newspapers, radio, and magazines), and public school textbooks.

7. The Appendix provides students with additional material on deduction and induction, including some interesting new material on the calculation of probabilities—for instance, the probability of winning the various state lotteries.

In addition, a section at the back of the book supplies answers to selected exercise items. But it should be remembered that most of the exercise items in this text are drawn from everyday life, where shades of gray outnumber shades of black and white. The answers provided thus constitute one person's responses rather than definitive pronouncements. (Similar remarks apply to the answers to the remaining exercise items provided in the *Instructor's Manual* that accompanies *Logic and Contemporary Rhetoric.*)

This book is unique in bringing together all of these apparently diverse elements, and unique among books on good reasoning in dealing so extensively with information sources. In this complicated modern world, all of us are laymen most of the time and with respect to most topics. The ability to evaluate effectively the mass of "expert" information available to us in the media—to separate the wheat from the chaff—is thus crucial to reasoning well about everyday problems, whether of a personal nature (health problems) or of a social/political nature (the qualifications of candidates or their stances on particular issues).

Although the text contains much discussion of theory, this is *not* a treatise on the theory of cogent and fallacious reasoning. Rather, it is designed to help students learn *how* to reason cogently and avoid fallacy. That is why so many examples and exercise items have been included and why most of them have been extracted from everyday rhetoric. Learning how to reason well and how to evaluate the rhetoric of others is a skill that, like any skill, requires practice, and in this particular case, practice on the genuine article—actual examples drawn from everyday life. Perhaps the most important exercises in the text are those that require students to do things on their own—to find their own examples from the mass media and do their own analyses of this material, or to write letters to their own representatives in Congress or to experts on various controversial topics. Classroom discussions of examples that students themselves have discovered is an excellent way to bring the topic of critical thinking to life. Another teaching device that dovetails nicely with the use of this text is to organize classroom debates on current social/political issues.

There is no term in general use for the concept labeled *cogent* reasoning or argument in this text. Most texts employ the related but somewhat different concept of *soundness*. Sound arguments are valid arguments that contain only true premises; cogent arguments are valid arguments that contain only *warranted* (justified) premises and do not suppress relevant evidence. Those who reason from unjustified premises, or even from premises that run counter to whatever evidence is available, may reason soundly if it turns out, luckily, that their unjustified premises are true, but they do not reason cogently. That luck provided them with the right answer does not prove they have reasoned well, and it is the notion of cogency, not soundness, that conforms to this fact. Our goal, of course, is sound reasoning that yields true conclusions, but the best mechanism available to mere mortals, lacking prevision, is cogent reasoning.

The word *fallacy* comes from the Latin *fallere,* to deceive. Latin commentators referred to the 13 kinds enumerated by Aristotle as *fallaciae,* no doubt because they were regarded as devices used to deceive others. Through the years, however, the term *fallacy* has taken on many different but related meanings. The use of the term in this book is much broader than in most, both in removing the idea of deliberate deception as a condition of fallacy and in extending the term to cover all *errors of reasoning.*

Fallacy classifications have also undergone many changes since Aristotle's time. The categories used here are fairly standard except for the employment of three master fallacies—*questionable premise, suppressed evidence,* and *invalid inference*—and in the inclusion of a few errors in reasoning not generally considered to be fallacies (for instance, *lack of proportion*). The classic text that comes closest to utilizing this sort of classification system is Richard Whately's *Elements of Logic,* written in 1826.

A true critical thinking course or textbook is unthinkable in a closed or authoritarian society and antithetical to the indoctrination practiced in that kind of culture. The author of this text takes very seriously the admonition that eternal vigilance is the price of liberty. Citizens who can think critically and for themselves rather than uncritically ingest what their leaders tell them are the foundation of any society that wants to remain truly free.

Acknowledgments

I'd like to thank the publisher's reviewers for this fifth edition: Professors R. V. Dusek, University of New Hampshire; Sidney Gendin, Eastern Michigan University; Patrick Maher, University of Pittsburgh; Thomas McKay, Syracuse University; and Robert Schwartz, University of Wisconsin–Milwaukee.

Many thanks also to the others who have aided in the preparation of this and previous editions, in particular, Leland Creer, Central Connecticut State University; Paul O. Ricci, Cypress College; Frank Fair, Sam Houston State University;

Robert Cogan, Edinboro University; Clayton Morgareidge, Lewis and Clark College; Monte Cook, University of Oklahoma; James Heffernan, University of the Pacific; Henry C. Byerly, University of Arizona; Donald Burrill, California State University, Los Angeles; Joan Straumanis, Kenyon College; Dana R. Flint, Lincoln University; J. Thomas Howald, Franklin College; Nelson Pole, Cleveland State University; Alan Hausman, Ohio State University; Paul A. Roth, University of Missouri; Douglas Stalker, University of Delaware; David Morgan, University of Northern Iowa; Ben Starr, Modesto Junior College; Paul J. Haanstad, University of Utah; Perry Weddle, California State University, Sacramento; James A. Gould, University of South Florida; Donald Lazere, California Polytechnic State University; Richard Paul, Sonoma State University; and Merrill Proudfoot, Park College.

Also many thanks to Nancy Cavender, College of Marin; Roye Templeton, University of Maryland Baltimore County; Linda C. Plackowski, Delta College; Daniel Van Gelder; John R. Lee, M.D., and, in particular to Professor Anne Brudno for her kind help in expanding the book's stock of examples. And finally, many thanks to students of the University of Kansas, Bernard Baruch College of CUNY, and the University of Maryland Baltimore County.

HOWARD KAHANE
Mill Valley, California

Logic and
Contemporary
Rhetoric

Drawing by Stevenson; © 1987 The New Yorker Magazine, Inc.

"Congratulations, Dave! I don't think I've read a more beautifully evasive and subtly misleading public statement in all my years in government."

Cartoon commentary on the state of contemporary rhetoric.

1

Introduction

There is much truth to the old saying that life is just one problem after another. That's why problem solving is one of life's major preoccupations. **Reasoning**—giving reasons in favor of this or that—is the essential ingredient in problem solving. When confronted with a problem, those who are rational reason from what they already know or believe to new beliefs useful for solving that problem. The trick, of course, is to reason *well*.

1. Reasoning and Arguments

Consider the following simple example of reasoning:

> Identical twins often have different IQ test scores. Yet such twins inherit the same genes. So environment must play some part in determining a person's IQ.

Logicians call this kind of reasoning an **argument.** In this case, the argument consists of three statements:

1. Identical twins often have different IQ test scores.
2. Identical twins inherit the same genes.
3. So environment must play some part in determining IQ.

The first two statements in this argument give *reasons* for accepting the third. In logic talk, they are said to be **premises** of the argument, and the third statement is called the argument's **conclusion.**

In everyday life, a few of us bother to label premises or conclusions. We usually don't even bother to distinguish one argument from another. But we do sometimes give clues. Such words as *because, since,* and *for* usually indicate that what follows is a premise. And words like *therefore, hence, consequently, so,* and *it follows that* usually signal a conclusion. Similarly, expressions like "It has been observed that . . . ," "In support of this . . . ," and "The relevant data . . . " generally introduce premises, while expressions like "The result is . . . ," "The point of all this is . . . ," and "The implication is . . . " usually signal conclusions. Here is a simple example:

> *Since* it's wrong to kill a human being, *it follows that* abortion is wrong, *because* abortion takes the life of (kills) a human being.

In this example, the words *since* and *because* signal premises offered in support of the conclusion signalled by the phrase *it follows that.* Put into textbook form, the argument reads:

1. It's wrong to kill a human being.
2. Abortion takes the life of (kills) a human being.
∴ 3. Abortion is wrong.[1]

(Of course, an argument may have any number of premises and may be surrounded by or embedded in other arguments.)

In addition to using transitional words like *since, because,* and *therefore,* we sometimes use other devices, such as sentence order, and may even mask a conclusion in the form of a question. For example, during the 1980 election a speaker gave all sorts of reasons for believing that Ronald Reagan would balance the budget if elected and then stated his conclusion in the form of a rhetorical question: "Can anyone doubt that Ronald Reagan will balance the federal budget?"

While we don't usually bother to label the premises and conclusions of our own arguments in daily life, it's sometimes useful to do so when evaluating the arguments of others. One quick way is to underline (or bracket) premises and conclusions, using a single underline to indicate a premise and a double underline to indicate a conclusion, like this:

> Since it's wrong to kill a human being, it follows that capital punishment is wrong, because capital punishment takes the life of a human being.

Notice that one of the premises is given *after* the conclusion. Psychological order doesn't always mirror logical order: Premises needn't come before conclusions. What makes a statement a premise of an argument is that it is offered in support of some other statement.

In everyday life, premises and occasionally conclusions are sometimes omitted as understood. Life is short, and we don't always bother to spell out the obvious or what is not at issue. In the IQ example just mentioned, we omitted the premise that IQ differences must be due to either genetic or environmental factors. In assessing an argument of this kind, we should by all means add such obvious premises when they are clearly relevant.

---

[1]The symbol " ∴ " is used as shorthand for the word *therefore* and thus indicates that a conclusion follows.

Exposition and Argument

Of course, not all groups of statements form arguments. Only those do that provide *reasons* for believing something. Thus, anecdotes are not usually arguments, nor are most other forms of *exposition* or *explanation*. But even in these cases, arguments often are implied. Here is a sales clerk explaining the difference between a 19-inch Sony and a 21-inch house brand: "Well, Sony has a one-gun picture tube, while our own Supremacy set doesn't; so the Sony picture will be a bit better in areas where reception is good to start with. Of course, if reception isn't that good in your area, the picture won't be that clear anyway—unless you have cable. On the other hand, our own brand, Supremacy, is $175 cheaper for a 21-inch set than Sony is for a 19-inch set."

While the clerk's remarks contain no explicit argument because no conclusion is drawn (no reasons are given in support of another statement), still a conclusion is *implied*—namely, you should choose the Sony if you're willing to pay $175 more for a slightly better picture (especially if you're on cable); otherwise you should choose the house brand.

The point is that explanations and expositions are not generally aimless: A good deal of everyday talk, even gossip, is intended to influence the beliefs and actions of others. In the television set example, the clerk gave information intended to convince the customer to draw either the conclusion, "I'll buy the 19-inch Sony because a small picture improvement is worth $175 to me," or the conclusion, "I'll buy the 21-inch Supremacy set because the difference in picture quality isn't worth $175 to me." In other words, the point of the chatter about Sony and the house brand was to *sell a TV set*.

Similarly, advertisements often restrict themselves to information about a product, rather than advancing any specific arguments. Yet clearly every ad has an implied conclusion—that you should buy the advertised product. Information given in an ad is thus offered as premises or reasons for drawing the conclusion that you should buy the product.

Still, it's important to understand the difference between rhetoric that is primarily expository or explanatory and rhetoric that is basically argumentative. A passage that contains only exposition gives us no reason to accept the "facts" in it other than the authority of the writer or speaker, whereas passages that contain arguments allege to give reasons for some of their claims (the conclusions) and usually call for a different sort of evaluation than merely an evaluation of the authority of the writer.

Exercise 1-1

Here are some passages from student papers and exams (modestly edited). Determine which contain arguments and which do not. Label the premises and conclusions of those that do, and *explain* your answers. (Starred [*] items are answered in a section at the back of the book.)

    *1. At the present rate of consumption, the oil will be used up in 20–25 years. And we're sure not going to reduce consumption in the near future. So we'd better start developing solar power, windmills, and other "alternative energy sources" pretty soon.

2. My thesis is that the doomsayers are wrong to believe we're going to run out of oil in the near future, because necessity is the mother of discovery (ha, ha), and my geology text says we have only discovered a small fraction of the oil in the ground.

*3. I don't like big-time college football. I don't like pro football on TV either. In fact, I don't like sports, period.

4. Well, I have a special reason for believing in big-time college football. After all, I wouldn't have come here if Ohio State hadn't gone to the Rose Bowl, because that's how I heard about this place in the first place.

5. Big-time football doesn't belong at a university. Look at Ohio State— everything here revolves around football, at least in the fall. You can't even park within a mile of campus on a football Saturday, and that's why this assignment is late.

6. My summer vacation was spent working in Las Vegas. I worked as a waitress at the Desert Inn and made tons of money. But I guess I got addicted to the slots and didn't save too much. Next summer my friend Hal and I are going to work in Reno, if we can find jobs there.

7. We've had open admission here at KU [the University of Kansas] ever since living memory can remember, and things work swell here, don't they? I suppose that's because those that don't belong here flunk out, or don't come here in the first place. So who needs restricted enrollment?

8. The abortion issue is blown all out of proportion. How come we don't hear nearly as much about the evils of the pill? After all, a lot more potential people are "killed" by the pill than by abortion.

9. People say too much is made of abortion. Hogwash. Didn't they say over a million babies don't get born every year because of it? Yes, they did. Boy, if they killed a million congressmen every year, they'd sure think it was important.

*10. You ask me what claims made by my textbooks are wrong. Well, I'll tell you. My science book says whales are mammals. But everyone knows whales live in the sea. And that's what a fish is, an animal that lives in the sea. So there.

11. I don't know of any claims in my textbooks that are wrong. But there must be some, because authors are human beings, just like everybody else. So I have to say there must be some wrong statements in my textbooks, even if I'm not smart enough to spot them.

12. I've often wondered how they make lead pencils. Of course, they don't use lead, they use graphite. But I mean how do they get the graphite into the wood? That's my problem. The only thing I can think of is maybe they

cut the graphite into long round strips and then cut holes in the wood and slip in the graphite.

2. Cogent Reasoning

Reasoning—and any argument into which reasoning is cast—is either **cogent** (good) or **fallacious** (bad). To reason cogently, we must satisfy three criteria: (1) We must start with **justified** or **warranted** premises; (2) we must include all available relevant information;[2] and (3) our reasoning must be **correct** or **valid**, which means roughly that being justified in accepting the premises justifies acceptance of the conclusion.[3] (The second criterion is important only with respect to what is called *inductive* reasoning, to be discussed in the next section and the Appendix.)

Consider the following argument:

1. No black person has ever been elected president of the United States.

∴ 2. Probably no black person ever will be elected to that office.

Everyone knows that the premise of this argument is true. And clearly, those who know nothing else relevant are justified in accepting the argument's conclusion. So the argument satisfies the first and third conditions of cogent reasoning.

But in fact, most of us do know other relevant facts that cast doubt on the argument's conclusion. We're aware, for instance, that times have been changing, in particular with respect to race discrimination and the distribution of political power. We know that a Catholic person (John Kennedy) was elected president after over 30 Protestant presidents in a row. We know that in 1984 a woman (Geraldine Ferraro) was the vice-presidential candidate on a major party ticket for the first time. And we know that a black person, Rev. Jesse Jackson, was for a short time the front runner in the race to receive the 1988 nomination of the Democratic party. Bringing this and related information to bear, we are not justified in accepting the conclusion that probably no black person will be elected to the highest office in the land. (Similar arguments apply to other minority groups that have as yet had no candidate with a serious chance to win the presidency.)

It is important to notice that the above argument is not cogent, *even though its reasoning is valid.* It is not cogent because it neglects known and relevant information, and thus violates the second rule of cogent reasoning that requires us to include everything relevant that we know. Although validity is a necessary condition of cogent reasoning, it is not sufficient to guarantee that we have reasoned intelligently. To obtain that guarantee, we must satisfy all three conditions of cogent reasoning.

---

[2]This is an extremely stringent requirement that in real life is beyond the ability of most of us most of the time. The point is to come as close as possible to satisfying it, bearing in mind the seriousness of the problem to be solved and the cost (in time and effort) of obtaining or recalling relevant information. (One of the marks of genius is the ability to recognize that information is relevant to a topic when the rest of us aren't likely to notice.)

[3]Provided we know nothing else relevant to the conclusion. For a more precise account of valid reasoning, see the author's *Logic and Philosophy,* 5th ed. (Belmont, Calif.: Wadsworth, 1986).

3. Two Basic Kinds of Valid Arguments

Philosophers have distinguished two basic kinds of correct or valid arguments: **deductive** and **inductive.** The essential property of a **deductively valid argument** is this: *If its premises are true, then its conclusion must be true also.* To put it another way, if the premises of a deductively valid argument are true, then its conclusion *cannot be false.*

On the other hand, the premises of an **inductively valid argument** provide good but not conclusive grounds for accepting its conclusion. The truth of its premises does not guarantee the truth of its conclusion, although it does make the conclusion *probable.* (That's why the expression "probability argument" is often used instead of "inductive argument.")

The key idea in induction is that of *learning from experience.* We notice *patterns* or other *resemblances* in our experiences and project them onto other experiences. Here is a typical example:

  1. The Indianapolis Colts were a losing team in their first few years of existence.
∴ 2. They'll be a losing team in their next year.

Anyone who accepts this argument's premise (and knows nothing else relevant) is justified in accepting its conclusion. Yet this conclusion *may* turn out to be false. The Colts could conceivably make some inspired trades and draft picks and start playing winning football.

Contrast this inductive argument with the following deductively valid argument:

  1. Every U.S. president has lied to us.
  2. Jimmy Carter was a U.S. president.
∴ 3. Jimmy Carter lied to us.

Assuming for the moment that the first premise is true (we all know that the second premise is true), it is inconceivable that the conclusion could be false. It would be inconsistent (contradictory) to believe both premises yet deny the conclusion. For in saying the two premises, we have implicitly said the conclusion.

We have here a fundamental difference between deductive and inductive reasoning: The conclusion of a deductively valid argument is just as certain as its premises, while the conclusion of an inductively valid argument is less certain than its premises. Inductive conclusions have that extra element of doubt, however slight, because they make claims not already made by their premises. In contrast, the conclusion of a deductively valid argument is no more doubtful than its premises because its conclusion is already contained in its premises, although often only implicitly. (Deduction and induction, and good reasoning in general, are discussed further in the Appendix, bad or fallacious reasoning in Chapters 2, 3, and 4.)

4. Background Beliefs and World Views

Background beliefs are crucial in assessing argument cogency. Untrue background beliefs lead to errors of the kind many Americans made in 1972 and 1973 when evi-

> God dwells in the details.
>
> —Mies Van der Rohe

dence linked high White House officials to the Watergate burglary during the 1972 presidential campaign. A great many Americans dismissed it as just campaign rhetoric—it couldn't be true because President Nixon himself said it wasn't, and presidents of the United States don't lie to the American people about such matters. But other Americans responded differently, dismissing Nixon's denials as what one would expect from a politician running for office, even a president of the United States. Nixon's earlier false denial that American forces had invaded Cambodia met with a similar mixed response.

Could it be true that officials of the American government, from the president on down, would lie about invading a foreign country? Yes, it could be true, and it was. Why then did so many Americans accept their government's denials, even in the face of clear-cut evidence to the contrary? Because of some of their basic beliefs about human nature, and in particular about how the American system works. Given these beliefs, which formed part of what might be called their **world views,** it *was* unlikely that Nixon, John Mitchell, and other top officials would lie about such a serious matter; it *was* sensible to believe what their government—in particular their president—told them and to reject what otherwise would have been overwhelming evidence.

World views are crucial. Accurate world views help us to assess information accurately; inaccurate world views lead us into error. A world view is like a veil through which we perceive the world, or a filter through which all new ideas or information must pass. Reasoning based on a grossly inaccurate world view yields grossly inaccurate conclusions (except when we're just plain lucky), no matter how good our reasoning may be otherwise.

This means that if we want to draw sensible conclusions, we must pay a good deal of attention to our world views or, as they are also called, our *philosophies*, constantly checking them against newly acquired information and revising them when necessary so that our evidence and beliefs form as coherent a package as possible.

A *world view* or *philosophy* is just the most general and theoretical part of what can be called our package of **background beliefs,** a package that includes particular facts as well as general theories. In judging arguments, we need to bring to bear *all* relevant background beliefs, particular as well as general. Thus, in trying to decide whether President Nixon was telling the truth about Watergate or Cambodia, intelligent citizens tried to bring to bear not only their overall world views but also particular facts they knew about Nixon (and about those who contradicted what Nixon said). For example, this writer tended not to believe the president, first because his overall world view told him that national leaders often do lie about such matters, second because of what he knew about Nixon's record as a shady liar,[4]

---

[4]See, for instance, page 55 for earlier Nixon chicanery.

and third because of what European and non–mass media correspondents in the Far East were claiming. But many Americans were fooled by Nixon, not just because of their defective world views, but also because they didn't know the details of Nixon's past record of dishonesty or hadn't heard (or believed) what European correspondents and the American non–mass media were saying.

Background beliefs clearly play a significant role in evaluating particular arguments, given that two of the three criteria of cogent reasoning require that they be consulted. The first criterion, you will recall, requires cogent arguments to have justified premises—justified, of course, by background beliefs. Take the argument heard in the early 1980s that AIDS must be a gay disease, given that in America only homosexuals had so far come down with that dread disease through sexual contact. This argument was accepted by many heterosexual people for some time because of wishful thinking. But eventually it became clear to virtually everyone that all of those who are "sexually active" are at risk, although some more so than others. Bringing this knowledge to bear, most people sooner or later rejected the idea that AIDS is some sort of homosexual curse or punishment because their background beliefs told them that arguments to justify this belief have questionable premises, in particular the premise that AIDS is transmitted by sexual contact only among homosexuals.

In addition, background information is relevant to the criterion for cogent reasoning that requires us to bring all relevant information to bear. Clearly, we can't

---

When major league baseball players started hitting home runs in extra large numbers in 1987, breaking all records, there was a revival of perennial claims that the baseball had been juiced up. Here is Reggie Jackson bringing his background knowledge to bear in skewering that idea:

I've heard that every year since 1980. If the ball had really been getting livelier since then, we'd be playing with Titleists (golf balls) by now. The ball is no livelier than it's always been. I got every bit of that pitch in Oakland (April 30), and it went 500 feet. But why didn't it go 550? Balls aren't going any farther. There's no rabbit ball.

Look at the size of these guys now. Look at Rob Deer, Pete Incaviglia, Mark McGwire, Jose Canseco. Look at the build on Eric Davis. These are some big dudes.

Eddie Mathews was a powerful home-run hitter, but he didn't have a body like Chris Brown of the Giants. And Bo Jackson is bigger than me.

Guys are in better shape now and take care of themselves better. When I came up we didn't have weight programs. It was almost illegal to lift weights. Now everybody's doing it.

People don't give enough credit to the athletes. It always has to be the balls or bats or something.

—*San Francisco Chronicle*
(May 15, 1987).

bring to bear what we don't know, so the extent of our background knowledge limits our ability to judge the cogency of particular arguments. Finding out that the principal ingredient in most nondairy creamers is coconut oil means nothing to those who don't know that coconut oil is a saturated fat, unlike most vegetable fats but like the saturated fat in milk that people are trying to avoid.

Further, without a background theory to guide us, we often have no way of knowing that some of what we do know is in fact relevant. Suppose we already know that coconut oil is a saturated fat but don't know about the theories and research linking saturated fats to strokes and heart disease. In such a case, we may know a relevant fact (that most nondairy creamers contain saturated fats) but not be able to bring that fact to bear on the argument in question because we lack a theory (concerning the connection between strokes and heart disease and intake of saturated fats) linking that fact to the argument in question.

It should be clear, then, that background beliefs are crucial in evaluating particular arguments. Those who know little, or worse "know" much that is false, cannot successfully evaluate arguments. They are fair game for every con artist, every shady politician, who comes down the pike, a group that (according to this writer's background beliefs) includes several recent presidents of the United States.

Exercise 1-2

Find at least one item in the mass media (a newspaper or magazine article or something from television) that reflects a typically American point of view, and explain what makes it typically American. (This is a difficult exercise that requires paying attention to the everyday and obvious in a way few of us are trained to do.)

5. Reading Between the Lines

A person who has a reasonably accurate world view and lots of background facts often can get more information from a statement or argument than is expressly contained in it. Doing this is called "reading between the lines" and often is the essential ingredient in assessing political rhetoric as well as (interestingly) advertisements.

Take the Bufferin ad, "No regular aspirin product reduces fever better." Reading between the lines of this ad, we should conclude that Bufferin does *not* reduce fever better than some competing products, because if it did, the ad would make that stronger claim ("Bufferin reduces fever better than any other aspirin product"), rather than the weaker one that none reduces fever better. The point is that we should expect an advertiser to make the strongest claim possible and thus conclude that a less strong claim is made because stronger ones are false.[5]

---

[5] Reading between the lines is the linguistic equivalent of "sizing up" a person. A good poker player, for instance, looks for telltale signs of bluffing in personal mannerisms, since some players systematically signal a bluff by increased chatter or nervousness, while others do so by feigning unconcern. Similarly, an intelligent voter sizing up a political candidate looks for nonverbal as well as verbal signs of that candidate's true intent once in office.

> A wise man hears one word and understands two.
>
> —Jewish proverb

Reading between the lines often requires great sophistication or subtlety, but sometimes it just requires adding or subtracting a few figures. Here is a quote from *Inquiry* magazine (October 15, 1979) illustrating this:

> Consider the state of agriculture between the Civil War and World War I, a period of immense growth in the American economy. Agriculture shared in that growth: The number of farms tripled, the number of acres of farmland doubled, the net farm income increased more than fourfold. Despite this growth, two stark figures stand out. Farm population decreased from 60 percent to 35 percent of the national total population, and agriculture's share of the national income dropped from 31 percent to 22 percent. In other words, agriculture did not keep pace with the rest of the economy.

Interesting figures. But by doing a little calculating, we can come up with two more interesting statistics. First, while lots of farmers must have gone broke, those that remained seem to have improved their financial position compared to non-farm workers. And second, surprisingly, the average farm, contrary to what one might think, seems to have decreased in size during the period in question (figure out why).

An alleged case of reading between the lines during World War II may have changed the course of human history. Here is the story, according to some

---

There is a technical reason why the intelligentsia in the Soviet Union consume more books than their Western colleagues. Where a Western scholar or writer can refer to just one source book, a Russian must often gather the same information bit by bit from various sources. Information about the history of religion is gleaned from quotes in antireligious brochures, the opinions of modern philosophers from Marxist articles condemning bourgeois or revisionist philosophy, and so on. For many years, for example, the only reference book on modern music was Shneerson's *Music Serving the Reactionaries,* which branded Stravinsky, Messiaen, Menotti, and others as agents of imperialism. But at least there one could pick up the names, dates, names of compositions, and a few ideas about these composers.

—Lev Lifshitz-Losev,
in *New York Review of Books (May 31, 1979)*

Reading-between-the-lines pickings are slim in the Soviet Union, but vital.

At certain moments, as we have seen, athletes have feelings of floating and weightlessness. Sometimes, in fact, they even have out-of-body experiences. Now we would like to consider the possibility that the athlete is literally able to suspend himself in midair. In the earlier chapters we discussed the athletes' subjective feelings that they were floating or outside themselves. But is there an objective reality involved, something that can be verified by others? We think that there is. We have collected many statements by sportswriters, coaches, and other observers that attest to the fact that some athletes actually can, for brief moments, remain suspended in the air. Basketball players and dancers, especially, seem to demonstrate this amazing ability.

—Human Behavior (March 1979)

This writer's world view tells him that if better evidence could have been obtained to prove this kind of levitation, it would have been—first, because really proving it exists would have created a sensation, and second, because it would have been so easy to get (motion pictures would show it). Since they didn't get this proof, it's reasonable to suppose they couldn't, because, as the basic laws of physics suggest, no one can suspend himself in midair, even for a brief moment.

sources:[6] "In May of 1942, . . . a young Soviet physicist noted the abrupt absence of articles on nuclear fission in the American journal *Physical Review*. He drew the obvious conclusion—security measures often point an unmistakable finger—and wrote Stalin a letter reporting that the Americans were trying to build an atomic bomb. Early in 1943, Stalin appointed the physicist Igor Kurchatov to run a small Soviet bomb project." Even supposing the story isn't true, the point about reading between the lines remains the same. The information was there for an astute physicist in the Soviet Union (or Germany! or Japan!) to discover by reading between the lines.

6. Wishful Thinking and Self-Deception

If human beings were simply rational animals, becoming a completely cogent reasoner would be a relatively easy task. We would simply learn which kinds of reasoning are good (*cogent*) and which bad (*fallacious*), and that would be that.

But we all are a good deal more complicated than that. The human animal has evolved with all sorts of emotions that play a serious role in determining actions and beliefs. Most of these nonrational tugs serve useful, even vital, purposes, for instance, in reducing anxiety and in fostering group loyalty. Unfortunately, they also often get in the way of straight thinking.

---

[6]See *The Atlantic* magazine (March 1983) book review of *The Soviet Union and the Arms Race* (New Haven: Yale University Press, 1982), or read the book.

Andy Capp by Reggie Smythe, ©1976 Daily Mirror Newspapers Ltd.
Dist. Field Newspaper Syndicate.

Self-deception at work.

Perceptive people recognize this tendency in others (for example, when some-one gives a high-minded reason for doing something when he is clearly motivated by selfish or immoral considerations). And it certainly is useful to be able to spot this in others. However, it is even more useful to be able to notice when we our-selves engage in these psychological tricks, since this kind of **wishful thinking** and **self-deception** interferes with cogent reasoning and indeed frequently leads us into serious, even death-dealing errors.

While no psychologist today would agree with the ancient Greek philosophers who defined human beings as essentially rational animals, they disagree as to ex-actly what mix of rational and nonrational (emotional) factors makes up a typical person. And they use different terms when talking about wishful thinking and self-deception. However, several (overlapping) terms (for instance, *rationalization, denial, prejudice,* and *superstition*) have become part of everyday speech in this post-Freudian age, and understanding a bit about them is crucial in overcoming the very human tendency to skew rational thought. (More will be said on this topic in Chapter 5.)

7. Revising Background Beliefs and World Views

By the time we reach adulthood, most of us have acquired a rather large stock of background beliefs, and our world views have been rather extensively fleshed out. We then filter our everyday experiences through all of these beliefs that we have ac-cumulated.

On the whole, it is all to the good that we do so, since information untied to the rest of what we believe is relatively useless, indeed, may be quite misleading even though completely true. The trouble is that, being human, once we have latched onto a particular belief, most of us are loath to revise it, no matter how much it is contradicted by experience. This is particularly true of beliefs that we find com-fortable. (See Chapter 5 for more on this point.) It is extremely important that our background beliefs, especially those that constitute our world views, continually be revised in the light of what we learn day to day. Failure to do so virtually guaran-tees poor reasoning.

> Knowledge not renewed quickly becomes ignorance.
> —Peter Drucker

While we want our background beliefs to be as *comprehensive* as possible, at least with respect to those areas with which we have a special interest, it is more important that we try to make our background beliefs *consistent* with each other. After all, one out of every pair of *inconsistent* beliefs has to be false. (Of course, complete consistency is beyond the ability of even the greatest geniuses. The point is to come as close to the ideal as possible.)

Theories About Information Sources

Two related parts of a person's world view are crucially important to critical thinking because they impinge so often on all sorts of other matters. One is our beliefs about the accuracy and truthfulness of the various available sources of information. As with computers, so also with the human mind, it's true that "garbage in, garbage out." We therefore need to constantly reassess our information sources (newspapers, the media in general, teachers, lawyers, ministers, elected officials, and so on). Under what conditions will these sources be likely to tell us the truth? We can't assume automatically that a source is reliable without some reason for doing so. And when is a source likely even to know the truth? Many people seem to believe that if it says so in print, or an elected official tells it to us, then it must be so. (Recall how many Americans were taken in by Richard Nixon on Watergate because he was, after all, the *president of the United States.*)

Sophisticated reasoners constantly revise their theories about when information sources can be trusted and when not in the light of their experiences with these information sources. (Regrettably, this applies even to close friends. Lots of otherwise fine friends are congenital bull slingers.)

Theories About Human Nature

The other crucial part of our world views concerns basic human nature. (Beliefs on this topic obviously are closely connected to those about the quality of various information sources, since it is people who write what we read or hear and people whom we elect to office and consult for professional advice.)

Fortunately, we don't have to start from scratch, since others have been at the task for some time now. Tapping this source has its risks, to be sure. But even common everyday sayings may yield a great deal of important truth. Blood *is* thicker than water, and power does tend to corrupt, even if it is questionable that the female of the species is any more vain than the male.

Science Provides the Most Accurate Information

While no information is absolutely reliable, and no theory exempt from doubt, the safest, the most reliable, the most accurate information comes from the well-established sciences such as physics, chemistry, and biology and to a lesser extent from the social sciences and psychology. The scientific enterprise is an organized, ongoing, worldwide activity that builds and corrects from generation to generation. The method of science is just the rigorous, systematic, dogged application of cogent inductive reasoning (mixed with all sorts of deductive—chiefly mathematical—reasoning) from what has so far been observed over countless centuries to theories about how the world as a whole functions and thus to expectations about future experiences. Theories falsified by experience are tossed out of science, no matter how comforting and no matter whose pet ideas thus are stepped on. Absolutely no one starting from scratch could hope to obtain in one lifetime anything remotely resembling the sophisticated and accurate conclusions of the physical and biological sciences, even if that person were a Galileo, Newton, and Einstein all rolled into one. It follows that it is the height of folly to believe what is clearly contradicted by well-established scientific theory in the physical sciences and foolish indeed to ignore what science has to say on any topic. (Note, however, that economics is not called the "dismal science" for nothing, and note also that psychology is still in its infancy, with lots of mistaken theories yet to be shaken out.)

Here is Isaac Asimov, one of the best known popularizers of science (also famous for his science fiction), explaining why cheating in science is so rare, why getting caught is almost inevitable sooner or later, and thus why scientists on the whole are so much more trustworthy (when they're doing science!) than, say, politicians and other "public servants."

Self-correction

Every once in a while—not often—scientists discover that one of their number has published false data or has plagiarized someone else's work.

This is always deeply embarrassing, especially since these days such news usually receives wide publicity in the nonscientific world.

In some ways, however, these scandals actually reflect credit upon the world of science. Consider:

1) Scientists are, after all, human. There is enormous pressure and competition in the world of science. Promotion and status depend on how much you publish and how *soon* you publish, for the lion's share of credit comes if you are *first* with an important theory or observation. Under these circumstances, there is great temptation to rush things; to make up some data you are sure you will eventually find anyway that will support your theory; or to help yourself to someone else's work. The surprise, really, is not that it sometimes happens, but that it doesn't happen much more often. Scientists resist the pressure marvelously well.

Summary of Chapter 1

Reasoning is the essential ingredient in solving life's problems. Chapter 1 concerns good (and bad) reasoning about such problems.

1. Reasoning can be cast into *arguments,* which consist of one or more *premises* supporting a *conclusion.* In real life (as opposed to in textbooks), rhetoric does not divide easily into arguments or have premises and conclusions neatly labeled. Still, clues are given (for example, the words *because, since,* and *for* usually signal premises, and *hence, therefore,* and *so,* conclusions). But remember that not all groups of sentences form arguments. They may, for example, form anecdotes or other types of exposition or explanation.

2. Reasoning is either *cogent* (good) or *fallacious* (bad). Cogent reasoning has to satisfy three criteria: it must (1) start with *justified* or *warranted* premises, (2) use all relevant available information, and (3) be *valid,* or correct.

3. There are two basic kinds of valid reasoning: *deductive* and *inductive.* An argument is *deductively valid* provided that if its premises are true, its con-

---

2) When it does happen, the mere fact that it is so publicized is a tribute to scientists. If it were a common event, or if people expected scientists to be corrupt, it would make smaller headlines and drop out of sight sooner. Single cases of scientific corruption, however, will be talked about for years and inspire articles and books by the score. It's really a compliment.

3) Cases of scientific misbehavior point out how difficult it actually is to carry them out successfully, or even for very long. . . . [A] vital principle in scientific research is that nothing counts until observations can be repeated independently and there, almost inevitably, anything peculiar is uncovered. Science is *self-correcting* in a way that no other field of intellectual endeavor can match.

4) It is scientists themselves who catch the frauds; no one else is equipped to do so. The point is that scientists *do* catch them. There is never any cover-up on the grounds that science itself must not be disgraced. However embarrassing the facts may be, the culprit is exposed pitilessly and publicly. Science is *self-policing* in a way that no other field is.

5) Finally, the punishment is absolute. Anyone who proves to have violated the ethics of scientific endeavor is ruined for life. There is no second chance, no vestige of status. He or she must drop out, forever disgraced.

Add to all this the fact that scientific ethics requires all scientists to labor to find flaws in their *own* observations and theories—and to publicize these flaws when they find them—and you will understand how stern the requirements are and how astonishing it is that scandal is so infrequent.

From *SciQuest* (February 1982). Reprinted by permission of the author.

clusion must be true. And, roughly, an argument is *inductively valid* when it projects a pattern gleaned from past experiences onto future ones. An inductively valid argument at best only makes its conclusion very probable— never certain.

4. Having accurate and extensive *background beliefs,* in particular, the most general of such beliefs called *world views,* or *philosophies,* is crucial in evaluating particular arguments. For one thing, they are needed in determining whether the premises of an argument are *justified* or *warranted.* And for another, they have to be used in deciding whether relevant information has been omitted or suppressed.

5. We often can glean more information from a passage or argument than it overtly contains by "reading between the lines" (for instance, by adding up the figures, drawing undrawn conclusions, or evaluating a person's character).

6. While it's true that human beings are in part rational animals, their reasoning is also influenced by nonrational (emotional) factors, leading to *self-deception* and *wishful thinking* in its various forms, such as *rationalization, denial,* and *prejudicial thinking.*

7. Background beliefs and, in particular, world views need to be revised on an ongoing basis, so as to be self-consistent and consistent with experience. This is especially true with respect to two parts of our world views that are particularly important for critical thinking (namely theories about the trustworthiness of information sources and about the fundamentals of human nature).

    The information that the physical sciences and mathematics provide is easily the most accurate we can obtain on these subjects. But the social sciences and psychology are less accurate on the whole because they are in their infancy. However, we ignore what they have to say at our peril.

Exercise 1-3

Find a magazine or newspaper article that *disagrees* with your world view on some point. Show either why you still think your world view is correct and the article wrong or how the article led you to change your mind.

Exercise 1-4

Find a magazine or newspaper article that involves some omission or misstatement of fact or theory that could pausibly be attributed to self-deception, wishful thinking, or other forms of bias on the part of the writer. Explain.

Exercise 1-5

Describe a situation in which you changed your mind on some more or less fundamental belief, and explain what convinced you. (Do *not* use the example you mentioned in answering Exercise 1-3.)

Truth Is Booty, Booty Is Truth

"There is already an inclination to trust the Veep-designate precisely because he is rich. 'When somebody is one of the wealthiest men in the world,' said Rep. John Rhodes of Arizona, the Republican leader in the house, 'he's got so much money there would be no point in cheating.' "

—*Newsweek* (September 2, 1974)

---

*Here is an Edward Sorel political cartoon (*Village Voice, *September 17, 1974) that nicely illustrates the foolishness in a fallacious appeal to the authority of former Vice-President Nelson Rockefeller's vast wealth.*

Half of being smart is knowing what you're dumb at.
                    —David Gerrold

Two wrongs don't make a right, but three do.
                    —Unofficial slogan of the
                    American military in Vietnam

It would be a very good thing if every trick could receive some short and obviously appropriate name, so that when a man used this or that particular trick, he could at once be reproved for it.
                    —Arthur Schopenhauer

2

Fallacious Reasoning—I

We said in Chapter 1 that to reason cogently, or correctly, we must: (1) reason from justified premises, (2) include all relevant information at our disposal, and (3) reason validly. *Fallacious reasoning* is just reasoning that fails to satisfy one or more of these three criteria. In other words, we reason **fallaciously** whenever we (1) reason from questionable premises, (2) fail to use relevant information, or (3) reason invalidly.

Of course, we must remember that the fallacious arguments encountered in daily life tend to be vague and ambiguous, and can thus be taken in different ways, depending on how we construe them. Consider the following line from a beer commercial:

> More people in America drink Budweiser than any other beer.

Taken literally, this isn't even an argument, much less a fallacious one. But it clearly implies that the listener should also drink Bud. So we can restate it to say:

1. More people in America drink Budweiser than any other beer. (Premise)
∴ 2. So you, too, should drink Budweiser. (Conclusion)

Stated this way, the argument is defective because it contains an *invalid inference.* Yet we could just as well restate it this way:

1. More people in America drink Budweiser than any other beer. (Premise)
2. The most popular beer is the best beer. (Premise)
3. You should drink the best beer.(Premise)
∴ 4. So you should drink Budweiser. (Conclusion)

Now the argument is valid but contains a *questionable premise*—that the most popular beer is the best beer. Interpreted this way, the commercial can't be faulted for *invalid reasoning,* but if we're persuaded by it, we become guilty of accepting a *questionable premise.*

Like the Budweiser example, most fallacious arguments can be restated in various ways. So there is no point in worrying too much about exactly which fallacy label we apply to a particular fallacious argument. Fallacy categories aren't built in heaven; they're just useful tools for spotting bad reasoning. The point is to recognize fallacious reasoning when we run across it and understand why it is fallacious.

Logically, all fallacies fall naturally into one or more of the three broad categories—*questionable premise, suppressed evidence,* and *invalid inference*—corresponding to the three ways that reasoning can be fallacious. But over the years a number of other fallacy categories have been invented that crosscut the three logical categories. These other categories have come into common use because experience has shown them to be helpful in spotting fallacious reasoning.[1]

Let's now look at some of these other fallacy categories, remembering that in the last analysis, what makes reasoning fallacious is that it uses *questionable premises* or *suppresses relevant evidence* or is *invalid.*

1. Appeal to Authority

Perhaps the most serious error in reasoning most of us regularly commit is to accept the word of someone, in particular an alleged authority, when we should not. None of us knows everything. So we all often have to appeal to other people or sources for information or advice. Improper appeals—in particular, improper appeals to alleged experts—constitute the fallacy called **appeal to authority.**

But which appeals are proper and which improper? Roughly speaking, an appeal to another person or source is proper (not fallacious) when we're reasonably sure that this "authority" has the knowledge or judgment we need, we can expect the authority to tell the truth, *and* we don't have the time, inclination, or ability to form an expert opinion on our own. The more sure we are of these three things, the more legitimate or proper is our appeal to an authority; the less sure we are, the more likely it is that our appeal is fallacious. (There are other complications, of course, particularly when dealing with "sensitive" questions that involve values or taste.)

This means that there are three basic questions that need to be asked when we seriously want to know whether a particular appeal to an authority would be legitimate:

1. Does this source have the information or judgment we need?
2. If so, can we trust this authority to tell it to us truthfully?
3. Do we have the time, the desire, and the ability to reason this out for ourselves (or to understand the expert's reasoning, so we don't have to merely accept his conclusion)?

---

[1]Several hundred different fallacies are discussed in one or another logic text, but no single book discusses them all. Only those that occur frequently are discussed in this text, which means our list is not exhaustive by any means. But the division into the master fallacies *questionable premise, suppressed evidence,* and *invalid inference* is exhaustive. (So far as this writer is aware, it is the only exhaustive fallacy classification in the literature.)

In everyday life, we usually know right away whether we've got the needed time and inclination. But the other questions can usually be answered only by bringing background information to bear. This process is often not easy, but the rules of thumb about to be discussed should prove useful.

Authorities in One Field Aren't Necessarily Experts in Another

Famous athletes and movie stars who endorse all sorts of products in television commercials are good examples of experts speaking out of their fields of expertise. They may know how to act or how to hit home runs, but there's no reason to suppose they know any more about beer or shaving cream than anyone else. The fact that Michael Jackson is paid to endorse Pepsi Cola proves nothing about Pepsi's quality.

Of course, many people are persuaded by celebrity commercials simply because they want to imitate famous people. Their main concern is fashion, not other sorts of quality. Looking good to other people is crucial in life, and one way to do this is to follow the lead of the rich, the powerful, and the famous. So if a movie star wears Jordache designer jeans, others will want to also. The error these people make in being persuaded by celebrity endorsements lies in assuming that celebrities actually prefer the products they endorse. Recommending a product and actually using it are two quite different things. It's very unlikely, for instance, that members of the "famed British wine tasting team" who endorsed Taylor Empire Cream Sherry actually serve that quite ordinary product when friends come over for dinner. Remember, celebrities are paid handsomely to tout these products. So if you really want to use the products famous people use, you'll have to find out what they are in some other way. (You'd also better be rich yourself.)

We Need to Become Experts on Controversial Topics

When experts disagree, the rest of us must become our own experts, turning to acknowledged authorities for evidence, reasons, and arguments, but not for conclusions or opinions. This is especially true with respect to political matters, because of the tremendous controversies they arouse. But it applies elsewhere, too. A judge, for example, rather than merely accepting a psychologist's opinion concerning the sanity of an accused person, ought instead to ask for the reasons that led the psychologist to this opinion. After all, a different opinion could be obtained just by asking another psychologist.[2] Similarly, American presidents need to go into the complex details that lie behind the opinions of their advisors, rather than confining themselves (as President Eisenhower is said to have done) to whatever can be typed onto one side of one page.

---

[2]This conforms to B. Duggan's Law of Expert Testimony: "To every Ph.D. there is an equal and opposite Ph.D." See Paul Dixon, *The Official Rules* (New York: Delacorte, 1978) for more on irreverent, pithy sayings like Duggan's Law.

Some Experts Are More Trustworthy than Others

Experts with an axe to grind are less trustworthy than just about anybody. It is to be expected, for instance, that corporation executives will testify to "facts" that place their corporations or products in a good light. Thus, we should expect that the executives of corporations dealing in products with harmful side effects (such as cigarettes, birth control pills, coffee, refined sugar, and nuclear power) will tend to deny or play down the unhealthy nature of their products if it is at all possible to do so.

Cigarette company executive denials that smoking their products is unhealthy are not believable precisely because they are so self-serving. By way of contrast, the continued claims by the medical profession that tobacco is deadly have been just the opposite of self-serving (because doctors make money when people get sick), which makes their claims all the more believable.

It is *believability* that always needs to be assessed. Lawyers speaking against no-fault auto insurance have to be less believable given that the point of no-fault insurance is to reduce litigation costs. Were they instead to come out on the other side, their judgment would have to be more respected because it is less likely to be biased by personal advantage.

©Al Ross/Rothco. Reprinted by permission.

"When Paul Newman says the arms race should stop, then the arms race *should* stop!"

Check the Past Records of Alleged Experts

Finally, anyone who has to appeal to an expert in a way that violates any of the previously listed rules should at least consult the past record of that authority. Experts who have been right in the past are more likely to be right in the future than those who have been wrong. It is surprising how often even this rule of last resort is violated. (Think of the many Americans who as late as the 1984 elections still believed President Reagan would balance the budget and significantly reduce the size of the federal bureaucracy.)

Avoid Wishful Thinking

Perhaps the principal reason that fallacious appeals to authority are so common in the public arena is that most of us have a much too high opinion of our leaders and what they know (not to mention what motivates them). We forget, if we ever knew, that elected government officials, in particular those holding high office, have to spend enormous amounts of time campaigning, mending fences, and other poli-

---

Experts on economic matters have notoriously poor track records; yet they are still listened to as though they have a direct wire to the truth. Here are a few predictions made by some of the nation's top money market experts in July 1982. The experts were asked to predict what interest rates would be at the end of 1982 (more precisely, what the prime rate charged by banks to top customers and the discount rate on three-month Treasury bills would be on December 31, 1982):[3]

	Prediction for:	
	Prime Rate	**TreasuryBills**
Irwin Kellner (Manufacturers Hanover Bank)	16%	12%
Donald Maude (Merrill Lynch)	15.5%	11.75%
Robert Parry (Security Pacific National Bank)	16%	12%
Thomas Thomson (Crocker Bank)	15%	11.75%
John Wilson (Bank of America)	14%	12%

The prime rate on July 2, 1982, was 16.5 percent, and three-month Treasury bills were paying 12.43 percent. At the end of the year, the prime was at 11.0–11.5 percent and T-bills were going at a discount rate of 7.9 percent. In other words, every one of these experts underestimated the decline in interest rates by a wide margin. (Note the implication of precision in a prediction like "11.75 percent"!) It's fiendishly hard to predict such things as how the economy is going to move. You should know that when you hear experts prognosticate.

---

[3]See Donald K. White's business column that appeared in the *San Francisco Chronicle* (among others) on April 13, 1983.

ticking, leaving too little time to think about or study the great issues on which they have to decide.

Here, for instance, is Congressman James M. Shannon of Massachusetts (*Parade* magazine, May 13, 1979) coming clean on the matter:

> Since taking office, the thing that really shocks me is how little time a Congressman has to devote to any one issue. There's simply no way you can cram your way to knowledgeability on any one subject in three or four hours. We have so many issues to contend with that, with all our research facilities, the best we can do is pick up information in bits and snatches.

Now here is an item (in an *Inquiry* magazine, March 30, 1981, review of Maine Senator William S. Cohen's book *Roll Call*) showing how elected officials who know next to nothing about a particular topic can become instant experts:

> [Maine Republican William S. Cohen's] first act after his Senate victory is a trip to Arizona to address the Traveling Salesmen of America. Then off on a whirlwind tour of the Far East. Then back to pose for *Life* magazine on the Capitol steps, dressed in a jogging suit.
>
> During this time he is playing intricate political games to position himself on the Armed Services Committee. Yet Cohen has not had the time to learn anything about military affairs before the committee actually meets—a fact he notes in passing as if it were a mere procedural detail. He boasts of confronting the secretary of defense with an impressive-sounding question about the AV-8B Harrier, an assault plane well-known to anyone with a modest interest in defense matters, even though "I had no idea what the AV-8B aircraft was." (Not to worry; little more than a month later, he is writing an Op-Ed piece about the intricacies of the SALT II treaty for the *Washington Post*.)

Finally, here is a snippet (*San Francisco Chronicle*, January 31, 1980) illustrating how appointed governmental officials can be completely ill prepared for their job:

> [U.S.] Ambassador [to Singapore] Richard Kneip didn't know there were two Koreas or that India and Pakistan had fought a war in 1971, says [Edward Ingraham,] a career diplomat dismissed by Kneip after eight months as his chief deputy.
>
> One day, during a discussion of the resurgence of Islam, Ingraham said Kneip had asked him, "What's Islam?"
>
> He said Kneip, shortly after his arrival, had asked senior staff members:
>
> "Did you say there are two separate Korean governments? How come?"
>
> "You mean there has been a war between India and Pakistan? What was that all about?"

Compare this ignorance with Ronald Reagan's remark, "Well, I learned a lot. . . . I went down [to Latin America] to find out from them and [learn] their views. You'd be surprised. They're all individual countries." No kidding?

It's not surprising that most of us have so overgenerous an evaluation of those we elect to power. Most people have not heard of Ambassador Kneip and his alleged ignorance and don't notice when members of Congress become instant experts on dozens of difficult topics. And anyway, don't *all* of us want very much to believe that things are being run at least tolerably well? To make our stock of beliefs less stressridden, we engage in wishful thinking and adopt generally higher opinions of those we elect than a fair appraisal would warrant. (See Chapter 5 for more on how wishful thinking and self-deception skew our judgments.)

The response of Americans to Ronald Reagan will undoubtedly become a textbook example of a people eager to think highly of their leader while he regularly provided evidence that he did not know what he was talking about, was making little effort to grasp even the rudimentary facts about important matters, and was at the very least flippant in his attitude toward the truth. Yet until the Iran-Contra scandal, he was perhaps the most popular president in recent years. A majority of Americans believed their amiable president, even though he continually uttered and was called down for uttering silly falsehoods like these (culled by *The Nation* magazine):

> *On the Contras in Nicaragua:* "They are the moral equivalent of our Founding Fathers and the brave men and women of the French resistance."
>
> *On Nazi soldiers:* "They were victims, just as surely as the victims in the concentration camps."
>
> *On the environment:* "There is today in the United States as much forest as there was when Washington was at Valley Forge."
>
> *On the military:* "You have to remember, we don't have the military-industrial complex we once had."

A majority of Americans also overlooked a constant stream of flatly false statements, including these (culled from the entertaining—and accurate—book *Ronald Reagan's Reign of Error*):[4]

> "There were two Vietnams, north and south. They had been separate nations for centuries." (January 1978) [Vietnam has been unified through most of its history.]

---

[4]Mark Green and Gail MacCall, *There He Goes Again: Ronald Reagan's Reign of Error* (New York: Pantheon, 1983). When examples are given, there is always the possibility that they are unrepresentative or are exceptional in some way. Anyone who thinks this might be true in this case should carefully read the Green and MacCall book or accounts in a *good* newspaper after the Reagan-Mondale debates or the Irangate press conference. The problem in revising this text was eliminating Reagan examples, not finding them.

"As for radiation, a coal-fired plant emits more radiation than a nuclear-powered plant. You even get more from watching TV or having your teeth X-rayed." (November 1978) [His figures aren't even close.[5]]

". . . [SALT II] is illegal, because the law of the land, passed by Congress, says that we cannot accept a treaty in which we are not equal." (October 28, 1980, during a debate with Jimmy Carter) [Such a treaty, good or bad, would be legal if ratified by the Senate.]

"Because Vietnam was not a declared war, the veterans are not even eligible for the G.I. Bill of Rights with respect to education or anything." (April 21, 1980) [That war was fought in "peacetime," but Vietnam vets are entitled to G.I. Bill rights anyway.]

"I've said it before and I'll say it again. The U.S. Geological Survey has told me that the proven potential for oil in Alaska alone is greater than the proven reserves in Saudi Arabia." (March 23, 1980) [U.S.G.S. figures at that time listed Saudi proven reserves at 17 times those for Alaska.]

"Now, the Soviets have 945 warheads aimed at targets in Europe in their medium-ranged missiles. And we have no deterrent whatsoever." (October 14, 1982) [To make this true, we have to say that 192 British and 98 French nuclear warheads then targeted on the Soviet Union constituted "no deterrent whatsoever." And we have to overlook the 400 or so U.S. warheads committed to NATO, not to mention the thousands of other nuclear warheads the U.S. might have used on the Soviets if it came to that. Other than that, the U.S. had no deterrent.]

"During the last ten years, the United States decreased its military spending." (January 14, 1982) ". . . in constant dollars, our defense spending in the 1960s went up because of Vietnam. And then it went downward through much of the 1970s." (November 22, 1982) [In constant dollars, U.S. military spending went up from about $180 billion in 1971 during the Vietnam War to about $194 billion in 1981 when we were more or less at peace.]

"I was the one who took the lead to begin bringing about the first real arms reduction talks that we've ever been able to hold with the Soviet Union." (February 16, 1983) [The SALT II arms reduction talks were supported by Presidents Nixon, Ford, and Carter.]

"Many New Dealers actually espoused what has become an epithet—fascism. . . . [Secretary of the Interior under Roosevelt] Harold Ickes, in his book said that what we were striving for was a kind of modified form of communism." (December 23, 1981) [Ickes says no such thing in his book, or elsewhere, for that matter.]

---

[5]For some supporting details showing Reagan was wrong on this fact and the others quoted here, see Mark Green and Gail MacCall, *There He Goes Again: Ronald Reagan's Reign of Error* (New York: Pantheon, 1983).

"John F. Kennedy authorized the sending in of a division of marines, and that was the first move toward combat moves in Vietnam." [The first U.S. combat division to go to Vietnam arrived there in March 1965, almost 18 months after Kennedy's assassination.]

"Those [nuclear weapons] that are carried in ships of one kind or another, or submersibles, you are dealing there with a conventional type of weapon or instrument, and those instruments can be intercepted. They can be recalled." (May 13, 1982) [Missiles fired from "submersibles" can be recalled. The president did lose some credibility because of this one.]

It may well be true that President Reagan has set some sort of record for false and/or foolish statements, at least for recent times. But the more important point is that most politicians stray from the truth, even if much less frequently, so that uncritical or automatic acceptance of what politicians tell us invites commission of the fallacy *appeal to authority*.

Appeal to Authority and Questionable Premise

As we mentioned before, the everyday fallacy categories like *appeal to authority* crosscut the three basic logical categories. But most fallacious appeals to authority happen to fall into the broad logical category *questionable premise*. In other words, they are fallacious precisely because they involve acceptance of a questionable premise, namely that the source or person appealed to has the information desired and will answer our appeal truthfully. In the case of fallacious appeals to authorities, this is often a very *questionable premise*.

Here are some excerpts from a talk given by President Reagan on February 24, 1982 (reported in the Columbia Journalism Review, May/June 1982) on his conception of truth:

More than forty years ago, I was a pioneer in radio, a sports announcer. And I found myself broadcasting major league baseball games from telegraphed reports. I was not at the stadium. . . . Now if the game was rather dull, you could say, "It's a hard-hit ball down towards second base. The shortstop is going over after the ball and makes a wild stab, picks it up, turns and gets him out just in time." Now I submit to you that I told the truth, if he was out from shortstop to first, and I don't know whether he really ran over toward second base and made a one handed stab, or whether he just squatted down and took the ball when it came to him. But the truth got there, and in other words, it can be attractively packaged. Well, we're justifiably proud that, unlike the Soviet broadcasts, the Voice of America is not only committed to telling its country's story, but also remains faithful to those standards of journalism that will not compromise truth.

It sounds as though President Reagan must have been a pretty good baseball announcer.

Soviet leader Mikhail Gorbachev will be seriously wounded in an assassination attempt by one of his own soldiers during Moscow's May Day parade.

Dean Martin will become a regular on "Dynasty"—and strike up a real-life romance with Linda Evans. They'll stun the world by announcing their engagement.

A massive White House investigation into UFOs will be launched after an entire fleet is sighted by thousands of fans at an open-air rock concert in northern California.

"Moonlighting" star Cybill Shepherd will wed a rock singer who's 10 years her junior—but the marriage will be short-lived.

A major hurricane will strike Miami in September—toppling a high-rise office block.

The biggest gold heist in history will be pulled in New York City. Thieves will get away with nearly $500 million worth of bullion from a warehouse at Kennedy Airport.

Parapsychologist buff Prince Charles will astound a TV audience by demonstrating a new ability—bending spoons using only the power of his mind.

America will launch a massive military attack on Iran—killing the Ayatollah—after agents learn the Mideast nation is planning a huge terrorist campaign against Americans overseas.

Three jet airliners will collide near a southern city, killing everyone aboard and making it the worst air disaster in aviation history.

These predictions were among several dozen made for 1987 by "10 top psychics" and reported in the National Enquirer. *This seer predicts, as of July 1987, that none of them will come true. The second edition of this text contained 13 predictions by perhaps the most famous of all alleged seers, Jeane Dixon. None of them came true (although two were so general and ambiguous that the faithful might claim they did. [Perhaps Ms. Dixon's finest work is her book* Horoscope for Dogs *(Boston: Houghton Mifflin, 1979).] The third and fourth editions contained similar predictions by people famous in the trade, including metal-bending watch-starter Uri Geller. None of them came true.*

You'd think that massive failure of this kind would tarnish the reputations of these "famous seers." But it doesn't. (Uri Geller has been exposed as an out-and-out fraud many times; yet he still has millions of followers.) Those who want to believe just because they want to believe, believe. Those of us who put our money on experience and the proper use of induction do not believe. Since the National Enquirer *and similar publications are read by over 20 million readers every week, and horoscopes by many more than that, it is clear that lots of people choose to ignore the evidence and accept the authority of con artists who pretend they can see into the future. Talk about committing the fallacy of* appeal to authority!

2. Two Wrongs Make a Right

The fallacy **two wrongs make a right** is committed when we try to justify an apparently wrong action by charging our accusers with a similar wrong. The idea is that if "they" do it, that justifies our doing it.

White South Africans have frequently been guilty of this fallacy when defending themselves against attacks on their system of apartheid. They like to respond to American attacks on their system by pointing out that the United States was the last major country to do away with legal slavery. While true, this is irrelevant to the charge against their country.

A variation of the fallacious idea that two wrongs make a right is that *many* wrongs do. [Polish leader] Wojciech Jaruzelski was guilty of this fallacy when he responded to U.S. criticisms of Polish policies by pointing out that the United States has no business blaming anyone, given our "reluctance for so many decades to condemn South Africa's regime, [our] support for other criminal regimes, [and our] waging an undeclared war against Nicaragua—in defiance of the protests of so many countries" (*Washington Post,* September 27, 1986). Jaruzelski may well have been right that U.S. hands were not clean, so that we were not ideally situated to lay blame. But this constituted not the slightest justification for Polish wrongdoings. Many wrongs don't make a right any more than do two (the U.S. Army not withstanding).

Fighting Fire with Fire

Like many other fallacies, *two wrongs* seems plausible because of its resemblance to a more sensible way of reasoning—in this case, to the plausible idea that we are sometimes justified in fighting fire with fire, or in getting our hands as dirty as our opponents'. A good example is the killing of someone in self-defense: We're justified in fighting one evil (the taking of our own life) with what would otherwise be another evil (the taking of our attacker's life).

So the fallacy *two wrongs make a right* is not automatically committed every time one apparent wrong is justified by appeal to an opponent's wrong; the crucial question is whether the second wrong indeed is necessary to fight or counteract the first wrong.[6] In the case of justified self-defense against physical attack, the evil of killing the attackers is necessary; in the case of South Africa and apartheid, the evil in that system has nothing to do with slavery in nineteenth-century America.

Two Wrongs and Hypocrisy

The fallacy *two wrongs make a right* also often seems pausible for another reason. Most of the time, someone arguing this way implies that his or her opponent is being hypocritical—and often this is correct, so that there is some justification in the attack. The town drunk isn't the one to tell us we've had too many and are making a fool

---

[6]This passes over the issue of retributive justice. If retributivists are right, then we're sometimes justified in inflicting harm (punishment) on those guilty of harming others, even though in doing so we fail to fight the original harm.

of ourselves, even it it's true. Similarly, the philanderer who finds out about his wife's infidelity is hardly the one to complain that she is deceiving him. But when we become outraged at the "chutzpah" of our accuser, we sometimes lose sight of the fact that our accuser's hypocrisy doesn't justify our own failures.

Common Practice and Traditional Wisdom

In addition to the fallacies of *appeal to authority* and *two wrongs make a right*, there are several similar, overlapping fallacies. One is *common practice,* where a wrong is justified by claiming lots of people do that sort of thing. An example is

---

A true expert is someone who knows a good deal more than most of us on a subject or who has acquired a skill most of us have not. Experts are not miracle workers. It is important to know the "state of the art" so that we can judge whether experts really know or can do what they (or others) claim. Here are some excerpts from an article showing the true limits to the expert ability of most wine tasters.

Challenged to identify a wine about to be served, the smart taster can learn much from details that have nothing to do with the wine itself. He will watch the cork being drawn, for instance, noticing its length, shape, firmness and branding. The shape of the neck and color of the glass of the bottle are also useful. So is the shape of the bottle.

A good example of this process occurred at one of the weekly tasting sessions I attend. One member presented a bottle from which cork and capsule — usually good hints to a wine's identity — had already been removed, and the label had been soaked off. It looked bad. But then I noticed that the label had left faint traces of glue on the bottle and that this glue had been applied in broad horizontal bands. I knew of only one winery doing that at the time. The outline of the glue showed that the label had been both tall and wide. Same winery. Finally, the bottle was of a dark tint not then widely used. Those three clues made it almost certainly a wine from Ridge Vineyards. . . .

After a bit of purely ceremonial peering, sniffing and tasting, I named the wine. Cheers all around! I had identified the wine "blind." But tasting had had little to do with it. I would have made the same guess without it. . . .

An exceedingly interesting experiment was conducted with nine of these judges not long ago to determine just how well they really could identify not specific wines, but simply the grape varieties from which certain wines had been made. Here was an experiment conducted under the best conditions, with some of the best judges in existence. These were no "wizard palates" on TV talk shows or "guest experts" performing at riotous public tastings. They were university professionals with an average of nineteen years of daily tasting experience each. Their task was simplified by the fact that all the wines in each group they tasted were of the same year. All the wines had been made at the university. Grape variety was the only variable.

the German soldier in World War II who justified machine-gunning unarmed civilian Russians by pointing out that lots of other German soldiers did the same thing.

A related fallacy is *traditional wisdom* or *past practice,* where the wrong is justified because it's the traditional or accepted way of doing things. Of course, we want to learn from the experiences of others. But we don't want to assume that *just because* something has been done in the past, it must be right.

However, we don't want to go overboard on this. Many organizations try to write their rules so as to conform to past practice because experience shows past practice has worked, while we can't be sure the new way will work as well, or have no good reason to think the new way will be better.

The judges failed. The only variety identified correctly more than half the time was the muscat—one of the most distinctive and easily recognizable grapes there is. Cabernet sauvignon was identified a bit more than a third of the time and chardonnay less than a quarter of the time. Zinfandel was correctly identified about a third of the time, but it was called cabernet almost as often. Cabernet wasn't called zinfandel as often, but it *was* called pinot noir, petite sirah and several other things.

These sobering results show how limited is the success to be attained when wine judges are rigorously denied all information about the wines they are considering. It is undoubtedly true that there are a few people with an extraordinary ability to identify wines, but this ability . . . is a matter of the elusive gift of taste memory and of specialization and luck—and . . . of the opportunity to sample vast numbers of wines.

A person who tastes, say, dozens of white burgundies of the Côte de Beaune every day will become adept at identifying these wines—but he still will not recognize them as one would recognize Lloyd George. He will have learned the personalities of each vintage, the characteristics of each district, the quirks of each producer, even details as specialized as the influence on the wine of various kinds of barrels. Faced with a sample, he begins to decide what it may be and what it may not be. Successively eliminating, he narrows down the possibilities to a few, or, with luck, to one. But take him to Bordeaux and he is as helpless as thee and me. . . .

The distinguished English wine taster Harry Waugh—himself a director of Château Latour—notes that he has been to many blind tastings in Bordeaux and elsewhere at which vineyard proprietors failed to pick out their own wines—and they had a great advantage over a true blind taster because they knew that their own wines were present. And once asked if he had ever confused bordeaux and burgundy, Waugh ruefully replied, "Not since lunch." That's the way an honest wine taster sounds.

Excerpts from Roy Brady, "Secrets of a Wine Taster Exposed," *New West,* Oct. 1978.
Reprinted with permission of Roy Brady.

Popularity

A related fallacy is that of *popularity,* where the fact that something is popular is taken to prove that it's right. This fallacy is committed, for instance, when someone argues that smoking marijuana must be physically harmful since most people think it is or that it isn't harmful since so many people smoke the stuff.

Of course, the usual precautions are in order. For instance, those who rushed out to see "Beverly Hills Cop" because it was so popular didn't necessarily commit a fallacy—they may have learned from experience that they tend to like popular movies, or they may just want to have seen the movie everyone is talking about so they can talk about it too.

3. Irrelevant Reason (*Non Sequitur*)

Traditional textbooks often discuss a fallacy called *non sequitur* ("it does not follow"), usually described as a fallacy in which the conclusion does not follow logically from the given premises. In this sense, any fallacy in the broad category *invalid inference* can be said to be a *non sequitur*. But other writers describe this fallacy more narrowly.

Let's replace the ambiguous term *non sequitur* with the expression **irrelevant reason** to refer to reasons or premises that are or come close to being totally irrelevant to a conclusion (provided another fallacy name, for instance, *appeal to authority,* does not apply).

As an example of *irrelevant reason,* consider those who replied to charges that the United States had no business in Vietnam, either morally or to satisfy our national interests, by arguing that such talk only prolonged the war by making the enemy believe America's will to fight was declining. This reply in all likelihood was true, but was irrelevant to the question of our justification for being in Vietnam.

(It should be noticed that a reason is not automatically irrelevant just because it is false. For instance, the old superstition that walking under a ladder brings bad luck is false, but it isn't irrelevant to the question whether a person should or shouldn't engage in that practice, because if true it would be a good reason not to walk under ladders.)

The fallacy of *irrelevant reason* fools us as often as it does because in typical cases the reasons presented support a conclusion that somehow resembles, or appears to resemble, the one supposedly argued for. Indeed, a special form of this fallacy, in which the issue is evaded deliberately while it appears not to be, is the stock in trade of many politicians. Their trick is to speak in favor of solving some general problem that all agree must be solved while ignoring the specific proposed solution that is in fact the issue in question. Everyone is in favor of freedom, equality, the elimination of poverty, and so on (politicians refer to this as being in favor of mom and apple pie). It's proposed ways for achieving these obvious goals that are controversial. So when we provide arguments in favor of mom and apple pie, our reasoning is generally irrelevant to what is at issue. (Recall Lt. Col. Oliver North's testimony about God and country in the Iran-Contra hearings or his attempt to introduce slides of events in Nicaragua.)

4. Equivocation

A term or expression is used *ambiguously* or *equivocally* in an argument when used in one sense in one place and another sense in another place. Clearly, an argument containing such an ambiguous use of language is invalid. Those who are convinced by such an argument are guilty of the fallacy called **equivocation** or **ambiguity** (which usually falls into the broad logical category *invalid inference*).

When an evangelist on TV said we all should stop sinning and "be like Jesus," a member of the audience expressed doubt that he was up to that. He pointed out that, after all, "Jesus was the son of God." In reply, the evangelist told the doubter that he could indeed stop sinning because, "You're the son of God, too." But the evangelist was guilty of *equivocation,* since the doubter meant that Jesus is the son of God in the special way that (according to Christian doctrine) only Jesus is held to be, while the evangelist had to mean that the doubter was the son of God in the metaphorical sense in which (according to Christian theology) we all are children of God.

Equivocation is a common fallacy because it is often quite hard to notice that a shift in meaning has taken place. But sometimes people are set up to commit this fallacy. For example, an ad touting sugar consumption (of all things) supported its pitch by stating, "Sugar is an essential component of the body . . . a key material in all sorts of metabolic processes." The ambiguity in this case centers on the word "sugar." If taken to mean glucose (blood sugar), the statement is true. But if taken to mean ordinary table sugar or sucrose (and the average reader could be expected to take it that way), then it is false. The advertiser can claim the ad tells the truth by construing the word *sugar* to mean glucose, knowing that most readers, taking it to mean ordinary table sugar, would conclude erroneously that table sugar is an essential food.

Ambiguity Serves Useful Functions

Students sometimes get the idea that every ambiguity, certainly every equivocation, is fallacious. But this is not so. Ambiguous uses of language, in particular

---

It is he that sitteth upon the circle of the earth.
—Isaiah 40: 22

Ambiguity

Almost any statement can be interpreted in various ways if we have a mind to do so. The Bible is a happy hunting ground for those intent on taking advantage of the ambiguity of natural languages because many people take what it says to be the word of the Ultimate Authority on most important issues. The above passage from Isaiah, one used to prove that the earth is flat, was cited after Copernicus, Kepler, and Newton as proof that it is a sphere.

metaphoric ones, have all sorts of good purposes. So do equivocations. Here is an example from the writings of oldster Carl Rogers in which the deliberate equivocation was successfully used to emphasize that he was still young at heart:

> As a boy I was rather sickly, and my parents have told me that it was predicted I would die young. This prediction has been proven completely wrong in one sense, but has come profoundly true in another sense. I think it is correct that I will never live to be old. So now I agree with the prediction. I believe that I will die *young*.[7]

Ambiguous uses of language also serve many other functions, such as the politeness needed to grease the skids of social intercourse. Benjamin Disraeli, nineteenth-century British prime minister, used ambiguity to soften his reply when someone sent him an unsolicited amateur manuscript: "Many thanks; I shall lose no time in reading it."

So-called token reflexive terms, such as *you* and *me,* are ambiguous in the sense that they refer to different people, depending on who uses them and who's listening. However, this ambiguity of reference fools very few people other than professional philosophers. But some terms that can be used either relatively or absolutely, like *rich* and *poor,* occasionally cause trouble for everybody. Poverty, for example, is exceedingly unpleasant anywhere, at any time. But the poor in America today are richer in absolute terms than most people were in nineteenth-century Europe (or are today in India or Africa). This important truth is masked by the fact that the term *poor,* in its relative sense, does apply to those Americans who are poor (in

---

So long as the economic system meets these demands [of the middle class for more jobs, higher income, more consumer goods, and more recreation], and so long as the demands take these forms, the perennial questions about *power* and *control* need never be asked. Or, better, those whose demands are being met can be congratulated on having "power," *for what is power but the ability to have one's demands met?*

—Ben Wattenberg*

The Real America (Doubleday, N.Y., 1974).

Ambiguity (Very Subtle)

Do we have power if we have the ability to get all of our demands met, some met, or even one? Just about everyone has some power. The political question Wattenberg evaded is whether average Americans have power equal to their numbers— Wattenberg's opponents don't deny that members of the middle class have power; they just deny they have their fair share.

---

[7]Carl Rogers, *Journal of Humanistic Psychology* (Fall 1980).

the relative sense) compared to most Americans although rich (in the absolute sense) compared to most non-Americans. (Clear?)

5. Appeal to Ignorance

When good reasons or evidence are lacking, the rational conclusion to draw is that we just don't know. But it's often tempting to take the absence of evidence for a claim as proof that the claim is false. Doing this sometimes leads to the fallacy called **appeal to ignorance** (traditionally known as *argumentum ad ignorantiam*). Thus, some have argued fallaciously that there is no intelligent life on other planets anywhere in the galaxy, given that no one has been able to prove that there is.

The fallacy in such reasoning is easily seen by turning such an argument around. If appeals to ignorance could prove that no intelligent life exists on other planets in the galaxy (since we haven't proved that there is), then they could also prove there is this kind of life on other planets (since we haven't proved that there isn't). In the absence of good evidence for a claim, the right thing to do is become *agnostic* on the issue and neither believe nor disbelieve it. Ignorance generally proves nothing, except, of course, that we are ignorant.

However, there are cases in which the failure of a search does count as evidence against a claim. These are the cases in which the thing searched for would very likely have been found if it were really there. Thus, if someone were to claim that a planet exists between Earth and Mars, the absence of favorable evidence would count against the existence of such a planet, given all the sky watching that has gone on in the last 10,000 years. Similarly, when a careful test fails to find blood in a urine specimen, a doctor is justified in concluding that no blood is there. These are not cases of reasoning from ignorance, but rather of reasoning from the *knowledge* that we've appropriately looked and yet failed to find the thing in question. (Note the importance of *appropriate* looking. The fact that telescopes have searched the sky for several hundred years, and naked eyes for thousands of years, without spotting God up there proves absolutely nothing about the existence of a God in the sky, since no one supposes you can see God just by looking through a telescope.)

In 1950, Senator Joseph R. McCarthy responded to a doubting question about the fortieth name on a list of eighty-one case histories he claimed were of communists working for the United States State Department by saying, "I do not have much information on this except the general statement of the agency that there is nothing in the files to disprove his Communist connections."

Many of McCarthy's followers took this absence of evidence proving that the person in question was not a communist as evidence that he was, a good example of the fallacy of appeal to ignorance.

6. Ad Hominem Argument

The fallacy of arguing **ad hominem,** sometimes called the **genetic fallacy,** consists of an irrelevant attack on an opponent, rather than his or her argument. (An *ad hominem* argument, literally, is an argument "to the person.")

Senator Jennings Randolph was guilty of *ad hominem* argument in a U.S. Senate debate on the Equal Rights Amendment to the Constitution (ERA) when he dismissed women's liberationists, and thus their arguments, with the remark that they constituted a "small band of bra-less bubbleheads." This may have been good for a laugh in the almost all-male Senate, but it was irrelevant to arguments the women's rights representatives had presented. Randolph attacked *them* (through ridicule) rather than their arguments. So he argued fallaciously.

In ridiculing women's liberationists as "bra-less bubbleheads," Senator Randolph resorted to name-calling on a rather low level. But ad hominem name-calling need not be so crude. Here is a famous example that has a good deal of literary merit, representing then Vice-President Spiro Agnew at his very best:

> A spirit of national masochism prevails, encouraged by an effete corps of impudent snobs who characterize themselves as intellectuals.[8]

Agnew attacked his intellectual opponents without bothering to consider their arguments.

Attacks on Character or Credentials May Be Cogent

Lawyers who attack the testimony of courtroom witnesses by questioning their character or expertise are not necessarily guilty of *ad hominem* argument. Courtroom witnesses, doctors, auto mechanics, lawyers, and other experts often present opinions against which we, as nonexperts, are unable to argue directly. Sometimes the best we can do is try to evaluate their honesty and judgment. Thus, testimony that a psychological expert has been convicted of perjury, or spends more time testifying in court than on any other job, would be good reason to prefer the conflicting opinion of an expert for the other side.

In these cases, we certainly do not prove that expert opinion is incorrect. At best, character attacks provide grounds only for canceling or disregarding the opinion of an expert, not for deciding that that opinion is false. If a doctor who advises operating on a patient turns out to be a quack, it's rash to conclude that no operation is necessary.

Further, in avoiding *ad hominem* reasoning, we don't want to also avoid assessing information partly in terms of its source. That someone is a genuine expert in a field or has a good record as a predictor is relevant to accepting or rejecting her or his claim, even though it's usually not conclusive.

---

[8]From a speech delivered in New Orleans (October 19, 1969).

Guilt by Association

One of the important variations on *ad hominem* arguments is **guilt by association.** Many believe that people are to be judged by the company they keep. Others hold that you should not judge people by their associates, any more than you judge books by their covers. Which view is correct?

The answer is that it *is* rational under certain circumstances to judge people by their associates. However, only rarely will such judgments have a *high degree of probability* attached to them. In the absence of other evidence, a man frequently seen in the company of different women known to be prostitutes is rightly suspected of being connected with their occupation. Similarly, a person who associates frequently and closely with men known to be agents of a foreign government is rightly suspected of being an agent of that government.

But caution is needed in dealing with indirect evidence of this kind. Suspecting that Smith uses the services of prostitutes is different from knowing that he does. (It is, of course, good reason for looking further—assuming we care enough to expend the effort.) The man who frequently associates with prostitutes may turn out to be a sociologist conducting an investigation. The close associate of foreign spies may be a friendly counterspy or just a friend of the family.

Summary of Chapter 2

We reason fallaciously when we: (1) reason from unjustified premises, (2) fail to use relevant information, or (3) reason invalidly. Standard everyday fallacy classifications, however, often crosscut these categories.

1. *Appeal to authority:* Accepting the word of alleged authorities when you shouldn't, either because it's not likely that they are in fact expert in the relevant field, or because they might not tell us truthfully, or because experts disagree on the issue (in which case we should become our own expert and form our own opinion). *Example:* Taking the word of power industry executives on the safety of nuclear power plants.

2. *Two wrongs make a right:* Defending a wrong by pointing out that our opponent has done the same (or an equally wrong) thing. *Example:* South Africans responding to charges against apartheid by pointing to our own past transgressions.

   However, sometimes two wrongs do make a right, in particular when "fighting fire with fire."
   a. *Common practice and traditional wisdom (or past practice)*: Claiming something isn't wrong, or at least is excusable, since it's commonly or traditionally done. *Example:* A soldier who defends his commission of atrocities on the grounds that soldiers commonly do such things.
   b. *Popularity:* Appealing to the crowd to determine truth. *Example:* Arguing that marijuana must be physically harmful since most people think it is.

3. *Irrelevant reason:* Trying to prove something using evidence that may appear to be relevant but really isn't. *Example:* Arguing against the claim that we shouldn't have been fighting in Vietnam on grounds that such talk only showed the enemy that America's will to fight was declining.

4. *Equivocation:* Using ambiguous locutions to mislead (or which in fact mislead). *Example:* The TV evangelist's use of the expression "son of God."
   It's important to note, however, that intentional ambiguity, and even equivocation, can be very useful and perfectly proper.

5. *Appeal to ignorance:* Arguing that since we can't prove something is false (true), we're entitled to believe it's true (false). *Example:* Arguing that no intelligent life exists on other planets in the galaxy on grounds that no one has proved there is.
   Note, however, that when an *appropriate* search has failed to turn up an item, we're generally justified in believing that it doesn't exist. *Example:* A doctor's failure to find blood in a urine sample.

6. *Ad hominem argument:* An irrelevant attack on one's opponent rather than his or her argument. *Example:* Senator Jennings Randolph's attacking women's libbers as "bra-less bubbleheads" instead of dealing with their arguments head-on.
   But note that in some circumstances, the best we can do is to attack (or evaluate) a person's character. *Example:* A courtroom expert or a doctor.
   a. *Guilt by association:* Judging a person by associates when more sensible evidence is available. *Example:* The CIA and FBI, during the 1950s, when they judged people who associated with "security risks" to themselves be security risks.

Exercise 2-1

Which of the fallacies discussed in Chapter 2 occur in the following passages? (Some may contain no fallacies.) Explain the reasons for your answers. (For instance, if the fallacy is *equivocation,* show the different senses that are involved and how they lead to fallacy; if the fallacy is *appeal to authority,* show what is unwise about this particular appeal—why we should not listen to this authority this time.) Remember that fallacy categories sometimes overlap, and that a given item may contain more than one fallacy. Remember also that some of the material is quite controversial and thus open to differing interpretations. Your *explanations* are therefore more important than the fallacy labels you put on an argument. Getting the label right but the explanation wrong means that you have answered incorrectly.

*1. *Article in college newspaper:* A committee on teaching evaluation in colleges is the coming thing.

2. *Senator Sam Ervin of North Carolina* (New York Times, *September 30, 1970*) *telling how he replied to women who were in favor of the Equal Rights Amendment to the Constitution:* I tell them, "Why, ladies, any bill

that lies around here for 47 years without getting any more support than this one has got in the past *obviously* shouldn't be passed at all. Why, I think *that affords most conclusive proof that it's unworthy of consideration.*"

3. *How:* Hey, what's with all this junk food you bought? You're always railing at me about eating healthily.
Aunt: Don't fuss. It was on sale.
How: Oh.

4. Atlantic *magazine article (January 1987) on the Chernobyl disaster's radioactive cloud that passed over most of Europe:* This agency [Italy's Civil Protection Agency] had arrived at its reassuring figure of twice background [radiation] by averaging the high radioactive levels of the north with those of the central and southern regions. The Civil Protection Agency's director defended himself by arguing that the authorities in Sweden, Austria, and Switzerland had also averaged regional data.

5. *Comment in the* Skeptical Inquirer *(Winter 1978) on astronaut Gordon Cooper's belief that some UFOs are ships from outer space:* What does Cooper do, now that he is no longer with NASA? He is currently employed, appropriately enough, by Walt Disney Enterprises.

6. *After the Soviet Union refused to accept a U.S. note demanding compensation for relatives of those in the Korean jet shot down by the Russians, the U.S. appealed to the Soviets to accept the note on grounds that it had been diplomatic common practice to do so for several centuries.*

*7. Hartford Courant *(December 20, 1972), in an article on the possibility of women priests in the Catholic Church:* Citing the historic exclusion of women from the priesthood, however, the study [of a committee of Roman Catholic bishops] said ". . . the constant tradition and practice, interpreted as of divine law, is of such a nature as to constitute a clear teaching of the Ordinary Magisterium [teaching authority]of the Church."

8. *Beginning of a book review:* Erich Segal's *Love Story—Romeo and Juliet* it isn't. But who cares. It's guaranteed to give you a good cry now and then. And it couldn't have gotten off to such a flying start for nothing. Everybody is going to be reading this novel, so you better go down to your nearest bookstore and pick up a copy.

9. It's all right for President Reagan to impound funds voted by the Congress. Every recent president—Carter, Ford, Nixon, Johnson—did so. In fact, Nixon did so on a grand scale.

10. *How:* Well, at least the post office is again working well, as it did years ago. We sent a whole bunch of packages and letters by regular mail across the country right before Christmas in three days.
Aunt: What's so hot about the post office? Years ago the mailman used to get here on foot by 10 in the morning. Now they've got a young girl driving in one of those *things,* and she never gets here till 3 in the afternoon.

11. *Robert Ringer in* The Tortoise Report *(September 1983) touting gold as an investment:* Two thousand years after the human flesh had disappeared, the gold that adorned it [an ancient Egyptian corpse] remained virtually unchanged. That's a real hard act for paper money to follow.

12. *Here is a reply on TV to political science professor Robert Lekachman's attack on "Reaganomics":* "What do these professors know? Have they ever met a payroll?"

13. *Mike Royko, in the* Chicago Sun-Times *(June 30, 1978), commenting on the very bad publicity Senator Edward Brooke of Massachusetts was getting because of the way he was handling his divorce:* What Brooke did was try to cheat his wife out of some money when they made a divorce settlement. In other words, he did what tens of thousands of desperate American men do every year. And for this perfectly normal effort at survival, his career is threatened with ruin. . . . I'm not siding with Brooke against his wife. I have no idea who was in the right or wrong. But lying during a divorce case is not unusual. If anything, it is the rule. Most people who come to divorce courts lie their heads off.

Momma by Mell Lazarus. Courtesy of Mell Lazarus and Field Newspaper Syndicate.

14. (In this case, the question is what fallacy Momma failed to perpetrate on her son.)

*15. *John P. Roche, in his political column (October 1970):* Every society is, of course, repressive to some extent—as Sigmund Freud pointed out, repression is the price we pay for civilization.

16. *Popular magazine article in 1874:* Louis Agassiz, the greatest scientist of his day, examined Darwin's claims for his theory of evolution very carefully and finally decided that it could not be true that man was descended from the ape and its earlier animal ancestry. Within six months the greatest German biologists, and the most learned anthropologists now living, have declared that the Darwin theory of the origin of man could not be true. In spite of the opinions of these, the . . . leading investigators of the century, the theory of Darwinism is being taught in the universities of

America. There is such a thing as a little knowledge leading to a great error, and this is an example.[9]

17. *American Medical Association ad against smoking:* 100,000 doctors have quit smoking cigarettes. (Maybe they know something you don't.)

18. *Lewis Carroll, in* Through the Looking Glass: "You couldn't have it if you *did* want it," the Queen said. "The rule is jam tomorrow and jam yesterday—but never jam *today.*"

"It *must* come sometimes to jam today," Alice objected.

"No it can't," said the Queen. "It's jam every *other* day: today isn't any *other* day, you know."

19. Washington Monthly, *June 1983:* According to Lou Cannon of *The Washington Post,* Fred F. Fielding recently objected to inviting Teamsters President Jackie Presser to a White House state dinner on the grounds that Presser's former Ohio local is under federal investigation for racketeering. An unnamed Reagan adviser rejected Fielding's advice by pointing out, "Teamsters are always under investigation."

20. *Vivekananda:* There is no past or future even in thought, because to think it you have to make it present.[10]

21. *Benedetto Croce, in* Philosophy of the Practical: The Inquisition must have been justified and beneficial, if whole peoples invoked and defended it, if men of the loftiest souls founded and created it severally and impartially, and its very adversaries applied it on their own account, [funeral] pyre answering to pyre.

*22. *Dr. Norman Geisler, witness for the state of Arkansas in the 1981 Creation-Evolution trial, testified in favor of belief in God, citing the line in the Bible to the effect that the Devil acknowledges but refuses to worship God, and then cinched his point by stating:* "The Devil believes there is a God!"

23. *St. Augustine, in* De Libero Arbitrio: See how absurd and foolish it is to say: I should prefer nonexistence to miserable existence. He who says, I prefer this to that, chooses something. Nonexistence is not something; it is nothing. There can be no real choice when what you choose is nothing.

24. [Secretary of Defense Caspar] Weinberger said [Israeli Premier Menachem] Begin's behavior [the bombing of Beirut, which killed 300 civilians] "cannot really be described as moderation," and [Deputy Secretary of State William] Clark added that the bombing had "embarrassed and disappointed" the Administration. Mr. Begin, however, was in no mood for

---

[9]Quoted in Richard L. Purtill, *Logic: Argument, Refutation, and Proof* (New York: Harper & Row, 1979).

[10]Quoted in Henry C. Byerly, *A Primer of Logic* (New York: McGraw-Hill, 1978).

moralizing from Washington. "I don't want to hear anything from the Americans about hitting civilian targets," he was reported to have said. "I know exactly what Americans did in Vietnam" (*New York Times,* July 26, 1981).

25. *Column by John Cunniff (July 1970):* Do Americans eat well in comparison with other nations? Millions of Americans still have poor diets, but generally speaking most Americans can afford to eat well. In the U.S. and Canada less than 20 percent of all "personal consumption expenditures" are for food. In less developed countries, the figures are much higher.

*26 ". . . Our own death is . . . unimaginable, and whenever we make the attempt to imagine it we can perceive that we really survive as spectators . . ."—Freud

The Smith Family by Mr. and Mrs. George Smith. Copyright 1986 Universal Press Syndicate. All rights reserved. Used by permission of Universal Syndicate.

27. (In this case, the question is to explain as carefully as you can why the logic exhibited in this Smith Family strip didn't deserve to get anyone anywhere.)

*28. *Nicholas von Hoffman, in the* New York Post *(October 1, 1974):* The trouble with such propositions [that there was a second murderer of John F. Kennedy] is that . . . they are seldom able to give us much of a clue as to who the "real" killer may be. It is for that reason that nobody has been able to discredit the Warren Commission report. If Lee Harvey Oswald didn't murder President Kennedy, then who did?

29. *Dialogue from the movie* Fun with Dick and Jane *about whether to keep the money Jane stole:*

> *Jane Fonda:* We've always done things the straight way.
> *George Segal:* Yeah. Well I'm tired of belonging to a minority group.

30. *From an interview with Ronald Reagan (taken from the* New York Review of Books):

> *Mr. Otis:* We would like to know . . . what the Bible really means to you.

President Reagan: I have never had any doubt about it being of divine origin. And to those who . . . doubt it, I would like to have them point out to me any similar collection of writings that have lasted for as many thousands of years and is still the best seller worldwide. It had to be of divine origin.

31. *President Reagan* (New York Times, *July 29, 1982*) *on how he could certify progress in human rights in El Salvador given that their government wasn't cooperating in the investigation of the murder of three American nuns:* I'm quite sure that there are unfortunate things that are going on and that are happening.

32. *E. F. Schumacher, famous economist, in an article in* The Atlantic *(April 1979):* Fifteen months [after I had advised that rural India should have a technology intermediate between the hoe and the tractor,] an all-India conference on intermediate technology was arranged. (They still didn't like the term [*intermediate*], so they called it appropriate technology. That's all right: when I come to India and somebody says, "Oh, Mr. Schumacher, I don't believe in appropriate technology," I just look him straight in the face and say, "Oh, that's splendid. Do you believe in inappropriate technology?")

33. *Asked how he could support a constitutional amendment requiring balanced budgets while his administration had the biggest deficits in history, President Reagan replied* (New York Times, *July 29, 1982*): The budget deficits I don't think can be laid at any individual's door.

34. Mother Jones *article (August 1983) on Ronald Reagan appointee Marjory Mecklenburg, whose legislative mandate was to promote chastity and self-discipline and "to explore family-centered approaches to the problem of adolescent sexual relations and adolescent pregnancy"* . . . she herself would just as soon keep quiet about those aspects of her personal history that do not conform to her "Little House on the Prairie" moral creed. Back home, where Mecklenburg was an outspoken opponent of abortion rights, sources have revealed to us that the chastity crusader was pregnant before she was married . . . How does Mecklenburg justify her efforts to impose an official morality on the nation's young when she herself conceived a child out of wedlock? "No comment . . . It's a family matter."

Exercise 2-2

Find examples in the mass media (television, magazines, newspapers, radio) of fallacies discussed in Chapter 2, and explain why they are fallacious.

"Having concluded, Your Highness, an exhaustive study of this nation's political, social and economic history, and after examining, Sire, the unfortunate events leading to the present deplorable state of the realm, the consensus of the council is that Your Majesty's only course, for the public good, must be to take the next step."

Question-begging advice, following oracular rule number one: make pronouncements as vague as possible to minimize the chance of being wrong.

Arguments, like men, often are pre-
tenders.

              —Plato

It don't even mak(

         remarl
        by Preside

Chapter 3

48

"The
the

*Too much doubt is much better than
too much credulity.*
              —Robert G. Ingersoll

3

Fallacious Reasoning—II

Let's now discuss some other common fallacies.

1. Provincialism

The fallacy of **provincialism** stems from the natural tendency to identify with our own group and to perceive experience largely in terms of "in-group" and "out-group." (It also stems from our identification with our own time and place.) This tendency has some good things to be said for it, since our own well-being so often depends on that of the group. But when it begins to determine the content of our beliefs, the result is fallacy.

    Provincialism influences our beliefs in basically two ways: (1) It tends to make us concentrate on our own society and what it knows and believes, to the exclusion of other cultures and what they know or believe; and (2) it tends, via *loyalty,* to influence our acceptance or rejection of alleged facts or theories, whatever the nature of the evidence.[1] Here is an example of the first, from an American newspaper series on Japan:

> The [Japanese] empire supposedly was founded about 600 B.C., but for the next 24 centuries the Japanese people lived in almost complete isolation from *the rest of the world.*[2] [Italics added]

---

[1]The fallacy of *provincialism* is similar to but different from that of *traditional wisdom.* The error in *traditional wisdom* results from assuming that traditional ways of doing things are right because they are traditional. The error in *provincialism* results from relative blindness to cultures and groups other than our own, or from loyalty to our own group. Being blind to other groups, for instance, does not imply accepting the traditions of one's own group.

[2]*Lawrence* (Kansas) *Daily Journal World* (August 8, 1970).

rest of the world," of course, meant the Western world. The writer ignored great influence of China on Japan during much of that 24-century period.

Provincialism is a problem for all of us, including experts. Countless psychological experiments conducted on American subjects have reached conclusions that could be shown wrong by observing even a few people of other cultures. The same is true of many commonly held ideas. When AIDS hit first in homosexual communities and among certain other small "high-risk" groups, many heterosex-

Garry Trudeau poking fun at American provincialism.

uals not in those groups, including some "experts," were lulled into thinking that heterosexuals would be largely passed over in this disaster. They believed this at a time when AIDS was running wild among heterosexuals in several African countries. For some Americans, Africa might as well have been on some other planet in another galaxy.

Loyalty

The second way our provincial natures push us into committing the fallacy of *provincialism* is by making us believe, or disbelieve, because of our *loyalty* to the group. We want to believe we're the greatest and the other guys are second rate, so we tend to make our beliefs conform to this desire, whatever the facts of the matter indicate.

The reactions of many Americans to the My Lai massacre in Vietnam are a good example.[3] On reading about My Lai, a teletype inspector in Philadelphia is reported to have said he didn't think it happened: "I can't believe our boys' hearts are that rotten." This response was typical, as was that of the person who informed the *Cleveland Plain Dealer,* which had printed photos of the massacre: "Your paper is rotten and anti-American." Surveys taken after wide circulation of news about the massacre revealed that large numbers of Americans refused to believe "American boys" had done such a thing. The myth of American moral superiority seems to have been a better source of truth for them than evidence at hand. They were like the clerics who refused to look through Galileo's telescope to see the moons of Jupiter because they *knew* Jupiter could not possibly have moons.

2. Lack of Proportion

One of the most overlooked errors of reasoning in the literature is the failure to see things in proper perspective or proportion. Let's name this the fallacy of **lack of proportion.** Here is an excerpt from a newspaper column by George F. Will making that very point:

> When polio was killing 300 people annually, parents feared for their children. Drunk drivers will kill 86 times that many people this year, yet few Americans are alarmed. They are rightly alarmed about violent crime, and about handguns, yet drunk drivers account for the most common form of violent death.
>
> When toxic shock killed some women, the publicity killed a product. A few instances of botulism destroyed a soup company. But the public that reacts swiftly to such dangers is not comparably aroused by the fact that a life is lost every 21 minutes in an alcohol-related crash, and one out of every two Americans will eventually be involved in an alcohol-related crash. . . .

---

[3]See Seymour M. Hersh, *My Lai 4: A Report on the Massacre and Its Aftermath* (New York: Random House, 1970), pp. 151–152.

> If Americans used seat belts, they would save 28,000 lives this year. But seat belt use is declining while anxieties about remote dangers are rising.[4]

Failure to see things in perspective is especially common among those who work for what they believe to be a worthy cause—they tend to get caught up in what they're doing and exaggerate its importance all out of proportion. Women caught up in the women's rights movement, blacks working for civil rights, and religious fundamentalists caught up in the fight against the theory of evolution all are good examples. Such people often become overzealous and tend to see the less concerned as callous, unthinking, or prejudiced, forgetting that there are plenty of other evils in the world, even some worse ones. (They also sometimes drive others crazy by turning every conversation into a political harangue.) Here is a magazine excerpt showing how our rhetoric often reveals a lack of a sense of proportion, generated by missionary zeal:

> "Genocide" was a word used to describe the Atlanta murders. "Fascist" was the word Norman Mailer used to characterize a society unwilling to take chances on literary murderers [the particular literary murderer Mailer had in mind proceeded to murder again when Mailer's efforts helped win him a chance]. Senator Larry Pressler was detained by the Polish police for half an hour during his visit to Warsaw a couple of weeks ago, and came back saying that now he understands how repressive martial law can be.[5]

Politicians can and often do take advantage of the failure of so many people to keep a sense of proportion about them. Richard Nixon was forced from office because he lied to the nation about subordinate wrongdoing he apparently learned about only after the fact. He was not driven from office for his much more serious crimes, such as authorizing illegal warfare in Cambodia that killed thousands of civilians (let's pass over the question of the legality of the Vietnam War, which Nixon inherited anyway).

During the first half of the 1980s, as the AIDS outbreak became more and more serious, it came close to being ignored by officials at the top of the Reagan administration (the president did not utter the word *AIDS* in public until May 1987). Instead, the masses were diverted from this and other serious problems in part by being whipped up on the comparatively minor illegal drug problem (on which they hardly made a dent), school prayers, and so on, modern day versions of bread and circuses.

Tokenism

One of the important variations on the fallacy *lack of proportion* is **tokenism**—mistaking a token gesture for the real thing. We do so, usually, because we fail to

---

[4] *Washington Post* (May 2, 1982).
[5] *New Republic* (February 10, 1982).

see the lack of proportion between the token gesture and the amount of effort actually required.

Tokenism is one of the politician's best friends. When action is demanded but is politically inexpedient, politicians frequently turn to it. They make a token gesture (set in motion only a small proportion of what is required) and shout about it as loudly as they can. For example, in 1970, an earthquake in Peru killed about 50,000 people and left an emergency of major proportions in its wake. (That many people have probably not been killed in the United States in all the earthquakes,

Doonesbury by Garry Trudeau. Copyright, 1973, G.B. Trudeau.
All rights reserved. Used by permission of Universal Press Syndicate.

Tokenism: Note that Clint equates his notion of half way with fairness.

hurricanes, and tornadoes in our history.) Relief aid was desperately needed by the Peruvians. The American response was a trip to Peru by Mrs. Nixon (widely publicized—a picture of Mrs. Nixon hugging a little earthquake victim appeared on page one in many newspapers around the country). But very little effective aid ever reached Peru from the United States.[6]

The Double Standard

We are guilty of the fallacy of the **double standard** when we judge or evaluate two or more things, groups, or people according to inconsistent standards (without some legitimate reason for doing so). Usually, this means holding our opponents to higher standards than we do our friends (or ourselves) just because they are our opponents. (And usually, we don't notice that we've used a double standard, because of *self-deception*.)

While the fallacy of the *double standard* is usually a variation of the fallacy *inconsistency* (to be discussed soon), a lack of proportion is often the psychological mechanism that puts it into motion. In other words, we often unwittingly adopt a double standard because we don't realize that a lack of proportion or perspective has led us into inconsistency.

The way the media portrayed Israel's role in the 1982 Beirut massacre is a good example. In the first place, "only" a few hundred people were killed in this massacre—many fewer than the number of Lebanese murdered by the PLO, the Syrians, and other Lebanese. Yet the coverage of the Beirut massacre was much greater (so

---

Names Change but Tokenism Never Does

Proctor & Gamble is making an all-out effort to eliminate sexist language from company reports and job titles. The firm is focusing its attention on a cake plant being built near Jackson, Tenn. There, "manpower curves" have become "effort curves," "man-hours" are now "effort hours" and "he"— "he/she."

Craftsmen became artisans but that term left the plant's building contractor speechless. Now they're crafters. Other terms have been harder to replace: Foremen are now called first-line supervisors, but they've yet to come up with a suitable replacement for journeyman.

As could be expected, the new terminology is not being taken too seriously by the people actually building the plant. And why should it be? Of the 340 wage earners at the cake factory, only five are women.

—*New Times* (October 2, 1978)
©1978 by New Times Publishing Co. Reprinted by permission.

Corporate tokenism on the women's rights front.

---

[6]See Roger Glass, *New Republic* (September 19, 1970).

was the public outrage). And second, while the Israelis surely were guilty of negligence (they expected the Lebanese Christian militia to kill PLO soldiers who were hiding in refugee camps in violation of the peace agreement just reached and didn't pay attention when civilians were killed), it was, after all, Lebanese Christian militia who committed the slaughter—in retaliation for previous atrocities that were, in turn, in retaliation for still prior atrocities. But it was the Israelis who received most of the condemnation.[7]

3. Questionable Premise

We're guilty of the fallacy of **questionable premise** when we violate the principle of cogent reasoning that requires us to use only justified or warranted premises. (Of course, what a given person finds justified depends on that person's background information and world view.)[8]

To become a pro at spotting questionable premises, we have to overcome certain natural tendencies and beliefs. Recall the misplaced faith many Americans had—almost to the end—that President Nixon did not take part in the Watergate coverup and therefore should not be impeached.[9] Why did they believe this in the face of increasingly strong evidence that he was lying? The answer spotlights several of the natural tendencies we need to hold in check.

In the first place, we all are strongly moved to accept the official "myths" about our own society, including the myth that our leaders, in particular our presidents, do not lie to us (the point of the George Washington cherry tree myth), except perhaps for very high-minded reasons (for instance, to keep vital secrets from the enemy). Good thinkers go beyond official myths to formulate more accurate theories as to how their societies actually function.

Second, when we're young, most of us accept our parents as genuine authorities, perhaps even the best authorities (when we're kids, *we* obviously don't know enough to survive without their knowledge). Other authority figures, such as religious ministers and especially leaders of nations, receive some of that parental aura by virtue of their positions of authority. Good thinkers learn from experience that authority figures come in all shapes, sizes, and qualities—our parents and leaders may be brilliant people of sterling integrity, but then again they may not. (Nixon, obviously, was not a leader of sterling integrity.)

---

[7]For more in this vein, see the Norman Podhoretz article that appeared in the *International Herald Tribune* and many other papers on September 27, 1982. And see Chapter 9 for more on the principles of news reporting that led the media to play the story the way they did.

[8]Some logicians, who conceive of the notion of fallacious reasoning more narrowly than we do in this text, refuse to call acceptance of a questionable premise a fallacy. They do, of course, admit that acceptance of questionable premises is a mistake in reasoning.

[9]Their fallacy was *questionable premise* because the conclusion Nixon wanted us to draw was that he shouldn't be forced out of office. (Premise: I'm innocent. Conclusion: Don't fire me.) In everyday life, however, it's often difficult to tell premises from conclusions—an argument should be questioned if it contains a questionable *statement*, whether or not we can figure out that it was a premise rather than a conclusion.

Third, our feelings get bound up with issues and personalities, making it hard for us to be objective. (Gamblers know, for instance, that in a stadium sports crowd, better odds can be obtained by betting *against* the home team.) Thus, the feelings of those who voted for Nixon became bound up with his innocence. It's hard, after all, to admit we voted for a liar. Good thinkers learn to give up discredited opinions.

Fourth, we tend to deceive ourselves in ways that favor our own narrow interests. Nixon, like any president, favored certain social and economic interests over others. Selfish desire led some people who had those interests to deceive themselves into believing in his innocence. Those who reason well don't let selfish desires influence their perception of reality.

Fifth, we tend to hang on to beliefs out of tenacity or loyalty, even in the face of contrary evidence (recall the earlier discussion of loyalty). Some diehard Nixon supporters didn't want to be "quitters" or "fair-weather friends," and thus they believed the president long after overwhelming evidence of his guilt was available. Loyalty is a wonderful human trait, but not for finding out the truth about things.

And, finally, most of us simply aren't trained in the art of critical thinking—in particular, in the knack of dredging up from memory old information relevant to current issues. Nixon should have been doubted on Watergate because of his past record (see below about the lies he told in campaigning against, say, Helen Gahagan Douglas in 1950); but even among those Americans who once knew this, there was a tendency to let the past rest. This tendency is the reason why, for instance, a sitting president can campaign for reelection on a platform contradictory to his actual record in the White House.

Reading between the lines, or adding up the figures, is one way to avoid accepting questionable statements. To take a lighter example, an article on Ann Landers (of advice column fame) stated that she personally read every one of more than 1,000 letters she received every day, considering it a sacred trust. The article states that this conscientious practice paid off for her not just with fame and a high salary but also with income from about 100 speeches she was asked to deliver every year. But even if she spent eight hours every day reading those letters, that would mean reading about two every minute (no time off for coffee breaks), a task even Ann Landers wasn't likely to be up to. And when would she have gotten time to write her column or prepare and deliver 100 speeches? The claim that she actually read every letter she received is questionable indeed.

4. Straw Man

While the broad fallacy category of *questionable premise* is seldom mentioned in traditonal logic texts, several specific varieties of that fallacy are quite common. One of these is the fallacy **straw man.**[10] We're guilty of this fallacy when we mis-

---

[10]Should a time-honored name such as this one be replaced by, say, *straw person,* on grounds of reforming sexist features of language? Is the name *straw man* derogatory to women? Would we do better chucking the "straw" altogether and referring to this fallacy as a kind of *caricature*?

represent an opponent's position to make it easier to attack, or attack a weaker opponent or position while ignoring a stronger one.

Politicians running for office frequently use this fallacy, Richard Nixon being one of the best examples. He used *straw man* (along with *ad hominem* argument and *false dilemma,* to be discussed soon) as the cornerstone of his rhetorical style in every campaign he waged. In 1950, when he ran for the Senate against Congresswoman Helen Gahagan Douglas, Nixon's speeches and political ads were full of *ad hominem* and *straw man* arguments.[11] Here is an example from a political ad:

> The real import of the contest between Mr. Nixon and Helen Gahagan Douglas is whether America shall continue to tolerate COMMUNIST CONSPIRACIES within our own borders and Government, persist in condoning BUREAUCRATIC PROFLIGACY and appeasing TOTALI-TARIAN AGGRESSION, or whether America shall victoriously resist these deadly dangers.[12]

The later Nixon played down communism in distorting his opponents' positions, preferring instead to associate them in the public eye with the views of "radical liberals," hippies, the youth counterculture, and militant left-wing groups like the Weather Underground. Here is an example from his acceptance speech at the 1972 Republican convention:

> Let me illustrate the difference in our philosophies. Because of our free economic system, what we have done is build a great building of economic wealth and might in America. It is by far the tallest building in the world, and we are still adding to it. Now, because some of the windows are broken, they say tear it down and start again. We say, replace the windows and keep building. That's the difference.

The "they" was the radical left; Nixon wanted voters to think the position of his opponent, George McGovern, was just like that of the radical left because Nixon's version of the radical left position was so easy to caricature and then attack. Nixon rarely mentioned the specifics either of McGovern's program or of his actual record. The straw McGovern was, after all, such an inviting target.

Why are *ad hominem* argument and *straw man* so powerful in the hands of a skilled practitioner like Richard Nixon? One reason is that voters rarely do the small amount of work necessary to discover that the position attacked is a straw one—a distortion of the position actually held. Those who fail to follow through on the facts are condemned to be easy marks for the clever politicians who hawk *straw man* and other fallacies as their stock-in-trade.

---

[11]Nixon is claimed to have engaged in straw man rhetoric against Mrs. Douglas only after she had used similar tactics against him. Can we argue that he thus was innocent because he was merely fighting fire with fire? Or would that constitute the fallacy of two wrongs make a right?

[12]For more on early Nixon campaign rhetoric, see the article on Helen Gahagan Douglas in *Ms* magazine, October 1973 and the book *The Strange Case of Richard Milhous Nixon* (New York: Popular Library, 1973) by former congressman Jerry Voorhis, Nixon's opponent in 1946.

Exaggeration

The fallacy of the *straw man* is perpetrated by distorting the argument of one's opponent and then attacking that distorted version. However, distortion itself is not necessarily bad or fallacious. In the form of *exaggeration,* for instance, it is a time-honored literary device used by most great writers for satirical or poetic effect. Great satirists, such as Jonathan Swift, use exaggeration in order to shock people into seeing what they take to be humanity's true nature, and in an attempt to reduce that strange gap in most of us between mere belief and belief that serves as an impetus to action.

So exaggeration in itself is not fallacious. The purpose of the exaggeration determines whether or ot a fallacy is committed. Satirists who exaggerate the evil in human nature don't intend us to believe that human beings are as bad as they portray them. They exaggerate to help us realize the actual extent of human evil. But when the intent is to make us believe that the exaggeration is literally true, then the fallacy *straw man* enters into the picture.

In the case of Richard Nixon, he got where he got by. . . dogged and intelligent perseverance: *ten million* town hall appearances for local candidates over a period of 20 years.

—William F. Buckley, Jr., *New York Post* (October 1974)

We don't want to be foolishly strict in labeling items fallacious. Obviously, Buckley didn't intend readers to take the 10 million figure literally. So he isn't guilty of a fallacy, although he surely did exaggerate. He used exaggeration to impress on us that, as vice-president and then president, Nixon made an unusually large number of appearances for local candidates, and in fact Nixon did just that.

---

5. False Dilemma

The fallacy called **false dilemma** (or the *either-or* fallacy) occurs when we reason or argue from the assumption that there are just two plausible solutions to a problem or issue, when in fact there are at least three. (However, it's convenient to stretch the term *false dilemma* to cover false "trilemmas," and so on.) *False dilemma* is a species of *questionable premise* because any statement that sets up a *false* dilemma ought to be questioned.

Here is the lead-in blurb for an article: "Society and Sex Roles":

Economics, not biology, may explain male domination.[13]

This statement suggests that there are just two possibilities: either biology explains male dominance, or economic success does so. And it suggests that the second pos-

---

[13]*Human Nature* (April 1978).

sibility, economic success, "may" (weasel word) be the true explanation of male domination. Yet there are many other possibilities, such as social custom, religious conviction, and various *combinations* of economic and biological factors. By tempting us to think of the cause of male domination as either economics or biology, the quote leads us to overlook other possibilities and thus to commit the fallacy of *false dilemma*.

Which brings to mind the familiar question whether it is differences in heredity or in environment (nature or nurture) that are responsible for individual differences in intelligence. Put as a question of heredity *or* environment, the problem becomes a *false dilemma* because it should be clear by now that heredity and environment both shape intelligence. The sensible question to ask is not whether heredity or environment is responsible, but rather how much effect each of these has on the various different kinds of intelligence.

Arguments or statements posing *false dilemmas* often mask the fact that they contain a dilemma of any kind, so that noticing their fallaciousness takes watchfulness. Here is an example, a 1978 statement by Harvard University President Derek Bok:

> If you think education is expensive, try ignorance.

This has lots of truth to it, of course; some sort of education is certainly more valuable than no education at all. But Bok's statement, in particular because uttered by the president of Harvard, invites us to think that our choice is either *formal* education or ignorance. So it invites us to accept the *false dilemma* of either getting a formal education or remaining ignorant—omitting the alternatives of *informal* education or becoming *self-taught* (as many important thinkers have been) as well as the alternative of less expensive formal education.

Since World War II, a good deal of the discussion in the mass media (as on the floor in Congress—but not nearly as much in the *non*-mass media) concerning the extremely serious question of military budgets has been based on some sort of *false dilemma*. The issue has usually been characterized in the media as though there are two basic positions on the question: increased defense spending, leading to increased military strength and safety, and decreased defense spending, leading to decreased military strength and safety.

Yet this has never been the way the forces have lined up. There have always been *several* camps on this issue. Some people have indeed favored increased military spending as the way to get increased military protection from the Russians (in terms of political power, this has been the dominant view). And a few have favored reduced military spending and reduced military capability—often on the grounds that an all-out war with Russia is unthinkable, but sometimes for strictly pacifistic reasons. However, others have argued not for an increase or decrease in military spending as much as for an improvement in the *quality* of the weapons and training we buy for all those billions spent. And still others have argued for both reduced spending and a (selective) improvement in our military might. Their point has been that we spend too much on atomic overkill and on a few very complicated ineffective weapons—battleships, the F-16 fighter plane, etc.—rather than on simpler, cheaper weapons. (The Reagan administration's view seemed to be that adequate defense requires spending more money.)

By reducing as much of the debate as possible into a simplistic *false dilemma* between more spending and better defense versus less spending and poorer defense, those favoring the first of these alternatives increase their chances of prevailing, since the other alternative in their dilemma is not acceptable to most Americans. (Note the connection between falling for this kind of *false dilemma* and simplistic, unsubtle, undetailed reasoning.)

6. Begging the Question

When arguing, it's impossible to provide reasons for every assertion. Some of what we say or do must go unjustified, at least for the moment. But if, in the course of a discussion or debate, we endorse without proof some form of the very question at issue, we are guilty of the fallacy generally called **begging the question**, a fallacy that falls into the broad category *questionable premise* (because a statement questionable as a conclusion is equally questionable as a premise). Here is an example excerpted from a magazine interview (during the days before the Argentine dictatorship was replaced by a more democratic government):

> *Question:* Why do you think Argentina will go socialist?
> *Answer:* Because of the force of "world historical circumstances."

In other words, we were told that the circumstances in the world that would lead Argentina to socialism were the historical circumstances in the world that would lead Argentina to socialism.

Now here is a little begged question from *Parade* magazine (December 15, 1985):

> *Question:* How old is John Kenneth Galbraith, the Harvard economist, and why was he never awarded a Nobel Prize in economics?—Fran Kay, Kansas City, Mo.
> *Answer:* Galbraith, 77, emeritus professor of economics at Harvard, is a learned and witty writer on many subjects including economics. Apparently the Nobel Memorial Prize committee has not judged his contributions to economics, at least at this point, to be sufficiently original to merit a laureateship.

Well then, why hasn't the prize committee considered Galbraith's work good enough for a Nobel prize? Because they judged it not original enough to warrant a prize. No kidding.

Political arguments frequently beg questions at issue. For example, some of those against abortion have argued that abortion is wrong since a baby shouldn't have to suffer because of the selfish desires or the illness of the mother. By calling the fetus a *baby*, they implicitly assert that it is a human being, thus begging one of the more serious points at issue (whether a fetus is a human being).

Question begging occurs frequently in disputes between partisans of extremely different positions. Thus, the rejoinder "But that amounts to socialism!" often is heard in disputes over public medical care, even though the other side is perfectly aware of this fact, and may even be attracted to the proposal precisely because it *is* socialistic. To avoid begging the question, the antisocialist must present *reasons* for rejecting anything that smacks of socialism. (This example illustrates the point that the fallacy of *begging the question* is relative. For instance, when two died-in-the-wool advocates of capitalism argue, the claim "But that amounts to socialism" doesn't beg a question *at issue* between them, and so isn't question begging.)

7. Inconsistency

One of the most important fallacies is that of **inconsistency.** We reason or argue *inconsistently* when we argue from contradictory premises, or argue for contradictory conclusions. Obviously, if two premises contradict each other, one of them must be false. So even though the argument in which they occur is *valid*,[14] we commit a fallacy in accepting its conclusion. (Similar remarks apply to cases in which we reason to inconsistent conclusions.)

It should be clear that the fallacy of *inconsistency* is a species of the larger fallacy category of *questionable premise*. This is because at least one of a set of inconsistent premises must be false, so that the set as a whole should be questioned.

Politics being what it is, government officials and other politicians are frequently (one might even say continually) inconsistent, although their inconsistency is not usually explicit or even exact (for one thing because political rhetoric is so vague and ambiguous). Their inconsistency is of several kinds, the simplest being to contradict themselves within a single speech, article, or news conference. Of course, such inconsistency is rarely explicit—that would be too obvious. Instead, it tends to be concealed in some way or other. Typical is the candidate who in the same speech favors large increases in government services (to attract voters who will benefit from them) and important tax reductions (to attract voters burdened by heavy taxes). Since government services cost money (and since most government expenditures are fixed), a package of increased services and decreased taxes can be regarded as inconsistent in the absence of a plausible explanation as to how it can be done. Requiring that figures "add up" is a way of requiring candidates to be consistent.

Inconsistency over Time

Another way in which politicians are often guilty of *inconsistency* is by saying one thing at one time and place and another thing at another, without justifying the change or retracting the earlier pronouncement. (The expression is "blowing with the wind.")

Politicians often are forced by circumstances to commit the fallacy of *inconsistency* when, by rising in office, they come to represent different constituencies with different viewpoints. Similarly, they often commit this fallacy in order to "keep up with the times"; what is popular at one time often is unpopular at another.

Lyndon Johnson's position on civil rights legislation illustrates both of these. As a congressman and (for a while) as a senator from Texas, he consistently voted

---

[14] *Valid* because contradictory premises validly imply any and every conclusion (for technical reasons).

Mike Peters, 1986. Reprinted by permission of United Feature Syndicate/United Media.

and spoke *against* civil rights legislation. But when he became a power in the Senate, his tune modified, and when he became president, it changed completely. Here are two quotes that illustrate Johnson's fundamental *inconsistency over time* on the question of race and civil rights legislation. The first statement was made in 1948 at Austin, Texas, when he was running for the Senate:

> This civil rights program [part of President Truman's "Fair Deal"], about which you have heard so much, is a farce and a sham—an effort to set up a police state in the guise of liberty. I am opposed to that program. I have fought it in Congress. *It is the province of the state to run its own elections.* I am opposed to the antilynching bill because the federal government has no more business enacting a law against one form of murder than another. I am against the FEPC [Fair Employment Practices Commission] because if a man can tell you whom you must hire, he can tell you whom you cannot employ.

But in 1964, Johnson was president of the United States. He had a larger constituency, and, equally important, the average American's views on race and civil rights were changing. In that year, Congress passed an extremely important civil rights act *at his great urging.* And in 1965, he delivered a famous speech at the predominantly black Howard University, in which he said in part:

> Nothing in any country touches us more profoundly, and nothing is more freighted with meaning for our own destiny, than the revolution of the Negro American.
>
> In far too many ways American Negroes have been another nation, deprived of freedom, crippled by hatred, the doors of opportunity closed to hope.
>
> In our time change has come to this nation, too. The American Negro, acting with impressive restraint, has peacefully protested and marched,

entered the courtrooms and the seats of government, demanding a justice that has long been denied. The voice of the Negro was the call to action. But it is a tribute to America that, once aroused, the courts and the Congress, the President and most of the people, have been the allies of progress. . . .[W]e have seen in 1957 and 1960, and again in 1964, the first civil rights legislation in this nation in almost an entire century.

As majority leader of the United States Senate, I helped to guide two of these bills through the Senate. And as your president, I was proud to sign the third. And now, very soon *we will have the fourth—a new law guaranteeing every American the right to vote.*

No act of my entire administration will give me greater satisfaction than the day when my signature makes this bill, too, the law of this land.

And on August 6, 1965, he did sign the Voting Rights Act into law. But he didn't explain why it was no longer ". . . the province of the state to run its own elections." He didn't explain his about-face on civil rights legislation.

During the Reagan administration, the Commerce Department investigated several Japanese electronics firms for "dumping" 64K RAM computer chips on the U.S. market. (*Dumping* means selling below cost in foreign markets.) At the same time, the Justice Department was investigating the same companies to determine if they'd violated antitrust laws by conspiring to set (presumably too high) prices.

Similarly, President Reagan said in a speech to the Costa Rican National Assembly that "any nation destabilizing its neighbors by protecting guerrillas and exporting violence should forfeit close and fruitful relations with . . . any

---

Here's an item from The New Republic, *September 28, 1987, showing Robert Dole blowing with the wind.*

Dole Sees AIDS Issue As Key One in '88 Race

"Senator Robert Dole said today that the AIDS issue would be a major one in the 1988 presidential race and that the government should consider spending several billion dollars to deal with preventing the spread of the disease."
—*New York Times* (March 21, 1987)

Dole Urges AIDS Not Become an Issue in Presidential Race

"Senator Robert Dole . . . urged that the issue of AIDS be kept out of the 1988 presidential race. . . . 'I just happen to believe it's not that kind of issue.' "
—*New York Times* (August 8, 1987)

(Thanks to Mr. Jack Kemp, Washington, D.C.)

people who truly love peace and freedom." But soon after, we learned that the CIA was recruiting, arming, and directing "clandestine military operations against Nicaragua."[15]

Because of the vagueness and ambiguity of most everyday language, organizations often can get away with what appears to be *inconsistency* simply by reinterpreting. For instance, in a nationally televised speech on July 27, 1981, President Reagan said, "I will not stand by and see those of you who are dependent on Social Security deprived of the benefits you've worked so hard to earn. You will continue to receive your checks in the full amount due you." Listeners certainly got the impression the president was against Social Security payment cuts. But the next day, David Gergen, a White House spokesman, "interpreted" Reagan's statement to mean that President Reagan reserved the right to decide who was dependent on Social Security benefits, who had earned such benefits, and who, accordingly, was due them.[16] (Since Reagan tended to wander from prepared texts, reinterpreting his remarks back on course became a common feature of the Reagan administration.)

Inconsistency Between Words and Actions

Another common variety of inconsistency is to *say* one thing but *do* something else. (Calling this a "fallacy" stretches that concept a bit to serve everyday purposes.) During the 1976 campaign, Jimmy Carter and his representatives kept assuring us that Carter would appoint "fresh talent" if elected. Here, for instance, is a statement by then campaign manager Hamilton Jordon:

> If we end up appointing people like Cyrus Vance and Zbigniew Brzezinski, we will have failed.

So after winning election, Carter appointed Vance secretary of state and Brzezinski head of the National Security Council. (His other appointments tended to be equally stale "fresh talent," like James Schlesinger as energy chief.)

Moon Mullins. Reprinted by permission of Tribune Media Services.

---

[15]*Philadelphia Inquirer* (December 5, 1982, and January 11, 1983).
[16]*Philadelphia Inquirer* (July 31, 1981); also reported in the *Quarterly Review of Doublespeak* (November 1981).

When Gerald Ford, chosen by Richard Nixon as his successor, became the first unelected president, he assured the Ameican people he would not run for president in 1976. But when the time came, he ran, an inconsistency between his words and actions that hardly caused a ripple.

During the hearings held before Ford's confirmation as vice-president, he was asked: "If a president resigned his office before his term expired, would his successor have the power to prevent or to terminate any investigation or criminal prosecution charges against the former president?" His reply was: "I do not think the public would stand for it," a clear indication that he would not use such power. And then, eleven days before issuing the pardon, when asked if he intended to pardon Mr. Nixon, he replied that until legal procedures had been undertaken, ". . . I think it's unwise and untimely for me to make any commitment." In the absence of an explanation of his change of mind, it's clear that President Ford was guilty of the fallacy of *inconsistency* when he pardoned Richard Nixon.

Of course, high government officials are not the only ones whose words are inconsistent with their actions. Cigarette smokers who argue against legalizing marijuana on the grounds that marijuana is unhealthy are inconsistent in this way. And so are those feminists who argue against different "roles" for each sex, yet play the feminine role when it's in their interest to do so (for instance, expecting men to drive on long trips, buy them expensive engagement rings, or spank errant children).

Like all candidates, Ronald Reagan promised all sorts of things to attract voters in his 1980 election campaign. Perhaps the nastiest example concerns the air traffic controllers. In October 1980, he wrote to Robert Poli, their union president, saying:

> I have been thoroughly briefed by members of my staff as to the deplorable state of our nation's air control system. They have told me that too few people working unreasonable hours with obsolete equipment has placed the nation's air travelers in unwarranted danger. In an area the Carter Administration has failed to act reasonably.
>
> You can rest assured that if I am elected President, I will take whatever steps are necessary to provide our air traffic controllers with the most modern equipment available, and to adjust staff levels and work days so they are commensurate with achieving the maximum degree of public safety. . . .
>
> I pledge to you that my administration will work very closely with you to bring about a spirit of cooperation between the President and the air traffic controllers. Such harmony can and must exist if we are to restore the people's confidence in the government. . . .

On the strength of this letter and Reagan's public pronouncements, the air traffic controller's union (PATCO) naïvely endorsed Reagan over Jimmy Carter. But when elected, Reagan sold the union and its striking members down the river in an especially brutal case of union busting (he had military personnel take over their jobs and barred strikers from ever again serving as air traffic controllers).

Inconsistency is often connected in people's minds with *hypocrisy*, with pretending to be or believe what one is not or does not believe. In 1986, when Nancy Reagan held a White House get-together in honor of handicapped children, Republican Senator Lowell Weicker blasted her for being hypocritical, given that her husband's administration had consistently tried to cut funds to aid the handi-

HIS FANTASY, TATTOO?... HE WANTS TO CUT TAXES, INCREASE DEFENSES AND BALANCE THE BUDGET ALL AT THE SAME TIME...

Mike Peters, *Dayton Daily News.* Reprinted by permission of Mike Peters.

capped. In leveling his charge that the White House party was "nothing but hypocrisy," Weicker commented, "Instead of advocating genuine opportunity for the disabled, this administration pushes nothing but photo opportunities."[17]

Organizational Inconsistency

Large organizations, such as governments, generally have several different people who can "speak for" the organization. Perhaps we can think of an organization as being guilty of *inconsistency* when different authorized representatives who are speaking or acting for that organization contradict each other.

While organizational inconsistency and inconsistency between words and actions are to be expected from governments on occasion, the 1987 Congressional Iran-Contra hearings publicized another aspect of this, if the testimony of President Reagan's National Security Agency advisor, Admiral John Poindexter, is to be believed. He claimed that in the case of certain covert actions it sometimes is the job of hired hands to lie about what is going on, even to Congress, as Lt. Col. Oliver North in fact did, and to conceal details from the president himself so that he will have "deniability"—the ability to deny in all honesty what his administration in fact is doing because he doesn't know what his administration is doing. (Of course, there were those who were not entirely convinced by Poindexter's testimony

---

[17]*San Francisco Chronicle* (February 22, 1986).

Over time, all politicians contradict themselves, some of course more than others. Ronald Reagan is a case in point, as illustrated by the following examples:[18]

On civil rights: "I favor the Civil Rights Act of 1964 and it must be enforced at the point of a bayonet, if necessary." (October 19, 1965). "I would have voted against the Civil Rights Act of 1964" (June 16, 1966).

On Redwood National Park: "I believe our country can and should have a Redwood National Park in California" (April 17, 1967). ". . . There can be no proof given that a national park is necessary to preserve the redwoods. The state of California has already maintained a great conservation program" (April 18, 1967—yes, that's the next day).

On the Soviet grain embargo: "I just don't believe the farmer should be made to pay a special price for our diplomacy, and I'm opposed to [the Soviet grain embargo]" (January 7, 1980). "If we are going to do such a thing to the Soviet Union as a full grain embargo, which I support, first we have to be sure our own allies would join us on this" (January 8, 1980).

On air pollution: "Air pollution has been substantially controlled" (October 8, 1980). "I don't think I've said anything of the kind" (October 20, 1980). "Isn't it substantially under control? I think it is" (October 20, 1980).

On Central America: "We have never interfered in the internal government of a country and have no intention of doing so, never have had any thought of that kind" (September 28, 1982). "We are not trying to do anything to try and overthrow the Nicaraguan government" (April 14, 1983). "Now, if they [House committee members] want to tell us that we can give money and do the same things we've been doing—money giving, providing subsistence, and so forth to these people [anti-Sandinista guerrillas in Nicaragua] and making it overt instead of covert—that's all right with me" (May 5, 1983).

Here now is an example of two members of the 1980 Reagan campaign team being inconsistent (at least) with each other:

Question: "Do you advocate a 'government to government relationship' with Taiwan?" *Candidate Reagan:* "Yes, I think that liaison—this is what I stress—that could be official" (August 16, 1980). *Candidate Bush:* "Governor Reagan hasn't proposed a two-Chinas policy, nor does he intend to propose such a policy. We don't advocate diplomatic relations with Taiwan, nor have we" (August 19, 1980). *Question:* "Are you still for 'official relations' with Taiwan, yes or no?" *Candidate Reagan:* "I guess it's a yes" (August 22, 1980). "I don't know that I said that or not, ah, I really don't" (August 25, 1980). *Candidate Bush:* "He did not say that. If you're referring to the press conference I attended, the Governor did not say 'government to government relations'." *Candidate Reagan:* "I misstated" (August 25, 1980).

---

[18]Marc Green and Gail MacCall, *There He Goes Again: Ronald Reagan's Reign of Error* (New York: Pantheon, 1983).

> *We have just gone to great lengths in describing* inconsistency *as a serious fallacy to be avoided at all costs and* consistency *as a requirement of good reasoning. Yet others have railed against being consistent, illustrated by Ralph Waldo Emerson's famous remark, "A foolish consistency is the hobgoblin of little minds, adored by little statesmen, philosophers and divines."*
>
> *But there need be no inconsistency in accepting both sides of this coin, provided we notice that consistency is an ambiguous concept. One sense requires us to be consistent with what we know at any given time. This is roughly the sense meant in this chapter. The other requires us to be consistent now and forever, to stick to our beliefs no matter what contrary evidence we encounter. This, presumably, is the sense intended by Emerson.*

that the president was not informed at least by implication of these covert activities.)

The Double Standard (Again)

Since the fallacy of the *double standard* (mentioned when discussing the fallacy *lack of proportion*) is a variety of *inconsistency,* let's look at one example here. When abortion and birth control became big issues a few years ago, many liberal pundits (such as *New York Times* columnist Anthony Lewis) attacked Catholic priests and bishops who spoke out against both of these measures on the grounds that the church and the clergy should stay out of politics; yet in the 1960s and 1970s, these same writers were loud in their praise of Catholic and other clergy who worked hard and risked their necks championing civil rights. They favored the clergy in politics when it suited their purposes but not when it didn't.

Summary of Chapter 3

1. *Provincialism:* Assuming that the familiar, the close, or what is one's own is *therefore* the better or more important. Also, the failure to look beyond one's own group, in particular to the ideas of other cultures. *Example:* Assuming that the AIDS epidemic would not hit the heterosexual community in America because it had not yet done so, thus ignoring the experience in Africa.
    a. *Loyalty:* Deciding the truth of an assertion on the basis of loyalty. *Example:* Refusing to believe the overwhelming evidence that U.S. soldiers had shot and killed defenseless women, children, and babies at My Lai 4 in South Vietnam.

2. *Lack of proportion:* The failure to see things in proper perspective or proportion.
    a. *Tokenism:* Mistaking a token gesture, usually ineffective, for an adequate effort. *Example:* Accepting General Motors' spending of 0.1 percent of its gross annual sales on air pollution research as a genuine effort at pollution control.

b. *Double standard:* Judging according to inconsistent standards, a variety of the fallacy of *inconsistency,* but often committed because of a lack of proportion. *Example:* Holding Israel to a higher standard of conduct than its enemies.

3. *Questionable premise:* Accepting a premise when there is no good reason to accept it (and the argument in question doesn't provide any). *Example:* Having believed the premise that President Nixon had no part in the Watergate coverup without having a good reason to believe it (leading to acceptance of his conclusion that he shouldn't be impeached).

4. *Straw man:* Attacking a position similar to but significantly different from an opponent's position (or attacking weaker opponents while ignoring stronger ones). *Example:* Richard Nixon branding his opponent, Helen Gahagan Douglas, as a pinko.

   Note that exaggeration of an opponent's position counts as a fallacy only if there is an implication that the exaggeration is literally true.

5. *False dilemma:* Erroneous reduction of alternatives or possibilities—usually a reduction to just two. *Example:* Implying that male domination is due to either economics or biology, while omitting all sorts of other possibilities.

6. *Begging the question:* Asserting without justification all or part of the very question at issue. *Example:* Answering the question why Argentina will go socialist by saying it's because of "world historical circumstances."

7. *Inconsistency:* Using or accepting contradictory statements to support a conclusion or conclusions. These statements may be presented: (1) by one person at one time; (2) by one person at different times (without explaining the contradiction as a change of mind and providing evidence to support the change); or (3) by different representatives of one institution. It also is committted by someone who *says* one thing but *does* another. *Example:* Lyndon Johnson's stand on racial questions as a candidate for the U.S. Senate and his stand on racial questions as president of the United States.

Exercise 3-1

Determine which fallacies (if any) occur in the following passages and state the reasons for your answers, following the instructions given for Exercise 2-1.

1. *Soviet sociologist Geunadi Gerasimov, quoted in the* Village Voice (*May 5, 1975*): Communism will replace capitalism because private ownership of the means of production is obsolete.

*2. *Private conversation:* I asked the doctor why my mouth was so dry, and he said it was because my salivary glands are not producing enough saliva. Some doctor.

3. *Henry J. Taylor, in the* Topeka Daily Capital *(July 1970):* The great Declaration of Independence begins: "When in the course of human events . . ."

and for the first time in man's history announced that all rights came not from a sovereign, not from a government, but from God.

4. *Polonius in William Shakespeare's* Hamlet:

> Your noble son is mad:
> Mad call I it, for to define true madness,
> What is't but to be nothing else but mad?

5. *Editorial in the* Hartford Times *(September 11, 1970) on the topic of an extra twenty minutes of school time for teachers (the extra time was objected to by the teachers' union):* Insisting that teachers be in school [twenty minutes] longer than children may seem to some teachers like a factory time-clock operation, but it probably troubles the conscientious teacher far less than those who leave school at the final bell.

*6. *Aristotle:* Oh my friends! There are no friends.

7. In March 1986, a Reagan administration spokesperson discussing the alleged dangers of "a communist base" in Nicaragua told members of Congress that they had to either stand "with Ronald Reagan and the resistance (the Contras) or with Daniel Ortega and the Communists."

8. How about a "Dear Abby" reply to a woman whose husband was dropping evidence here and there indicating he was having an affair (which he denied)? She asked Abby, "Is this man a saint or a sinner?" Abby's reply was, "If your suspicions are correct, he's a sinner."

9. *Lyndon B. Johnson:* I believe in the right to dissent, but I do not believe it should be exercised.

10. *Bumper sticker:* America—Love It or Leave It!

*11. Although traditional Jewish practices forbid eating the meat of the pig, a large minority of Jews in Israel have developed a taste for bacon, pork, and the rest. This offended Orthodox Jews, who wanted to pass a law prohibiting the sale of these forbidden products. Explained Rabbi Avraham Shapira, a leader of Orthodox Jews, (Fall 1985): "Our law is not to forbid people to eat pork. We are very democratic here. What we want is people not to be able to sell pork. It hurts every religious man when he passes through a city in Israel and he sees a shop with pork in the window."

12. *John F. Kennedy:* Why, some say, the moon? Why choose this as our goal? They may [as] well ask why climb the highest mountain? Why thirty-five years ago fly the Atlantic? Why does Rice play Texas?

13. High Times *magazine interview with once-Deputy Director of the Bureau of Narcotics and Dangerous Drugs John Finlator (Fall 1974):*

> *High Times:* One of the excuses for keeping grass illegal is that it causes fatal car accidents.
> *Finlator:* I'd rather be riding with a guy who's stoned than with a guy who's drunk, or on heroin.

14. *Patient:* Doctor, my wife left me four months ago, and I've been shot ever since. I'm beginning to wonder. Will I ever pull out of this?
    Shrink: It's normal to feel a lot of anxiety and depression after a severe loss. But let me assure you that everyone does recover from this sort of thing. So you will too. Unless, of course, the trauma has been so severe that the ego is shattered.

*15. *From "Intelligence Report" by Lloyd Shearer, in* Parade *magazine (November 5, 1978);* This past September, [Bob Hope] refused to cross a picket line at the Chicago Marriot Hotel, where 1500 guests were waiting for him at a dinner of the National Committee for Prevention of Child Abuse. W. Clement Stone, the insurance tycoon who contributed $2 million to the Nixon campaign fund in 1972, tried to negotiate a temporary halt of picketing so that Hope could enter the hotel. When Stone failed, Hope returned to the Drake Hotel, where he videotaped a 15-minute spot to be shown at the dinner. Hope, who belongs to four show business unions, later explained that he had crossed a picket line many years ago and subsequently had to apologize to labor leader George Meany. He promised then never to cross another.

*16. *From the television show* The Advocates *(December 1972), a story on a proposed "shield law" granting reporters immunity from prosecution if they refuse to reveal their sources to the police or courts:* Contempt of court is a crime for an ordinary citizen. Since it is a crime for every citizen, it ought to be a crime for a news reporter who refuses to disclose his sources to a court which has subpoenaed him.

17. *South African Premier P. W. Botha (October 10, 1985) honoring an old war hero:* "General De laRey, after whom this town is called, laid down his life in the service of freedom and the principles of justice. Later, for the sake of these same principles, he revolted against the unfair attempt on South West Africa." [He was serious.]

18. *From a student exam in critical thinking:* The problem with this is that anyone can quit smoking if they have enough willpower and really want to do it.

19. *Newspaper article entitled "Reagan's Remedy for His 'Woman Problem' ":* The Reagan administration has launched a campaign to close the political "gender gap" by attempting to improve its negative image to women. In recent days the administration has appointed two women to Cabinet positions, filed a brief supporting women's pension benefits and is hinting at taking further initiatives.
    At the same time, there is no indication that President Reagan plans to change his opposition to many fundamental rights that would strengthen women—from abortion to equal pay.

20. *Howard Smith and Brian Van derHorst, in the* Village *Voice (October 18, 1976):* Sri Swami Swanandashram, Hindu holy man from India, after criticizing other Hindu swamis [for instance, Maharishi Mahesh Yogi of

TM fame, Swami Muktananda, Sri Chinmoy, and Baba Ram Dass (Richard Alpert)] for making lots of money in the United States from their teaching: "They should have no house, no foundation, no bank accounts. . . . Our laws strictly forbid selling spirituality. But that's what they're doing." When asked what will happen when *he* starts making money, his chosen ally, the Divine Mother Swami Lakshmy Devyashram Mahamandaleshwari, responded: "Money itself is not bad. It's how it's used. Money should all be given away to schools, hospitals, and needy children, or something. It shouldn't be held on to." When asked if it wasn't against their own rules to criticize anyone else's spiritual path, that each must find his own way, Swami Swanandashram answered: "Oh, yes, it's true. Nobody is supposed to do it. But I'm in America. In India we wouldn't criticize. But we are not actually criticizing here. When they are deviating from the real path, we are just telling the truth."

21. An article in *New Times* (May 30, 1975, p. 13) on the Catholic Church reported its efforts to reduce the divorce rate among Catholics by instituting rules that prospective couples must satisfy to gain the Church's blessing for their marriage. A church spokesman stated that the right to marry is a natural right, but restrictions are justified when the proposed marriage "poses a threat to the common good of society."

22. *Ad for a debate at North Texas State University:* The arena has been set. The contestants are preparing themselves. The event—the Warren-Barnhart debate. On the timely question of ethics and morality.

    Dr. Barnhart's position is that if an act brings pleasure, then it is right. If an act is unpleasant, then it is wrong. But if two actions bring pleasure, then the one with the greatest amount of pleasure should be adopted.

    Dr. Warren's position is that an act is right or wrong based upon God's word—the New Testament.

    The stances have been made. The time is drawing nigh for the confrontation. The only thing lacking now are the spectators. And their judgment of which position is right.

23. *From a high school civics exam:* The white settlers brought civilization to the Indians in America. So now their descendants are suing everybody in sight—total injustice, I say—even ingratitude.

24. *Congressman Frank T. Bow:* How did this so-called leak get out with regard to Kent State?
    FBI Director J. Edgar Hoover: That did not come from the FBI. But it did cause me great concern. The first time I knew of it was when the *Akron Beacon-Journal* had a great headline—it is part of the Knight chain of newspapers—saying "FBI: No Reason for Guard to Shoot at Kent State." I knew this was untrue. We never make any conclusions. . . . These were certainly extenuating circumstances which caused the guard to resort to the use of firearms. Perhaps they were not as completely trained as they should have been, but certainly some stated they feared for their lives and

then fired; some of the students were throwing bricks and rocks and taunting the National Guardsmen.

Congressman Bow: Do you mind this being on the record?

Hoover: Not at all.[19]

25. *Thomas A. Porter, Dean, School of Arts and Sciences, Central Connecticut State College (in a November 1970 report titled "School of Arts and Sciences: 1970–1980"):* Each department of the school should begin at once to plan how to utilize various instructional patterns and/or new instructional techniques so as to make quality instruction available to all students who seek it. The problem of closing students out of classes which they want and need can only become more serious as our enrollments increase. Efforts in this direction by departments may include the creation of large lecture classes (not always at the lower division level) and utilization of TV, auto-instructional labs, and other technological aids. It can be argued, of course, that this approach sacrifices individual communication between faculty and student and dehumanizes education. On the other hand, nothing sacrifices communication so much as being closed out of a class entirely.

*26. *Pope Pius XII (in 1944):* If the exclusive aim of nature [for sexual intercourse] or at least its primary intent had been the mutual giving and possessing of husband and wife in pleasure and delight; if nature had arranged that act only to make their personal experience joyous in the highest degree, and not as an incentive in the service of life; then the Creator would have made use of another plan in the formation of the marital act.

Exercise 3-2

Find several examples in the mass media (television, magazines, newspapers, radio) of fallacies discussed in Chapter 3 and explain carefully why they are fallacious.

---

[19]House Appropriations hearings on the 1971 supplemental (released December 8, 1970). Reported in *I. F. Stone's Bi-Weekly* (December 28, 1970).

Doonesbury by Garry Trudeau. Copyright, 1975, G. B. Trudeau.
All rights reserved. Used by permission of Universal Press Syndicate.

It's dangerous to conclude that A *is the cause of* B *just because* B *follows* A.

Figures don't lie, but liars figure.
                        —Old saying

There are lies, damn lies, and statistics.
                        —Benjamin Disraeli

How happy are the astrologers, who are believed if they tell one truth to a hundred lies, while other people lose all credit if they tell one lie to a hundred truths.
                        —Guicciardi

It is a well-known fact that in human memory the testimony of a positive case always overshadows the negative one. One gain easily outweighs several losses. Thus the instances which affirm magic always loom far more conspicuously than those which deny it.
                        —Bronislaw Malinowski

===================== **4** =====================

Fallacious Reasoning—III

Let's now continue our discussion of common fallacies.

1. Suppressed Evidence

We commit the fallacy of **suppressed evidence** when we fail to use relevant information that we should have thought of or known to look for or deliberately neglect evidence we know or suspect contradicts our theory.

Politicians distort the truth when, for one thing, they are confident that the mass of people either will not know the refuting facts (sheer ignorance) or know them but not see that they are relevant. In these cases, politicians get away with suppressing evidence that might persuade people to reject their views of the matter. Of course, *we,* their audience, are guilty of the fallacy *suppressed evidence* only if we know or at least should suspect that information is being suppressed. (Complete ignorance at least has the virtue that it gets one off the fallacy hook of *suppressed evidence.*)

At a press conference in March, 1982, President Reagan said the poor would not suffer from his budget cuts because the federal budget was increased by $32 billion. The evidence the president suppressed (let's assume he knew, for gosh sakes) was that all of the budget increases were going for military expenditures (along with funds transferred out of other projects). In fact, less money was directed to the poor than before. (Lawyers refer to this kind of suppression of relevant evidence as a *material omission.*)

On a less earth-shaking topic, the American Automobile Association argued in an advertisement that:

> OVER 23,000,000 CAN'T BE WRONG!
> YOU OWE IT TO YOURSELF TO INVESTIGATE!

The evidence they suppressed could be put this way:

> OVER 47,000,000 CAN'T BE WRONG!
> THEY DIDN'T JOIN, SO NEITHER SHOULD YOU!

Now here is a nonverbatim account of an argument heard on TV's "Nightline": All nations with research stations in Antarctica, including the U.S. and the Soviets, have agreed not to establish military bases on that continent and have lived up to that agreement. This shows that an arms control agreement is possible between these two most powerful nations.

As often is the case when an argument fails to take account of some relevant information, listeners or readers will be taken in if they do not know or suspect the catch in the argument. In this case, those with even a modest idea of what a globe of the Earth looks like could see right away that Antarctica is at the other end of the globe, so to speak, from both the U.S. and the U.S.S.R. and about as far as one can get from virtually all strategic military areas. In other words, neither the Americans nor the Ruskies have very much interest in establishing a military base in Antarctica anyway, so why not agree to a treaty? The problem with nuclear arms reduction talks is that the issue touches matters vital to both parties. Each side wants to make sure it has at least as much nuclear power as the other, if possible more, and can't completely trust the other side on this matter. So the case is not comparable to the one about Antarctica, something it takes only a modest amount of background information to know.

One good way to avoid being taken in by arguments that suppress evidence is to ask yourself whether additional information isn't needed to come to a sensible conclusion. Take the *Soviet Life* article, "About Millionaires, Family Budgets and Private Business, Soviet Style," which implied that Soviet citizens can indeed become rich, even millionaires:[1]

> Can Soviet citizens accumulate considerable savings? Of course they can. Here are some figures to prove it:

Savings Bank Deposits

Item	1970	1976
Total accounts (in millions [of accounts])	80.1	113.1
Accounts in urban banks (in millions)	58.9	84.0
Accounts in rural banks (in millions)	21.2	29.1
Total deposits (in billions of rubles)	46.6	103.0

---

[1]April 1978. *Soviet Life* is a Soviet magazine published especially for American readers and distributed in the United States in accord with a reciprocal agreement between the U.S. and U.S.S.R.

In cases where inconclusive evidence or reasons are given to us when it would be reasonable to expect something more conclusive—for instance, when some easily obtained fact necessary to prove a point is omitted from an argument—we should suspect that the arguer didn't provide us with the information because he didn't have it or perhaps because he knew it to be false. The question we should ask is why that relevant fact hasn't been given to us.

When the New York Times *settled a sex discrimination suit for $350,000 (plus promises to hire more women), it tried to reduce its guilt by pointing out that the $350,000 was less than female employees at the* Readers Digest *and NBC received from their suits. But before we can accept their implied conclusion (that they discriminated less than the others), we need to know whether there are as many women employed by the* Times *as by these other corporations, so as to calculate average compensation. Since the* Times *didn't provide this needed information, we should suspect that negative evidence was suppressed and therefore not accept their conclusion that they discriminated less. (This turned out to be a suspicion confirmed: In fact,* New York Times *women received more per person than the women at the other organizations, which certainly does not support the* Times *in its claim to have discriminated less.)*

But taken alone, these figures don't prove much of anything. For example, simple calculation yields the information that the average deposit was about 910 rubles. But, first, how much was a ruble worth? (In Italy, 910 lira won't buy much more than a can of garbanzo beans at the local grocery.) It turns out that 910 rubles were worth about $1,400 in U.S. dollars in 1975. That should buy a lot of borscht but hardly make anyone rich. Second, how many people, if any, had savings of, say, 1,000,000 rubles (a bit over $100,000)? (That amount would at least make a person paper rich.) Third, what can be bought in the Soviet Union for 1,000,000 rubles? (Being paper rich without much to buy doesn't make a person actually rich.) Finally, does even one private person have a million rubles saved up? (The article wants very much for you to conclude that there are such persons in Russia, but it doesn't say that there are.) Until we get the answers to questions like these, suppressed by *Soviet Life*, we're in no position to evaluate their claims about all those rich people in Russia.

2. Slippery Slope

The fallacy of **slippery slope** consists of objecting to a particular action on the grounds that once that action is taken, it will lead inevitably to a similar but less desirable action, which will lead in turn to an even less desirable action, and so on down the "slippery slope" until the horror lurking at the bottom is reached. (Members of the Texas State Legislature sometimes refer to this fallacy as "the camel's nose in the tent," since once the camel's nose enters, the rest of the camel, it is alleged, will follow close behind.)

According to a slightly different version of *slippery slope,* whatever would justify taking the first step over the edge also would justify all the other steps. But, it's argued, if the last step isn't justified, then the first step isn't either.

People frequently argued against Medicare in the late 1960s on the grounds that it was socialized medicine for the aged and would lead to socialized medicine for all, and then to socialized insurance of all kinds, socialized railroads, airlines, and steel mills. It was also argued that whatever justified socialized medicine for the aged justified it for everyone, and justified as well socialized railroads, and so on, all the way down the slope to a completely socialistic system.

The *slippery slope* fallacy is committed when we accept *without further argument* the idea that once the first step is taken, the slide all the way down is inevitable. In fact, the first step sometimes does and sometimes doesn't lead to more steps. Further argument is needed to determine the facts in particular cases (like that of Medicare). The mistake in all these cases is *not* that the slope isn't slippery. Without more information, we can't know whether it is or isn't. The error is to assume *without good evidence* that the slope *is* slippery.

The Domino Theory

The variations on *slippery slope* are almost limitless. One, the **domino theory,** was especially popular during the Vietnam war. It was argued that if South Vietnam was taken over by the communists, Laos, Cambodia, and other places in southeast Asia would then fall one by one, like dominoes, and result, according to extreme versions—for instance, Bob Hope's—in the commies "looking off the coast of Santa Monica" (California).

Today, one of the commonly heard domino theories alleges that if Nicaragua is allowed to go communist, so will El Salvador, Honduras, and the other Central American countries until we have a communist Mexico at our doorsteps. (This argument cropped up during the 1987 Congressional Iran-Contra hearings.)

A Quick About-Face

Perhaps intimidated by flack from Capitol Hill, the Social Security Advisory Council has backed away from a proposal to increase the maximum pay subject to Soc-Sec taxation from $14,000 to $24,000 to keep the plan on a pay-as-you-go basis. Instead, it has recommended shifting the cost of Medicare to the general fund.

The proposal, if adopted, would begin the process of transforming Social Security into an out-and-out welfare program. Once we start in that direction, where do we stop?

—*New York Daily News* (January 21, 1975)

Slippery slope, a favorite of the New York Daily News. *(The answer to the* News's *question, by the way, is that we can stop whenever—collectively—we want to.)*

3. Hasty Conclusion

The fallacy of **hasty conclusion** is generally described as the use of an argument which presents evidence that, while relevant to its conclusion, is not sufficient by itself to warrant acceptance of that conclusion. This fallacy is committed by all sorts of people in many different ways. Examples range from those who judge politicians running for office on the basis of a few 30-second campaign spots on TV to "good neighbors" who conclude that the woman next door is having an affair on the basis of one or two suspicious clues.

Of course, if we mere human beings were as lucky as Hercule Poirot, Miss Marple, J. B. Fletcher, or the other famous fictional detectives, our overly hasty conclusions would almost always turn out to be correct. Here is the archetype of the great fictional detective, Sherlock Holmes, at work when first introduced to Dr. Watson (in *A Study of Scarlet*):

> Here is a gentleman of the medical type, but with the air of a military man. Clearly an army doctor, then. He has just come from the tropics, for his face is dark, and that is not the natural tint of his skin, for his wrists are fair. He has undergone hardship and sickness, as his haggard face says clearly. His left arm has been injured. He holds it in a still and unnatural manner. Where in the tropics could an English army doctor have seen much hardship and gotten his arm wounded? Clearly in Afghanistan.

What Holmes observed about Watson was consistent with all sorts of other possibilities that in real life might have been realities. Medical types are not really that different from other professional types. Some men with a military air aren't in the military and may never have been. Among Englishmen in those days, naval military men were just as common as army types. Tanned faces can result from exposure to nontropical sunlight. A still and unnatural arm carriage may be the legacy of a childhood accident, a haggard expression due to anguish at the loss of a close relative. And even supposing the person described turned out to be an army doctor who had been wounded in battle in Afghanistan, he still might in this case have just come from a funeral in Italy, South Africa, or Timbuktu. The conclusion drawn by Holmes may have been a good guess, but stated with the typical Holmes air of correctness surely was hasty.

4. Small Sample

Statistics frequently are used to project from a sample to the "population" from which the sample was drawn. This is the basic technique behind all polling (as well as a good deal of inductive reasoning), from the Gallup poll to the Nielsen television ratings. But if the sample is too small to be a reliable measure of the population,[2] then to accept it is to commit the fallacy of the **small sample,** a variety of the fallacy of *hasty conclusion.*

---

[2]An extremely well-conceived poll, which takes care to obtain a truly representative sample, may be quite small and still be reliable. (How small depends on the nature of the sample.) The trouble with most small samples is that they're not selected with sufficient care, because it's too expensive to do so.

An interesting related fallacy concerns statistical trends in small populations. An article in the University of Maryland Baltimore County *Retriever* (September 19, 1977) argued that the "crime wave" on campus was decreasing. Aggravated assaults decreased by 50 percent from 1975 to 1976 and car thefts by 20 percent. This sounded convincing until we read that the 50 percent decrease was from four to two aggravated assaults, and the 20 percent decrease was from five to four cars stolen.

Scientists, of all people, aren't supposed to commit statistical fallacies. But they're human too. An interesting article on vocal responses during mating among different primate species in *Human Nature* (March 1979) turned out to be based on a sample of three human couples (each observed engaging in sex exactly once), a pair of gibbons, and one troop of chacma baboons.

5. Unrepresentative Sample

In addition to being large enough, a good sample must be *representative* of the population from which it is drawn. (Indeed, the more representative it is, the smaller it can be and still be significant.) When we reason from a sample that isn't sufficiently representative, we commit the fallacy of the **unrepresentative sample.** (This fallacy is sometimes called the fallacy of **biased statistics,** although that name also applies to cases where known statistics that are unfavorable to a theory are deliberately suppressed.)

The previous example about primate mating responses illustrates the fallacy of the *unrepresentative sample* as well as the *small sample.* For one thing, only three of dozens of primate species were checked—chimpanzees, gorillas, tarsiers, and so forth may be quite different. For another, there is reason to believe that no sample of three human couples could possibly be representative of human beings, given the tremendous variety our species exhibits in its sex habits.

Notice that, as usual, without relevant background knowledge, there is no way to know whether a sample is representative of the population from which it was drawn. Good reasoning *always* requires good background information.

6. Questionable Classification

The fallacy of **questionable classification** or **questionable correlation** is committed when we classify something incorrectly, given the evidence we have or could have. The program of NOW (National Organization for Women) once included in its list of recommendations for securing equality of the sexes the proposal that facilities be established to rehabilitate and train divorced *women.* They further recommended that the ex-husbands in question, if financially able, should pay for the education of divorced *women.*

But stated this way, their recommendation exhibited *questionable classification* (to say nothing of female chauvinism). The group in need of rehabilitation clearly was not divorced women but divorced *persons,* or better yet, divorced *homemakers.* For if a man happened to be the partner who took care of the home while his wife earned the bread, surely he would be entitled to help in the event of a divorce, just as a woman would in the same situation. Of all groups, NOW, with its concern for equality between the sexes, should not have classified the needy group as divorced *women.*

Note that in this example of *questionable classification,* the correct and incorrect classes (divorced homemakers and divorced women) are close to being identical in membership: There are relatively few divorced males in the United States who fit the classification *divorced homemaker.* Close overlap of this kind is frequent when the fallacy of *questionable classification* occurs and is a major reason why this fallacy is so common.

But it also is a major reason why avoiding questionable classifications is so important. In some areas of the United States, the overwhelming majority of "deprived children" (whatever that means) are nonwhite (whatever *that* means). Deprived children, as a group, do less well in school than nondeprived children. Hence, nonwhites do less well than whites. But to classify backward students as nonwhites leads naturally to the conclusion that their being nonwhite is the *cause* of their backwardness. And we are all familiar with the way in which this conclusion has been used to defend racial prejudice in the United States.

7. Questionable Cause

We commit the fallacy of **questionable cause** when we label a given thing as the cause of something else on the basis of insufficient or inappropriate evidence, or in the face of reasonable contrary evidence.

The fallacy of *questionable classification* frequently entails *questionable cause* because we classify partly in order to determine causes. As just stated, once we classify slow learners as mostly nonwhite, it's easy to take the next step and conclude that their being nonwhite is the *cause* of their being slow learners. But even when the classification is correct, it doesn't follow that we've discovered a causal connection; the correlation we've discovered may be *accidental.*

For example, a *Parade* magazine "Intelligence Report" (May 6, 1984) on the decline in birthrate in France from 2.9 per family in 1964 to 1.9 in 1984 asked the question, "Why the decline?" and answered, "Most probably a lack of confidence in the nation's future." Assuming for the moment that there had been a correlating decline in confidence (something that is very hard to measure), it is questionable that this was the cause of the reduced birthrate. For one thing, France's experience of a post–world War II baby boom followed by a severe reduction in birthrate is mirrored in most industrial countries, including the United States. It's unlikely that the citizens of all these countries lost confidence at the same time (did the Japanese, for instance?), especially since they were at the same time becoming much richer. Of course, it's not impossible that the French did lose some confidence in the future of their society and that this was the cause of their reduced birthrate. But we cannot accept this unlikely explanation without solid evidence in its support.

On a level not much higher, a *Newsweek* article on the My Lai massacre raised the question whether the GIs involved "should be punished for, in effect, *trying too hard*—by gunning down civilians in a village long sympathetic to the Viet

Cong?"[3] But is it reasonable to say that the *cause* of the massacre of tiny babies in mothers' arms at point blank range was overconscientiousness on the part of the soldiers in question?

Statistical Versions

Perhaps the most common variety of *questionable cause* is the statistical one—taking a mere statistical correlation as proof of a causal connection. Of course, every statistical connection has some significance and increases the probability, however slightly, that there is also a causal connection between the things correlated. But when we have background information strongly opposed to such a causal connection, or the statistical sample in question is too small or unrepresentative, then we make a mistake in jumping to the conclusion that we've found a causal connection.

Sometimes alleged causal connections of this kind are so silly hardly anyone who is thinking takes them seriously (*silly* here means obviously contrary to well-supported background beliefs). The idea that dope smoking causes better grades, seriously proposed by some researchers on the basis of one statistical correlation, is an example. But sometimes the dubious connection is quite appealing and indeed leads to serious disputes within the scientific community.

An interesting and timely case (more complicated than most) is the dispute concerning the relationship between the intake of high-cholesterol fats and heart disease. According to recent studies, there was a decline of 27 percent in heart disease in the United States between 1968 and 1977, a time when Americans were seriously reducing their intake of fatty foods and serum cholesterol (indicated as linked to heart disease by other studies). This shows that there is certainly a statistical correlation between fat intake and heart disease in the sample in question (the American population between 1968 and 1977).

On the other hand, lots of evidence points in the other direction. First of all, during the period in question, Americans also reduced their cigarette smoking significantly (and there is independent evidence linking smoking and heart disease), did more strenuous exercise, and took greater care to reduce high blood pressure (also associated with heart disease). Further, in both Switzerland and Japan, fat intake increased during that period while heart disease decreased. And finally, a report, in spring 1980, of the Food and Nutrition Board of the National Research Council of the National Academy of Science (a name like that would snow anybody) said they had found no persuasive reason for healthy people to eat less fatty foods containing cholesterol. One serious factor leading them to this conclusion was summed up as follows:

> The distinct differences that emerge when one population is compared with another tend to vanish among people *within* a population. The Japanese, for example, will show marked differences from Americans in fat

---

[3]*Newsweek* (August 31, 1970). (Recall the discussion in Chapter 3 of American reactions to news of this massacre.)

intake, serum cholesterol, and heart disease rates. But when Japanese are compared to other Japanese (in Japan), or Americans to other Americans, differences in fat intake or dietary habits show no consistent relationship to either serum cholesterol levels or heart disease incidence. In part, this is because the range of dietary variation within a country tends to be relatively narrow. Countries, on the other hand, may vary greatly from one another in eating habits and lifestyles.[4]

Perhaps we should add here that the latest fat controversy concerns fish oils high in omega-3 fatty acids and olive oil, claimed to reduce heart disease and strokes.

Confronted with statistical jungles like the one above concerning fat intake and heart disease, many people throw up their hands and just accept the latest "expert" opinion. And sometimes that's all the nonexpert can do. But we can learn a few simple ways to evaluate statistical classifications alleged to indicate causal connections. The following excerpt from an article on statistical reasoning illustrates one such method:

"What do the other three cells look like?" This slogan should always be invoked to assess covariation [statistical connection] of events. . . . To determine the effectiveness of chiropractic treatment, for example, one needs numbers from four "cells." How many people were cured after being treated by a chiropractor? How many were not cured after such treatment? How many people got better without treatment? How many people didn't get better and went untreated?

—*Psychology Today* (June 1980)

Most of us are impressed when we see statistics on the first cell and fail to realize that we usually need to know about one or more of the others to determine whether we've found a causal connection as well as a mere statistical one. For example, finding out, say, that two-thirds of those treated by chiropractors get better proves nothing about the effectiveness of chiropractors; it may be that two-thirds of those with similar complaints who weren't *so treated also got well, or even that three-quarters of them did (in which case we would have evidence that chiropractors harm patients more than they help them). We might, of course, find that chiropractors cure nine-tenths of their patients, which would indicate that they do help some patients. (Similarly, before going to a chiropractor with a certain kind of ailment, it would be useful to know not just the success rate of chiropractors in these cases but also that of MDs and osteopathic physicians. Of course, figures like these are often hard to come by.)*

---

[4]*Consumer Reports* (May 1981).

8. Questionable Analogy

We reason by analogy (discussed further in the Appendix) for much the same reason that we classify and assign causes, namely, to understand and control ourselves and our environment. In fact, analogical reasoning is a common way in which we reason to causes. But analogical reasoning can go wrong, and when it does, the result is the fallacy of **questionable analogy, false analogy,** or **faulty comparison.**

Here is North Carolina Democratic Congressman Charles Rose answering (in part) the arguments of opponents of government-sponsored research intended to develop "remote viewing—the ability to see a distant place telepathically." Said Rose, "It seems to me that it would be a hell of a cheap radar system, and if the Russians have it and we don't, we are in serious trouble. This country wasn't afraid to look into the strange physics behind lasers and semiconductors, and I don't think we should be afraid to look into this."

Rose's analogy is between developing a telepathic system and the development of lasers and semiconductors. To be an apt analogy, the items compared must be alike in all or at least most relevant respects. In this case, the items are more different than they are alike. The "strange physics" behind lasers and semiconductors grew out of the main body of extremely well-confirmed physical science and was itself confirmed by experimental evidence at every step along the path of development. In the case of telepathy, there is no "strange psychology" that has grown from conventional psychology. There is no scientific theory that lends the slightest support to the idea of telepathy. So the analogy between the possible development of telepathy and the actual development of lasers and semiconductors is completely questionable.

(One suspects that, like most people, Congressman Rose hasn't the faintest idea what science is up to. He seems to think of it as some kind of magic that can produce results on demand. His mind-set is political, and his comment, "if the Russians have it and we don't, we are in serious trouble," reminds one of the "mineshaft gap" in the film "Dr. Strangelove.")

If we have to teach the Bible account of creation along with evolution theory, we ought to have to teach the stork theory of creation along with biological theory.

> —Response to a demand that the Bible account of creation get equal time with evolution theory in biology classes.

This is a typical case in which our opinion about whether the fallacy of ques-tionable analogy *has been committed depends almost entirely on our world view. Those whose religious convictions lead them to literal acceptance of the Bible will tend to find this analogy questionable; others will tend to find it apt.*

Faulty Statistical Comparisons

Although they are just variations on the general theme, mistaken statistical comparisons are so widespread that they deserve special mention. For example, because statistics are often cited showing that the percentage of births to adolescent mothers compared to more mature women has increased significantly since 1960, it is widely believed that American teenage women have become more promiscuous. Various sets of statistics showing an increase in births to teenagers from about one-seventh or one-eighth to one-sixth or one-fifth of all births are often cited by those pining for the "good old days" when, they say, morality meant more than it does now.

But even though the statistics cited are no doubt reasonably accurate, this sort of comparison is faulty, to say the least. Here is an excerpt from an article in *Atlantic* explaining why it is faulty and showing that the correct comparison indicates a significant *decline* in births to American teenage women:

> Amid all the anxious words that have been published, few people have considered . . . the fact that the rate of births to teenagers is actually lower now than it was in 1976, and lower still than it was in the 1950s. The birthrate among adolescents peaked in 1957, when there were 96.3 births per thousand young women, married and single, between the ages of fifteen and nineteen. Since then, the rate for this age group has fallen sharply and steadily; by 1980 it had dropped to 53 births per thousand. But over the same period there was a still sharper decline, of almost 50 percent, in births to women between the ages of twenty and twenty-nine. Thus, when the number of childbearing teenagers is expressed relative to the population of childbearing women as a whole ("one out of six"), it appears inordinately high. In fact, however, it accounts only for a significant fraction of a shrunken total.[5]

Washington Star Syndicate, Inc.

1-26 BRICKMAN

The Small Society. Reprinted by permission of the Washington Star Syndicate, Inc.

It's not easy to determine what is the cause of what.

[5] Jo Ann S. Putnam-Scholes, *Atlantic* (July 1983).

The

General Surgeon

has determined that breathing

is dangerous to your health.

This conclusion

was drawn from a survey

of 100 Canadian rats

that have died

within the past 5 years.

All were

habitual breathers.

Reprinted by permission of Gibson Greeting Cards, Inc., Cincinnati, Ohio.

Greeting card humor illustrating some fallacy or other, no doubt.

Virtually all governments engage in a bit of statistical juggling of one kind or another, and often are guilty of comparing apples with oranges. That's one reason why the price of liberty is eternal vigilance.

Consider the Reagan administration attempts to gloss over its extremely poor record in enforcing civil rights legislation. In a 1983 speech before the American Bar Association (ABA), the president stated that his administration had filed more than 100 cases concerning criminal violations of civil rights legislation and added, "That's not just a respectable number; it's substantially more than any prior administration during a comparable period."

This was a sneaky use of statistics for two reasons. First, it implied that the number of cases filed is the most significant statistic, and as we shall see, this is not necessarily true. And second, it misdirects listeners to the less important statistic involving *criminal* cases while ignoring the civil cases that, with respect to civil rights violations, are the more important.

The correct statistics comparing the Reagan record at that point with that of President Carter, for whatever such numbers may prove, are as follows:[6] The Carter administration filed 101 criminal and 225 civil rights cases in its first 30

---

[6]Taken from James Nathan Miller, "Ronald Reagan and the Techniques of Deception," *Atlantic* (February 1984). If you think that title sounds unnecessarily hostile, reading the article may change your mind.

months, compared to Reagan's 156 civil and 114 criminal cases. Overall then, again for whatever it is worth, Carter wins over Reagan by 326 to 270.

In a speech in July 1983, Reagan cited his record on aggressively combating segregation in schools, "We have authorized for filing three desegregation cases, more than were authorized by the previous administration during its first thirty months in office." This little gem contains three serious "semantic deceptions," pointed out in the following:[7]

> First, did Reagan actually file more school-desegregation cases than Carter? No. He filed only one, and Carter filed two. Second, why then did Reagan say he had filed more cases than Carter? He didn't say so— he just seemed to. What he actually said was that three suits had been *"authorized"* for filing. . . . Third, had Carter, like Reagan, merely *authorized* filings without filing the suits? No. Carter had actually filed the two suits. Then why did Reagan say he had "authorized" them? [Justice Department spokesman William Bradford] Reynolds answered the question this way: Carter couldn't have *filed* them without first *authorizing* their filing; therefore, the sentence was "absolutely accurate."

Now here is administration voting rights enforcement official William B. Reynolds, when asked why the administration had filed only two fair housing suits in two and a half years: "We actually have filed nine housing cases—as compared, by the way, to eight housing cases that were filed in 1980, the comparable period of the prior administration."

And here is a knowledgeable reply (by James Miller in the *Atlantic* article):

> First, Reynolds suggested that a twelve-month period under Carter was comparable to a thirty-month period under Reagan. Second, Carter filed *twelve* housing suits in 1980, not eight, whereas Reagan filed *six* suits during his first thirty months, not nine. Third, the cases Carter filed were in no way comparable to those Reagan filed. Beginning in 1979, Carter's Justice Department began a new policy in fair-housing enforcement, abandoning its former practice . . . concentrating its legal resources on a small number of nationally significant, precedent-setting cases. As soon as Reagan took office, the department abandoned this policy and resumed the scatter-gun approach. . . . Finally, if Reynolds had given his listeners the figures for the truly comparable periods—the first thirty months of each administration, . . . the comparison would have reflected even more unfavorably on Reagan: forty-six cases filed by Carter, six by Reagan.

How to cope with this kind of sleazy rhetoric? According to James Miller, the best advice one can offer to both press and public is the suggestion Ronald Reagan himself gave to students in Chicago right after delivering two whoppers in a row: "Don't let me get away with it. Check me out. Don't be the sucker generation."

---

[7]Again, from the *Atlantic* article by James Nathan Miller. Used with permission of the author.

Quality of Statistics Differs Widely

Comparisons using statistics may also be faulty because the quality or accuracy of statistics differs so widely from time to time and place to place. Crime statistics are a good example. In many parts of the country, apparent increases in the crime rate can be achieved simply by changing the recording habits of police officers—for instance, by recording minor crimes by blacks against blacks, Chicanos against Chicanos, or Indians against Indians. In New York City, police can increase the crime total simply by walking down almost any main street and arresting hot dog, pretzel, or ice cream vendors; if a decrease is desired, they simply become blinder than usual to these everyday violations of the law. The same is true of prostitution, gambling, and homosexual activity, areas of crime in which the police generally have a special interest (a euphemistic way of indicating that police often get their "taste"of this kind of action). Police statistics simply do not accurately reflect the actual incidence of lawbreaking. Hence, if we compare figures on lawbreaking for one place or time with those for another, the result is apt to be ludicrous.

Equally silly are many of the statistical comparisons that fail to take account of inflation or (occasionally) deflation. Perhaps the classic inflation example is the one inadvertently furnished by Marvin Kitman in his book, *Washington's Expense Account* (New York: Simon & Schuster, 1970). Mr. Kitman was trying to prove that George Washington had lived relatively high on the hog during the Revolu-

---

Bookkeeping Le(d)gerdemain

In the long gone days when business books were kept primarily for the purpose of informing owners about how things were going, profit and loss statements may have been relatively easy to read and no doubt generally revealed simple facts about things like profit and loss. Today, the situation is much different. All sorts of "creative" accounting methods exist so that corporation and industry brochures can minimize or maximize profits as desired, or minimize losses, or even turn profits into losses.

Take profits and losses for the insurance industry in 1985. If you consider what the insurance industry calls "operating income"—income from insurance premiums plus interest and dividends from the investment of insurance premiums minus operating expenses, taxes, claims paid, and so on—it will seem as though the insurance industry lost $5.6 billion in 1985, which is what they want us to believe.

But if you consider net income (the true bottom line), calculated as operating income plus realized capital gains (profits made from the sale of securities), the $5.6 billion loss turns into a $1.9 billion profit.

—Figures taken from an interesting *Philadelphia Inquirer* article of January 6, 1987.

tionary War, which is true,[8] and also that he padded expense accounts, which is possible but not proved by Kitman's figures.

Washington's accounts were kept primarily in Pennsylvania pounds. Mr. Kitman translated them into dollars via the Continental (Congress) dollar, equating twenty-six Continental dollars with one Pennsylvania pound. The trouble is that the value of the Continental dollar fluctuated widely, mostly downward, eventually becoming just about worthless (the origin of the phrase "not worth a Continental").

Kitman listed Washington's total expenses as $449,261.51 (note the aura of authority in that last 51¢!). An "expert" (who preferred to remain anonymous—perhaps because of the amount of guesswork involved) suggested $68,000 was a better figure.

In these examples, the comparisons themselves are faulty. Often, however, while the comparison is on the up and up, the *conclusion* is misleading. It is sometimes stated that the American Indian has less to complain about than is usually supposed—that we can't have treated the Indian all that badly—since there are more Indians in the United States now than when Columbus "discovered" America. (This is disputed by some experts, who think the standard estimates on the Indian population in 1492 are too low. But in any event, the population then was probably not greatly different from what it is now.)

But even supposing the cited figures are correct, what do they prove? A more significant figure would be this (but still not terribly significant, given the immense amount of direct evidence that white men mistreated Indians): Take the number of whites and blacks in the United States in, say, 1783 (the end of the Revolutionary War), and compare that to the number of their descendents alive today (that is, don't count later immigrants and their progeny—a good trick because of interbreeding, but not impossible to estimate). Now compare this increase with that of the American Indian. What we would no doubt find is that the white and black populations doubled many times over, while the number of Indians remained fairly stable.[9] If we had no direct evidence, then this comparison would be significant; but it would support the idea that the white man did, after all, mistreat the Indian.

9. Unknowable Statistics

Statistics always seem precise and *authoritative*. But statistical facts can be just as unknowable as any others. Here is a letter received several years ago that contains examples of **unknowable statistics** that would be hard to top:

> Dear Friend: In the past 5,000 years men have fought in 14,523 wars. One out of four persons living during this time have been war casualties. A nuclear war would add 1,245,000,000 men, women, and children to this tragic list.

---

[8] But you won't find this truth in public school history textbooks because it runs counter to an official myth.

[9] Actually, the Indian population steadily declined until the Indians were completely conquered at the end of the nineteenth century. But in the past 75 years or so, their number has increased.

It's ludicrous to present such precise figures as facts. No one knows (or could know) the exact number of wars fought up to the present time, to say nothing of the number of war casualties. As for the number of casualties in some future nuclear war, it would depend on what kind of war, and in any event is a matter on which even so-called experts can only speculate.

10. Questionable Statistics

But it is not just *unknowable statistics* that should be challenged. Some kinds of statistics are knowable in theory but not in fact. Business statistics, a case in point, often are **questionable.**

Take the statistics published by the federal government on business conditions in the United States. One of the major problems with these statistics is that their *margin of error* (not usually reported) is often greater than the "significant" differences they report. This becomes evident when we consider the government's revisions of its own figures, since they occasionally show a larger change than the supposed margin of error. Add to this the fact that even the officially corrected figures cannot take account of the deliberately misleading or false figures businessmen sometimes provide the government (to cover their tracks or to mislead rival companies), and it becomes clear that the margin of error on figures for the gross national product has to be fairly large.

In addition, there is the problem arising from the need to use a base year (because of price fluctuations). Those who want to show, for instance, that a given year had a high rate of growth choose a low base year, and vice versa for a low growth rate. Meanwhile, the true rate of growth remains unknown, except for broad, long-term trends.

Statistics on employment and the gross national product are subject to another (little noticed) problem, namely, that a good deal of employment and industry in the United States is illegal (racketeering, gambling, drugs, prostitution, migrant farm labor), so that figures on these activities must be either guesswork or based on tangential evidence (for instance, legal sales of gambling and marijuana equipment or records of convictions for prostitution). Further, the amount of otherwise legal commerce that is done "off the books," so that no taxes need be paid, has

---

The average American child by age eighteen has watched 22,000 hours of television. This same average viewer has watched thousands of hours of inane situation comedy, fantasy, and soap opera and an average of 4,286 separate acts of violence.

> —D. Stanley Eitzen, *Social Structure and Social Problems in America* (Boston: Allyn & Bacon, 1975)

Statistics—knowable or unknowable? And if knowable roughly, what about that precise figure of 4,286?

It has recently been said that the Warsaw Pact nations (the Soviet Union and its Eastern European satellites) have surpassed their NATO rivals (the United States and its Western European allies) in military strength in Europe. (This claim is sometimes used to prove that the Warsaw Pact countries are planning an invasion of Western Europe.) President Reagan lent support to this hypothesis in his 1981 State of the Union address:

> I believe my duty as President requires that I recommend increases in defense spending over the coming years. Since 1970, the Soviet Union has invested $300 billion more in its military forces than we have.

His administration then attempted to counter this trend by increasing United States military spending.

But is there such a trend to counter? It all depends on how you throw figures around. As pointed out in an article in the Atlantic,[10] *much of this speculation is based on CIA estimates that the U.S.S.R. is currently outspending the U.S. in military matters by about 50 percent—$300–400 billion more in the past decade. However, reviewed more closely, these figures appear to be misleading. For one thing, our NATO allies (West Germany, France, Britain, etc.) are much richer than the Soviets' East European puppets (East Germany, Romania, Poland, etc.) and spend much more on military forces. Comparing the total NATO military expenditures (instead of just the U.S. effort) with total Warsaw Pact expenditures (not just Soviet military spending), even the CIA estimates that NATO is the bigger military spender (by about $250 billion in the last ten years).*

Further, the CIA estimates that about 12–20 percent of the Soviet military effort is directed against China, and thus is not easily available for combat in Europe.

In addition, CIA estimates of Soviet versus American expenditures are calculated both in rubles and in dollars, but the figures generally quoted are those calculated in dollars. Yet for several reasons, the dollar calculations are much higher than those in rubles; for one thing, Soviet spending for complicated military equipment is calculated on the basis of higher American costs. Therefore, both figures should be used—one to give the highest estimate, one the lowest. As the CIA itself has said, "Dollar cost calculations tend to overstate Soviet defense activities relative to those of the United States."

Adjusting the often quoted figures in the three ways just described, it appears that NATO outspent the Warsaw Pact in the ten years in question by about $550 billion. (Of course, this doesn't prove we've spent enough, or too much, since dollar figures say nothing about what is bought for all that money.)

---

[10]Franklyn D. Holzman, "Are We Falling Behind the Soviets?" *Atlantic* (July 1983). Most of the facts and figures quoted here can be found in this article.

been increasing rapidly in recent years in the United States. (In some other countries, this has been the custom for a long time.) No one can be sure of the true value of such transactions, in particular since money usually doesn't change hands (one sort of goods being bartered for another). And even rough estimates are bound to be mainly educated guesses (for instance, by insiders in the barter trade).

All of this does not mean that government statistics on commerce and the gross national product should be tossed in the wastebasket. But it does mean that precise official figures should be taken as merely rough approximations of true business activity, valuable primarily in showing long-term trends.

Polls

A well-conceived and well-executed poll is a useful way to find out all sorts of things, from the voter strength of a political candidate to Fido's tastes in canned dog food. Unfortunately, all polls are not created equal.

For one thing, many polls ask biased or loaded questions. That is, they ask their questions in such a way as to get more or less the answers they want to hear. Evangelist Billy James Hargis conducted a poll of 200,000 "subscribers to various publications . . . a sampling of 200,000 average Americans," and reported the results in a letter to the *Houston Post* (April 1979). Here are a few of the questions and the responses:

3. Are you in favor of the diplomatic death of Taiwan as the price of recognizing Red China? 111 said yes; 16,889 said no.

4. Do you favor retaining loud-mouthed, pro-terrorist, racial agitator Andrew Young as a U.S. ambassador to the United Nations? 564 said yes; 16,436 said no.

Dissecting the notion that continuous growth in the gross national product is *per se* desirable, he emphasizes that the GNP is the sum of very different quantities. Those quantities include costs associated with economic "throughput," such as mining of ores and the cleaning up of polluted rivers; additions to capital stock, such as the production of automobiles; and services rendered by the capital stock, such as auto rental fees. ("Throughput," a word difficult to avoid in such discussions, refers to the flow of raw materials processed by the economic system.) "It makes no sense," Daly writes, "to add together costs, benefits, and changes in capital stock. It is as if a firm were to add up its receipts, its expenditures, and its change in net worth. What sense could any accountant make of such a sum?" And yet, in spite of numerous critiques of the value of the GNP as a measure, both from economists and others, one continually hears economists talking solemnly about how important it is for the GNP to grow. If its name were changed to the equally accurate gross national *cost.* . . .

From a book review in *Human Nature* (August 1978) of Herman E. Daly's *Steady-State Economics* (San Francisco: W. H. Freeman, 1978).

5. Are you willing to pull U.S. troops out of Korea and risk surrendering the country to the Communists after our boys bled and died on the Korean battlefield? 503 said yes; 16,497 said no.

9. Are you ready to surrender our way of life in order to "accommodate" left-wing forces here in America? 52 said yes; 16,780 said no.

While the extremely lopsided results are almost certainly due in part to an unrepresentative sample, in large part, they result from the loaded nature of the questions. It takes some nerve to favor retaining a "loud-mouthed, pro-terrorist, racial agitator" or to be "ready to surrender our way of life in order to accommodate left-wing forces here in America."

While the Hargis poll contained grossly loaded questions, poll questions can be biased in more subtle, even unintentional ways. During the Watergate scandal, a Gallup poll question asked:

> Do you think President Nixon should be impeached and compelled to leave the presidency, or not?

Thirty percent said yes. But a Pat Caddell private poll asked the question this way:

> Do you think the President should be tried, and removed from office if found guilty?

Fifty-seven percent answered yes to that one. How a question is worded is crucial to what sorts of answers will be obtained.

DOLLAR$ AND NONENE

"The Net National Product—the total output of all the goods and services minus the total output of all the bads and disservices—rose slightly last month."

Doonesbury by Garry Trudeau. Copyright, 1980, G. B. Trudeau.
All rights reserved. Used by permission of Universal Press Syndicate.

Another problem with polls is that respondents don't want to sound stupid (or prejudiced). A 1981 Cambridge Reports poll conducted for Union Carbide asked:

> Some experts say that there are 50,000 toxic and poisonous chemical waste sites around the country that pose serious health and safety threats to the public. Other experts say that . . . only a few of these sites pose a risk to the public. . . . In general, which view is closer to your own?

Common sense tells us that most Americans know next to nothing about the number of such sites, yet 52 percent answered that there were 50,000, 25 percent that there were hardly any, and only 23 percent admitted that they didn't know.[11]

---

[11]For more on this, see "The Art of Polling," *The New Republic* (June 20, 1981).

An article in *Parade* magazine, "Keeping Up with Youth" (March 11, 1979), contained the following gem:

> Census takers point out that the percentage of those [in census surveys] who say they voted is considerably higher than the official count.

People lie when they answer poll questions for all sorts of reasons—in addition to not wanting to look stupid—as this bit from *Scientific American* (August 1978) illustrates:

> The University of Arizona . . . project is an effort to get quantitatively reliable data on household food input and output. Some of the earlier results are striking. Poor people interviewed in Tucson say they never buy beer, but their garbage gives them away. The point is that beer cannot be lawfully acquired with food stamps.

Polls often are misleading because they tap an *unrepresentative* or *biased sample* of the population. Perhaps the most famous case of this is the 1936 *Literary Digest* poll, based on names lifted from telephone directories and auto registration lists. This poll predicted that Alf Landon would defeat Franklin Roosevelt, but the actual result, of course, was a tremendous landslide for Roosevelt. The magazine failed to realize that relatively few people with low or average incomes owned cars or had telephones in those depression days, so that their poll was far from representative of the voting population as a whole.

Of course, the art of polling has come a long way since 1936, or even 1948, when polls predicted Thomas E. Dewey would easily defeat Harry Truman. (The *Chicago Tribune* was so sure Dewey would win that it misinterpreted early returns and

---

In a test of beer drinkers:

Drinking from a six-pack without labels, beer lovers decided the quality of the beer was not very good and showed no particular preference for one bottle over another—even though their favorite brand was included as one of the unlabeled bottles. Later, given the same six-packs, this time with the proper brand labels, the taste rating improved immeasurably and drinkers showed a definite preference for their own brand.

Jeffrey Schrank, *Snap, Crackle, and Popular Taste* (New York: Delacorte, 1977)

In assessing poll results, we have to bear in mind the various peculiarities of human nature which lead respondents to stray from the truth. Since most popular brands of beer of a given type (for example, regular, as compared to low-calorie) taste pretty much the same, factors such as snob appeal, pandered to by advertising ("Tonight, let it be Lowenbrau"—trading on the snob appeal of the name of a famous old, and excellent, German beer applied to an ordinary American beer), determine most beer preferences. But few beer drinkers are aware of being snobs—that's the sort of thing we tend to deceive ourselves about.

> *Statistics seem to baffle almost everyone. Here is a choice item illustrating that fact:*
>
> ---
>
> We once gave a test to 200 educators, asking what percent of children read at grade level or below. Only 22 percent answered correctly—50 percent of children.
>
> —*Human Behavior* (April 1977)
>
> ---
>
> *Even teachers have a hard time keeping straight on the difference between comparative and absolute scales.*
>
> *Another comparative rating that causes confusion is the IQ rating: Half of all who take the test must be rated below 100, given that 100 merely marks the halfway point in results.*

printed one of the most famous headlines in newspaper history—"Dewey Defeats Truman"—which an exultant Truman held up to the crowd at his victory celebration.) Nevertheless, it still is difficult to get a representative sample of the U.S. voting population by polling only 1,500 or so people, which is the standard practice today. In theory, a very carefully selected sample of roughly this size should be almost as reliable as one of 15,000 people (polls this large would be much too expensive and are never conducted). But in practice, for all sorts of reasons, it doesn't always work that way. The result is that political polls occasionally are wrong by significant amounts.

In the 1980 presidential election, for instance, a *New York Times* and CBS News survey conducted between October 30 and November 1 showed Carter and Reagan only one percentage point apart. This was "too close to call," since the alleged margin of error of the poll was 2 percent. Yet on November 4, Reagan won in a landslide.[12]

11. Common Gambling Fallacies

The most common gambling fallacy, of course, results from the widespread belief in luck. Statements like "Today is my lucky day" or "My lucky number is going to *win* today" express this foolish attitude. Luck is by definition that which we are not able to predict, so even though it is true that some people have so far had good luck, we can't know this in advance or have any reason to believe it will continue.

But there are also some other very common fallacies that cost foolish gamblers millions of dollars every year, in particular two. The first is the belief that by dou-

---

[12]See the *Washington Star* or almost any major newspaper on November 1, 1980, for more on this.

bling the bet after a losing play, victory is assured in the long run. Suppose you bet $2 at even money and lose. Using this system, simply bet $4 on the next play.[13] If you win, you're ahead $2. If you lose, bet $8 on the next play, $16 on the next, and so on, until you finally win, at which time you're ahead of the game.

The trouble with this scheme and all variations on it is that sooner or later a streak of bad luck will wipe out the gambler who tries this for any length of time. Two factors work against the player and assure defeat in the long run. First, the odds are still against the player on every play; doubling the bet or any other method cannot change this fundamental fact. And second, unless the gambler is a Rockefeller, Getty, or Mellon, the house always has much greater reserves than the gambler and can therefore withstand a greater run of losses than can the gambler, who therefore will almost certainly get wiped out first. (There are famous old stories about "the man who broke the bank at Monte Carlo," but if it ever happened, it wasn't in recent memory.)

Suppose you start out with, say, $1,030 (to make the figuring easier). Doubling the bet will wipe you out on the ninth play if you lose from the start. And how often, on an average, does someone lose nine times in a row at fair odds of even money? The answer is the chance of losing on the first play times the chance of losing on

---

Women in West Germany are limiting their families to an average of only 1.4 children. If that rate continues, the current population of West Germany will decline to about 49 million by the end of this century, and to 22 million 100 years from today. [The article implied that it will continue if West Germany doesn't do something about it.]

— Lloyd Shearer, in "Intelligence Report," *Parade Magazine* (March 1979)

A common trick of some "experts" is to make predictions simply by continuing current trends into the future. Population trends are a good example. But why assume they will continue? Who knows? We do know that some factors are very likely to change, the death rate being an important example. (If the death rate in West Germany continues to decline from now until the year 2000, and it's more likely that it will than that it won't, West Germany's population will have increased, assuming no nuclear war or other unknown factor arises.) Imagine trying to guess the population of the United States in 1980 simply on the basis of the 1880 birth and death rates. The result wouldn't be anywhere near the true figure. (This is one of those cases where background knowledge should lead us to suspect the results of low-level induction.)

---

[13]In some systems, the bet is not doubled but just increased some amount, say $1, so that the second bet is for $3 instead of $4. You can last longer on an average using this variation, but the end result is exactly the same—you get wiped out.

the second times the chance of losing on the third, and so on, which means ½ × ½ × ½ × . . . × ½ = 1/512. (See the Appendix for details on how to calculate odds.) Of course, some gamblers will lose on the first nine plays in a row and be wiped out rather quickly; others will last longer than 512 plays. Theoretically, a rare player will walk away from the gambling table a big winner, although the author of this text has never heard of anyone actually doing so using the doubling the bet method.[14]

The other cute fallacy gambler's fall for is to believe, say, that the less often seven has shown up lately at a dice table, the more likely it will show up on the next toss. The odds have to "even out," gamblers are fond of saying. So some gamblers wait until seven has not shown up for a specified number of tosses, say ten in a row, and then bet heavily that seven will occur on the next toss.

The trouble with this is that each toss of the dice is *independent* of every other toss (as discussed in the Appendix). The dice don't know what has shown up on previous tosses. So the conditions that determine the odds on any toss determine them to be the same on this toss. After all, the dice are still the same symmetrical devices obeying the same laws of physics when tossed. But all sorts of gamblers simply will not believe this and continue to drop bundles on this system at Las Vegas and Atlantic City. A true critical thinker, on the other hand, does not even need to know the correct odds to be pretty sure these methods do not work, simply on the grounds that the house is in business to *win;* if they let you play, as they do *not* let card counters play blackjack, it must be because your "system" is no good.

12. False Charge of Fallacy

It's often easy, perhaps too easy, to charge others with fallacy. This is particularly true when they change their minds and embrace positions they previously denied. The temptation in these cases is to charge them with the fallacy of *inconsistency*. But someone who makes a certain statement at one time and a contradictory statement later is not automatically guilty of the fallacy of *inconsistency*. That person may have rational grounds for a change of mind.

Take the person who argues, "I used to believe that women are not as creative as men, because most intellectually productive people have been men; but I've changed my mind, because I believe now (as I didn't then) that *environment* (culture, surroundings), and not native ability, has been responsible for the preponderance of intellectual men." Surely, that person cannot be accused of *inconsistency,* since he (or she!) has explained the change of mind, as say, Lyndon Johnson did not explain his switch on the question of civil rights.

Consider the charge that the philosopher Bertrand Russell was guilty of *inconsistency* soon after World War II, when he advocated attacking the Soviet Union if

---

[14]Of course, it's perfectly possible to win at this game if you happen to be the one out of two who wins on the first play and you then quit. (This writer can truthfully say that he was a winner at Monte Carlo, because he placed one bet on red at the roulette table, won, and then quit forever.) Similarly for very short runs, some people will win, although most will lose. The point is that in the long run, the odds are very great that you will lose your bankroll.

Exercise item from the second edition of a textbook on logic and contemporary rhetoric:

Newspaper Story: Thor Heyerdahl has done it again, crossing the Atlantic in a papyrus raft designed according to ancient Egyptian tomb carvings. Landing in the Western Hemisphere on the island of Barbados, he was greeted by the Barbados prime minister, Errol Barrow, who declared, "This has established Barbados was the first landing place for man in the Western World."

The correct answer was supposed to be hasty conclusion, *but a student from Barbabos pointed out that the prime minister was known for his sense of humor. Another* false charge of fallacy.

the Russians failed to conform to certain standards and yet in the 1950s supported the "better Red than dead" position. Russell *would* have been guilty of *inconsistency* if he had not had, and stated, what he took to be good reasons for changing his mind about how to deal with the Russians. He felt, and stated, that Russian acquisition of the atomic bomb made all the difference in the world. Before they had the bomb, he believed it to be rational to deal with them in ways that become irrational after they had acquired such great power. Hence, Russell was not guilty of the fallacy of *inconsistency.*

On the contrary, it is his critics who are guilty of a fallacy, which we might as well call the **false charge of fallacy.** (Of course, falsely charging a person with *any* fallacy, not just *inconsistency,* makes one guilty of a *false charge of fallacy.*)

Quibbling

In deciding whether someone has committed a fallacy, we don't want to **quibble.** For instance, we don't want to take advantage of the fact that life is short, and in everyday life, we don't spell out every detail. Consider the AMA ad: "100,000 doctors have quit smoking. Maybe they know something you don't." Some students have said this ad is fallacious because it suppressed evidence as to what kind of doctors had quit ("Maybe it was horse doctors," "They don't say if they were doctors of medicine"). These students were *quibbling,* like the student who objected to Shakespeare's wonderful line, "He jests at scars that has never felt a wound" (*Romeo and Juliet*), on grounds that *he* had felt a wound (a mere scratch) and still jested at scars.

This concludes our account of fallacies. We've discussed only a few of the more common ones from among the hundreds mentioned in the literature (many others have never been catalogued). The point is to become sufficiently critical in your reading and reasoning so that you can spot fallacies more easily. But we'll soon see that spotting fallacies is only part of a larger enterprise, namely, the analysis of more extended passages containing related arguments that are intended to form a *coherent* whole. *Extended arguments* of this kind are discussed in Chapter 7.

The Handbook of Political Fallacies, *by the English political philosopher and reformer Jeremy Bentham (1748–1832) is one of the classic works on political rhetoric and fallacies. Here are excerpts from his account of the first two of four "causes of the utterance of [political] fallacies" (taken from Chapters 2 and 3 of Part Five):*

First Cause . . . : Self-Conscious Sinister Interest

. . . [I]t is apparent that the mind of every public man is subject at all times to the operation of two distinct interests: a public and a private one. . . .

In the greater number of instances, these two interests . . . are not only distinct but opposite, and that to such a degree that if either is exclusively pursued, the other must be sacrificed to it. Take for example pecuniary interest: it is to the personal interest of every public man who has at his disposal public money extracted from the whole community by taxes, that as large a share as possible . . . should remain available for his own use. At the same time it is to the interest of the public . . . that as small a share as possible . . . should remain in his hands for his personal or any other private use. . . .

Hence it is that any class of men who have an interest in the rise or continuance of any system of abuse no matter how flagrant will, with few or no exceptions, support such a system of abuse with any means they deem necessary, even at the cost of probity and sincerity. . . .

But it is one of the characteristics of abuse, that it can only be defended by fallacy. It is, therefore, to the interest of all the confederates of abuse to give the most extensive currency to fallacies. . . . It is of the utmost importance to such persons to keep the human mind in such a state of imbecility that shall render it incapable of distinguishing truth from error. . . .

Second Cause: Interest-Begotten Prejudice

If every act of the will and hence of every act of the hand is produced by interest, that is by a motive of one sort or another, the same must be true, directly or indirectly, of every act of the intellectual faculty, although the influence of interest upon the latter is neither as direct or as perceptible as that upon the will.

But how, it may be asked, is it possible that the motive by which a man is actuated can be secret to himself? Nothing, actually, is easier; nothing is more frequent. Indeed the rare case is, not that of a man's not knowing, but that of his knowing it. . . .

When two persons have lived together in a state of intimacy, it happens not infrequently that either or each of them may possess a more correct and complete view of the motives by which the mind of the other is governed, than of those which control his own behavior. Many a woman has had in this way a more correct and complete acquaintance with the internal causes by which the conduct of her husband has been determined, than he has had himself. The reason for this is easily pointed out. By interest, a man is continually prompted to make himself as correctly and completely acquainted as possible with the springs of action which determine the conduct of those upon whom he is more or less dependent for the comfort of his life. But by interest he is at the same time diverted from any close examination into the springs by which his own conduct is determined. From such knowledge he would be more likely to find mortification than satisfaction.

When he looks at other men, he finds mentioned as a matter of praise the prevalence of . . . social motives. . . . It is by the supposed prevalence of these amiable motives that he finds reputation raised, and that respect and goodwill enhanced to which every man is obliged to look for so large a proportion of the comforts of his life. . . .

But the more closely he looks into the mechanism of his own mind, the less able he is to refer any of the mass of effects produced there to any of these amiable and delightful causes. He finds nothing, therefore, to attract him towards this self-study; he finds much to repel him from it. . . .

Perhaps he is a man in whom a large proportion of the self-regarding motives may be mixed with a slight tincture of the social motives operating upon the private scale. In that case, what will he do? In investigating the source of a given action, he will in the first instance set down the whole of it to the account of the amiable and conciliatory motives, in a word, the social ones. This, in any study of his own mental physiology, will always be his first step; and it will commonly be his last also. Why should he look any further? Why take in hand the painful probe? Why undeceive himself, and substitute the whole truth, which would mortify him, for a half-truth which flatters him?

Summary of Chapter 4

1. *Suppressed evidence:* The omission from an argument of known relevant evidence (or the failure to look for evidence likely to be available). *Example:* The American Automobile Association ad that told how many people have joined AAA but neglected to give us the larger figure of those who have not joined.

2. *Slippery slope:* Failure to see that the first step in a possible series of steps does not inevitably lead to the rest.
   Example: Claims—unargued for—that Medicare would inevitably lead to complete socialism.
   a. *Domino theory:* The conclusion that if *A* fails, so will *B*, then *C*, and so on.
      Example: The belief that if South Vietnam went Communist, so would Laos, Cambodia, Thailand, the rest of the Far East, and so on.

3. *Hasty conclusion:* The use of relevant but insufficient evidence to reach a conclusion.
   Example: Sherlock Holmes' conclusion that Dr. Watson was an army man just back from Afghanistan.

4. *Small sample:* Drawing conclusions about a population on the basis of a sample that's too small to be a reliable measure of that population.

Example: Conclusions drawn about primate mating habits based on a sample of three humans, a pair of gibbons, and one baboon troop.

5. *Unrepresentative sample:* Reasoning from a sample that isn't representative (typical) of the population from which it was drawn.
Example: Same sample cited above as too small.

6. *Questionable classification:* Placing items in the same class although they aren't relevantly similar.
Example: NOW's classification of divorcees in need of rehabilitation as divorced *women* instead of divorced *homemakers*.

7. *Questionable cause:* Labeling something as the cause of something else on the basis of insufficient evidence or contrary to available evidence.
Example: A magazine's suggestion that Vietnamese civilians were massacred by American soldiers because the soldiers were "trying too hard."

8. *Questionable analogy:* Use of analogy where the cases seem relevantly different.
Example: Congressman Rose's analogy between development of a telepathy system and lasers and semiconductors.

9. *Unknowable statistics:* Presenting unknowable statistics as though they are established facts.
Example: Stating that in the past 5,000 years men have fought in 14,523 wars.

10. *Questionable statistics:* Using or accepting statistics that are questionable without further proof or support.
Example: Statistics on illegal or off-the-book transactions.
a. *Polls:* Statistics generated by polls should be questioned when their sample: (1) is too small, or (2) is unrepresentative, or (3) asks loaded questions, or (4) asks questions likely to embarrass respondents, or (5) asks questions respondents are not likely to know how to answer.
Example: The Billy James Hargis poll that asked loaded questions about American attitudes.

11. *Common gambling fallacies:* Gamblers tend to fall for certain kinds of fallacies.
Example: Doubling the bet or waiting for an unusual run to "change the odds" (such a run doesn't change the odds).

12. *False charge of fallacy:* Fallaciously charging someone with a fallacy.
Example: The charge that Bertrand Russell was *inconsistent* in advocating the use of force against the Russians at one time, while adopting a "better Red than dead" position at another. Russell explained this switch several times as being due to changing circumstances. (Quibbling often leads to commission of this fallacy.)

Exercise 4-1

Determine which fallacies (if any) are committed by the following, and carefully explain why you think so, following the instructions for Exercise 2-1. (Some of these contain fallacies discussed in previous chapters.)

1. *Bob Schwabach, "On Computers," San Francisco Chronicle, February 24, 1986:* There aren't just a couple of brands [of IBM compatibles] for those [very low] prices; there are dozens. Do they work? Someone I know has been running one continuously for five months, and it's never missed a beat.

2. *John F. Keenan, New York Off-Track Betting Corporation chairman, responding to a question about whether licensed gambling casinos would cut into OTB revenue, in the* Washington Monthly (*August 1979*): "Big business thrives on competition. When night baseball came, they didn't stop sex."

*3. Hartford Courant, *"Sunday Parade" (August 20, 1972):* [There was] a judge in Salisbury, Rhodesia, who had never driven a car. Someone in his court wanted to know how [he] could rule on motor accidents without first-hand knowledge of driving. "It's really no handicap," the magistrate explained. "I also try rape cases."

4. *Letter in the* Huntsville (*Texas*) Item (*September 27, 1974):* The Chamber [of Commerce] proposes taxing occupancy of the hotels to build occupancy [by advertising for tourists]. If the city adopts this policy, then it should tax bank deposits and use the proceeds to advertise for more bank depositors; it should tax professors' salaries and use the proceeds to try to attract more students; it should tax retail sales and use the proceeds to advertise for more shoppers.

*5. *Start of letter from Anita Bryant Ministries arguing for harsh laws against homosexuals:* "When the homosexuals burn the Holy Bible in public . . . how can I stand by silently?" Dear Friend: I don't hate the homosexuals. But as a mother, I must protect my children from their evil influence. . . .

6. In 1978, the National Highway Traffic Safety Administration placed a value on human life, for purposes of assessing the costs to society of an accidental death, of $287,175.

*7. Smoking marijuana definitely leads to heroin use. A report by the U.S. Commissioner of Narcotics on a study of 2,213 hardcore narcotic addicts in the Lexington, Kentucky, Federal Hospital shows that 70.4 percent smoked marijuana *before* taking heroin.

8. People think just because they're insured, they aren't paying for medical expenses for marginal tests and the like. But they are. One way or another, you end up paying. You pay for your insurance—directly or via your employer.

9. *Thomas O. Enders, Assistant Secretary of State for Inter-American Affairs under the Reagan administration (late 1981):* There is no question that the decisive battle for Central America is under way in El Salvador. . . . If after Nicargua El Salvador is captured by a violent minority, who in Central America would not live in fear? How long would it be before major strategic United States interests—the Panama Canal, sea lanes, oil supplies—were at risk?

10. *Magazine article: Amen, Deacon.* It's time Christian people stand up for our rights. If we don't stand up for creation against evolution, we soon won't have any opportunity to worship. It'll be like Russia.

11. Texas Observer *(March 16, 1973), quoting State Senator Walter Mengden:* The base cause of inflation is an unbalanced federal budget. . . . "If the rate of inflation becomes too excessive, the result of this inflation is that the economy will stop . . . because the dollar will be losing value so fast people will stop exchanging goods of real value for dollars. . . . Now this isn't conjecture; this has happened before, many times. . . . If you don't control inflation, . . . you will destroy the economy, and in a few weeks there will be no food to buy, little water, no electricity and services, and there will be such panic and disaster that some hard-pants general is going to move in and say, 'I am now running the show,' and the Army or some-body like him will take over, and that's the end of the Constitutional Republic. And that's what's going to happen if we don't control infla-tion."

12. What do you think of the analogy illustrated by this cartoon?

13. National Review *(June 11, 1982):* They were rudely rebuffed by the ruling feminist clique. The [Women's] Center's [of Princeton] director, Lila

©Adrian Raeside, *Victoria Times-Colonist*/Rothco. Reprinted by permission.

Karp, asked hostile questions about the supplicants' religion, and her cohorts screeched that for women to be against abortion was like Jews favoring Nazism. [The *National Review*, obviously, didn't agree with this sentiment.]

14. *From Dr. Joyce Brothers's column, in the* Houston Post *(October 3, 1976): Question:* You should be more fearful of rape at home because rapes occur more frequently in private homes than in back alleys. *Answer:* TRUE. Studies indicate that more rapes are committed in the victim's home than in any other place. Almost half took place in either the victim's home or the assailant's; one fourth occurred in open spaces; one fifth in automobiles; one twelfth in other indoor locations.

15. *From article claiming to prove a causal link between junk food diets and antisocial behavior, in* Moneysworth *(November 1977)*: If you project a curve showing the increase in behavioral disturbances and learning disabilities over the past 25 years, you will find that it parallels the increase in the dollar value of food additives over that time. . . .

*16. Defense Secretary Caspar W. Weinberger objects to a House-passed bill that would require the military to seal the border against drug traffickers as "pretty absurd." Weinberger compared the directive in the House legislation to the effort by the eleventh-century monarch King Canute of England "to order the tides back."

17. *Allan Grant, president of the American Farm Bureau Federation, in the* Houston Post *(October 5, 1976), lamenting the forced resignation of Secretary of Agriculture Earl Butz for telling offensive ethnic jokes:* It's unfortunate and it shouldn't have been said, but most people are guilty of telling ethnic jokes at one time or another.

18. The universe, like a watch, must have a maker.

19. *From the* American Sociological Review *(October 1950)*: One of woman's most natural attributes is the care of children. Since the ill and infirm resemble children in being physically weak and helpless as well as psychologically dependent and narcissistically repressed, women are also especially qualified to care for the sick.

20. *From a* New Republic *(September 5, 1983) review of the James Michener book* Iberia: Michener leads off his chapter on bullfights with an argument between your quintessential American and Spaniard about brutal sports—which the Spaniard wins by pointing out that more young men get killed and maimed every year playing American football than in the bullring.

21. Parade *magazine (September 25, 1983):* For a while, doctors argued over whether bypass surgery prolonged patients' lives. . . . Dr. [Michael] DeBakey recently completed a study of 3500 patients. "About 80 to 85 percent survived 10 years after their surgery," he told me, "and half of the

people under 65 years of age are working full time." [The implication is that bypass heart surgery does prolong life.]

22. *Overheard in the halls (not verbatim):* Every other new weapon of increased power or effectiveness in killing the enemy has been used, including some that are pretty ghastly. The atomic bomb is no exception. The plutonium bombs dropped on Hiroshima and Nagasaki are just a continuation of this fact. And the hydrogen bomb will be used too, and on a much larger scale.

*23. *Peter Singer in* Animal Liberation: The racist violates the principle of equality by giving greater weight to the interests of members of his own race when there is a clash between their interests and the interests of those of another race. The sexist violates the principle of equality by favoring the interests of his own sex. Similarly the speciesist allows the interests of his own species to override the greater interests of members of other species. The pattern is identical in each case.

Exercise 4-2

Follow the instructions for Exercise 2-1.

*1. *W. Allen Wallis and Harry V. Roberts, in* Statistics: A New Approach: After the New Hampshire preferential primary in 1952, it was reported that Senator Taft, Ohio, had received a slightly higher percentage of the total vote in a group of 17 cities in which he had not campaigned personally than in a group of 15 cities in which he had. One newspaper jibed that "Senator Taft should have stayed at home."

2. *Here is a student answer to the earlier question about 100,000 doctors having quit smoking:* "This ad is fallacious in its appeal to authority. The ad is made to make the reader think that the expert (the doctor) knows something the reader doesn't because he is a doctor. The problem with this is anyone can quit smoking if they have enough will power and really want to do it. The doctors don't know any more on the subject than the people."

*3. Vancouver (*British Columbia*) Sun (*July 10, 1975*): Britain has a strong socialist tradition more preoccupied with the distribution than the production of wealth. But distributionist preoccupations are a luxury for rich nations, which Britain no longer is. Since 1945, while world living standards tripled and productivity increased more than it did in the preceding 10,000 years, Britain went from being the second richest nation in northwest Europe (behind Sweden) to being the second poorest (behind Ireland).

4. *From a National Rifle Association membership letter (objected to by the Reverend James Atwood in a letter to the* Washington Monthly, *June, 1983):* We all know their Master Plan: First, outlaw all handguns. Then

register all rifles and shotguns. . . . Make no mistake, these anti-gun and anti-hunting forces are working feverishly for the day when they can gather up your rifles, handguns, and shotguns and ship them off to gun melting furnaces.

A letter in the same issue by Frank N. Egerton stated in part: Ten to 15 percent of the murders committed each year in the United States with guns are actually committed with shotguns and rifles. If we ever succeed in banning handguns in America, the number of crimes committed with shotguns and rifles is apt to increase. There might then be a new demand from liberals to ban all private ownership of guns.

5. *Robert Sherrill, in* Inquiry *(May 14, 1979):* The myth of Franklin D. Roosevelt as the savior of a depressed nation has been pretty thoroughly debunked. The welfare capitalism of his New Deal, his Keynesian orgy, has left us with a federal government dedicated to waste and corruption and corporate favoritism.

6. *Item in* Playboy *(February 1983), above a picture of Anita Bryant dancing with Russ McCraw: Shake it, Anita!* We all remember what Anita Bryant used to say about homosexuals, but here she is, discoing with gay evangelist Russ McCraw.

*7. *Michael H. Hart, in* The 100: A Ranking of the Most Influential Persons in History, *1980:* It's worth noting that over the past fifteen years—a period during which American women began using the pill regularly—life expectancy among American women has *increased* significantly. That fact alone should make it obvious that the pill is not a *major* health hazard.

*8. *Article in* Science 80 *(November/December 1979):* The chief trouble with the word "superstition" is that it always applies to the beliefs of someone else, not your own. The entire history of science shows that, in varying degrees, much that even the greatest dead scientists believed to be fact is today either false or else somewhat less than factual, perhaps even superstitious. It follows that what the best scientists today believe to be fact will suffer the same fate.

9. National Review *(April 2, 1982):* El Salvador is more decisively crucial than Vietnam ever was. If it is allowed to fall into Communist hands, the strategic balance in the Western Hemisphere will be dangerously, perhaps irretrievably, tilted against the United States. The credibility of American power would be gravely, perhaps fatally, affected. For if the U.S. were seen to be incapable of stopping a direct challenge in a minor country in its own backyard, what credence would be commanded by its will to act, say, in the European theatre?

10. *Article in the Marin County, California,* Independent Journal *(February 4, 1983) on a proposed regulation of "prescription drugs or prescription devices" of a sexual nature:* We are stuck with trying to communicate two

contradictory messages: Don't do it because it's premature, dangerous, stupid or immoral; but if you do, make certain that you use a contraceptive. It's like saying to your son: Don't shoplift; it's illegal, immoral and extremely dangerous. But if you do, here's how to avoid getting caught.

*11. *Article in* New York *magazine (September 12, 1972) on alcoholism:* A genetic biochemical deficiency could be the reason some persons become alcoholics while others don't. Dr. Stanley Gitlow, President of the American Medical Society on Alcoholism, [stated] that more than 80 percent of the alcoholics he has seen had a blood relative who also was an alcoholic.

12. *Richard C. Gerstenberg, General Motors board chairman, arguing against more stringent auto exhaust emission standards:* [The Clean Air Act would force auto makers to put out a car which] would emit fewer hydrocarbons per day than would evaporate from two ounces of enamel you might use to paint your shutters.

13. *Item from* Detroit Free Press, *by Ronald Kotulak, entitled "When Doctors Struck, Death Rate Fell":* If surgeons performed fewer operations more people would still be alive.

  This controversial conclusion, by a public health expert from the University of California at Los Angeles, is the latest and perhaps most serious attack on the surgical field. . . .

  The newest charge was made by Dr. Milton I. Roemer, professor of health-care administration at UCLA, after studying the effects of a five-week doctor strike in Los Angeles in 1976.

  Roemer and Dr. Jerome L. Schwartz from the California State Department of Health found that the death rate in Los Angeles County declined significantly during the strike.

  They said that fewer people had non-emergency surgery, so there was less risk of dying.

  "These findings . . . lend support to the mounting evidence that people might benefit if less elective (non-emergency) surgery were performed in the United States," said Roemer. "It would appear, therefore, that greater restraint in the performance of elective surgical operations may well improve U.S. life expectancy."

*14. It's a well-known and much pondered-over fact that every United States president elected at 20-year intervals died in office, starting with William Henry Harrison, elected in 1840, and continuing with Lincoln in 1860, Garfield in 1880, McKinley in 1900, Harding in 1920, Franklin D. Roosevelt in 1940, and Kennedy in 1960. Only one other president, Zachary Taylor, has ever died in office. So the odds are pretty bad for Ronald Reagan.

15. *Jane B. Lancaster, in "Carrying and Sharing in Human Evolution,"* Human Nature *(February 1978), in which she argued that some other primates are much more vicious than homo sapiens:* During the five years of

observing the habits of a community of chimpanzees at the Gombe Stream Reserve in Tanzania, researchers witnessed eight attacks between the community and neighboring groups. These fights resulted in the deaths of at least two elderly males, an adult female, and four infants, the equivalent of an annual murder rate of 1,400 per 100,000 chimpanzees. The murder rate in the United States, 88 per 100,000 people in 1976, becomes insignificant in comparison.

16. *Article in* Baltimore *magazine (March 1979) on the social costs of drug use in the state of Maryland:* Start with the understanding that a so-called "dime" ($10) bag of heroin . . . today sells for $50. Some addicts need six bags per day to keep from going into physical withdrawal. Cost: $300 daily. At 365 days a year, this amounts to $109,500. . . .

    How do you support a $110,000-a-year habit? One 28 year old . . . prostitute with three children . . . explains:

    Normally, I'll turn anywhere from 6 to 12 tricks a day and shoplift at Hutzler's or any large department store. Other times we'll spend the day over in Rockville at White Flint Mall boosting [shoplifting] at Bloomingdales and Lord and Taylor's. Once a month we'll try and pull a con game . . . and at least once a week I'll pull a stick-up either around the Block or down off Park Avenue."

    Suppose every addict supports his or habit by stealing every day. Multiply, then, the $110,000 it costs the heroin addict to support his yearly habit by the 32,625 known narcotic addicts in the state and you get a figure of over $3.5 billion a year.

17. *Note from* High Times *magazine:* Even though they contain an illegal drug, *Psilocybe* mushrooms are legal in Great Britain, held the Reading Crown Court. . . . Judge Blomefield reasoned: "Psilocybin is a chemical; these mushrooms are mushrooms."

18. Public school textbooks inculcating the idea that the United States is a peace-loving nation point with pride to the fact that the border between the United States and "our friendly neighbor to the north," Canada, is the longest unprotected border in the world.

19. *Wayne W. Dyer, in* Your Erroneous Zones (New York: Avon Books, 1977): Here is a logical exercise that can forever put to rest the notion that you cannot take charge of your own emotional world.
    MAJOR PREMISE: I can control my thoughts.
    MINOR PREMISE: My feelings come from my thoughts.
    CONCLUSION: I can control my feelings.
    Your major premise is clear. You have the power to think whatever you choose to allow into your head. . . . You alone control what enters your head as a thought. If you don't believe this, just answer this question, "If you don't control your thoughts, who does?" Is it your spouse, or your boss, or your momma? . . .

20. *William Harsha, in the* Congressional Record: The city of Boston, the city of Philadelphia, the city of Chicago, the city of New York, all have rapid rail transit systems, and they have the highest congestion and traffic tie-ups in the country. Rail mass transit has not solved their problems. It is not the solution . . . to the problem.

21. A letter to the *San Francisco Examiner* from a physician argued that if juries award sums like $10.5 million to plaintiffs who have contracted toxic shock syndrome—even though that disease wasn't known to medical science when the damage took place—perhaps we can now expect lawsuits against pharmaceutical companies and physicians by the relatives of people who died of pneumonia before 1943, on the grounds that as yet undiscovered penicillin hadn't been prescribed.

22. *Delta Rubber Company Chairman Richard Moe, quoted in* This World *(March 27, 1983), defending his ban on the parking of Japanese cars in the company parking lot:* As Communism has taken one country at a time, . . . so the Japanese are taking over one industry at a time: automobiles, motorcycles, television, electronics, clothes, lawn mowers, machine tools—you name it. They are making Scotch whisky now. It's the same way with the Communists. We just sit idly by and say: 'Oh, well, there goes Afghanistan.'

23. *William Shakespeare, in* As You Like It: Why, if thou never wast at court, thou never sawest good manners; if thou never sawest good manners, then thy manners must be wicked; and wickedness is sin, and sin is damnation. Thou art in a parlous state, shepherd.

24. *Huck in* Huckleberry Finn: I've always reckoned that looking at the new moon over your left shoulder is one of the carelessest and foolishest things a body can do. Old Hank Bunker done it once, and bragged about it: and in less than two years he got drunk and fell off the shot-tower and spread himself out so that he was just kind of a layer, as you may say; and they slid him edgeways between two barn doors for a coffin, and buried him so, so they say, but I didn't see it. Pap told me. But anyway it all come of looking at the moon that way, like a fool.

25. *William Safire column, December 22, 1986:* Lt. Colonel [Oliver] North, who put on his Marine Corps uniform to plead the fifth [Amendment], has tried to put his personal interest ahead of the public interest by declaring how "people have died face down in the mud . . . protecting those individual rights [the Bill of Rights, including the right under the Fifth Amendment to refuse to provide self-incriminating testimony]. [In this case, the question is what you think of Colonel North's justification in taking the Fifth Amendment about what he did while on military duty? Remember this was well before North was granted limited immunity and testified before a Congressional committee.]

26. *R. J. Reynolds' counsel, John L. Strauch, tossed off the following statistics for thought by those opposed to cigarette smoking (from an article in*

the Washington Post, *November 10, 1986):* The average age of the start of lung cancer is 67 in people who smoke heavily, in people who smoke lightly, in people who smoke a short time, and in people who smoke a long time, and—this is significant—in people who have never smoked at all. Tobacco has been declared more addictive than alcohol or heroin by a House [of Congress] subcommittee. But what has the test [for addiction] traditionally been? It's traditionally involved increasing the dose. . . . Does that apply to cigarette smoking? Obviously not. . . . What's happening here in recent years is that the addiction definition has been expanded and changed and broadened by some people in an effort to throw a very, very wide net that's going to pick up tobacco. And the problem with that is that the definition of addiction loses its credibility and it ends up picking up chocolate and coffee and tea and jogging and things like that.

27. Would enactment of a national sales tax do any better at improving the U.S. trade balance? Sales-tax advocates offer a beguiling argument. Since the sales tax would be collected only on goods entering the United States, not on those leaving, they say, the result would be to encourage exports and penalize imports. (*The* Atlantic, *January 1987. This is more difficult than it may appear.*)

Exercise 4-3

Find examples in the mass media of fallacies discussed in Chapter 4, and carefully explain why they are fallacious.

Rationalization *in the comic strips.*

5

Impediments to Cogent Reasoning

If human beings were completely rational animals, learning how to reason well would be a relatively easy task. We would simply learn which patterns of reasoning are good and which bad, and then make all of our reasoning conform to good patterns while avoiding reasoning according to the bad. Even if we started out with poor background beliefs, repeated uses of valid inductions based on what we have experienced so far would soon solve that problem.

Unfortunately, human beings are not completely rational, although rationality is an important part of our makeup. This chapter is concerned with the other part of human nature, the nonrational aspect of being human that prevents us from being perfect reasoners. While no one can eliminate these things from our nature, any more than a leopard can change its spots, understanding this part of our nature can help us reduce the harm that it introduces into our attempts at completely rational thought.

1. Loyalty, Provincialism, and the Herd Instinct

Throughout history, individual chances for success at most things, from getting enough food to attracting and holding a mate to successfully raising children, have depended on two fundamental factors—namely, the success of the group we belong to and our success within that group. Being successful within our own group means little if the group as a whole loses out to other groups. But being in a successful group also is not sufficient if others in the group do not allow us reasonable chances for success in whatever it is we want to do.

One result of these facts is that all of us have natural tendencies toward group **loyalty**, because a society composed primarily of disloyal people would have little chance against other, more cohesive groups.

In addition, success within our society requires that we get along with others and relate successfully with them in various ways (depending on what sorts of things we try to do). The person who is completely out of step with everyone else in the group is not likely to be successful, even if the group as a whole thrives and multiplies. Enter the **herd instinct**, which tends to keep us within the bounds of what society as a whole will accept. Finding ourselves in a culture in which everyone covers certain parts of the body, we feel uncomfortable leaving those parts naked. But had we grown up, say, in a typical tropical hunting and gathering society, our feelings on this matter would be quite different. Of course, this is true with respect not just to appropriate dress but also to what sorts of food seem right (people in Hindu societies are repelled by the idea of eating cows; those in Moslem and orthodox Jewish groups dislike eating pigs) and to many other things as well.

The trouble is that this tendency to conform to group standards of propriety influences what sorts of beliefs we will seriously entertain. We find it easy and natural to believe what everyone else in our society believes and to find foolish what others find foolish. This is no doubt one reason for what sociologists call *cultural lag*, the tendency of a practice or belief to hang on in a society long after whatever conditions made that practice or belief useful or sensible have disappeared.

In addition, there is the fact that hardly any large societies are completely cohesive. Nations such as the United States, Canada, India, and the Soviet Union are composed of all sorts of diverse subgroups, the United States probably being the most diverse culture in history. Those completely loyal, say, to the United States may thus have a special interest in the fates of several subgroups and thus tend to see things not just from the point of view of the larger culture but also from that of "minorities" within it. We see the results of this in current politics, with politicians appealing to "special interest" groups such as religious fundamentalists, women, blacks, Hispanics, Jews, and so on.

Most people have a special loyalty to groups of this kind in addition to the nation as a whole, to say nothing of the loyalty felt toward their own families. Blacks are more likely to notice injustices perpetrated against blacks, Jews against Jews, and women against women, just as virtually all Americans tend to see things from the point of view of the United States when there is conflict with other groups. The result is a kind of **belief provincialism** operating at various levels (for instance,

> Man is a social animal; only in the herd is he happy. It is all one to him whether it is the profoundest nonsense or the greatest villainy—he feels completely at ease with it—so long as it is the view of the herd, and he is able to join the herd.
>
> —Sören Kierkegaard

leading Americans frequently to misconstrue what is happening in the rest of the world). Thus, a great many Americans have failed to notice that while we stand for democracy at home, since World War II our government has supported quite a few authoritarian regimes that suppressed democratic factions (for example, in South Korea, Nicaragua, and the Philippines), helped overturn democratically elected governments (for instance, in Chile) and was involved in the murder of some leaders of other countries (for example, Diem in Vietnam—but, of course, we were instrumental in installing him in power in the first place). It is difficult to arrive at unpleasant truth when others are shouting something else from the housetops and when loyalty and provincialism reinforce what others vehemently assert.[1]

The herd instinct is no doubt related somehow to the hysteria that grips the members of mobs and perhaps even to the buying frenzy that moves bull markets to price stocks at figures far higher than their true value warrants. In a wonderful book, *Memoirs of Extraordinary Popular Delusions and the Madness of Crowds*, first published in 1841,[2] Charles MacKay attempted to show us "how easily the masses have been led astray, and how imitative and gregarious men are, even in their infatuations and crimes," by recounting several rather amazing examples in Western history, including the witch mania, the Crusades, and the South-Sea bubble. Here are excerpts from his account of the tulip mania that struck Europe, in particular Holland, in the seventeenth century:

> In the course of ten or eleven years after [the introduction of the tulip into Europe], tulips were much sought after by the wealthy, especially in Holland and Germany. Rich people at Amsterdam sent for the bulbs direct from Constantinople, and paid the most extravagant prices for them. . . . In 1634, the rage among the Dutch to possess them was so great that the ordinary industry of the country was neglected, and the population, even to its lowest dregs, embarked in the tulip trade. As the mania increased, prices augmented, until, in the year 1635, many persons were known to invest a fortune of 100,000 florins [a suit of clothes could be bought for about 80 florins, 1,000 pounds of cheese for 120] in the purchase of forty roots. . . . A tulip of the species called *Admiral Liefken*, . . . was worth 4,400 florins; an *Admiral Van der Eyck*, . . . 1,260 florins, . . . and most precious of all, a *Semper Augustus*, . . . 5,500 florins. . . .
>
> The demand for tulips of a rare species increased so much in the year 1636, that regular marts for their sale were established on the stock Exchange of Amsterdam, . . . and other towns. Symptoms of gambling now became, for the first time, apparent. . . . At first, as in all these gambling mania, confidence was at its height, and every body gained. The tulip-jobbers speculated in the rise and fall of tulip stocks, and made large profits by buying when prices fell, and selling out when they rose. Many individuals grew suddenly rich. A golden bait hung temptingly out before

---

[1]Another reason is that public school textbooks don't tell it to us this way. See Chapter 10 for more on this.

[2]Recent edition by Harmony Books (New York, 1980), with a foreword by Andrew Tobias.

the people, and one after the other, they rushed to the tulip-marts, like flies around a honey-pot. Everyone imagined that the passion for tulips would last forever. . . . People of all grades converted their property into cash, and invested it in flowers. . . . [F]or some months Holland seemed the very antechamber of Plutus.

At last, however, the more prudent began to see that this folly could not last for ever. Rich people no longer bought the flowers to keep them in their gardens, but to sell them again at cent per cent profit. It was seen that somebody must lose fearfully in the end. As this conviction spread, prices fell, and never rose again. Confidence was destroyed, and a universal panic seized upon the dealers. A had agreed to purchase ten *Semper Augustines* from B, at 4,000 florins each, at six weeks after the signing of the contract. B was ready with the flowers at the appointed time; but the price had fallen to 300 or 400 florins, and A refused either to pay the difference or receive the tulips. Defaulters were announced day after day in all the towns of Holland. Hundreds who, a few months previously, had begun to doubt that there was such a thing as poverty in the land suddenly found themselves the possessors of a few bulbs, which nobody would buy, even though they offered them at one-quarter of the sums they had paid for them. . . . The few who had contrived to enrich themselves hid their wealth from the knowledge of their fellow-citizens. . . . Many who, for a brief season, had emerged from the humbler walks of life were cast back into their original obscurity. Substantial merchants were reduced almost to beggary, and many a representative of a noble line saw the fortunes of his house ruined beyond redemption. . . .

The example of the Dutch was imitated to some extent in England. In the year 1636 tulips were publicly sold in the Exchange of London. . . . In Paris also the jobbers strove to create a tulipomania. In both cities they only partially succeeded. However, the force of example brought the flowers into great favour, and amongst a certain class of people tulips have ever since [this was written in 1841] been prized more highly than any other flowers of the field. The Dutch are still notorious for their partiality to them, and continue to pay higher prices for them than any other people.

2. Prejudice and Stereotypes

Loyalty and provincialism are related to **prejudice**, in particular, prejudice against members of other groups, and to the thinking in terms of unverified **stereotypes** that supports prejudicial thinking.

But being prejudiced against members of another group is quite different from simply having a bad opinion of them. We are prejudiced only when our nasty beliefs about others are not justified by sufficient evidence.

It is very important that we see the foolishness in prejudice against *every* member of some other group. After all, no group is composed of people who resemble each other as do peas in a pod. It is silly to think that the French are all great lovers, Jews and Scots all unusually frugal, or women all more emotional than men, even if, as is very unlikely, these stereotypes apply to a majority in these groups.

But the problem with thinking in terms of stereotypes is not that members of various groups are not typically different from others in some way or other. The French as a group are different from the Germans, something anyone can notice simply by going from one of these countries to the other. The trouble with stereotypic thinking is, rather, first, that most stereotypes are woefully off the mark and, second, that even when accurate with respect to a group as a whole, they fail to take account of the differences between particular members of a group, as just mentioned. Many older white Americans are a bit embarrassed when they see movies made prior to about 1950 that portray blacks as foot-shuffling, obsequious children in the Stepin Fetchit mold, as most movies made by whites pictured blacks in those days.

3. Superstitious Beliefs

Prejudice against members of other groups at least has loyalty to one's own group to say for it. But even that can't be said for **superstitions**, although most superstitions are based on some small scrap of evidence. Bad things obviously sometimes occur on Friday the thirteenth. Coincidences do happen. And even newspaper astrology columns occasionally are moderately accurate.

The difference between superstitions and sensible beliefs, say of the kind we find in science, is that sensible beliefs are based not on carefully chosen scraps of support but rather on *sufficient evidence* that justifies those beliefs. In particular, superstitious beliefs are generally based on *biased* or *suppressed evidence* (discussed a bit in Chapter 4), which means evidence from which all negative cases have been removed. Bad things do happen on Friday the thirteenth, but so do lots of good things. And bad things happen on other days also, so that there is nothing remarkable about the fact that they also happen on Friday the thirteenth.

4. Wishful Thinking and Self-Deception

As we have just seen, loyalty, prejudice, the herd instinct, superstition, and so on tend to give us beliefs that do not square with reality. When this happens, we have engaged in a kind of **wishful thinking** or **self-deception**. But as we shall see, there are other forces at work leading us to believe what we wish were true, whether the evidence supports such beliefs or not. It is a very human trait indeed to believe that which we want very much to believe and to deny what we find too unpleasant. Most people admit that this is so in extreme cases, at least with respect to others. A classic example is British Prime Minister Neville Chamberlain, who signed an agreement with Hitler in 1938 to bring, in his words, "peace in our time." (Those of us alive then remember seeing the prime minister happily waving the agreement in the air on his return to Britain from Munich.) Poor Mr. Chamberlain was so conscious of the horror another world war would bring and so desperately anxious to spare his nation and the civilized world from such a disaster that his judgment was destroyed, and he failed to see Hitler's intent in spite of all sorts of evidence that many others, including Winston Churchill, perceived for what it was.

Of course, most of us luckily have no opportunity to commit horrendous mistakes of this nature. Our deceptions tend to result in less global evils. Take tobacco use, still engaged in by a significant percentage of adults in every industrial country. The evidence linking tobacco to all sorts of fatal illnesses, including lung cancer, heart disease, lip cancer (from chewing tobacco), and emphysema, is overwhelming. Yet millions of people everywhere continue to puff or chew away, undeterred even by warning labels on the product like this one:

> SURGEON GENERAL'S WARNING: Smoking Causes Lung Cancer, Heart Disease, Emphysema, And May Complicate Pregnancy.

The **rationalization, denial,** and other forms of self-deception involved in smoking cigarettes, cheating on diets, and so on are typical of the way human beings often handle situations in which immediate desire for something gratifying is pitted against a possible long-term harm. In general, the more likely or more serious the long-run harm, the less likely that an intelligent person will choose immediate gratification. The trouble is that most of us tend to weigh long-term harms or losses too lightly when compared with short-run gains.

The current and extremely serious AIDS epidemic provides a case in point. As the disease has spread and people have become increasingly aware of its menace, many "sexually active" people have altered their sexual behavior to at least some extent—for instance, by using condoms (thus reducing but not eliminating the risk). But as this was being written (mid-1987), many other heterosexuals not in high-risk groups still tended to regard their chances of getting AIDS as sufficiently small to make serious changes in their sexual behavior unnecessary.[3] "Be careful and you'll be all right" seems to have become a common motto, even though the

---

Here is an excerpt from an analysis by N. W. Ayer of a Daniel Yankelovich opinion survey.

Women are in unanimous agreement that they want to be surprised with gifts. . . . They want, of course, to be surprised for the thrill of it. However, a deeper, more important reason lies behind this desire, . . . "freedom from guilt." Some of the women pointed out that if their husbands enlisted their help in purchasing a gift (like diamond jewelry), their practical nature would come to the fore and they would be compelled to object to the purchase.

Quoted by Edward J. Epstein in *The Atlantic* (February, 1982)

Typical example of self-deception—allowing selfish motives to overcome more high-minded ones of familial cooperation.

---

[3]See, for instance, "Heterosexuals and AIDS," *Atlantic* (February 1987), from which the following example was taken.

only way to take sufficient care is to have one's partner pass a blood test (still not proof because testing errors occur). Of course, blood tests are impractical in the heat of, . . . ah, battle; so plenty of people have been kidding themselves into believing that they are able to "tell" who is clean and who may not be. Even among those at high risk (intravenous drug users, homosexuals, prostitutes, Haitians), self-deception has been rampant. Some of the husbands and wives of those who had tested positive for the AIDS virus continued to have unprotected intercourse with their mates even after they themselves had tested negative and thus knew they probably did not have the virus.

Here is an active bisexual kidding himself about what he knew: "What dating I do, I trust my judgment. I am extremely intuitive about people's wellness and their participation in their wellness processes; I would intuit if someone had something as degenerative as the AIDS virus. . . . wellness is a process of being. I don't buy into the Western-model germ theory that germs attack us.[!] I am more attracted to the Eastern model, which has to do with a person's energy. Someone may be AIDS susceptible because of abuse of their basic wellness process." Unfortunately, truth isn't decided by what one is "attracted to," but by a reality that will exist no matter what we want to believe. (Let's hope that this person has been lucky and is still alive and well.)

Wishful thinking of this kind has been widespread in the United States, Canada, and other industrial countries since the beginning of the AIDS crisis. But it has been even worse in parts of the world where most people have no understanding of modern science and medicine: "We tell people this disease is caused by sexual intercourse and they laugh," says Louis Ochero, who heads Uganda's AIDS education program. "They say, 'But we've been having that for years and never got such a thing.' " A frank lecture last year to a group of medical students [!] at the University of Zambia on the dangers of taking too many sexual partners was greeted with jeers and derision.[4] In the case of these African people, there is at least the excuse that they are not taught a scientific germ theory as part of their education (except for those medical students). Most Westerners who chose sex over safety were simply guilty of a deadly game of head in the sand, or as we have been calling it, *wishful thinking*.

Of course, not all those who played down the problem were guilty of wishful thinking. Swinger club officials who claimed they successfully screened applicants without giving them a blood test may simply have been talking out of the self-interested sides of their mouths. But when a president of the United States goes for months without even mentioning a health disaster of such great magnitude, we can suspect that political considerations have clouded his judgment. And when *patrons* of swinger clubs believe that customers are adequately screened without a blood test, in the face of the constant reminder that this can't be done, some sort of wishful thinking must be involved.

The moral in all of this is that it is very human indeed to engage in self-deception and wishful thinking. We all do it on occasion, some more than others, and it takes great determination and effort over a long period of time to make a dent in the self-

---

[4] *Time* (February 16, 1987).

Populus vult decipi (the people want to be deceived).

—Ancient Roman saying

deceptive web we weave around ourselves as protection against the harsh realities of life. But that effort is very much worthwhile, given that truths denied so often return to haunt us (in the cases of tobacco and AIDS, perhaps to kill us). Straight thinking, unlike wishful thinking, pays off by giving us better estimates of what life has to offer, of what we should seek or avoid, and of our strengths and weaknesses, so that we will have a better chance to succeed at whatever it is we want to do with our lives.

Yet many people prefer the comfort of fantasy to the harshness of reality. They seem to reason this way: "How can I arrange my beliefs so I'll feel most comfortable?", rather than trying to make them agree with reality.

Reduction of Anxiety

Our account of human beings as self-deceivers as well as rational agents has been objected to on several grounds, one being that such an apparently harmful device could not have evolved, and if it did, it should have been weeded out by natural selection.[5]

There are at least two responses to this objection. First, whatever any theory may say, it seems clear that human beings do in fact deceive themselves and do engage in wishful thinking that sometimes results in harmful behavior. Those who accept a theory of evolution and natural selection on other grounds have to make their theory conform to this fact. They cannot deny the fact because of their theory. The second response is that self-deception and wishful thinking also have great survival benefits, in addition to harms, and we may suppose that it was because of them that self-deception evolved as a mechanism furthering genetic survival. While these benefits are not yet clearly understood, we are beginning to grasp how this side of human nature works.

One important benefit of self-deception seems to be the reduction of *anxiety*, or *stress*, which gives us the ability to come to a decision and *act* when delay might be a disaster. For example, this writer was in a serious accident a few years ago in which he felt no fear whatsoever (until the accident was over and he pretty much fell apart emotionally). He was thus able to control the car during the crucial moments in a way that would have been impossible had he been paralyzed by fear.

Anxiety reduction also is crucial with respect to long-term dangers and potential failures. Scientists are beginning to understand the biological effects of long-term anxiety on the body, and they are not good, to say the least. Stress is related to a lowering in effectiveness of the immune system and perhaps also of other impor-

---

[5]That the rational, intelligent side of our nature should have evolved seems quite natural, given its immense value in solving life's problems. This idea was held even in the nineteenth century, for instance, by Charles Darwin and Charles Peirce, among many others.

tant bodily functions.[6] The relationship between anxiety or stress and belief systems is still not very well understood by scientists, but this much seems to be true. Doubt, in particular doubt about important matters, produces anxiety in most people. Settling doubt and coming to some beliefs or other thus reduces anxiety and makes us feel better. So it isn't only the need to act, to do something, that sometimes leads us to premature or unwarranted beliefs. Even when there is nothing to be done right now, doubt may produce ongoing anxiety (sometimes referred to as "generalized anxiety"), and wishful thinking that eliminates this doubt may reduce harmful ongoing anxiety.

However, while it is useful to understand the good functions of self-deception and wishful thinking, we don't want to forget how they can lead us into false beliefs and thus into foolish actions.

One of the functions of great humorists—in particular great satirists, like Jonathan Swift and Henry Fielding—is that they effectively puncture our self-deceptive defenses and reveal true human nature with all its warts. Here is Mark Twain skewering the naïve idea that human beings are essentially honest and truthful.

As I understand it, what you desire is information about "my first lie, and how I got out of it." I am well along, and my memory is not as good as it was. If you had asked about my first truth it would have been easier for me and kinder of you, for I remember that fairly well. I remember it as if it were last week. The family think it was the week before, but that is flattery and probably has a selfish project back of it. . . .

I do not remember my first lie, it is too far back; but I remember my second one very well. I was nine days old at the time, and had noticed that if a pin was sticking in me and I advertised it in the usual fashion, I was lovingly petted and coddled and pitied in a most agreeable way and got a ration between meals besides.

It was human nature to want to get these riches, and I fell. I lied about the pin—advertising one when there wasn't any. You would have done it; George Washington did it, anybody would have done it. During the first half of my life I never knew a child that was able to raise above that temptation and keep from telling that lie. Up to 1867 all the civilized children that were ever born into the world were liars—including George. Then the safety pin came in and blocked the game. But is that reform worth anything? No; for it is reform by force and has no virtue in it; it merely stops that form of lying, it doesn't impair the disposition to lie, by a shade. . . .

---

[6]For an excellent and very readable account of the relationship of self-deception to anxiety reduction and of how the unconscious mind selects what comes into consciousness, see Daniel Goleman's *Vital Lies, Simple Truths* (New York: Simon & Schuster, 1985). For a short account of one theory concerning the relationship between stress and the immune and endocrine systems, see *Scientific American* (May 1987), pp. 68B–68D.

To return to that early lie. They found no pin and they realized that another liar had been added to the world's supply. For by grace of a rare inspiration a quite commonplace but seldom noticed fact was borne in upon their under-standings—that almost all lies are acts, and speech has no part in them. Then, if they examined a little further they recognized that all people are liars from the cradle onward, without exception, and that they begin to lie as soon as they wake in the morning, and keep it up without rest or refreshment until they go to sleep at night. If they arrived at that truth it probably grieved them—*did,* if they had been heedlessly and ignorantly educated by their books and teachers, for why should a person grieve over a thing which by the eternal law of his make he cannot help? He didn't invent the law; it is merely his business to obey it and keep still; join the universal conspiracy and keep so still that he shall deceive his fellow-conspirators into imagining that he doesn't know that the law exists. It is what we all do—we that know. I am speaking of *the lie of silent assertion;* we can tell it without saying a word, and we all do it—we that know. In the magnitude of its territorial spread it is one of the most majestic lies that the civilizations make it their sacred and anxious care to guard and watch and propagate.

For instance. It would not be possible for a humane and intelligent person to invent a rational excuse for slavery; yet you will remember that in the early days of the emancipation agitation in the North the agitators got but small help or countenance from anyone. Argue and plead and pray as they might, they could not break the universal stillness that reigned, from pulpit and press all the way down to the bottom of society—the clammy stillness created and maintained by the lie of silent assertion—the silent assertion that there wasn't anything going on in which humane and intelligent people were interested.

From the beginning of the Dreyfus case to the end of it, all France, except a couple of dozen moral paladins, lay under the smother of the silent-assertion lie that no wrong was being done to a persecuted and unoffending man. . . .

Now there we have instances of . . . prominent ostensible civilizations working the silent-assertion lie. Could one find other instances . . . ? I think so. Not so very many perhaps, but say a billion—just so as to keep within bounds. Are those countries working that kind of lie, day in and day out, in thousands and thousands of varieties, without ever resting? Yes, we know that to be true. The universal conspiracy of the silent-assertion lie is hard at work always and everywhere, and always in the interest of a stupidity or a sham, never in the interest of a thing fine or respectable. Is it the most timid and shabby of all lies? It seems to have the look of it. For ages and ages it has mutely labored in the interest of despotisms and aristocracies and chattel slaveries, and military slaveries, and religious slaveries, and has kept them alive; keeps them alive yet, here and there and yonder, all about the globe; and will go on keeping them alive until the silent-assertion lie retires from business—the silent assertion that nothing is going on which fair and intelligent men are aware of and are engaged by their duty to try to stop.

What I am arriving at is this: When whole races and peoples conspire to propagate gigantic mute lies in the interest of tyrannies and shams, why should we care anything about the trifling lies told by individuals? Why should we try to make it appear that abstention from lying is a virtue? Why should we want to beguile ourselves in that way? Why should we without shame help the nation lie, and then be ashamed to do a little lying on our own account? Why shouldn't we be honest and honorable, and lie every time we get a chance? That is to say, why shouldn't we be consistent, and either lie all the time or not at all? Why should we help the nation lie the whole day long and then object to telling one little individual private lie in our own interest to go to bed on? Just for the refreshment of it, I mean, and to take the rancid taste out of our mouth. . . .

Mr. [William Cullen] Bryant said, "Truth crushed to earth will rise again." I have taken medals at thirteen world's fairs, and may claim to be not without capacity, but I never told as big a one as that. Mr. Bryant was playing to the gallery; we all do it. Carlyle said, in substance, this—I do not remember the exact words: "This gospel is eternal—that a lie shall not live." I have a reverent affection for Carlyle's books, and have read his *Revolution* eight times; and so I prefer to think he was not entirely at himself when he told that one. . . .

To sum up, on the whole I am satisfied with things the way they are. There is a prejudice against the spoken lie, but none against any other, and by examination and mathematical computation I find that the proportion of the spoken lie to the other varieties is as 1 to 22,894. Therefore the spoken lie is of no consequence, and it is not worth while to go around fussing about it and trying to make believe that it is an important matter. The silent colossal national lie that is the support and confederate of all the tyrannies and shams and inequalities and unfairnesses that afflict the peoples—that is the one to throw bricks and sermons at. But let us be judicious and let somebody else begin.

And then—But I have wandered from my text. How did I get out of my second lie? I think I got out with honor, but I cannot be sure, for it was a long time ago and some of the details have faded out of my memory. I recollect that I reversed and stretched across someone's knee, and that something happened, but I cannot now remember what it was. I think there was music; but it is all dim now and blurred by the lapse of time, and this may be only a senile fancy.

—Mark Twain, "My First Lie and How I Got Out of It,"
in *Mark Twain on the Damned Human Race,*
edited by Janet Smith (New York: Hill & Wang, 1962)

Many of us are very much aware of the "lie of silent assertion," acquiesced in by the great majority of Germans during the Nazi period, that there was nothing going on with respect to Jews, Gypsies, political prisoners, and others, nothing happening in concentration camps that needed to concern responsible citizens. They had no need to know because in their minds there was nothing untoward to know. But when it comes to our own time and place, we have a hard time noticing what is happening.

Summary of Chapter 5

Human beings are not completely rational animals. There is also a nonrational component to our makeup, which sometimes interferes with our ability to argue or reason correctly.

1. Our reasoning is sometimes skewed from the truth because of *loyalty, provincialism,* and a *herd instinct* that makes us tend to see our own society and its beliefs in a more favorable light than the evidence may warrant and to find it easy and natural to believe what most others in our society believe.

   Example: Failing to notice some of the undemocratic and nasty things our government has done around the world since World War II. In addition, we tend to pay attention to what is going on in our own culture to the neglect of others.

2. Loyalty and provincialism are related to *prejudice,* in particular, prejudice against members of other groups. Such prejudice often is supported by thinking of members of other groups in terms of unverified *stereotypes.*

   Example: The stereotype that was common in the United States until recently that pictured blacks as foot-shuffling, obsequious children.

   But merely believing bad things about others does not constitute prejudice. We are prejudiced in such cases only if these beliefs are not justified by the evidence.

   Being prejudiced against *every* member of a group is particularly foolish. No group is composed of people who are absolutely alike. Of course, average members of different groups do tend to be different in various ways, for instance, as Americans are from Italians. Noticing these differences is not a matter of prejudice, first because the differences are supported by evidence and second because (let us hope) we don't conclude that, say, every American is different from every Italian with respect to dress, typical gestures, or what have you.

3. *Superstitions* often are based on some small amount of evidence. What makes them superstitions is that we believe them although we lack sufficient evidence. In addition, a typical superstition is supported by *biased* evidence from which all negative cases have been carefully suppressed.

   Example: Overlooking the cases when the daily horoscope column badly misses the mark.

4. Superstitious or prejudicial beliefs generally have a certain amount of *wishful thinking* or *self-deception* to them. But believing what we wish were true, even though the evidence indicates otherwise, is common in many other kinds of cases.

   Examples: People who are sexually active with many partners during the AIDS epidemic and cheaters on diets.

   The *rationalization* and *denial* that often are involved in self-deception may allow us immediate gratification, but at the risk of serious long-run harm.

Example: Cigarette smoking.

While we can't at this stage be sure why these nonrational mechanisms have evolved, we are beginning to understand certain good functions they perform. Loyalty has the obvious advantage of making a cohesive group better able to hold its own against competing groups, as do provincialism and the herd instinct. The herd instinct also helps us get along with others in our culture, which has obvious advantages for us.

In addition to these obvious advantages, self-deceptive mechanisms seem to aid in reducing *anxiety,* or *stress*, thus helping to keep our immune systems up to par. Doubt tends to be stressful; thus, coming to a firm belief reduces the ongoing stress that results from long-term doubt.

Exercise 5-1

1. Explain how, according to the text, loyalty may skew a person's beliefs away from what the evidence will support. Do you think the text is mistaken in what it says about this? If so, support your belief with evidence; for instance, show that the examples given in the text are somehow mistaken, or present counterevidence. If you agree with the text, explain what experiences you have had that seem to support the text on this point.

2. Do human beings really have a herd instinct, or is that just true of cows and such? Defend your answer.

3. How does the text use the expression "belief provincialism"? Give some examples not mentioned in the text, and explain why they are examples.

4. According to the text, what is wrong with categorizing, say, the French as great lovers, the Germans as obedient, automatons, and so on? After all, doesn't experience show that members of a group tend to be different from members of other groups, as Germans are different from Americans?

5. Give at least two examples of other people engaging in self-deception or wishful thinking, and explain why you think it is. Do you ever engage in such a thing? Explain and defend your answer.

6. What are some of the good consequences of wishful thinking and self-deception that are mentioned in the text? Explain.

7. Some people argue that there is indeed something called luck, that some people have been quite lucky so far, and that they are therefore entitled to argue by induction that they will be lucky in the future. Critically evaluate this line of reasoning.

Jules Feiffer. Copyright 1978. Distributed by Field Newspaper Syndicate.
Reprinted by permission.

It makes a great deal of difference what we call something. Political cartoonist Jules Feiffer suggests that military bureaucrats know this just as much as any other bureaucrats.

6

Language

Language is the indispensable tool used in formulating arguments. But it can be used just as well to construct bad arguments as good—all the more reason to understand a few things about language and how it can be used.

1. Cognitive and Emotive Meaning

If the purpose of a sentence is to inform, or to state a fact, some of its words must refer to things, events, or properties. Some of its words thus must have what is commonly called **cognitive meaning**. The sentences made up of them also may be said to have cognitive meaning—provided, of course, that they conform to grammatical rules.

But words may also have **emotive meaning**—that is, they may have positive or negative overtones. The emotive charges of some words are obvious. Think of the terms *nigger, wop, kike,* and *fag,* or think of four-letter "sex" words, which even in this permissive age rarely appear in textbooks.

The emotively charged words just listed have negative emotive meanings. But lots of words have positive emotive overtones. Examples are *freedom, love, democracy, springtime,* and *peace*. On the other hand, many words have either neutral or mixed emotive meanings. *Pencil, run,* and *river* tend to be neutral words. *Socialism, politician,* and *whiskey* tend to have mixed emotive meanings.

In fact, almost any word that is emotively positive (or negative) for some may be just the opposite for others, perhaps because one person's meat is another's poison. *God,* for instance, has quite different emotive overtones for a sincere believer and for an atheist. Similarly, *dictatorship,* a negative word for most Americans, in some contexts has positive overtones in the Soviet Union. (The U.S.S.R. is said to be a "dictatorship of the proletariat." Dictatorship it surely is, but not of the proletariat.)

Terms that on first glance appear neutral often turn out to be emotively charged. The terms *bureaucrat, government official,* and *public servant,* for instance, all refer to roughly the same group of people and thus have roughly the same cognitive meaning. But their emotive meanings are quite different. Of the three, only *government official* is close to being neutral.

2. Emotive Meaning and Con Artistry

There are several ways in which the emotive side of language can be taken advantage of. One is to use emotively charged words to mask cognitive import. Another is to take an emotively favorable or "pro" word, like *democracy* or *republic,* and change its cognitive meaning while keeping its emotively "pro" overtones. Thus, the East German Communist dictatorship is called the *German Democratic Republic,* although it is neither democratic nor a republic; and the Communist dictatorship in China is officially known as the *People's Republic of China.* (This makes the straightforward and accurate *State of Israel* and *Kingdom of Saudi Arabia* sound almost refreshing.)

Doublespeak, Jargon, Bureaucratese, . . .

And then there is the use of emotively dull or euphemistic language of the kind favored by many government officials and by professionals like doctors, lawyers, and academics. There are several names for this kind of language, each with slightly different cognitive and emotive meanings; *doublespeak, jargon, bureaucratese, newspeak, academese, professionalese, bafflegab, gobbledygook,* and so on.[1]

Take the bureaucratic language of war—remembering that war, the real thing, is unvarnished hell. During the Vietnam War, we used particularly nasty weapons (for example, fragmentation bombs and napalm) in areas where they were certain to kill thousands of civilians. We dropped far more bombs on that small nation than on Germany and Japan combined in World War II. To make all this palat-

---

[1]Some writers have introduced the term *hedgetalk* to refer to doublespeak designed to hedge one's response to a question so as to be able later to deny having said what one appeared to have said.

Here is George Orwell in his 1948 classic, Politics and the English Language, *explaining one reason why politicians favor doublespeak:*

In our time, political speech and writing are largely the defence of the indefensible. . . . Thus political language has to consist largely of euphemism, question begging, and sheer cloudy vagueness. Defenceless villages are bombarded from the air, the inhabitants driven out into the countryside, the cattle machine-gunned, the huts set on fire with incendiary bullets: This is called pacification. Millions of peasants are robbed of their farms and sent trudging along the roads with no more than they can carry: This is called *transfer of population* or *rectification of frontiers.* . . .

The inflated style is itself a kind of euphemism. A mass of Latin words falls upon the facts like soft snow, blurring the outlines and covering up all the details. The great enemy of clear language is insincerity. When there is a gap between one's real and one's declared aims, one turns as it were instinctively to long words and exhausted idioms, like a cuttlefish squirting out ink. . . .

And here is Albert Joseph in the Quarterly Review of Doublespeak *(July 1981) giving three reasons why so many people use this obfuscatory language:*

People everywhere enjoy making their messages sound more complicated than necessary. In all professions, people enjoy using language to convey the feeling, "my field is so complex ordinary mortals could never understand it." Children establish superiority over peers with pig Latin. Lawyers do it with gobbledygook, truck drivers with citizens-band jargon, and scientists (and educators) with the language of grantsmanship.

Now my main point is this. Misrepresentation is not the only reason so many people write in impossibly difficult language. In fact, years of study have convinced me it is not even the main reason. Many perfectly honorable people write in heavy language because it is an ego trip; they are writing to impress, not to express. They many not be writing doublespeak, in the sense that they are not deliberately concealing weak information, but the effect on language style is the same.

But the most common reason for heavy writing style is still more innocent: *most people honestly think they are supposed to write that way.* Who can blame them? They see it all around them—in government regulations, legal documents, and in their professional books and journals. They see it, alas, even in the writings of their teachers of English, who set the model.

able, a doublespeak language was developed. Here are a few examples (with translations):

Pacification center	Concentration camp
Incursion	Invasion (as in the "Cambodian incursion")
Protective reaction strike	Bombing
Surgical strike	Precision bombing (itself euphemistic, since bombings by their nature tend to be imprecise)
Incontinent ordinance	Off-target bombs (usually used when they kill civilians)
Friendly fire	Shelling friendly village or troops by mistake
Specified strike zone	Area where soldiers can fire at anything—replaced *free fire zone* when that became notorious
Interdiction	Bombing
Strategic withdrawal	Retreat (when our side does it)
Tactical redeployment	Retreat (when our side does it)
Advisor	Military officer (before we admitted "involvement" in Vietnam) or CIA agent
Termination	Killing
Infiltrators	Enemy troops moving into the battle area
Reinforcements	Friendly troops moving into the battle area
Selective ordinance	Napalm (also known as *selective explosives*)

George Orwell was probably right in arguing that much bureaucratese is intended to numb the reader into submission by replacing succinct, pungent locutions with long-winded or dull ones. Typical examples seem to support his view: Bureaucrats speak of *undocumented workers,* not illegal aliens; of *termination with prejudice* rather than assassination (CIA lingo); of *end use allocation* instead of rationing; and of *diversion,* rather than theft (as in "200 pounds of highly enriched uranium *diverted* by Israel"). They speak of *plausible deniability* (as in "Once the White House tapes became known, Nixon lost his *plausible deniability* on the Watergate coverup"—the tapes were said to be a *smoking gun*). They write of being *selected out,* not fired (as in "Foreign Service Officer Smith was again passed over for promotion, and is therefore to be *selected out*"). And they use the phrase *program misuse and management inefficiency* in place of the old *fraud, abuse, and waste.*[2]

---

[2]See the *Washington Monthly,* "Memo of the Month" (March 1981).

But Albert Joseph is also right that people often think they're supposed to write that way.[3] How else explain this example from the Internal Revenue Code:

> The term "taxable distribution" means any distribution which is not out of the income of the trust, within the meaning of section 643(b), from a generation-skipping trust to any younger generation beneficiary who is assigned to a generation younger than the generation assignment of any other person who is a younger generation beneficiary.[4]

One of George Orwell's main points in his attacks on "insincere" language was that so long as we let our leaders get away with doublespeak and the like, democracy and representative government are in danger. Perhaps this is an exaggeration, but there is a good deal of truth in it. It is no accident that this kind of obfuscatory language flourishes best in dictatorships and minority ruled governments. Orwell would not have been surprised when Chilean dictator Augusto Pinochet defended his decision to impose a state of seige in Chile by saying, "It is precisely in order to safeguard democracy and liberty that today more than ever it is necessary to be inflexible," or when South African Prime Minister P. W. Botha denied having violated an agreement to respect the sovereignty of neighbor Mozambique, calling serious breaches of this agreement mere "technical violations." Orwell's point was that if we let politicians get away with talk like this, our leaders will no longer be accountable to us for their actions.

Apropos Al Smith's famous remark that law school is where you learn to call a bribe a fee, here is an item from *New Times* on illegal bribes by big business:

> Asked by a *New York Times* reporter about the recent bribery disclosures, a professor of management and business at the University of California replied, "At a high level of abstraction, it's clear that American companies should not engage in wholesale bribery abroad, but I can't pass judgment until I get down to the operating details and ask when a bribe is a tip or a commission."

Misleading language is apt to crop up almost anywhere. Cod liver oil contains no liver and may contain no cod or any liver oil of any kind. The name refers to a mixture primarily of fish oils from various fish. Even *The Congressional Record* isn't an accurate record of what goes on in Congress, or of what is said on the floors of the House and Senate. Members of Congress have power, so they also have privileges—one being the privilege of changing what they actually say in Congress or adding to the "record" things they might have liked to say but didn't. (The folks back home will never know.)

The Group Health Association says that it believes "it is important for [ex-schizophrenic] patients to realize they are normal, average people who happen to have a medical illness called schizophrenia." That's like saying Siamese twins are

---

[3]For instance, see Gregory M. Jones', "Confessions of a Reg Writer," *Quarterly Review of Doublespeak* (July 1981).
[4]IRS Code, Chapter 13, Subchapter B, Section 2613.

"normal, average people" who just happen to be physically joined together at the hip so that they share the same circulatory system.

When in 1984 Tip O'Neill suggested moving U.S. troops in Lebanon offshore, President Reagan called it *surrender*. But when the president moved the troops offshore a few days later, he first called it *redeployment* and then *reconcentration*.

The nuclear age has generated a *nukespeak* to mask the risky nature of atomic energy plants and the horror of atomic war. In this lingo, *spent fuel* means radioactive waste, *thermal enrichment* means heat pollution, *breach of containment* means a leak of radioactive poisons, *nuclear exchange* is used instead of atomic war, and *anticipatory retaliation* for first strike (itself a euphemism for nuking the enemy without warning). Similarly, atomic weapon accidents are called *bent spears* or *broken arrows,* and the Three Mile Island near-disaster an *event, incident,* or *normal aberration* (literally contradictory, since by definition an aberration is abnormal). The Indians call their bomb a *peaceful nuclear device.* And in Washington, D.C., we encounter the phrase *fallout sojourn in the countryside* to describe people fleeing cities under atomic attack.[5]

Here are a few more doublespeak examples:

Singularities	Miracles (used by "creation scientists"— itself a euphemistic expression employed to make a religious doctrine appear to be scientific)
Democratic Personnel Committee	Name of the U.S. House of Representatives Democratic party patronage committee (*patronage* has a foul odor)

From a memorandum that was issued last August by the office of Army Chief of Staff General John A. Wickham Jr.

FM: HQDA WASHDC
TO: ALARACT
SUBJECT: Addressing Soldiers

The Chief of Staff, Army, has directed that all military members of the U.S. Army be called soldiers. The term "soldier" has connotations of valor, duty, honor, sacrifice: noble values of a noble profession. The term "SM" (meaning Service Member) is a vapid construct which evokes sensings of computer-jargon ciphers, or worse: an 8-hour-per-day "employee" of the U.S. government.

—Harper's (April 1987).

Score one for the Army!

---

[5]For more on this topic, see Stephen Hilgartner, Richard Bell, and Rory O'Connor, *Nukespeak: Nuclear Language, Visions and Mindset* (San Francisco: Sierra Club Books, 1982).

Unacceptable borrowing	Plagiarism (used by the *New York Times* in investigating alleged plagiarism of some of its writers)
Developmental class	Remedial class (itself once a euphemism)
Poorly buffered precipitation	Acid rain
Scheduled person	Nonblack (in South Africa)
Cult[6]	Group with a doctrine most "respectable" people reject (as in "the *cult* founded by James Jones" or "the Moonie *cult*")
Life insurance	Death insurance
Price enhancement	Inflation
Disinformation	Lies against one's enemies told to the press (as in "The Reagan administration engaged in a policy of disinformation.")
Lost enrollments	Students who flunk out or drop out
Receipts strengthening	Tax increase
Revenue enhancement	Tax increase
Internal Revenue Service	Tax collector

Who's on First?

From House debate of Oct. 11:

MR. KASTENMEIER. Mr. Speaker, I ask unanimous consent that it shall be in order to consider in the House, any rule of the House to the contrary notwithstanding, a motion to take from the Speaker's table the bill (H.R. 5479) to amend section 504 of title 5, United States Code, and section 2412 of title 28, United States Code, with respect to awards of expenses of certain agency and court proceedings, and for other purposes, with a Senate amendment to the House amendment to the Senate amendments thereto, and to concur in the Senate amendment to the House amendment to the Senate amendments with an amendment, and that the previous question be considered as ordered on the motion.

THE SPEAKER PRO TEMPORE. Is there objection to the request of the gentleman from Wisconsin?

—*Washington Post* (October 14, 1984)

---

[6]This isn't really doublespeak, but rather an ordinary term whose bias isn't generally recognized. The same is true of the example that follows.

High mobility multipurpose wheeled vehicle	Jeep (official Army name)
Negative economic growth	Recession
Member of a career offending cartel	Mobster (as in "Don Corleone was a member of a *career offending cartel*")
Incomplete success	Failure (used by Jimmy Carter to describe the failed Iran hostage rescue mission)
Vertical Transportation Corps	Insignia on uniforms of elevator operators at Hahnemann Hospital in Philadelphia
Ecology, Inc.	Name of the old *Nuclear Engineering Co.,* which runs waste disposal sites for chemical and atomic wastes
Freedom fighters	The Contras—our guys in Nicaragua (how much freedom they were fighting for, indeed how much effective fighting they were doing, is a very political question)

And then, in a class by itself, the crowning achievement of Nazi phraseology, purified of the stench and horror of extermination camps: *The Final Solution.*

Academese

Now for a bit of *academese,* which has a sleep-inducing quality all its own. First, a tiny snippet from Zellig Harris's well-known text *Structural Linguistics,* to give a feel for the genre:

> Another consideration is the availability of simultaneity, in addition to successivity as a relation among linguistic elements.

Which may or may not mean simply that we can simultaneously do things like wink an eye and talk and can also say words one after another. You didn't know that, did you?

Shoe. Reprinted by permission of the Tribune Media Services.

In his book, *The Dragons of Eden,* Carl Sagan explains a bit of academese:

> With this evidence, paleontologists [titles in the professions rival those in government] have deduced that "bipedalism preceded encephalization" by which they mean that our ancestors walked on two legs before they evolved big brains.

The *Washington Monthly* (February 1979) noted that writer Tom Wolfe referred to what he perceived as a very self-centered generation in America as the "me generation," but that when social scientists picked up the idea, they translated it as "the culture of narcissism."

It might be naïvely supposed that academics who write in academese would as a consequence not be read and thus have little influence in their fields. But that isn't the way it works. Here is a typical example of the writing of a very famous and extremely influential sociologist, Talcott Parsons:

> Skills constitute the manipulative techniques of human goal attainment and control in relation to the physical world, so far as artifacts for machines especially designed as tools do not yet supplement them. Truly human skills

---

When newspaper columnist Richard Cohen was a cub reporter, he was assigned the job of interviewing someone described in print as ruddy-faced *and discovered at the interview what this meant: the guy was a drunk. Over the years, he has kept track of other code words used by reporters that should not generally be taken literally. Here are a few of his items:*

Jolly: This means fat.

Controversial: This is a word used to describe people like Idi Amin, the controversial [ex] leader of Uganda. The newspaper meaning of the word is abominable. People or issues that are really controversial are called complex.

Linked to: A sexual term when applied to a woman. In this context it means that the woman is sleeping with whomever she is linked to.

Eye for the ladies: Another sexual term. It does not refer to a man who has an esthetic appreciation of the female form. Instead, it refers to a man who will sleep with anything that walks.

Attractive: All women mentioned in newspapers are attractive. The word tells you nothing. The word handsome, however, means that the woman looks like a horse but has money.

Crony: The friend of someone the writer does not like.

Associate: The friend of someone the writer likes. Sometimes the same person can be both a crony and a friend. See George Allen—Truman's crony and Eisenhower's associate.

—*Washington Post* (November 9, 1976).

are guided by organized and codified *knowledge* of both the things to be manipulated and the human capacities that are used to manipulate them. Such
knowledge is an aspect of cultural level symbolic processes, and . . . requires
the capacities of the human central nervous system, particularly the brain.
This organic system is clearly essential to all the symbolic processes.

This passage was cited by Stanislav Andreski,[7] who translated it into: "A developed brain, acquired skills, and knowledge are needed for attaining human
goals." Which sounds about right.

A common feature of academese, as of all jargon, is padding—adding significant-
sounding sentences here and there that in fact say little or nothing. Here's one that
occurs over and over, in this case in a *Human Nature* article (August 1978) on psychological causes of illness: "Although the effects of mental attitudes on bodily
disease should not be exaggerated, neither should they be minimized." True. And
here's one from *Psychology Today* (July 1979): "As soon as there are behaviors
you can't generate then there are responses you can't elicit." Yes. And finally, in
their article "Needs Assessment and Holistic Planning," in *Educational Leadership* (May 1981), Roger Kaufman and Robert Stakevas point out that "in order to
achieve products, outputs, and outcomes through processes, inputs are required."
Absolutely.

Some words are born pretentious (*ongoing ambience*). Some words achieve
pretentiousness (*situation*). And some have pretentiousness thrust upon
them (*charisma, parameter*).

—Philip Howard, *Weasel Words*

Inside Woody Allen. From *Non-Being and Something-Ness,* by Woody Allen. Drawn by Stuart
Hample. © 1978 by IWA Enterprises, Inc. and Hackenbush Productions, Inc. Reprinted by
permission of Random House, Inc.

---

[7]In *Social Science as Sorcery* (London: Andre Deutsch, 1972).

1986 Doublespeak Award Winner

First place in the Committee's voting went to officials of the National Aeronautics and Space Administration (NASA), Morton Thiokol, and Rockwell International. The language used by officials of these organizations in discussing the tragedy of the *Challenger* accident and in the subsequent investigation of that accident was filled with doublespeak. When one NASA administrator was asked if the performance of the shuttle program had improved with each launch or if it had remained the same, he answered, "I think our performance in terms of the liftoff performance and in terms of the orbital performance, we knew more about the envelope we were operating under, and we have been pretty accurately staying in that. And so I would say the performance has not by design drastically improved. I think we have been able to characterize the performance more as a function of our launch experience as opposed to it improving as a function of time." Another official said that "the normal process during the countdown is that the countdown proceeds, assuming we are in a go posture, and at various points during the countdown we tag up the operational loops and face-to-face in the firing room to ascertain the facts that project elements that are monitoring the data and that are understanding the situation as we proceed are still in the go direction." An engineer for Morton Thiokol, the maker of the rocket, said he had expressed concern about the possible effect of cold weather on the booster rocket's O-ring seals the night before the launch: "I made the comment that lower temperatures are in the direction of badness for both O-rings, because it slows down the timing function." Another NASA official responded to a question assessing whether problems with the O-rings or with the insulation of the liner of the nozzle posed a greater threat to the shuttle by saying, "The criticality in answering your question, sir, it would be a real foot race as to which one would be considered more critical, depending on the particular time that you looked at your experience with that." After several executives of Rockwell International, the main contractor to build the shuttle, had testified that Rockwell had been opposed to launching the shuttle because of the danger posed by ice formation on the launch platform, one official added, "I felt that by telling them we did not have a sufficient data base and could not analyze the trajectory of the ice, I felt he understood that Rockwell was not giving a positive indication we were for the launch." Officials of Morton Thiokol, when asked why they reversed earlier decisions not to launch the shuttle, said the reversal was "based on the reevaluation of those discussions." The presidential commission investigating the accident suggested that this statement could be translated to mean that there was pressure from NASA. NASA also called the accident an "anomaly," the bodies of the astronauts "recovered components," and the astronauts' coffins "crew transfer containers."

—*Quarterly Review of Doublespeak* (January 1987). © 1986 by the National Council of Teachers of English. Reprinted by permission of the NCTE.

BEDTIME PRAYERS BEFORE MOMMY WENT TO LAW SCHOOL.

AT THE PRESENT JUNCTURE, THIS DAY AND AGE, THIS HOUR, ON THIS, THE PRESENT OCCASION; I, MYSELF, THIS PARTICULAR INDIVIDUAL AND ENTITY, ALLEDGED TO BE MARY JOYCE HARCOURT AND SOMETIMES REFERRED TO AS "JOYCIE" OR "MOMMY" (MOTHER TO THE ALLEDGED LIBERTY REESE HARCOURT); REPOSIT, ASSIGN AND CONSIGN, FIX AND ESTABLISH THIS SAID PERSON, THE ABOVE AND AFORE-MENTIONED (SEE PARAGRAPH 1. LINE 3. WORDS 26, 27, 28) WHO SHALL BE REFERRED TO AS THE PARTY OF THE FIRST PART FROM THIS TIME FORWARD, IN A LOWERED (AS COMPARED TO UPRIGHT) RECLINED AND/OR PROSTRATED POSITION, FOR THE SOLE PURPOSE OF SLUMBER, REPOSE REST IN THE ARMS OF MORPHEUS, SOUNDLY AND/OR HEAVILY, LIKENED TO A TOP AND/OR LOG; NOT TO THE EXCLUSION OF DREAMING AND/OR SNORING WHICH SHALL REMAIN TO BE SEEN ON THE EVIDENCE OF THOSE WHO SHALL REMAIN ANONYMOUS AT THIS TIME; I, MYSELF, THIS PERSON, THIS PARTICULAR INDIVIDUAL AFOREMENTIONED AND NOW REFERRED TO AS THE PARTY OF THE FIRST PART, PROPOSE, REQUEST AND PETITION, MAKE BOLD TO ASK, PUT TO AND CALL UPON, COURT, SEEK TO ENTREAT, AND IMPLORE, BESIEGE, IMPORTUNE AND ADJURE, BEG AND BESEECH THE DIVINE DEITY, GODSHIP, GODHEAD, OMNIPOTENT AND OMNISCIENT SPIRIT I.E. SUPREME BEING, SOUL, HIGHER POWER, PROVIDENCE, KING OF KINGS, QUEEN OF QUEENS, LORD OF LORDS, ALMIGHTY ONE, ABSOLUTE BEING, INFINITE CAUSE, SOURCE, UNIVERSAL MIND, NATURE, ALL POWERFUL, ETERNAL BEING, ALL KNOWING, ALL WISE, ALL MERCIFUL, ALL HOLY, THE PRESERVER, MAKER, CREATOR, AUTHOR AND/OR CREATOR OF ALL THINGS, TRUTH AND LOVE; MY, THE AFOREMENTIONED PARTY OF THE FIRST PART, ESSENCE, FUNDAMENTAL TRUE BEING, INMOST NATURE, CORE, INNER AND ESOTERIC REALITY, VITAL CENTER, ESSENTIAL QUALITY AND SUCHNESS, QUIDDITY PITH, KERNEL, NUCLEUS, INMOST RECESSES OF THE HEART, SPIRIT, PRANA, LIFE FORCE; TO TAKE CUSTODY OF GUARD, WATCH OVER, SUSTAIN AND PRESERVE FOR THE SAFE KEEPING OF, AUSPICIOUS AND SECURE AND CAUTIOUS SURVEILLANCE OF, TO PROTECT, HOLD AND KEEP. SHOULD CIRCUMSTANCES WARRANT THAT I, THE AFOREMENTIONED ONE, NOW KNOWN AS THE PARTY OF THE PART, SHOULD EXPIRE, END, CEASE TO LIVE, EXTINGUISH THE MORTAL LIGHT, LEAVE THIS PHYSICAL PLANE, EXPERIENCE MY DEMISE, DESIST, QUIT THIS WORLD, MAKE MY EXIT, PASS ON, PASS AWAY, MEET MY END, SHUFFLE OFF THIS MORTAL COIL, RELINQUISH OR SURRENDER MY LIFE, YIELD THE GHOST, GIVE UP MY BREATH, GO OUT LIKE THE SNUFF OF A CANDLE, BEFORE OR AT A TIME PRIOR TO THE TIME I REGAIN CONSCIOUSNESS, PASS FROM THE SLEEPING TO THE WAKING STATE, ROUSE MYSELF, WARM TO THE DAY, OPEN MY EYES, I, THE PARTY OF THE FIRST PART, IMPLORE, BEG, AND BESEECH, INVOKE AND ENTREAT, HUMBLY ASK THEE ALMIGHTY, EVER PRESENT UNIFYER OF ALL PERSONS, PLACES AND THINGS, MAMMALS, FISH, BIRDS AND INSECTS, GIVER OF BOONS, INSTILLER OF FAITH, HEALING SOURCE, ONE WHO GIVES ENDLESS LOVE UNCONDITIONALLY, MY, AS IN ME AND MINE, AS IN I, THE PARTY OF THE FIRST PART, OF LOWER OR MORTAL NATURE, SPIRIT, ATMA, BUDDHI, VITAL FORCE, INNER PRINCIPLE, HEART, MIND AND EMBODIED BREATH, ANIMATING PRINCIPLE AND TRUE SELF, ESSENCE AND SUBSTANCE OF LIFE, THE DIVINITY THAT STIRS WITHIN, INNER FLAME AND SEAT OF CONSCIOUSNESS TO; (IF IT PLEASES THEE) APPROPRIATE, CAPTURE, SEIZE, ABDUCT WITH AND ACQUIRE FOR, AN INFINITE PERIOD OF TIME, ENTER INTO POSSESSION OF, AND TAKE RESPONSIBILITY FOR, OBTAIN AND RESCUE, PICK UP, GLEAN, GATHER IN, CAPTURE AND SEIZE AND HOLD UNTIL SUCH TIME   AS IT SHALL BE RELINQUISHED BY THE SAID HOLDER. AMEN.

BEDTIME PRAYERS AFTER MOMMY WENT TO LAW SCHOOL.

Reprinted with permission from *29 Reasons Not to Go to Law School,* by Ralph Warner and Toni Ihara, illustrated by Mari Stein. © 1982 Nolo Press/Folk Law, Inc., 950 Parker Street, Berkeley, CA 94710.

Perhaps the deadliest variety of professionalese is legalese.

But Euphemisms Often Serve Good Purposes

Our desire to cleanse language of bad uses shouldn't blind us to the fact that euphemisms often serve good purposes. Those used to replace offensive four-letter words are an example. Why, after all, should we shock or offend others when we don't have to? Similar remarks apply to the euphemistic expressions *put to sleep, passed gas,* and *for the mature figure.*

3. Those Who Control the Definitions . . .

Calling something by just the right name, or legally shifting the meaning of a term in just the right way, is crucial when you want to bend the law to your own purposes. For instance, employers who want to pay employees less than the minimum wage laws require can call them "subcontractors" instead of "employees." *Employees* is a bad name, and *subcontractors* a good one, because the minimum wage laws apply to employees but not to subcontractors. Yes, the law in the United States does sometimes work that way.[8]

Of course, it operates pretty much the same way everywhere else. In Moslem Saudi Arabia, for example, the commandment not to make graven images is taken quite seriously; photography was therefore forbidden—until recently. But aerial photography is such a boon to oil exploration that something had to be done. So:

> King Ibn Saud convened the Ulema [a group of Moslem theologians who have great power over public morals] and eventually prevailed over them with the argument that photography was actually good because it was not an image, but a combination of light and shadow that depicted Allah's creations without violating them.[9]

All sorts of organizations twist words for profit when they can get away with it. A certain large corporation defended the judgment of one of its employees whose mistake caused a great deal of trouble by arguing that the person was a "trained employee"—the implication being that a "trained employee" ought to know the right thing to do, so the company was not negligent. But as they were using the expression, *trained employee* meant just "employee put through a company training program." Whether the program was any good, or whether the employee actually learned what was being taught, is another matter. By the way, did you notice that among the tools used by the Reagan administration to fight unemployment was the redefinition of terms, so that 6.5 percent unemployment or less suddenly became known as *full employment*?

The Roman Catholic Vatican Council II declared that marriage is a permanent covenant of love resulting in an intimate union of persons and their actions, so many Catholic priests and bishops have concluded that where love never existed, or has been extinguished, a marriage covenant never existed, or no longer exists.[10]

---

[8]But chicanery of this kind is often challenged in court, sometimes successfully.
[9]Peter A. Iseman, "The Arabian Ethos," *Harper's* (February 1978).
[10]See Francis X. Murphy, C.S.S.R., "Of Sex and the Catholic Church," *Atlantic* (February 1981).

So they remarry divorced people in some circumstances without in their own eyes violating the Catholic doctrine that marriage is forever and divorce impossible. They've reasoned that "till death do us part" refers to the death of love as well as physical death. And Church courts have sometimes declared that no marriage existed even when the legally married couple had several children.

The United States Constitution grants Congress the sole right to declare war. But a president who wants to engage in a military venture without getting the consent of Congress need only *rename* his military escapade. Since our last war declared by Congress (World War II), United States military forces have been ordered to fight in several wars, the most prominent being the Korean and Vietnam "engagements." (The Supreme Court decided that the Vietnam War was legal even though no declaration of war had been made by Congress.)

For years, psychologist Thomas Szasz has been campaigning against the use of the expression "mental illness." Declaring John Hinkley "not guilty by way of insanity" in his attempt to assassinate President Reagan is for Szasz just an extreme example of what happens when we take the analogy between physical illness and mental illness seriously. His view is that there is no such thing as mental *illness*. (He would say, however, that sometimes "mental illness" is really physical disfunction.)

Another consequence of this mislabeling, he claims, is that close relatives of the "mentally ill" (and others who don't want them around) often are able to have them "hospitalized for treatment" against their will. Forcing people into institutions in this way is a practice some see as not unlike the Russian habit of confining dissidents in "mental institutions." In a similar vein, Szasz argues, "we call self-starvation either anorexia nervosa, a hunger strike, a suicide attempt, or some other name, depending on how *we* want to respond." (Szasz's view is not the dominant one in psychology today, although a number of psychologists—and this writer—find it modestly persuasive.)

Finally, let's mention the Alabama judge who in 1987 ordered several dozen textbooks removed from Alabama schools on the grounds that they favored the establishment of a particular religion—*secular humanism*—over Christianity, Judaism, and so on, thus violating the provision in the Bill of Rights forbidding the establishment of a government-sanctioned religion. (His ruling was later overturned.) Secular humanists, of course, promote moral principles and social institutions not based on any religious convictions.

You can consistently win debates if you consistently use two words: "baby" and "kill."

> —Dr. J. C. Willke, vice-president, National Right to Life Committee, at a pro-life (which means antiabortion) convention, teaching others to teach the pro-life position (St. Louis, 1978)

Choosing words and phrases with just the right emotive force is a vital part of the art of rhetoric.

4. Common Rhetorical Devices

Mind-numbing language of the doublespeak variety is only one of many kinds of rhetorical devices used to obfuscate, deceive, or otherwise manipulate via language. Emotively loaded language is, obviously, another. Let's now consider a few more common rhetorical tricks.

Slanting

Slanting is a form of misrepresentation. In one version, a true statement is made in such a way as to imply or suggest something else (which usually is either false or not known to be true). For example, a defense lawyer may try to blunt damaging testimony by stating, "All this proves is that . . ." or "Since we willingly admit that . . .," implying that the testimony was of little importance when in fact it was quite damaging. Or an advertisement may say, "Try our best quality knife, *only* $9.95," implying that the price is very low, whether it is or not.

Slanting also can be accomplished by a careful selection of facts. (So slanting often involves the fallacy of *suppressed evidence,* discussed in Chapter 4.) School textbooks are almost always written so as to slant the history of a nation and its leaders. For example, history texts used in American public schools select facts so as to make the United States look as good as possible in the eyes of young readers. The point of public school history texts is, after all (note that slanting expression), to turn young people into good citizens by making them proud of their nation. (See Chapter 10 for more on this point.)

Obviously, writers and speakers aren't going to tell you how they've slanted what they say very often. Perhaps the best defense against slanting (as against the fallacy of *suppressed evidence*) is to ask yourself whether there are some unmentioned things you would need to know before making an intelligent judgment. If so, would the author be likely to know them? If he would, but didn't reveal them, that's good reason to think the information may be damaging to his claim. Another important question to ask is whether the slanted material would convince you if you wanted very much to believe it *false*. If the answer is "no," then perhaps there would be self-deception or wishful thinking involved in the acceptance of that material.

Weasel Words

Weasel words are words or phrases that appear to make little or no change in the content of a statement while in fact sucking out all or most of its content.[11] For example, an anthropology student, apparently unsure of her facts, wrote that "Economic success *may be* the explanation of male dominance over females" (italics added). Using the expression *may be* instead of the usual verb *is* protected the

---

[11]This expression, which originated with Theodore Roosevelt, suggests the practice weasels have of making a small hole in eggs and sucking out their contents, so that what appears to be a normal egg is in fact just an empty shell.

student from error by reducing the content of her statement to close to zero. After all, given what she said, the economic success of males may *not* be the explanation of male dominance. (Note the assumption that males *do* dominate females in the last analysis, something some of us—in particular hen-pecked males—would deny.)

Fine Print Disclaimers

Another common device is to unobtrusively take back in the (usually) unread fine print what is claimed in the most easily read part of an argument or document. Schlock insurance policies are notorious for using this device. They tout wonderful coverage in large type while taking away most of it in the small-print explanatory qualifications. Advertisements regularly do this by using a small asterisk to direct you to the bottom of the ad—where you find, for instance, that you have to buy the ticket 30 days in advance and stay over at least one Saturday to qualify for the low fare shouted in the headline.

Monroe C. Beardsley was one of the first to write a textbook dealing strictly with critical thinking (as opposed to formal logic). In this excerpt from Thinking Straight, *he explains an example of what he calls "suggestion" (a kind of slanting):*

On November 30, 1968, the *New York Times* reported on the construction site for a new jetport in the Everglades, 40 miles from Miami:

> Populated now by deer, alligators, wild turkeys, and a tribe of Indians who annually perform a rite known as the Green Corn Dance, the tract could someday accommodate a super jetport twice the size of Kennedy International in New York and still have a one-mile buffer on every side to minimize intrusions in the lives of any eventual residents.

A more horrible example of suggestion could hardly be found. First, note that by putting the Indians in a list with deer, alligators, and wild turkeys, the writer suggests that they belong in the same category as these subhuman species. This impression is reinforced by the allusion to the "Green Corn Dance," which . . . (since it is irrelevant to the rest of the story) can only suggest that this kind of silly superstitious activity sums up their lives. And the impression is driven home sharply at the end when we get to the need to "minimize intrusions on the lives of any eventual residents"—the Indians, of course, can hardly be counted as real residents.

—Monroe C. Beardsley, *Thinking Straight* (4th edition)
Englewood Cliffs, N.J.: Prentice-Hall, 1975)

Here is an item that illustrates how the way things are counted can be used to mask unfavorable information:

. . . , the committee [on doublespeak] voted a third place award to the Nuclear Regulatory Agency for its method of counting accidents at nuclear power plants and reporting them to Congress. In one report the agency detailed 400 "events" at nuclear plants, naming two of them "abnormal occurrences." But one of those "abnormal occurrences" included accidents at 19 different reactors. The 19 plants had a common design problem and the agency counts "generic" problems such as design flaws built into many different reactors as one problem, not 19. Another "abnormal occurrence" ocurred so frequently (in 12 different reactors) that it was called a "normally expected occurrence."

—*Quarterly Review of Doublespeak* (January 1981)

Obfuscation

When confronted with a tough issue or question, people frequently try to evade it, or at least soften the blow, by some sort of *obfuscation*. One way to do this is to wander from the point onto safer topics. Another is to snow listeners with an immense amount of details.

Several witnesses at the 1987 Congressional Iran-Contra hearings resorted to this sort of rhetoric on a grand scale, in particular, Lt. Col. Oliver North and Admiral John Poindexter. For example, when Col. North was asked "who in the United States government chose to structure the transaction [of money collected from the sale of arms to Iran] so that there would be $17 million left in Mr. Secord's bank accounts?" his first reply was:

> Well I don't know that it was structured to leave $17 million in the account, to start with. It was structured so by the time we got to the February transaction, it was structured in such a way that General Secord would become the person who actually conducted the transactions, that the government of the United States would be paid exactly what it asked for whatever was shipped. And that was what we did with the 1000 TOWs in February, and that's what we did with the Hawk parts that were shipped in May. And eventually the Hawks—excuse me, the Hawk parts—and TOWs later in the Autumn. In each case, the decision was made to allow General Secord to be the broker, if you will, for that transaction, that it would be his accounts that would then transfer monies to the Israelis, to the various people who needed to be paid, to include the government of the United States. I initially thought the money was coming from the Israelis in the person of Mr. Ghorbanifar—who was widely regarded in our government, at least in the CIA people I talked to, as an Israeli agent—to Mr. Secord's account, to the CIA, and then to the

The October 1987 issue of the Quarterly Review of Doublespeak, *a publication of the National Council of Teachers of English, contained a very interesting article by William Lutz on the doublespeak nature of Lt. Col. Oliver North's Iran-Contra congressional testimony. Here are a few of Lutz's points:*

North said that he "cleaned things up," he was "cleaning up the historical record," he "fixed" things up, and that he "took steps to ensure" that things never "came out"—meaning he lied, destroyed official government documents, and created false documents. Some documents weren't destroyed; they were "non-log" or kept "out of the system so that outside knowledge would not necessarily be derived from having the documents themselves."

North also implied that those who opposed aid to the Contras were assisting the cause of Communism: "And thank God somebody put money into that account and the Nicaraguan resistance didn't die, as perhaps others intended; certainly the Sandinistas, and Moscow and Cuba intended that. . . ." The use of the word "others" coupled with the independent clause beginning "certainly" lumps together all who oppose aid to the Contras, and aligns Congress with promoting the aims of the Communists.

One of North's most interesting uses of language occurred when he declared that "the American people ought not to be led to believe . . . that we intentionally deceived the American people, or had that intent to begin with. The effort to conduct these covert operations was made in such a way that our adversaries would not have knowledge of them, or that we could deny American association with it, or the association of this government with those activities. And that is not wrong." North never did explain how the American people were to be informed of these covert operations, especially since he testified that "I didn't want to show Congress a single word on this whole thing."

North also insisted that "the president could authorize and conduct covert actions with unappropriated funds." When asked, "And in such an event, to whom would the president be accountable?" North answered. "To the American people . . . that elected him . . . they can vote him out of office." But, North was reminded, if "covert action is secret and he [the president] doesn't tell them about it, there's no way the American people can know about it to be able to vote him out of office on that basis, is there?" To this North replied, "I believe the president has the authority to do what he wants with his own staff. . . ."

Welcome to the world of doublethink, a world where North could participate in drafting a letter to Congress saying that "we are complying with the letter and spirit of Boland" while admitting what the letter really meant was that "Boland doesn't apply to us and so we're complying with its letter and spirit." A world where noncompliance is compliance.

Pentagon, to pay for the weapons—or the materiel, whatever it wa[s]
was being shipped.

That was done for a number of purposes. One, to accrue sufficient
funds to pay for Israeli replenishments for what had been shipped in '8[5;]
second of all, to generate revenues to support the Nicaraguan resistance;
and third, to cover the costs of these transactions; and ultimately, further
the cause of the approach that we made with the second channel.

Since this didn't quite answer the question, it was repeated, leading Col. North
into a reply that takes up almost three pages, including the following:[12]

> If I—and I'm going to ask you for the latitude to make a more—a longer
> discourse than ten words. When Mr. Nir arrived in the United States in
> the end of December or early January of 1985, early '86, the principal
> concern that he had, as he expressed it to me, was to keep this initiative
> moving, to further the goals that we—that I clearly understood of an
> opening to a more moderate regime in Iran, to get beyond the obstacle of
> the hostages—in other words, to recover them safely, because they were
> both a—a—a legitimate political problem here in the United States—you
> couldn't deal with the Iranians without getting beyond that—and to carry
> out a hoped for, and I think successful while we did it, program of reduc-
> ing Shia-sponsored terrorism. He also had as a—as a very obvious goal,
> insurance that the Israeli TOWs that had been shipped in September be
> replenished, and that the Hawks, which were sitting in Iran at the time,
> be returned to Israel.
>
> I had, by this time, had absolutely come to the conclusion that there
> was no way to do it by having the Israelis walk into the Pentagon and
> buy 508 new TOWs without it becoming a public issue. They knew that,
> and I knew that. And so Mr. Nir is the first person to suggest that there
> be a residual, and that the residual be applied to the purpose of purchas-
> ing replenishments, and supporting other activities. Now, at that point in
> time in early January, he did not raise with me the specifics of supporting
> the Nicaraguan resistance. That proposal came out of a meeting in, as I
> recall, later in January, where I met with Mr. Nir and Mr. Ghorbanifar—
> I'm gonna say London, but it may have been Frankfurt or it may have
> been elsewhere—and in that meeting, I expressed our grave reservations
> as to how the structure, which at that point in time focused on several
> thousand TOWs, would result in what we wanted. And, what we wanted
> were laid out very clearly in the January findings, and what we wanted
> was a more moderate regime, ultimately, in Iran, the cessation of Iranian
> Shia fundamentalist terrorism, and the return of the American hostages,
> which I viewed as an obstacle, and we had to overcome as a first step.
>
> I expressed our reservations that the arrangements that were being
> made by Mr. Ghorbanifar, and by then acting in our behalf as well as the
> Israelis, were not going to lead to what we wanted. What we wanted, as a

---

[12]In *Taking the Stand: The Testimony of Lt. Colonel Oliver L. North.* (New York: Pocket
Books, 1987).

rall program, was to establish a higher level meeting, well
ade. In fact, I suggested a number of people, and I'm
in my messages to my superiors, a number of people
h senior Iranian officials, in various ways in which

questioning took a new turn, and Col. North had man-
 cring the question put to him about who in the United States
decided to have $17 million remain in General Secord's bank

Here are excerpts from "Psychological Operations in Guerrilla Warfare," by "Tayacan," a manual prepared by the CIA for the Nicaraguan Contras and made public in October 1985. The translation is by the Congressional Research Service (reprinted in Harper's, *January 1986).*

Below we enunciate many of the literary devices in frequent use in oratory. We recommend that those interested use them in moderation, since an orator who overuses literary devices loses credibility.

Anaphora is the repetition of a word at the beginning of each clause. For example, "Freedom for the poor, freedom for the rich, freedom for all."

Antithesis involves a play on words in which the same word is used with different meanings to give an ingenious effect. For example, "The greatest wealth of every human being is his own freedom, because slaves will always be poor but we poor can have the wealth of our freedom."

Concession involves skillfully conceding something to an adversary in order to better emphasize another point. This is done through the use of expressions such as *but, however, although, nevertheless, in spite of the fact that,* etc. For example: "The mayor here has been honest, but he is not the one controlling all the money of the nation." It is an effective form of rebuttal when the opinions of the audience are not entirely one's own.

Irony is a way to get across exactly the opposite of what one is saying. For example, "The divine mobs that threaten and kill, they are indeed Christians."

Apostrophe consists of addressing something supernatural or inanimate as if it were a living being. For example, "Mountains of Nicaragua, make the seed of freedom grow."

Paralipsis involves the pretense of discretion. For example, "If I were not obligated to keep military secrets, I would tell you about all the armaments we have, so you would feel even more confident that our victory is assured."

Litotes is a way of conveying a lot by saying little. For example, "The nine commanders haven't stolen much, just the whole country."

Interrogation consists of asking a question of oneself. For example, "If they have already murdered the members of my family, my friends, my peasant brothers, do I have any path other than brandishing a weapon?"

Blending Value Claims into Factual Assertions

One way to get value judgments across to others without the need to justify them is to slip them in with other statements in the hope that they won't be noticed and thus not be challenged. The fewer words used to do this, the better. Here is a snippet (*Parade* magazine, March 25, 1984) in which one word does the trick:

> President Reagan's re-election [remember, this was in 1984] is predicated on the continued recovery of the U.S. economy for which he *justifiably* takes credit. (Italics added)

Lots of us thought at the time that the recovery had little if anything to do with Reagan administration policies.

Or consider this little item containing an unfair manipulative expression most readers probably never noticed:

> *Self-appointed* consumer advocate Ralph Nader . . . . (Italics added)

5. Sexism in language

In the last 15 to 20 years, a minor language revolution has been taking place as a result of the demands of women's rights advocates and because of a quickly evolving consensus against sexist language. An early sign of this consensus was the publication of "Guidelines for Equal Treatment of the Sexes . . ." by the McGraw-Hill publishing company, guidelines that were quickly adopted by most publishers. Here are some dos and don'ts listed in various places in the guidelines that show how far this part of the language revolution has come:[13]

NO	YES
mankind	humanity, human beings, human race, people
If a man drove 50 miles at 60 m.p.h., . . .	If a person (or driver) drove 50 miles at 60 m.p.h., . . .
manmade	artificial, synthetic, manufactured, constructed of human origin
manpower	human power, human energy, workers, workforce

NO	YES
grow to manhood	grow to adulthood, grow to manhood *or* womanhood

(1) Reword to eliminate unnecessary gender pronouns.

---

[13]Reprinted by permission of the McGraw-Hill Book Co.

NO	**YES**
The average American drinks his coffee black.	The average American drinks black coffee.
(2) Recast into the plural.	Most Americans drink their coffee black.

(3) Replace the masculine pronoun with *one, he or she, her or his,* as appropriate. (Use *he or she* and its variations sparingly to avoid clumsy prose.)

(4) Alternate male and female expressions and examples.

NO	**YES**
I've often heard supervisors say, "He's not the right man for the job," or "He lacks the qualifications for success."	I've often heard supervisors say, "She's not right for the job," or "He lacks the qualifications for success."
congressman	member of Congress, Representative (but Congress*man* Koch and Congress*woman* Holzman)
businessman	business executive, business manager
fireman	fire fighter
mailman	mail carrier; letter carrier
salesman	sales representative; salesperson; sales clerk
chairman	the person presiding at (or chairing) a meeting; the presiding officer; the chair; head, leader, coordinator, moderator

Cathy by Cathy Guisewite. Copyright 1984 Universal Press Syndicate. All rights reserved. Used by permission of Universal Press Syndicate.

NO	YES
the men and the ladies	the men and the women; the ladies and the gentlemen; the girls and the boys
man and wife	husband and wife

NO	YES
Bobby Riggs and Billie Jean	Bobby Riggs and Billie Jean King
Billie Jean and Riggs	Billie Jean and Bobby
Mrs. Meir and Moshe Dayan	Golda Meir and Moshe Dayan or Mrs. Meir and Mr. Dayan

NO	YES
the fair sex; the weaker sex	women
the girls or the ladies (when adult females are meant)	the women
girl, as in: I'll have my *girl* check that.	I'll have my *secretary* (or my *assistant*) check that. (Or use the person's name.)

NO	YES
Pioneers moved West, taking their wives and children with them.	Pioneer families moved West. Or Pioneer men and women (or pioneer couples) moved West, taking their children with them.

On the other hand, things can be carried too far. It would be silly, for instance, for Germans to stop referring to their homeland as the "Fatherland," or Englishmen—that is, ah, citizens of England—to their "mother tongue." Nor does there seem to be anything wrong with the predominantly male members of a ship referring to their particular tug as *she.* There are also questions of aesthetic taste—of what sounds right, or wrong, rolling off the tongue. The expression *her or his,* for instance, rings false, perhaps because it calls attention to the avoidance of *his or her,* or *his* (used to mean his or her), and thus distracts from what's being said. Similar remarks apply to the term "Congressperson" (avoided in this text in favor of "member of Congress").[14]

---

[14]Interestingly, no one seems perturbed by the fact that liberty is always portrayed as a woman on American coins, never a man. And while there are lots of complaints about sexist terms like "waitress" and "aviatrix," no one seems bothered by the equally sexist "widower." Double standard?

A *Wilmington Comment* on Governor Tribbitt's appointment of Irene Sha-
doan of the Associated Press as his press secretary at $20,000 a year: "If he
wants to pay $10,000 a mammary, that's his business."

> —*Delaware State News,* reprinted in *Ms.* magazine

Can you imagine a similar remark about paying a man $10,000 a testicle?

Summary of Chapter 6

1. Most words have emotive meanings (in addition to cognitive meanings).
   Words like *oppression, kike,* and *bitch* have more or less negative (con)
   emotive overtones: words like *spring, free,* and *satisfaction* have positive
   (pro) emotive overtones; and words like *socialism, marijuana,* and *God*
   have mixed emotive overtones.

   Words that have roughly the same cognitive meaning often have radically
   different emotive meanings; the words *bureaucrat, government official,*
   and *public servant* illustrate this.

2. Con artists use the emotive side of language (1) to mask cognitive meaning
   by whipping up emotions so that reason is overlooked and (2) to dull the
   force of language so as to make acceptable what otherwise might not be.
   The latter often is accomplished by means of euphemisms (less offensive
   expressions used in place of more offensive ones) or a kind of doublespeak
   that lulls the unwary into acceptance.

3. It should also be noted that the meanings of words and expressions sometimes are changed so as either to get around or to take advantage of laws,
   rules, or customs.
   Example: Calling an employee a *subcontractor* to avoid paying a minimum
   wage or social security.

4. Common rhetorical devices are often used to obfuscate.
   Examples: Slanting words and expressions ("All this proves is that . . ."),
   weasel words that suck the meaning out of a sentence ("Economic success
   may be . . ."), fine print disclaimers that take back part of what was originally claimed, and unsupported value judgments embedded in factual
   assertions.

5. The English language contains features that mirror sexist attitudes of our
   past. The McGraw-Hill guidelines have been adopted by most publishers to
   rid written English of these locutions.
   Example: They require us to replace the word *man* by *person* whenever gender is not an issue.

Exercise 6-1

1. Discuss what you think (and why, of course) of the following explanation (in Robert J. Ringer's *Looking Out for Number One*) of President Kennedy's famous statement, "And so, my fellow Americans, ask not what your country can do for you; ask what you can do for your country":

   > Ask what you can do for your *country?* Does this mean asking each of the more than 200 million individuals what you can do for him? No, individuals are not what Kennedy or any other politician has ever had in mind when using the word *country*. A country is an abstract entity, but in politicalese, it translates into "those in power." Restated in translated form, then, it becomes: Ask not what those in power can do for you; ask what you can do for those in power.

2. Try to find some examples of inappropriate names being applied to things so that the law, custom, or whatever will deal with these things differently, and explain the chicanery.

3. Here is a passage from a United States history textbook, *America: Its People and Values,* by Leonard C. Wood, Ralph H. Gabriel, and Edward L. Biller:

   > A friendly Indian named Squanto helped the colonists. He showed them how to plant corn and how to live in the wilderness. A soldier, Captain Miles Standish, taught the Pilgrims how to defend themselves against unfriendly Indians.

   > How is language used to slant this account? In what other ways is it slanted?

*4. Translate the following excerpt from *Usable Knowledge: Social Science and Social Problem Solving,* by Charles F. Lindblom and David K. Cohen (mentioned in a book review in the *Washington Monthly*):

   > By social problem solving, we mean processes that are to eventuate in outcomes that by some standard are an improvement of the previously existing situation, or are presumed to so eventuate, or are conceived of as offering some possibility to so eventuate.

5. Translate the following quotation from Woodrow Wilson into the most succinct form you can, and compare both versions for persuasive power and understandability:

   > The men who act, stand nearer to the mass of man than the men who write; and it is in their hands that new thought gets its translation into the crude language of deeds.

6. Check your local newspaper, a magazine, a television program, etc., find one or two examples of doublespeak or jargon, and translate them into plain English.

7. The memo below was used by the *Washington Monthly* as a "Memo of the Month." Translate the body of the memo into plain English, coming as close to the original meaning (so far as it can be determined) as possible.

Sacramento City-County Library

Intra-Department Correspondence

Date: October 14, 1971

To: ALL LIBRARY PERSONNEL — Shirley Louthan

From: HAROLD D. MARTELLE
CITY-COUNTY LIBRARIAN

Subject: PERSONNEL PROFILE FORM AND TELEPHONE DIRECTORY ATTACHMENT

The newly devised Personnel Profile form comprises a very necessary and integral function in the intellection of personnel services to this library system by providing data not currently available, by synthesizing employee qualifications and by projecting the basis for a comprehensive codification of all library staff experience and talent.

Although some of you have questioned the requirement for such a form by referring to application forms or Civil Service records, retrospection reveals that when the library's administrative offices were relocated to 930 T Street in February 1967, a significant portion of extant personnel files accidentally was eliminated and has never been replaced. Therefore, institution of the Personnel Profile will eliminate the paucity of available data while expending a minimum of time and expense. This form also will assist in the efficacious programming of manpower skills to related positions and/or need. In addition, the form will facilitate the immediate retrieval and expeditious articulation of available skills and personnel through an extensive codification of data.

In order to implement this form as soon as possible, please complete and return both the Profile and the attached sheet relating to the projected telephone directory of library personnel to the Personnel Office by Wednesday, October 27, 1971.

Thank you for your cooperation and immediate attention.

Harold D. Martelle, Jr.
City-County Librarian

8. Check the media for sexist uses of language, and translate so as to remove the sexist connotations.

9. Check your automobile insurance policy (or somebody's insurance policy). If it isn't written in the new clear style, rewrite the first 250 words or so to say the same thing in plain English. (Lots of luck.)

10. What do you think of the following remark by Michael Armacost, then Reagan's under secretary of state for political affairs:

> It's impossible for somebody to defect from the United States. [Former CIA agent] Edward Lee Howard is not a defector. He's a traitor.

11. Translate into plain English the following quote by Admiral Isaac C. Kidd, chief of Navy material (*Washington Monthly,* May 1972):

> We have gone with teams of competent contract people from Washington to outlying field activities to look over their books with them . . . to see in what areas there is susceptibility to improved capability to commit funds.

12. Defend your opinion concerning the action by Glenn Dean Davis described in the following AP news item:

> SHAMOKIN, PA.—A plaque etched with a lesser-known Benjamin Franklin quotation was removed from a wall at a vocational school here at the order of the state civil rights coordinator, who said the slogan's use of "he" was sexist. The official, Glenn Dean Davis, was inspecting the Northumberland County Vocational-Technical School during the summer when he noticed the plaque, which reads, "He who hath a trade, hath an estate," said school director James Buggy.
>
> Davis contended the use of "he" discriminated against women and the school removed it, Buggy said.

Drawing by H. Martin; © 1974 The New Yorker Magazine, Inc.

"If the coach and horses and the footmen and the beautiful clothes all turned back into the pumpkin and the mice and the rags, then how come the glass slipper didn't turn back, too?"

Two important factors in critical or creative thinking are the ability to bring relevant background information to bear on a problem and to carry through the relevant implications of an argument or position to determine whether they hang together. The above cartoon illustrates the second of these factors: The child carries through the reasoning in the Cinderella story and finds it wanting. The first factor might be illustrated by a child who brings relevant background information to bear on the Santa Claus story (for instance, a child who realizes there are millions of chimneys for Santa to get down in one night and wonders how he could manage to do so in time).

7

Analyzing and Constructing Extended Arguments

Our topic in this chapter is the evaluation of extended passages, or *essays,* that argue to a conclusion. Up to this point, we've considered mainly short arguments, and these primarily to illustrate fallacious reasoning. But in daily life, we usually encounter longer passages of the kind we now need to consider.

However, it should be noted first that there are different kinds of persuasive essays in addition to the argumentative variety. Even simple *description* or *narration* may be used for this purpose. For example, in his famous short story "A Hanging," George Orwell argued with some force against capital punishment simply by graphically describing a hanging and one person's gut-wrenched response to it. (Current abortion debate is studded with detailed descriptions of aborted fetuses.) And just explaining something may be used effectively to persuade others to our own point of view. For instance, an article on fluorocarbons and depletion of the ozone layer may simply describe how the ozone layer is being depleted, increasing the chances of getting skin cancer, and yet convince many readers of the implied conclusion that something needs to be done about freon and all that.

But our main concern here will be everyday rhetoric in which there is at least some attempt to present reasons for some conclusion or other. These reasons may be of the textbook variety, deductively or inductively supporting the essay's conclusion, in some straightforward way, or of some other kind. *Examples* are often convincing reasons (example: George Orwell's "A Hanging," illustrating how a story can persuade). And so are legitimate *appeals to authority* (example: Einstein's letter to F.D.R. conveying his belief that it was possible to build an atomic bomb).

In addition, we should remember that a conclusion can be argued for by reasons in different ways. We may weigh the merits and demerits of a possible course of action, instead of concentrating on the merits alone, to come to a judgment about whether to take the action. A **pro and con argument** of this kind can be very effective because it tends to answer questions the reader or listener may raise against the thesis. This is also true, of course, with respect to arguments that explicitly provide a **refutation to counterarguments,** as in the case of a politician who says something like, "Now my opponent will no doubt respond _____; but I say __ __ __ __ __." And an essay may also argue for a course of action by showing that alternatives are less desirable, that is, argue by a **comparison of alternatives.**

Of course, a typical essay may employ more than one persuasive strategy. It may argue first by a general comparison of alternatives and then, finding the alternative that seems to be the most attractive, zero in on it for a more careful analysis. Or it may provide reasons that deductively support the essay's thesis and are in turn supported by expert opinion, or perhaps by examples.

1. Analyzing Extended Passages

There are almost as many ways to analyze extended arguments as there are analyzers. What works best for one person may not work well for someone else. And time and interest also play a role. Even so, there are guidelines that are useful for most people, in particular for those who initially have a bit of trouble handling lengthier arguments.

Find the Thesis and Keep It in Mind

The most important thing, obviously, is to find the author's main conclusion or **thesis.** (Occasionally there is more than one.) The thesis isn't always obvious because the passage may be poorly written, or the author may build up to it and put it near the end. The thesis is the point of the passage, so you have to keep it in mind to determine whether the author provides sufficient *reasons* for accepting it. In sports, the trick is to keep your eye on the ball. In analyzing extended passages, it is to keep your mind's eye on the thesis.

Find the Reasons Supporting the Thesis

The next thing to do, obviously, is find the *reasons,* or *premises,* supporting the author's thesis, or main conclusion. Again, this will be hard or easy, depending on the author's style and competence. But it may also be hard because the reasons themselves are supported by reasons, and so on. A simple example is the newspaper columnist who argued that cigarettes should be made illegal because they kill so many people, and anything so bad for us should be illegal. He then went on to argue for his claim that cigarette smoking is indeed deadly by providing overwhelming statistical evidence. So the logical structure of his extended argument was something like this:

> *Thesis:* Cigarettes should be made illegal.
> *Reasons:* (1) Cigarettes are deadly.
>   (2) anything so deadly should be illegal.
> *Reasons for (1):* Statistical proof linking smoking cigarettes with lung cancer, emphysema, and heart disease.

He assumed most people would accept his second reason without further justification.

Skip Whatever Doesn't Support the Thesis

People write to persuade other people. So they include irrelevant material whenever they think that it will help convince others. This kind of "flavoring" material makes reading more fun, but you don't want to be influenced by it when analyzing a passage that you're serious about. Anecdotes and especially introductory flavorings are great but generally irrelevant to the job of proving the thesis.

Add Relevant Information

Everything needed to prove a thesis is never—that means *never*—included in any argument, no matter how long. To do that would require dragging in big chunks of a writer's world view, as well as proving things that are obvious or generally accepted. Good writers try to provide just the information their audience will need. Someone writing about education, say for an audience of teachers, generally wouldn't bother to prove that a great many public school students graduate from high school today without a solid background in reading, writing, and arithmetic. Proving this for that audience would amount to useless overkill.

In addition, being human, writers often neglect a point that they should have included or (worse) argue fallaciously when a cogent argument is available. So you should provide whatever reasons you know that support the thesis of the passage (as well as the things you know that contradict it). That is, you should analyze the best version of an argument you can think of, even if the writer's argument is less good.

Come to an Evaluation

While evaluation is logically the last thing we need to do in argument analysis, good argument analyzers tend to start evaluating as soon as they come across the thesis. They keep in mind questions like, Do I already accept this thesis? Does it fit well with what I already know? If not, what sort of evidence or reasons might change my mind? And they continue to evaluate as they go along, bearing in mind such questions as, Is this reason acceptable without further argument? Does that reason defend the thesis or just a straw version of it? Do the facts referred to seem plausible, given my background beliefs? Is there some serious counterargument the writer seems to be forgetting? Of course, a completely confident judgment can't be reached until the whole extended argument has been gone through, and at least something of its structure has been figured out.

When the entire structure of an extended argument has been figured out, all of its relevant passages will divide into those that are argued for within the argument as a whole and those that are not. The latter are the writer's basic "starting points"—assumed without being justified. When thoroughly evaluating an extended passage, you need to ask and answer three basic questions, corresponding to the three basic requirements of good reasoning (discussed in Chapter 1 and in the Appendix): (1) Are the writer's starting points justified by what you already believe? (2) Do you know other relevant reasons or arguments? (If so, you should add them, of course.) (3) Do the starting points (plus any relevant material you may have added) justify acceptance of the thesis? That is, is the reasoning valid?

If there is a starting point that isn't justified by your background beliefs, or if you know of relevant information that refutes or casts doubt on the thesis, or if the reasoning is not completely valid, then clearly you should not be convinced by that particular argument.

A note of caution: It's common for some of the subsidiary arguments in a lengthy passage to be cogent while others are fallacious. In these cases, the right thing to do is to accept only the untainted portions of the overall argument. You don't want to automatically toss out the whole extended passage because, in many cases, other relevant information can be added from your store of background beliefs to make the main thesis of the whole passage acceptable.

Exercise 7-1

For each of the following, find the thesis, find the reasons, explicit or implicit, supporting the thesis (and any reasons supporting the reasons), and isolate the extraneous material (whatever doesn't support the thesis or the reasons). Then rewrite the passage in your own words, as in the following example.

Example: Original Passage (from a speech by President Reagan):

As many of you know, our administration has . . . strongly backed an amendment that will permit school children to hold prayer in our schools. (Applause) We believe that school children deserve the same protection, the same constitutional consensus that permits prayer in the Houses of Congress, chaplains in our armed services, and the motto on our coinage that says, "In God We Trust." (Applause) I grant you, possibly, we can make a case that prayer is needed more in Congress than in our schools, but. . . . (Laughter, applause)

Rewritten passage:

Thesis: We should pass an amendment permitting prayers in public schools. *Reason:* School children deserve the same protection (he meant "the same *rights*") under the Constitution as it gives to Congress, the armed services, and coins. *Extraneous material:* We can probably make out a better case for the need for congressional prayers.

1. *Richard Nixon:* Some people, quite properly appalled at the abuses that occurred, will say that Watergate demonstrated the bankruptcy of the American political system. I believe precisely the opposite is true. Water-

gate represented a series of illegal acts and bad judgments by a number of individuals. It was the system that has brought the facts to light and that will bring those guilty to justice.[1]

2. *Baruch Brody* [on the abortion issue]: There is a continuity of development from the moment of conception on. There are constant changes in the foetal condition; the foetus is constantly acquiring new structures and characteristics, but there is no one state which is radically different from any other. Since this is so, there is no one stage in the process of foetal development after the moment of conception which could plausibly be picked out as the moment at which the foetus becomes a living human being. The moment of conception is, however, different in this respect. It marks the beginning of this continuous process of development and introduces something new which is radically discontinuous with what has come before it. Therefore, the moment of conception, and only it, is a plausible candidate for being that moment at which the foetus becomes a living human being.[2]

3. *Florida Democratic Senator Lawton Chiles:* Citizens have the right to know how their Government works; yet, lobbying is largely hidden from public view even though it has enormous impact on legislation. Of an estimated 15,000 lobbyists in Washington, only about 2,000 are registered and little of an estimated $2 billion a year spent for lobbying is being reported. This is allowed by current law loopholes, loopholes that legislation I am sponsoring would plug. The public understandably is suspicious of that which is hidden from it, and this suspicion creates doubt about the integrity of both lobbyists and the legislative process. We must have greater lobbying disclosure.[3]

*4. *Thomas Paine, in his classic* The Age of Reason: Revelation is a communication of something which the person to whom that thing is revealed did not know before. For if I have done a thing, or seen it done, it needs no revelation to tell me I have done it or seen it, nor to enable me to tell it or to write it. Revelation, therefore, cannot be applied to anything done upon earth, of which man himself is the actor or the witness; and consequently, all the historical and anecdotal parts of the Bible, which is almost the whole of it, is not within the meaning and compass of the word 'revelation,' and therefore, is not the word of God.

5. *Astronomer Fred Hoyle:* Perhaps you may think that the whole question of the creation of the Universe could be avoided in some way. But this is not so. To avoid the issue of creation it would be necessary for all the material in the Universe to be infinitely old, and this it cannot be for a very practical reason. For if this were so, there could be no hydrogen left in

[1]*The White House Transcripts* (New York: Bantam Books, 1974).
[2]Robert Perkins, *Abortion: Pro and Con* (Cambridge: Schenkman Publishing, 1974).
[3]*Family Weekly* (March 4, 1980).

the Universe. . . . ⓐHydrogen is being steadily converted into helium throughout the Universe and this conversion is a one-way process—that is to say, hydrogen cannot be produced in any appreciable quantity through the breakdown of other elements. ⓑHow comes it then that the Universe consists almost entirely of hydrogen? ⓒIf matter were infinitely old this would be quite impossible. So we see that the Universe being what it is, the creation issue simply cannot be dodged.

6. *John Locke, in his classic* The Second Treatise on Government: Though the earth and all inferior creatures be common to all men, yet every man has a property in his own person; this nobody has any right to but himself. The labor of his body and the work of his hands, we may say, are properly his. Whatsoever then he removes out of the state that nature has provided and left it in, he has mixed his labor with, and joined to it something that is his own, and thereby makes it his property. It being by him removed from the common state nature has placed it in, it has by this labor something annexed to it that excluded the common right of other men. For this labor being the unquestionable property of the laborer, no man but he can have a right to what that is once joined to, at least where there is enough and as good left in common for others.

7. It also appears that suicide no longer repels us. The suicide rate is climbing, especially among blacks and young people. What's more, suicide has been appearing in an increasingly favorable light in the nation's press. When Paul Cameron surveyed all articles on suicide indexed over the past 50 years in the *Reader's Guide to Periodical Literature,* he found that voluntary death, once portrayed as a brutal waste, now generally appears in a neutral light. Some recent articles even present suicide as a good thing to do and are written in a manner that might encourage the reader to take his own life under certain circumstances. Last year, a majority of Americans under 30 told Gallup pollsters that incurable disease or continual pain confer on a person the moral right to end his life.[4]

8. *Ayn Rand:* By what conceivable standard can the policy of price-fixing be a crime when practiced by businessmen, but a public benefit when practiced by the government? There are many industries in peacetime—trucking, for instance—whose prices are fixed by the government. If price-fixing is harmful to competition, to industry, to production, to consumers, to the whole economy, and to the "public interest"—as the advocates of the antitrust laws have claimed—then how can that same harmful policy become beneficial in the hands of the government? Since there is no rational answer to this question, I suggest that you question the economic knowledge, the purpose and the motives of the champions of antitrust.[5]

9. *From a speech by President Ronald Reagan:* I . . . strongly believe, as you have been told, that the protection of innocent life is, and has always

---

[4]Elizabeth Hall and Paul Cameron, *Psychology Today* (April 1976).
[5]*Capitalism: The Unknown Idea* (New York: New American Library, 1966).

been, a legitimate, indeed, the first duty of government. Believing that, I favor human life. (Applause) And I believe in the human life legislation. The Senate now has three proposals on this matter from Senators Hatch, Helms, and Hatfield. The national tragedy of abortion on demand must end. (Applause) I am urging the Senate to give these proposals the speedy consideration they deserve. A Senate Committee hearing was held recently to determine, if we can, when life actually begins. And there was exhaustive testimony of experts presenting both views. And, finally, the result was declared inconclusive. They could not arrive at an answer. Well, in my view alone, they did arrive at an answer, an answer that justifies the proposed legislation. If it is true we do not know when the unborn becomes a human life, then we have to opt in favor that it is a human life until someone proves it isn't. (Applause)

10. Segregation of white and colored children in public schools has a detrimental effect upon the colored children. The impact is greater when it has the sanction of the law; for the policy of separating the races is usually interpreted as denoting the inferiority of the negro group. A sense of inferiority affects the motivation of a child to learn. Segregation with the sanction of law, therefore, has a tendency to [retard] the educational and mental development of negro children and to deprive them of some of the benefits they would receive in a racially integrated school system.[6]

11. *B. F. Skinner:* The concept of responsibility is particularly weak when behavior is traced to genetic determiners. We may admire beauty, grace, and sensitivity, but we do not blame a person because he is ugly, spastic, or color blind. Less conspicuous forms of genetic endowment nevertheless cause trouble. Individuals presumably differ, as species differ, in the extent to which they respond aggressively or are reinforced when they engage in sexual behavior or are affected by sexual reinforcement. Are they, therefore, equally responsible for controlling their aggressive or sexual behavior, and is it fair to punish them to the same extent? If we do not punish a person for a club foot, should we punish him for being quick to anger or highly susceptible to sexual reinforcement? The issue has recently been raised by the possibility that many criminals show an anomaly in their chromosomes. The concept of responsibility offers little help. The issue is controllability. We cannot change genetic defects by punishment; we can work only through genetic measures which operate on a much longer time scale. What must be changed is not the responsibility of autonomous man but the conditions, environmental or genetic, of which a person's behavior is a function.[7]

12. *Thomas Szasz:* Psychiatry is conventionally defined as a medical specialty concerned with the diagnosis and treatment of mental diseases. I submit

[6]From the 1954 U.S. Supreme Court decision in *Brown v. Topeka Board of Education,* which declared segregated schools inherently unequal and thus unconstitutional.
[7]B. F. Skinner, *Beyond Freedom and Dignity* (New York: Alfred A. Knopf, 1971).

that this definition, which is widely accepted, places psychiatry in the company of alchemy and astrology and commits it to the category of pseudoscience. The reason for this is that there is no such thing as "mental illness." Psychiatrists must now choose between continuing to define their discipline in terms of nonexistent entities or substantives, or redefining it in terms of the actual interventions or processes in which they engage. . . .

Until the middle of the nineteenth century, and beyond, illness meant a bodily disorder whose typical manifestation was an alteration of a bodily structure: that is, a visible deformity, disease, or lesion, such as a misshapen extremity, ulcerated skin, or a fracture or wound. Since in this original meaning of it, illness was identified by altered bodily structure, physicians distinguished diseases from nondiseases according to whether or not they could detect an abnormal change in the structure of a person's body. This is why, after dissection of the body was permitted, anatomy became the basis of medical science: by this means physicians were able to identify numerous alterations in the structure of the body which were not otherwise apparent. As more specialized methods of examining bodily tissues and fluids developed, the pathologist's skills in detecting hitherto unknown bodily diseases grew explosively. . . .

It is important to understand clearly that modern psychiatry—and the identification of new psychiatric diseases—began not by identifying such diseases by means of the established methods of pathology, but by creating a new criterion of what constitutes disease: to the established criterion of detectable alteration of *bodily structure* was now added the fresh criterion of alteration of *bodily function;* and, as the former was detected by observing the patient's body, so the latter was detected by observing his behavior. This is how and why conversion hysteria became the prototype of this new class of diseases—appropriately named "mental" to distinguish them from those that are "organic," and appropriately called also "functional" in contrast to those that are "structural." Thus, whereas in modern medicine new diseases were *discovered,* in modern psychiatry they were *invented.* Paresis was *proved* to be a disease; hysteria was *declared* to be one.[8]

2. Quick Appraisals

In real life, outside of the classroom, people seldom spend a lot of time on any particular extended argument. This is certainly true of the mass of readers. Exact analysis is regularly done only by lawyers and such types, or by someone commenting on or replying to someone else's arguments (as in a debate or school assignment).

---

[8]R. E. Vatz and L. S. Weinberg, eds., *Primary Values and Major Contentions* (Buffalo, N.Y.: Prometheus Books, 1983). ©1983 by Thomas Szasz: Prometheus Books, Buffalo, New York. Reprinted with permission.

The key to good, quick appraisals is the ability to do the basic processes of a more systematic appraisal informally and quickly.

First, you want to find the *thesis* so that you can keep it in the back of your mind when reading the passage. Some people like to make a mark in the margin where the thesis occurs, others underline, still others just keep the thesis firmly in their mind.

When the thesis is stated right off, there's no problem in finding it. In other cases, you may have a pretty good idea what the thesis is anyway. For instance, if the first few sentences of an essay describe how human an aborted fetus looks, you can figure the thesis is going to be antiabortion. But if in doubt, skip around, especially to the last paragraph or two, to find the main point. That's one of the great advantages of written material over speeches, television, and radio, so take advantage of it. You don't have to read an essay in the order it was written.

Second, read the passage with an eye for the *reasons* given to support the thesis (and, when the reasons aren't acceptable to you straight off, for the reasons supporting the reasons). Again, some people like to place marks in the margin next to the important reasons, others underline, and still others just firmly plant them in their mind. The point is to get an idea of the basic thrust of the extended argument without working out its complete structure and without putting anything down on paper.

And third, as you read, bring to bear your *background knowledge and beliefs,* making preliminary evaluations as you go along. Reasons pro or con may occur to you that the author of the argument has overlooked entirely. Bringing to bear what you already believe should guide your reading by helping you to know what you want to look out for.

Remember, in real life people read critical essays to find out things they didn't know before or to correct old ideas. Suppose, for instance, the thesis of an essay is that abortion should be made illegal because it is murder. You have probably already heard quite a few arguments pro and con and come to some conclusions on the issue. Perhaps you feel that abortion is all right—that arguments against it are wrong because they consider the fetus to be a human being (a baby), while you're inclined to think it isn't. If so, then for you the key question when reading an antiabortion tract is whether it gives any good reasons for thinking a fetus is indeed a human being. If it does, you may have to change your mind on the abortion issue (which means reading the article was very profitable, since the point of reading critical material is either to expand or to change your opinions). If it doesn't, you probably won't have to change your mind (which means reading the article wasn't very useful, although it may have been comforting). Of course, there's always the possibility that the author will take a completely original tack, say by arguing that abortion is wrong even though a fetus isn't human. In that case, you want to bring your background beliefs to bear on the reasons presented for this unexpected way of looking at the issue.

So, quick appraisal boils down to swiftly doing the things that any good analysis must do: Keeping your eye on the thesis; looking for reasons that support it; and bringing your background beliefs to bear in evaluating or supplementing the reasons. This means not getting distracted or moved by flavoring material, fancy language, or irrelevant asides. Keep your mind's eye on the issue!

Oh, yes. One of the reasons for developing the knack of quick appraisal is to save time—to keep you from struggling through a whole extended essay only to find out that you've learned next to nothing. Quickly getting to the nub of an article often lets you know that the best thing to do is toss it aside and go on to something else. There are wonderful things out there to read on almost any topic, but there's much more chaff than wheat. Skipping the chaff is half the battle.

Let's now do a quick appraisal of excerpts from comedian and movie director Woody Allen's testimony before the U.S. Senate Judiciary Subcommittee on Technology and the Law (May 12, 1987). The issue was whether to legally ban the colorization of old black-and-white movies, a process that computer technology had just made possible. But Mr. Allen also had the broader question in mind of whether it is "right," whatever the legalities may be, to tamper with a work of art in ways that are contrary to the intent of the artist. In reading Mr. Allen's testimony, the question to remember is whether what he says provides sufficiently good reasons for adopting his position on the matter:

> . . . You might get the impression . . . that I am against colorization of black and white films, but . . . you'd be wrong. If a movie director wishes his film to be colorized, then I say by all means, let him color it. If he prefers it to remain in black and white then it is sinful to force him to change it. If the director is not alive and his work has been historically established in black and white it should remain true to its origin. . . .

We now know, as of course we should have suspected, that director Woody Allen thinks it is wrong to color the old black-and-white films, and, because this is testimony before a Congressional committee considering legislation, we can assume he wants this codified into law.

> The colorizers will tell you that it's proven no one wants black and white but this is not true. . . .

Woody engages in a bit of *straw man* argument here, because his opponents did not claim that no one wants black-and-white versions of the films to be colorized, but rather that a large majority of people prefer these films in color. For instance, they pointed out that only 11,000 video copies of the Jimmy Stewart movie *It's a Wonderful Life* were purchased in black and white compared to 60,000 in color when home video owners were offered both versions. Notice that background knowledge is needed to catch this little slip on Woody's part. (But the point is not central to his argument.)

> . . . [A]nd even if it were [true that people prefer colorization]—if audiences who have grown up on mindless television were so desensitized that a movie like *It Happened One Night,* which has been delighting people in black and white for generations, now had to be viewed in color to be appreciated—then the task would be to cultivate the audience back to some level of maturity rather than to doctor the film artificially to keep up with lowered tastes. . . .

Well, this certainly lays the cards on the table. Woody thinks that if people really prefer colored versions of these old movies, then their taste isn't very good and instead of coloring the movies we should reeducate the audience. So Woody Allen is no democrat when it comes to aesthetic matters. People shouldn't get what they want if what they want is aesthetically poor but rather should be educated to want what is better. (He doesn't say what we should do if most people can't be educated to his taste in movies.) In any event, whatever people may want, it is what the director, the artist who created the film, wishes that counts.

Whether you should accept this view depends on your view as to whether it is somehow wrong to do things with a work of art that the artist does not intend and also whether you believe that matters of this kind should be legislated. (There also is the question whether very many of these old black-and-white films are works of art.)

In any case, notice the distortion in his remark about people needing to view these movies in color to appreciate them. No one ever denied that people can appreciate black-and-white films. The point made by his opponents was that most people prefer color versions.

Notice also that Woody believes those whose taste in movies is different from his lack maturity and also that he has begged the serious question about whether aesthetic goodness is an objective feature of a movie rather than a matter of personal preference. Whether you should accept his view depends in part on whether you agree with him on this matter or perhaps instead agree with the adage that there is no disputing about taste.

> A large number of American movies are classics both at home and all over the world. Thinking they were making popular entertainment, American film makers have produced numerous motion pictures that are considered genuine works of art comparable to fine literature, painting, and music. . . .

That a movie like *It Happened One Night* (Woody Allen's own example) should be considered a work of art "comparable to fine literature, painting, and music," that it is a classic in the sense, say, in which Mozart's music is classic, strikes this writer as false. There is no general agreement on this topic, and you must make your own judgment, but surely most musicians would prefer to compare these movies to works like those of Rogers and Hammerstein or Cole Porter, not to the greats of serious music. They would think it makes more sense to consider the majority of these old movies as classics only of popular taste. At best, Woody Allen is just telling us something about his own aesthetic sensibilities and not providing us with the opinions of serious musicians, painters, or film buffs.

> The colorizers also tell us that a viewer can simply turn off the color and see the film [*The Maltese Falcon*] in black and white. The fact that the man who made the film wants no one at all to see it in color [because it would make this "hard-boiled Bogart film silly-looking"] means nothing to them. . . .

The issue here is whether the wishes of the director take precedent over all other considerations, for instance, over the wishes of the general public and the rights of those who own these old movies. This writer doesn't see why the director's opinion should overrule everything else and so finds this not a good reason for accepting Woody's thesis that black-and-white films should not be colorized. But those who believe that it is always wrong to go against an artist's wishes should count this as a reason in favor of Woody's position. (But see the comment below about some of the other artists involved in making movies.)

> If members of the public had the right to demand alterations to suit their taste the world would have no real art. Nothing would be safe. Picasso would have been changed years ago, and James Joyce and Stravinsky and the list goes on. . . .

Whether he intended it or not, this passage suggests that colorizing old black-and-white movies is like defacing old masters. But the issue is not whether we should or shouldn't allow the mutilation of old movies! Making color versions of old black-and-white films renders the originals just as safe as does the making of black-and-white magazine copies of old masters. Does Mr. Allen object to such reproductions of the works of the great masters? It is a common practice when performing Hayden, Mozart, and many other great composers to ignore the artist's instructions to repeat a section. Would Woody like to see a law against this practice? The point is that there already is general acceptance of several different kinds of alterations in great aesthetic works, without regard to what the artist might have wished. Virtually everyone accepts reproductions of the works of old masters although they are inferior to the originals and by analogy should not object to reproductions in color of old black-and-white films given that colorization does not destroy the original versions. Those who adopt Mr. Allen's position must either go against this commonly held view or show what is different about the colorization of movies.

> . . . [T]he different effect between color and black and white is often so wide it alters the meaning of scenes. If I had portrayed New York City in color rather than black and white in my movie, *Manhattan,* all the nostalgic connotations would have vanished. All the evocation of the city from old photographs and films would have been impossible to achieve in glorious technicolor. . . .

This is surely Woody's best point, because most film buffs would agree that filming *Manhattan* in color would not have worked nearly as well as in black and white. But does what works better take precedence in the law? Imagine what it would be like if it did. We would need boards of experts to decide what is better. All inferior reproductions of paintings, that is, virtually all reproductions, would be forbidden. Performances of great works by inferior orchestras or under second-rate conductors would become illegal. And so on.

Similarly, does what works better make production of the inferior somehow wrong? Suppose that people like Muzak versions of the second movement of Mozart's Twenty-First Piano Concerto. Is there something wrong in allowing masses of people the enjoyment of the aesthetically inferior product, given that this in no way takes away the possibility of hearing that music in something closer to its original form? (We very rarely hear symphonic music from that period in its original form: For one thing, musical instruments have changed; and for another, modern ears prefer shortened versions.)

Woody's response would no doubt be that we should look to the intent of the artist. If John Huston intended and still wants *The Maltese Falcon* to be viewed only in black and white, then that should settle the matter. But if we carry this out in other cases, we get results that are a bit hard to swallow. We don't know what Beethoven would say about performing his Ninth Symphony with either a larger or smaller chorus than was originally intended or about playing it on an ordinary phonograph. And supposing he wouldn't want us to play just one movement of one of his symphonies without playing the rest of the work, say while sitting in our living room listening to a stereo set, would we really want his wishes attended to on this matter? (In the case of movies, there also is the question of the wishes of the other artists, who together with the director make the finished product, not to mention those of the people who provide the money without which movies would not be made.)

> If a producer insists on color and if a helpless director is forced to film it the studio's way, despite his own feelings that it should be black and white—well a deal's a deal. But once a film exists in black and white and has been thrilling audiences for years, then to suddenly color it seems too great an insult. . . .

The fact is that very few, if any, directors have ever had carte blanche when making a film. Those who put up the money have always had a great deal of say, and that has always been part of the deal. (Woody Allen is one of a handful of directors who have been able to wrench significant concessions from those who put up the money.) Part of the deal in the case of the old movies in question was that the financiers would own the finished product, with the director receiving a salary and perhaps a percentage of the proceeds. Woody now wants to force revisions of these old deals, which means he doesn't want a deal to be a deal. He thus contradicts himself. (Of course, this doesn't touch his view that there is still something wrong with the colorization of these old films, even if nothing legally wrong.)

> Only in America are films so degraded. In other countries the artist is often protected by the government. No one can change a French film director's film without his consent. They have too much respect for people who contribute to the society by doing creative work to allow anyone to subvert their creations at random.

Well, few of us outside of France have enough background information to know about French law on the matter, but this writer certainly knows that there are many other countries in which the artist has no more say about the matter than in the United States and suspects that France is at best a rare exception to the general rule. But more importantly, he knows that even in France directors do not have the final say as to film content while a movie is being made. (Francois Truffaut illustrated this fact nicely in his film *Day for Night*.) Nor did famous writers (for example, William Faulkner) who wrote some of the scripts for the old Hollywood black and whites have control over what they wrote. Few, if any, financiers would put up money to make a movie without a good deal of control over the way in which it is made. (We pass over the point that when color became an option, the directors of the old black and whites jumped on the bandwagon with everyone else and made color movies much like the black-and-white ones they had turned out. And we pass over the question whether most of the old black-and-white movies aren't improved by colorization.)

Woody Allen sums up his position by saying:

> My personal belief is of course that no one should ever be able to tamper with any artist's work in any medium against the artist's will . . .

Not even when a deal is a deal? This writer's quick conclusion is that Woody Allen makes great movies but rather poor arguments. His reasons for his conclusion, if carried out in other cases, would result in foolish restrictions on the reproduction of all works of art (as the examples mentioned above suggest). Of course, there may be reasons why the colorization of old black-and-white movies is somehow different from these other cases, but if so, Woody has not shown what this difference is.

Whether readers should agree with Woody Allen on this matter or with the author of this text depends on their background beliefs, particularly as to legislating aesthetic taste and to the rightness or wrongness, independent of legal matters, of changing an artist's work in ways that he or she may not desire. Woody hasn't really argued in favor of his view on these two matters but taken it as assumed, for instance, that the artist should have the last word.

Quick appraisals are useful not just in deciding whether to accept an essay's thesis but also in deciding whether a topic is worth pursuing further. In today's complicated world in which so much depends on high-powered science or technology, a good deal of what we read is beyond our ability to evaluate directly. The question in such cases is whether something sounds sensible enough to be worth pursuing further.

When the issue is completely beyond our reach, the only thing we may be able to do is consult the best authorities we can find. Hardly anyone who is not a nuclear physicist has the ghost of a chance of being able to make a sensible judgment on whether "star wars," or SDI, is a practical idea, and so we have to resort to consulting as unbiased an authority as possible, such as the Union of Concerned Scientists (who believe, incidentally, that SDI is impractical now and will be for quite a long time into the future).

Often, however, we may have enough relevant background information at least to know whether something is worth pursuing further. Coming across an article claiming that an "inventor" has discovered how to make a perpetual motion machine, anyone with even a tiny bit of knowledge of the basic principles of science will immediately toss it aside.

Recently, however, a student asked the author of this text for an opinion on some excerpts she had taken from a book titled *Stop Dieting—Start Living!*[9] Stop

---

[9]Sharon Greene Patton, *Stop Dieting—Start Living!* (New York: Dodd, Mead & Co., 1982, 1983). Copyright © 1982, 1983 by Sharon Greene Patton. Reprinted by permission of Dodd, Mead & Co., Inc.

dieting and start living! There is an idea, everyone who has ever dieted and failed wants to believe, whose time has come. But it certainly smacks of wishful thinking.

What should the student be told? Not being an expert on how the human body functions, this writer could not evaluate the excerpts and come to any well-reasoned conclusion. But he could at least tell whether this marvelous sounding idea was worth pursuing, and for this purpose a quick appraisal would be sufficient, while a more thorough analysis would be a waste of time for him (and anyone who is not a medical expert). So let's do a quick appraisal of the guts of this argument against dieting, keeping in mind that the issue for us nonexperts is whether the matter is worth pursuing further, not whether to accept the essay's thesis. (And remember that these are just excerpts from a whole book on the topic.) Here are the first two paragraphs:

> If we accept the premise that if dieting worked people would be getting thinner, we must consider dieting a failure. We have only to look at the statistics to realize that the plain, simple fact is: Diets don't work. Statistics show that less than five percent, or possibly as few as two percent of people who diet lose weight permanently.

We now know, if the title of the essay didn't tell us already, that the thesis of the essay is going to be antidieting. And we know one reason to be presented, namely that hardly anyone is able to diet, lose weight, and keep it off. Note, however, that the spread between 2 and 5 percent indicates that these statistics at best result from educated guesswork, which we should have suspected anyway, because of the difficulty of obtaining accurate statistics on a subject like this. Nevertheless, that most people who go on diets don't lose much if any weight in the long run seems plausible, given our everyday experiences with dieters. And this does count as a reason against dieting, although not a conclusive reason all by itself.

> Everyone says diets don't work because people don't stay on diets. That is partly true; however, if people are unable to stay on diets there must be a reason. If 10,000 people go on a diet and 9,900 eventually go off, that is a good indication that it is nearly impossible to stay on a diet.

Well, that is surely some reason for this conclusion, but by itself it doesn't prove the point. Do people in other cultures find it equally hard to stay on diets? Perhaps failure to stay on diets reflects a generally indulgent way of life and not some physiological mechanism.

> Dieting upsets the biochemical balance of your body and makes it more difficult to lose weight. Dieting, in physiological terms, can make you fatter, and not just because you "cheat" and go off your diet and overeat, but the actual process of dieting can cause you to gain weight.

Now we see that the thesis is stronger than we might have expected; not only do diets not work, but they may actually make us fatter! A reason such as this one itself needs to be supported by reasons.

> Your body is a wonderfully balanced machine, and it does not like to be mistreated. It compensates for your negligence. If you starve yourself, it will find a way to store food for its own protection.

You might not like it on your hips and thighs, but the ability of the body to store food as fat is a great advantage to living things. You need fat to protect your body, to burn as fuel and to repair tissue. Your ancestors could not always count on a constant food supply, so the body stored fat for the lean times. The people who survived through those times were the ones best able to store extra fat that they could live on. . . .

Your body does not know, however, whether you are a cavewoman facing occasional famine, or a Beverly Hills matron on a self-induced famine—a diet. . . . It is only logical that if you starve your body, it will compensate by storing food when it gets a chance, which is when you resume eating. That is why you usually regain your weight so rapidly—your body is replenishing its fat stores. And it is not necessarily storing fat at its previous rate. Your body has been threatened, so it can become efficient at building up its reserves, to be ready for the next famine—or the next diet. . . .

Fat not only protects you against possible loss of food, it also helps in times of stress. Your body stores fat to help you through times of stress, and because food is the basis of survival, there is very little that is more stressful to your body than dieting, and the more severe the diet, the more severe the stress. Therefore, if you are dieting, you are more than likely increasing your body's ability to store fat and decreasing your body's ability to use fat.

In addition to becoming more efficient at making fat, your body also adjusts to less food when you diet and needs fewer calories to survive. After dieting, you can actually require less food than when you started. . . .

Scientists think this is similar to hibernation. Animals' metabolisms slow down to nearly zero so that they can live off their reserves while sleeping through the winter. . . . [When we diet, we lose] muscle mass, and the problem with losing muscle is that it requires five times more calories than fat does to maintain itself. That means, when you are finished dieting, you may actually need fewer calories to support the same weight than when you started, because you have less muscle mass to maintain.

Whatever the merits of the main thrust of her argument, this point seems off the mark. The point of a diet is to lose fat, not muscle mass. Of course, if we both diet and stop exercising our muscles, we will also lose muscle mass. But we don't need to reduce physical exertion, and so her argument about losing muscle mass would seem to be wrong. Also, it seems odd to suppose that the body can somehow learn how to be more efficient than it normally is in burning calories, because efficiency at any time would seem to be biologically advantageous.

Finally, hundreds of hormones and enzymes affect the metabolism and dieting can upset the balance of these hormones and reduce the number of enzymes that burn fat. Various studies have shown that many of these chemicals are lacking in fat people, and to continue to diet is to make the problem worse. . . .

In evaluating this mass of supporting evidence, note first the "hedging" expressions and words, such as ". . . you *can* actually require . . .," "you are *more than likely* increasing . . .," and so on. These indicate that the author is not on the firmest scientific ground, and that while there may be good evidence, the matter is not proved. Still, the question for us is whether we should bother to pursue the matter further. Does it seem plausible, given what we already know, that there is scientific support for these claims?

Those who accept an evolutionary point of view, seeing human mechanisms in terms of their survival value (what biologists call "genetic inclusive fitness"), ought to find this a rather reasonable support for the idea that heavy dieting tends to be self-defeating, while those who reject this way of looking at things ought to find it less compelling. (But note that expression "tends to." We know that some people do in fact diet successfully, even if they are in a small minority.) This writer likes the idea of looking at human mechanisms in terms of their survival value and so found much of the above quite plausible. In any case, it does seem reasonable that the body reacts to a strict diet as it would to a famine, making it more tempting for us to eat greater amounts of food and harder to resist the temptation.

Of course, it is another matter whether this is true in fact. At this point, the question was whether the matter was worth pursuing further, and this writer's background beliefs supported the idea that it was.[10]

Exercise 7-2

What is your quick appraisal of the following item? Remember that you must defend your answer:

Letter to the editor of the *San Francisco Chronicle* (slightly expanded):

> Editor:
> The scare tactitioners have been getting so much space in your publication for their anti-smoking diatribes that I have come to the conclusion that you are using these articles to distract your readers from the disgust-

---

[10]Consulting expert medical opinion revealed that most of the claims made in the excerpts above are controversial, but nevertheless are accepted by many experts in the field *with respect to crash diets*. A majority of doctors seem to be against crash diets except for medical reasons (for instance, when a serious operation is required). The concensus seems to favor dieting in which small modifications in food intake are coupled with increased physical activity in an ongoing, indeed lifelong, program. Typical comment: "The problem of rebound weight gain is not an argument against dieting; it is an argument against sporadic crash diets. One can argue that conditioning the body by maintaining a constant diet will gradually defuse its propensity to reestablish excessive fat stores." (It also should be remarked that perusal of the rest of Ms. Patton's book reveals that the title of her book is a bit misleading and that her overall view isn't that far away from the general medical consensus.)

ing antics of the Washington prevaricators. [The reference was to Iran-gate figures.]

In 1955, I was working for an internist, M.D. in Reno, Nevada. He received a request from Mutual of Omaha (I think) for statistical records of 100 lung cancer patients, deceased. The percentage of heavy smokers, light smokers and nonsmokers. It was my assignment to ferret out and submit our record. These numbers I recall clearly: 3 percent were heavy smokers, 15 percent were light smokers, and 82 percent were nonsmokers.

I am 70 years old and have smoked for 50 of my years and shall continue to do so. One distinct advantage for me has been the ability of the nicotine to curb my hyperactivity. Smoking has not wrinkled my skin unduly as had been predicted.

I seem to recall a piece you printed some time ago that stated that a person standing on a street corner for five minutes waiting for a bus would inhale more toxic fumes in five minutes than a cigaret smoker inhales in a year. Or have the antismokers convinced you that you are not going to die?

Of course you are going to die. We all are. Non-smokers die of lung cancer, diabetes, heart failure, uremic poisoning, AIDS, peritonitis, influenza, etc. Fear of death is the driving force with its fear of retribution after death. The guilt trips fill the church's bank accounts. Salvation always seems to cost money. Death is as natural and necessary as birth to keep our species in balance. Smoking is not going to deter the inevitable one whit.

Juneau A. Wilkinson[11]
Susanville

3. The Margin Note and Summary Method

When an evaluation absolutely has to be right, margin notes can be used to construct a summary of the essay to be analyzed. The idea behind this *margin note and summary method* is that a summary can be more easily digested than the longer essay from which it was drawn. Of course, you want to make sure your summary is *accurate*. There are four basic steps in the margin note and summary method:

1. Read the material to be evaluated.

2. Read it through again, this time marking the important passages with an indication of content written in the margin, taking advantage of what was learned from the first reading. (Margin notes need not be full sentences, or grammatically correct, and may contain abbreviations or shorthand notations.)

3. Use the margin notes to construct a summary of the passage.

---

[11]Letter to the Editor, *San Francisco Chronicle* (February 4, 1987). Reprinted by permission of the author.

4. Evaluate the original material by evaluating the summary, checking the original to be sure there are no differences between the two that are relevant to the evaluation.

Two things need to be said about using the margin note and summary method. First, when we skip part of a passage, we make a value judgment that the skipped material is relatively unimportant. It takes practice and skill to know what to include and what to omit, and "experts" will differ on such matters. And, second, margin notes and summaries are shorthand devices and should thus be briefer than the passage analyzed. But any shortening runs the risk of falsification. When using margin notes or summaries to aid in reasoning, remember that we don't want to be guilty of the *straw man* fallacy by drawing conclusions from the shortened version that would not be valid for the original.

A Closer Look at an Important Political Address

Let's now try the margin note and summary method on a very important recent political speech. But let's kill two birds with one stone and also say a few words about political rhetoric in general and the problems politicians and their speech writers have to deal with.

Those who think of human beings as essentially rational animals may suppose that appeals to reason constitute the best way to get an audience to believe political promises or to identify with a political candidate. But in fact, purely rational appeals are seldom successful, particularly when dealing with a mass audience. Emotional appeals, and especially appeals that are both emotional and rational, are much more effective. Slogans (Jimmy Carter: "I will never lie to you.") and humor (Ronald Reagan's "one liners") tend to be more successful than complicated arguments.

Exactly what sorts of rhetoric a politician should use depends on many factors, the most important of which is the nature of the intended audience. An effective address to a large audience cannot be as complicated, detailed, or logically rigorous as, say, a journal article in *Foreign Affairs* magazine. Large masses of people cannot, or at least will not, follow such reasoning or evaluate it on its logical merits and demerits.

Similarly, an effective speech must take account of audience prejudices, values, and personal interests. A speech delivered to an audience of senior citizens cannot as vigorously attack the Social Security system or Medicare as one addressed to an audience of yuppies. We need to remember these basic facts about human nature and what sorts of rhetoric are most effective when dealing with the pronouncements of political candidates and elected officials.

While persuasion is the chief function performed by political rhetoric, it is by no means the only one. Ceremony and ritual, for instance, often play an important role, as in an acceptance speech by a newly nominated candidate or an address by a newly sworn in United States president. Indeed, a single political speech may perform several different functions, and most in fact do. For instance, the *mea culpa* speech given by President Reagan at the height of the Irangate scandal contained portions that were primarily ceremonial, a section that on the whole was argumentative, and several paragraphs whose very enunciation on national television amounted to the performance of a ritual act of contrition. (This speech will be examined in more detail shortly.)

Nonargumentative portions of political addresses—ceremonial remarks, symbolic gestures, flattery—serve very important functions. They signal friendliness on the part of the speaker, put an audience at ease, unite members of a group behind shared values and myths, and bid the audience to give a fair hearing to the politician and his or her point of view.

All this is to the good; indeed, it is hard to imagine a democratic society and its political system functioning well without this kind of political rhetoric. The trouble is that gracious compliments, gestures of solidarity, bows to the hometown audience, and the like invite soft-headedness rather than a fair hearing when the time comes to evaluate the more substantive portions of a political speech. Overcoming this unfortunately almost universal tendency in human nature takes a good deal of self-awareness (of actual cases when we mentally shoot ourselves in the foot in this way) combined with persistent effort at reform.

Let's now take a closer look at the Ronald Reagan speech just mentioned. It was delivered on March 4, 1987, when the Irangate mess threatened to topple the Reagan administration or at least completely hamstring its last two years in office.

The television audience for this speech was extremely large. Americans wanted to know whether their aging president still could be trusted with the power of office. They wondered if his performance up to that point had been as bad as the Tower Board report of the week before had indicated, and in particular wanted Reagan to stop stonewalling and admit his share of the guilt in this fiasco. (This demand for atonement on Reagan's part is not something to be dismissed lightly. Failure to own up was an important reason why Richard Nixon had been driven from office only a dozen years before. Every one of Reagan's advisors had for some time been telling him that he had to do this.)

The crafting of a speech that would satisfy the demands and allay the fears of the general public posed serious problems for the president, his advisors, and in particular his speech writers.[12] The Tower Board report had fanned the flames of suspicion. *Time* magazine wrote that Reagan "stands exposed as a President *willfully* ignorant of what his aides were doing, *myopically* unaware of the glaring contradictions between his public and secret policies, *complacently* dependent on advisors who never once, from start to finish, presented him with any systematic analysis of aims, means, risks and alternatives. And in the end, as a President *unable* to recall when, how or even whether he had reached the key decision that started the whole arms-to-Iran affair"[13] (italics added). Any president who could be treated so roughly by the press had to be in serious trouble. To get out of it, Reagan had to accept the damning charges of the Tower Board report, or at least accept its main thrust, while at the same time satisfying doubts concerning

---

[12]Many people have the quaint idea that presidents still compose their own orations, as Lincoln composed his famous Gettysburg Address. But in fact no president since Woodrow Wilson has done so. Of course, presidents still control the general content and tone of their speeches.

[13]*Time* (March 9, 1987).

his ability to manage the executive branch of the government and to tell truth from falsehood.

The address his speech writers composed can conveniently be divided into 34 paragraphs. The first two consist primarily in introductory remarks of a ceremonial nature, much like saying "How do you do?" to the audience. While custom and indeed common courtesy require an introduction of this kind, by their very nature introductory bows to the audience cannot be relevant to whatever happens to be the main business at hand.

In this case, however, the introductory remarks were salted with a nice compliment designed to warm up the audience for the more serious business ahead. Here are the first two paragraphs (printed without margin notes because there is nothing in them relevant to the main question concerning Reagan's guilt and his ability to run the government).

[1] My fellow Americans, I've spoken to you from this historic office on many occasions about many things. The power of the presidency is often thought to reside within this Oval Office. Yet it doesn't rest here; it rests in you, the American people, and in your trust.

[Nothing relevant here, and so nothing we need to keep track of or put into a summary.]

[2] Your trust is what gives a president his powers of leadership and his personal strength, and it's what I want to talk to you about this evening.

The third paragraph asked and the fourth then answered a question that must have occurred to many citizens:

[3] For the past three months, I've been silent on the revelations about Iran. You must have been thinking, "Well, why doesn't he tell us what's happening? Why doesn't he just speak to us as he has in the past when we've faced troubles or tragedies?" Others of you, I guess, were thinking, "What's he doing hiding out in the White House?"

Q.: Why hasn't the president spoken to us on the Iran business during the past three months?

[4] I've paid a price for my silence in terms of your trust and confidence. But I have had to wait, as have you, for the complete story. That's why I appointed Ambassador David Abshire as my special counselor to help get out the thousands of documents to the various investigations. And I appointed a special review board, the Tower board, which took on a chore of pulling the truth together for me and getting to the bottom of things. It has now issued its findings.

A.: Because he had to wait for the Tower Board report.

Note that in asking and answering this question right after flattering his audience, the president continued the process of softening audience resistance to the important message to follow: that he could be trusted to continue running the government. (It was expected that the audience would not notice the half-truth, the small lie, in the president's remarks. Reagan had been *relatively* silent on the issue for about three months before delivering this speech; but he had spoken out on a few occasions, for example, in his state of the union address to Congress, and his underlings speaking for the government had said much more. This little fib passed by relatively unnoticed.)

Now the president had to speak to the Tower Board report and its charges of incompetence and unconcern. The speech allows him to jump in gingerly by starting out with the one point in the report favorable to Ronald Reagan:

[5] I'm often accused of being an optimist, and it's true I had to hunt pretty hard to find any good news in the board's report. As you know, it's well stocked with criticisms, which I'll discuss in a moment, but I was very relieved to read this sentence, ". . . the board is convinced that the president does indeed want the full story to be told." And that will continue to be my pledge to you as the other investigations go forward.

The Tower Board affirms that RR wanted the full story told.

The sixth paragraph contains more ceremonial material irrelevant to the main questions we want to hear about:

[6] I want to thank the members of the panel—former Senator John Tower, former Secretary of State Edmund Muskie, and former National Security Adviser Brent Scowcroft. They have done the nation, as well as me personally, a great service by submitting a report of such integrity and depth. They have my genuine and enduring gratitude.

[Nothing relevant here.]

Now it's time for Reagan to perform his act of contrition, his admission of guilt (paragraphs 7 through 11):

[7] I've studied the board's report. Its findings are honest, convincing, and highly critical, and I accept them. Tonight I want to share with you my thoughts on these findings and report to you on the actions I'm taking to implement the board's recommendations.

RR accepts the Tower Board findings, critical as they are.

[8] First let me say I take full responsibility for my own actions and for those of my Administration. As angry as I may be about activities taken without my knowledge, I am still accountable for those activities. As disappointed as I may be in some who served me, I am still the one who must answer to the American people for this behavior. And as personally distasteful as I find secret bank accounts and diverted funds, as the Navy would say, this happened on my watch.

RR takes "full responsibility" and admits there were "secret bank accounts and diverted funds."

Notice the quick switch from his taking "full responsibility" to his anger at underlings who acted without his knowledge. This tends to shift responsibility from Reagan to his staff and masks the contradiction in his acceptance of the Tower Board's assertion that he authorized his staff to engage in this activity while now saying they acted without his knowledge. The implication of this paragraph is that it happened on his watch, so he was responsible, but he did not know what they were doing.

Notice also that Reagan accepted the board's report but did not enumerate its negative contents. Saying that the report was "highly critical" does not convey the flavor of that report's damning picture of an uncaring and incompetent president. Of course, he could not be expected to wallow in the sordid details; the point is that he softened the blow as much as it could be softened while still doing what he had to do, namely, accept the report and admit that he was guilty.

[9] Let's start with the part that is the most controversial. A few months ago I told the American people I did not trade arms for hostages. My heart and my best intentions still tell me that is true, but the facts and the evidence tell me it is not.

RR doesn't remember (authorizing) an arms trade for hostages, but admits the facts show he did so.

[10] As the Tower Board reported, what began as a strategic opening to Iran deteriorated in its implementation into trading arms for hostages. This runs counter to my own beliefs, to administration policy, and to the original strategy we had in mind. There are reasons why it happened, but no excuses. It was a mistake.

TB report: what began as "strategic opening" to Iran "deteriorated" into trade for hostages. RR didn't want that, but it happened and was a mistake. No excuses.

[11] I undertook the original Iran initiative in order to develop relations with those who might assume leadership in a post-Khomeini government. It's clear from the board's report, however, that I let my personal concern for the hostages spill over into the geopolitical strategy of reaching out to Iran. I asked so many questions about the hostages' welfare that I didn't ask enough about the specifics of the total Iran plan.

RR authorized Iran approach to develop post-K. relations. But his concern for the hostages led him to ask too much about them and not enough about the total plan.

Having ruffled feathers by admitting he may have been too concerned about the hostages, he then had to placate those who may have been offended:

[12] Let me say to the hostage families, we have not given up. We never will. And I promise you we'll use every legitimate means to free your loved ones from captivity. But I must also caution that those Americans who freely remain in such dangerous areas must know that they're responsible for their own safety.

[Nothing relevant here.]

Since the Tower Board report did not settle the question of the transfer of funds to the Nicaraguan Contras, it apparently was felt that the president had to say something about this, and he did in the next paragraph, where he again adopted the *mea culpa* tone of paragraphs 7 through 11 (the tone of the first half of the speech):

[13] Now, another major aspect of the board's findings regards the transfer of funds to the Nicaraguan Contras. The Tower board was not able to find out what happened to this

RR didn't know of funds "diverted" to the Contras, but takes responsibility.

money, so the facts here will be left to the continuing investigation of the court-appointed independent counsel and the two congressional investigating committees. As I told the Tower Board, I didn't know about any diversion of funds to the Contras. But as president I cannot escape responsibility.

Next the president returned to his management style and admitted that it didn't work in this case while at the same time claiming it was a good and successful style:

[14] Much has been said about my management style, a style that has worked successfully for me during eight years as governor of California and for most of my presidency. The way I work is to identify the problem, find the right individuals to do the job, and then let them go to it. I have found this invariably brings out the best in people. They seem to rise to their full capability and in the long run you get more done.

RR's management style was to identify a problem, find the right person to solve it, and "then let them go to it." This style had been successful in the past.

Reagan could expect that most people would not see this for the simpleminded theory of management that it was, and in particular not notice that it said nothing about checking up on underlings to see that they carry out their work correctly.

[15] When it came to managing the NSC staff, let's face it, my style didn't match its previous track record. I have already begun correcting this. As a start, yesterday I met with the entire professional staff of the National Security Council. I defined for them the values I want to guide the national security policies of this country. I told them that I wanted a policy that was as justifiable and understandable in public as it was in secret. I wanted a policy that reflected the will of the Congress as well as the White House. And I told them that there'll be no more free-lancing by individuals when it comes to our national security.

RR's style didn't work managing the NSC in the Iran business, but he's already begun to correct that by meeting with the NSC staff and telling them what to do now.

Notice how "my style didn't match its previous track record" is used here as a euphemism for "I mismanaged."

This last paragraph introduced a new tone and a new subject to the president's speech. The *mea culpa* went into the background, and we were shown a new Ronald Reagan who was in charge again and could be trusted to run the government, having learned from experience. This is the theme of the rest of the speech after ceremonial paragraph 16:

[16] You have heard a lot about the staff of the National Security Council in recent months. I can tell you, they are good and dedicated government employees, who put in long hours for the nation's benefit. They are eager and anxious to serve their country.

[Not relevant.]

In paragraphs 17 through 31, Reagan listed one after another of the changes and actions he had accomplished to get the ship of state back on course, all designed to show that he could be trusted with the power of the presidency. Since they said simply that Reagan endorsed the Tower Board recommendations and had appointed several new people to replace the ones who had been discredited, let's omit margin notes at this point, remembering, of course, that we'll have to include something on this in any summary. (It could be argued that this material is irrelevant, since anyone can appoint people to office, and what Reagan said did not tell us anything about the quality of those appointed. But some will find this material relevant, so we'll include it in our summary.)

[17] One thing still upsetting me, however, is that no one kept proper records of meetings or decisions. This led to my failure to recollect whether I approved an arms shipment before or after the fact. I did approve it; I just can't say specifically when. Rest assured, there's plenty of record-keeping now going on at 1600 Pennsylvania Avenue.

Reagan here glossed over his inability to remember even the most basic facts in the case. Earlier he had said he did not remember *whether* he had approved the shipments, but at this point, he said he could not remember *when,* a much less serious matter. This passage also is interesting in its employment of a standard *mea culpa* device: admitting error in the context of announcing its correction. (Reagan also passed over all sorts of inconvenient evidence indicating that he was not on top of the situation, for instance, his having allowed Col. North and his secretary to shred relevant evidence well *after* the scandal had broken.)

[18] For nearly a week now, I have been studying the board's report. I want the American people to know this wrenching ordeal of recent months has not been in vain. I endorse every one of the Tower board's recommendations. In fact, I'm going beyond its recommendations so as to put the house in even better order.

[19] I'm taking action in three basic areas—personnel, national security policy and the process for making sure that the system works.

[20] First, personnel. I've brought in an accomplished and highly respected new team here at the White House. They bring new blood, new energy and new credibility and experience.

[21] Former Senator Howard Baker, my new chief of staff, possesses a breadth of legislative and foreign affairs skills that's impossible to match. I'm hopeful that his experience as minority and majority leader of the Senate can help us forge a new partnership with the Congress, especially on foreign and national security policies. I'm genuinely honored that he has given up his own presidential aspirations to serve the country as my chief of staff.

[22] Frank Carlucci, my new national security adviser, is respected for his experience in government and trusted for his judgment and counsel. Under him, the NSC staff is being rebuilt with proper management discipline. Already, almost half the NSC professional staff is comprised of new people.

[23] Yesterday I nominated William Webster, a man of sterling reputation, to be director of the Central Intelligence Agency. Mr. Webster has served as director of the FBI and as a U.S. district court judge. He understands the meaning of "rule of law."

[24] So that his knowledge of national security matters can be available to me on a continuing basis, I will also appoint John Tower to serve as a member of my Foreign Intelligence Advisory Board.

[25] I am considering other changes in personnel and I will move more furniture as I see fit in the weeks and months ahead.

[26] Second, in the area of national security policy, I have ordered the NSC to begin a comprehensive review of all covert operations. I have also directed that any covert activity be in support of clear policy objectives and in compliance with American values. I expect a covert policy that if Americans saw it on the front page of their newspaper, they'd say, "That makes sense."

[27] I have had issued a directive prohibiting the NSC staff itself from undertaking covert operations—no ifs, ands, or buts.

The president didn't remind us that the NSC is strictly an advisory body and was never authorized to engage in covert activity. And he glossed over the strong disagreements about both the kinds of covert activities the CIA has engaged in since World War II, of which this case was an example, and whether the CIA should engage in any covert hanky-panky at all, rather than restricting itself to what its name and original mission imply—the gathering of information:

[28] I have asked Vice President Bush to reconvene his task force on terrorism to review our terrorist policy in light of the events that have occurred.

[29] Third, in terms of the process of reaching national security decisions, I am adopting in total the Tower report's model of how the NSC process and staff should work. I am directing Mr. Carlucci to take the necessary steps to make that happen. He will report back to me on further reforms that might be needed.

[30] I've created the post of NSC legal adviser to assure a greater sensitivity to matters of law.

[31] I am also determined to make the congressional oversight process work. Proper procedures for consultation with the Congress will be followed, not only in letter but in spirit. Before the end of March, I will report to the Congress on all the steps I've taken in line with the Tower Board's conclusions.

Having outlined the host of changes he had instituted in his administration, the president then went into his socko ending, tying together his admission of past mistakes with his current forthright actions: He had learned from his past mistakes and was better able to lead now *because* of what he had learned:

[32] Now what should happen when you make a mistake is   *[Nothing relevant.]*
this: You take your knocks, you learn your lessons and then you move on. That's the healthiest way to deal with a problem. This in no way diminishes the importance of the other continuing investigations but the business of our country and our people must proceed. I have gotten this message from Republicans and Democrats in Congress, from allies around the world—and if we're reading the signals right, even from the Soviets. And, of course, I have heard the message from you, the American people.

[33] You know, by the time you reach my age, you've made   *[Nothing relevant.]*
plenty of mistakes if you've lived your life properly. So you learn. You put things in perspective. You pull your energies together. You change. You go forward.

[34] My fellow Americans, I have a great deal that I want   *[Nothing relevant.]*
to accomplish with you and for you over the next two years. And, the Lord willing, that's exactly what I intend to do.

It's hard to imagine how this speech could have been improved. It allowed the president to say what he had to say (that he was guilty) while presenting him in as nice a light as possible. It allowed him to own up to past errors while appearing to have regained control. It was an excellent speech from the point of view of rhetoric, but like fine music, one that required a masterful job of delivery, with just the right facial expressions, attitude, and tone of voice (no Jimmy Carter unction and no hesitant voice cracks suggesting indecision). Ronald Reagan outdid himself with a remarkable performance for anyone, much less someone well into his seventies, showing that he could still handle the rhetorical part of the job of being president of the United States (a necessary part of the governing process in this age of television and the common citizen).

Let's now draw together the relevant margin notes of the speech and see whether it should have persuaded people to be more trusting of Ronald Reagan. Here are the main arguments Reagan provided for trusting him with the highest office in the land:

1. The Tower Board affirmed that RR wanted the whole story to be told.

2. Their report was very critical of RR, but he accepted it and took full responsibility.

3. RR doesn't remember trading arms for hostages, but admits the facts show that he did so.

4. The board's report said that the Iran business began as a strategic opening to Iran but turned into a trade, which was wrong, and RR admits this is so.

5. RR's concern for the hostages led him to skew his monitoring of the situation from developing post-K. relations to swapping arms for hostages.

6. He has moved to correct the situation and to prevent further difficulties from arising by appointing new people and instructing them to obey the law and do what the people will approve.

What is there here that might influence a sensible person to trust the president?

1. He wanted the Tower Board to find and reveal the truth (that is, unlike Richard Nixon, he didn't want a coverup).

2. He admitted his guilt and took full responsibility for what had happened.

3. He had moved to correct the situation and make things work right by appointing new people.

And what is there in the president's speech that might count as reasons for *not* trusting him?

1. He admitted that he can't remember facts that happened to be vital to matters of state with which he was concerned.

2. He admitted that he was unable in this case to keep his mind on his own plan of action and became diverted to a disastrous course of action.

3. The Tower Board report that he accepted was very critical of his performance in this case.

There also were reasons pro and con that lay outside the speech itself. Favorable to the president was the fact that he seemed in control of himself and displayed no signs of senility. Whatever his other qualifications for fulfilling the duties of his office, he definitely still was able to deliver a speech in a first-rate manner.

Unfavorable to him was the actual content of the Tower Board's report, which was not just critical of the president, as his speech indicated, but rather was *damning* in its criticism and in effect described a president who was not competent to hold the office. In addition, there was the fact that for over three months Reagan had denied guilt in this matter before finally coming clean in this speech. The implication of this delay was that either he had lied to the people for over three months or else himself had not known and for three months was unable to determine what he had authorized or how his staff had carried out his orders.

The upshot of this speech was a small but significant change in the national mood of sad hostility and disappointment. Large numbers of people seemed to be somewhat less hostile and more willing to give the Reagan administration another chance to do something effective and regain some of its lost power and respect. (Later disclosures eroded that power and respect, but that is another matter.)

Although few people had actually read the Tower Board report, a great many Americans at the time had a pretty good idea of what it said because of the massive coverage given to the report by the media. They also knew that the president had denied his role in this affair before owning up in this speech. While it is difficult to know why people responded as they did to Reagan's speech, it is a good guess that the large number of people who were inclined to go easy on the president were primarily those who had been favorable to Reagan before the Irangate mess and responded to his seeming to be in control of himself again. Their worries about his age and the possibility that he was becoming senile were dispelled, and so they were inclined to give him another chance.

But the minority of people who prior to the scandal had regarded Reagan as over his head in the office of the president of the United States apparently were reinforced by the Tower Board report and were not swayed by the president's speech.

The odd thing is that most of those who responded favorably would not have continued to have faith in an accountant, doctor, or lawyer who could say no more in self-defense than Reagan was able to. *Analogy:* President of a large bank to board of directors and depositors, "Trust me to remain as president of this bank because I take full responsibility for the extremely foolish and illegal loans that I authorized, as the facts show, although I've forgotten myself, and got carried away in my zeal to do good to the point of authorizing secret bad loans made contrary to my own publicly announced policy, causing serious damage to the bank's solvency. However, I've now appointed new people to run the bank." Very few would be moved by such remarks to put their money back into a bank whose president had found it necessary to own up in this way. Yet that is what millions of perfectly intelligent Americans in fact seem (metaphorically) to have done. Whether or not we profess to understand why they responded in this way, we have to come to see that people do think differently when assessing social and political matters, much as they behave differently when part of a mob. They can be manipulated by clever rhetoric that plays on their emotions and wishful thoughts, and we have to remember that when we listen to or evaluate political rhetoric.

Exercise 7-3

Here are two items on the question of forcing private service clubs to open their membership rolls to women. Your job, naturally, is to critically evaluate each one, using whatever method you wish.

1. **Court ruling opens doors for women**

   Ten years ago, the men-only Rotary club in tiny Duarte, Calif., was languishing. Women had begun to occupy the community leadership slots that Rotary had traditionally turned to for members-to-be. So Duarte's Rotarians did the gentlemanly thing: They opened the door for the ladies.

   And a very ungentlemanly squabble ensued.

Rotary International banished the club. Both sides went to court. The fisticuffs ended last week when the Supreme Court ruled 7-0 for the Duarte Rotarians.

Echoing an earlier ruling that ended the men-only status of the Jaycees, the court said states have the right to forbid sex discrimination by local Rotary clubs.

Why? Because, while truly private clubs have a constitutional right of free association, the Jaycees and the Rotary clubs aren't "private," the court said: They are too big, too business-related, too community service-oriented.

Does this spell the end to men-only clubs? The court said decisions must be made case by case. But across the USA, die-hard men's clubs are manning the barricades:

- In Salt Lake City, when a judge warned he would yank the beer license if the Alta Club didn't stop discriminating, the club quit selling beer—rather than admit women.
- In Bethesda, Md., the men-only Burning Tree Club forfeited $186,000 in tax breaks—rather than admit women.
- In New York City, the Century Association is so afraid that its income from non-members will jeopardize its private status that it is considering selling its art collection to substitute for that revenue—rather than admit women.

How *un*gentlemanly.

Professional and business people use private clubs to make contacts and clinch deals. Women should have the same opportunities. Today, 44 percent of the work force is female. There are 130,000 women bankers, 104,000 women lawyers. It is unfair that they must stand outside while their male clients and competitors dine in the clubroom.

Now that the Supreme Court has sent the message that Rotary and the Jaycees must accept women, other men-only service groups should follow suit.

And what of the smaller, more exclusive private clubs where the socially prominent eat and play?

The court's message was less clear. But there's no mistaking the moral message: Closing the doors of opportunity to women is just plain wrong.

Clubs that have evolved into meeting places where members transact business must admit members without regard to race, religion, or sex.

The gentlemen of Duarte found that welcoming women helped their club. So did the men of Philadelphia's Union League Club, Washington's University Club, Pittsburgh's Duquesne Club, and others that have recently stopped discriminating. Old members say that since the ladies joined, the change has been negligible.

But for women, the change can be dramatic and positive. When opportunity knocks, they're there to answer.

It's time to open the door for the ladies.[14]

---

[14]*USA Today* (May 12, 1987). Copyright 1987 *USA Today*. Reprinted by permission.

2. **This ruling threatens the rights of women**

SPRINGFIELD, VA.—The latest feminist victory against discrimination—the Supreme Court's ruling that the state of California can force the Rotary club to admit women—is a major blow against everyone's freedom.

The government may still allow small, independent clubs to set their own admission standards if, in the court's words, the group involves "the kind of intimate or private relation that warrants constitutional protection." But organizations like the Lions, Kiwanis, and Elks apparently have lost control over their memberships.

While forcibly opening up such clubs obviously benefits women, it vastly increases state interference with the most minute and personal of social and business relationships.

Indeed, in the name of nondiscrimination, governments have banned discounts for women during "ladies' nights" at bars and restaurants. A children's hair salon in Los Angeles was sued for charging girls, who tend to have longer hair, more than boys. Price breaks for women at a car wash have been ruled discriminatory and illegal. One male patron even sued a night club that barred men, but not women, from wearing shorts.

In none of these cases was the discrimination invidious. Irritating, perhaps. But nothing like the old Jim Crow rules that treated blacks as subhumans.

And while there's no logical reason for organizations like Rotary to exclude women, human relationships are not logical. Which is why freedom of association—a right protected by the First Amendment—is so important.

Indeed, there are women's-only organizations, like the Cosmopolitan and Colony clubs in New York and the Spa Lady chain of fitness centers. They, along with establishments that cater to homosexuals, are threatened by rules that ban all discrimination.

In a free society like ours, the government should stay out of interpersonal relations whenever possible. Social change may take longer as a result, but it will still occur.

In fact, the Rotary case arose after the local club in Duarte, Calif., decided to induct women to help counteract a declining membership. Three dozen Kiwanis clubs have also defied their international organization by admitting women. And many women's colleges have gone coed because of economic pressure.

This sort of voluntary movement toward non-discrimination is preferable to heavy-handed government regulation. Where innocuous discrimination persists, whether it be men's business clubs or ladies' discount nights, it should be accepted as inevitable in a pluralistic society.

A free people must tolerate intolerance, for the cost to liberty of trying to expunge every last vestige of discrimination from society is too high.[15]

---

[15] *USA Today* (May 12, 1987). Copyright 1987 *USA Today*. Reprinted by permission.

Exercise 7-4

Here are two more items to evaluate, following the instructions for exercise 7-3. The second is rather difficult.

1. **Stockman vs. Amtrak**

   David Stockman, the boy genius of the Reagan administration, threw a tantrum the other day before a Senate subcommittee. If senators did not have "the courage, the foresight, the comprehension" to "pull the plug" on what he called an "irredeemable" Amtrak rail passenger system, he saw little hope for deficit reduction or for avoiding a "whopping tax increase."

   There, there, little man. It won't be as bad as all that, if Amtrak survives. Take Elizabeth Dole's word for it.

   As secretary of transportation, she affirmed last September that she shared the view of Federal Railroad Administrator John H. Riley that Amtrak had made "great strides" toward "modern, cost-efficient intercity rail passenger service"—running in 1985 "more route miles than it did in 1981 at approximately 28 percent lower funding."

   Mrs. Dole had asked for a $765 million Amtrak subsidy for fiscal 1986. But that was before the youthful budget director began to drum his heels.

   He and President Reagan squawk frequently about a $35-per-head subsidy that each Amtrak passenger supposedly receives. This prestidigitation requires adding the Amtrak subsidy to the amount that Amtrak business travelers can deduct from their income taxes, and dividing by 20 million passengers; presto! $35 a head.

   Young David is so distraught that he apparently forgets some of the other numbers he might be expected to crunch. For example:
   - Sixty-five percent of airline revenues are for business travel; so for each airline passenger, business travel deductions *alone* provide a subsidy of $33. In 1984, moreover, air-traffic control cost the federal government $2.1 billion, or $9 for each of 221 million air passengers; so by young David's arithmetic, the federal subsidy per air passenger was $42.
   - From its ticket revenues—which pay 60 percent of its costs—and subsidy, Amtrak is required to spend $116 million annually to maintain the Northeast Corridor right-of-way, over which also move the freight trains of Conrail and every rail commuter service from Boston to Washington.

   If, as young David urges, Congress pulls the plug on Amtrak—a House subcommittee voted Thursday to continue the rail system in operation—the government will have to pay $2.1 billion in labor termination costs over the next six years, an obligation inherited from the private railroads; $3 billion in modern locomotives, equipment, specialized shops and Northeast Corridor plant will be scrapped, with little market for salvage; and about 150,000 jobs in affected business sectors will be jeopardized (25,000 railroad employees will be thrown out of jobs).

But the young genius told the senators that few programs ranked lower than Amtrak "in terms of the good they do, the purpose they serve and the national need." Boyish overstatement again—Amtrak carried 20 million passengers last year, while receiving a smaller federal subsidy (in current dollars) than in 1978; and in the Northeast Corridor 160,000 commuters on various services rode over Amtrak-maintained right-of-way *every day.*

So young David shouldn't get so wrought up about Amtrak; and returning White House colleagues might calm him with news that the West German government, planning its transit investments for the next decade, has decided to put 34 billion marks into its railroads and only 28 billion into its highway network. Now that's a grown-up decision.[16]

2. Why We Need the Tobacco Program

In a recent editorial entitled "Smoke," The Post asks why the federal government should be sponsoring a program that supports a product such as tobacco, a major health hazard and thus a contributing factor in health-care costs.

The answer is simply that the federal tobacco program has absolutely nothing to do with whether people smoke, or even whether tobacco is grown. What this program does is to limit the amount of tobacco grown and to determine what price the tobacco manufacturers should pay the growers for their product.

Without the federal tobacco program, tobacco would still be grown. But under a free-market system, more tobacco would be grown, most likely by corporate agribusiness rather than by small family farmers, as is now the case. This would happen because the production allotment aspect of the program has served as a barrier to the entry of large corporate farms into tobacco production.

Does The Post really believe that the anti-smoking cause would be better served by allowing more tobacco to be grown and tobacco production to be taken over by big business?

The federal tobacco program should be retained, even if one disagrees with its purposes, also because the economy of the tobacco-producing regions of the country is dependent on it. This program has been in existence for over 50 years. Farm values and thus local property tax revenues are directly linked to the existence of the program.

Does The Post really believe that it is enlightened or rational public policy to disrupt the economy of the tobacco-producing regions of the country?

Counting past years and the immediate future, tobacco growers will have contributed more than $100 billion in excise tax revenues to our country. In contrast, over the 50-year history of the federal tobacco program, the total cost to the taxpayers has been only about $50 million.

[16]Tom Wicker, "Young David's Tantrum," *New York Times* (May 3, 1985). Copyright © 1985 by the New York Times Co. Reprinted by permission.

In view of the enormous excise tax revenue contributions that tobacco growers have made to our country and will continue to make, is it too much for them to ask that a federal program, which they find beneficial and which has absolutely nothing to do with whether people smoke, is continued?

> Stephen T. Yelverton[17]
> Arlington

*Exercise 7-5

Here are several excerpts from Adolf Hitler's famous tract, *Mein Kampf* (from the chapter titled "Nation and Race").[18] Critically evaluate Hitler's arguments, using whatever method you care to use.

There are some truths which are so obvious that for this very reason they are not seen or at least not recognized by ordinary people. They sometimes pass by such truisms as though blind and are most astonished when someone suddenly discovers what everyone really ought to know. Columbus's eggs lie around by the hundreds of thousands, but Columbuses are met with less frequently.

Thus men without exception wander about in the garden of Nature; they imagine that they know practically everything and yet with few exceptions pass blindly by one of the most patent principles of Nature's rule: the inner segregation of the species of all living beings on this earth.

Even the most superficial observation shows that Nature's restricted form of propagation and increase is an almost rigid basic law of all the innumerable forms of expression of her vital urge. Every animal mates only with a member of the same species. The titmouse seeks the titmouse, the finch the finch, the stork the stork, the field mouse the field mouse, the dormouse the dormouse, the wolf the she-wolf, etc. . . . .

Any crossing of two beings not at exactly the same level produces a medium between the level of the two parents. This means: the offspring will probably stand higher than the racially lower parent, but not as high as the higher one. Consequently, it will later succumb in the struggle against the higher level. Such mating is contrary to the will of Nature for a higher breeding of all life. The precondition for this does not lie in associating superior and inferior, but in the total victory of the former. The stronger must dominate and not blend with the weaker, thus sacrificing his own greatness. Only the born weakling can view this as cruel, but he after all is only a weak and limited man; for if this law did not prevail, any conceivable higher development of organic living beings would be unthinkable.

The consequence of this urge toward racial purity, universally valid in Nature, is not only the sharp outward delimitation of the various races,

---

[17]Letter to the Editor, *Washington Post* (October 5, 1985). Reprinted by permission of the author.

[18]From Ralph Manheim's translation (Boston: Houghton Mifflin, 1971), pp. 284–287. Copyright 1943 and renewed 1971 by Houghton Mifflin Company. Reprinted by permission of Houghton Mifflin Co. and Hutchinson Publishing Group Ltd.

but their uniform character in themselves. The fox is always a fox, the goose a goose, the tiger a tiger, etc., and the difference can lie at most in the varying measure of force, strength, intelligence, dexterity, endurance, etc., of the individual specimens. But you will never find a fox who in his inner attitude might, for example, show humanitarian tendencies toward geese, as similarly there is no cat with a friendly inclination toward mice.

Therefore, here, too, the struggle among themselves arises less from inner aversion than from hunger and love. In both cases, Nature looks on calmly, with satisfaction, in fact. In the struggle for daily bread all those who are weak and sickly or less determined succumb, while the struggle of the males for the female grants the right or opportunity to propagate only to the healthiest. And the struggle is always a means for improving a species' health and power of resistance and, therefore, a cause of its higher development. . . .

No more than Nature desires the mating of weaker with stronger individuals, even less does she desire the blending of a higher with a lower race, since, if she did, her whole work of higher breeding, over perhaps hundreds of thousands of years, might be ruined with one blow.

Historical experience offers countless proofs of this. It shows with terrifying clarity that in every mingling of Aryan blood with that of lower peoples the result was the end of the cultured people. North America, whose population consists in by far the largest part of Germanic elements who mixed but little with the lower colored peoples, shows a different humanity and culture from Central and South America, where the predominantly Latin immigrants often mixed with the aborigines on a large scale. By this one example, we can clearly and distinctly recognize the effect of racial mixture. The Germanic inhabitant of the American continent, who has remained racially pure and unmixed, rose to be master of the continent; he will remain the master as long as he does not fall a victim to defilement of the blood.

Exercise 7-6

Here are two letters to the editor on related topics. In your evaluation of each one, be sure to take account of whatever is relevant in the other, and be sure to apply background information consistently.

1. To the Editor:

In "A Prescription for Heroin," his Nov. 19 Editorial Notebook article, Peter Passell writes about the benefits to be gained from a British-type model of supplying heroin legally to addicts. Fortunately for the British, they had our American-type model of heroin prohibition to study before they formulated their own policy.

In 1914, the United States Congress passed the Harrison Narcotic Act, which effectively stopped doctors from supplying heroin to patients. In 1922, the British sent Dr. Harry Campbell to the United States to observe what had been happening during the seven years of enforcement of the Harrison Act.

His report to the Rolleston Committee, a group of distinguished medical authorities set up by the British Government to study various policies, stated that ". . . not only has the Harrison law failed to diminish the number of drug takers—some contend, indeed, that it has increased their numbers—but, far from bettering the lot of the opiate addict, it has actually worsened it; for without curtailing the supply of the drug, it has sent the price up tenfold, and this has had the effect of impoverishing the poorer class of addicts and reducing them to a condition of such abject misery as to render them incapable of gaining an honest livelihood."

The Rolleston Committee wisely recommended that, since heroin addiction is an illness, physicians could legally treat it by supplying heroin to addicts. This medical model, that heroin is an illness, has been the overarching philosophic approach to British policy.

Unfortunately for America, we will persist in using the criminal justice model—and thus turn the heroin problem into the heroin disaster. As Peter Passell points out, American society has asked for a great deal of government control of heroin, and in the process gotten nothing at all.

The British saw the error of our ways and responded cleverly and humanely. Now, 60 years later and with no improvement in the "colonies," isn't it about time we look to heroin maintenance for addicts as a viable alternative to our present system?

Martin H. Levinson
Assistant Professor of Urban Health
Management, St. John's University
Jamaica, NY, Nov. 22, 1982[19]

2. To the Editor:

Peter Passel argues in his Nov. 29 Editorial Notebook article for "regulation and taxation" of marijuana. Legalization would, he writes, produce tax revenues of up to $2 billion a year and provide uncontaminated and even "low tar" pot.

Many readers may have wondered, "Why not?" There are answers.

Before getting to them, however, several facts need to be understood. In the last decade, the catalogue of negative health effects of marijuana—once thought to be a "harmless giggle"—has grown alarmingly, to include serious damage to the lungs, brain and reproductive organs as well as a wide range of behavioral toxicities whose ultimate effects range from decreased school and work performance to highway fatalities.

Along with the growing awareness of these serious health effects, marijuana use among the young, which had risen relentlessly for two decades, peaked in 1978 and now appears to be declining. Public support for legalization and even the less extreme "decriminalization" also peaked in 1978 and is now declining. No state has decriminalized marijuana possession since 1978.

Still, marijuana use remains unacceptably high. In 1979, 4 million of the nation's 12- to 17-year-olds smoked marijuana, while "only" 2.8 million smoked tobacco cigarettes. In 1981, 7 percent of American high school sen-

---

[19]*New York Times* (December 12, 1982). Reprinted by permission of the author.

iors smoked an average of 3½ marijuana cigarettes a day; "only" 6 percent of this group drank alcohol daily.

When considering legalization of marijuana, it is well to remember that the arguments favoring it apply to all other drugs, including cocaine, PCP and even heroin. If we are willing to legalize pot to provide possible tax revenues and to give the users a "pure" product, why not do the same for other drugs? It was once believed that marijuana was significantly less toxic than other illegal drugs. This comforting thought has been shown to be dangerously wrong.

What would the effect of legalization of marijuana be on the levels of use in our society?

For those who think legalization will not increase use, the American experience with repeal of Prohibition is instructive: Levels of alcohol use and the health problems associated with that use have risen steadily since 1933.

How many more children are we willing to lose to marijuana to get that hypothetical $2 billion tax windfall? How many more families will we wreck? How much less productivity, how many more highway fatalities?

Any thought of legalizing marijuana leads to thoughts of our national experience with the two traditional legal drugs, alcohol and tobacco.

While these drugs are so common as to seem almost trivial, as a physician concerned with the public health I cannot dismiss the fact that fully 30 percent of all American deaths in 1982 will have been premature because of these two drugs. Is that a precedent we should follow with another drug, a drug that appears to be more toxic than either alcohol or tobacco?

But one answer to the question "Why not?" stands out beyond all others: Why give up the effort to turn around the epidemic of marijuana use in the U.S. just as it is, for the first time, declining?

I can think of only one reason: the marijuana lobbyists are desperate. The "reforms" of permissive marijuana laws touted in the 1970's are now politically dead, so all pretense of compromise is being dropped. With it goes the one best argument the pro-pot forces had, namely that legalization is inevitable.

Mr. Passell makes this argument clear when he concludes, ". . . marijuana is here to stay. Some day, some way, a prohibition so unenforceable and so widely flouted must give way to reality." Would he use the same argument in regard to highway speed limits, which are surely more "widely flouted"?

It is unlikely that marijuana will be eliminated from the American scene, but major reductions in its use, and in the problems caused by that use, are now being achieved. Why quit while we're winning?

> Robert L. DuPont, M.D.
> President, American Council
> on Marijuana and Other
> Psychoactive Drugs
> Washington, Dec. 3, 1982[20]

---

[20] *New York Times* (December 12, 1982). Reprinted by permission of the author.

Exercise 7-7

Here are two more items to evaluate that are very appropriate given the discussion of the Ronald Reagan speech a few pages back. The first is by *New York Times* pundit James Reston and appeared on March 8, 1987, shortly after President Reagan's "mea culpa" speech:

1. **We Bought the Package**

   Everything has been examined now about what happened to the U.S. government except the role of the American people. We have blamed everybody but ourselves. It's almost as if the American people had taken the Fifth Amendment or been granted immunity from explaining why they elected Ronald Reagan in the first place.

   We couldn't really say he deceived us. The Tower Commission complained about his ignorance of the facts, his carelessness with the truth, his excessive reliance on subordinates, but we knew all that back yonder when he was governor of California.

   He was the good-looking, easy-talking type out of Hollywood every mother warned her daughter to avoid—irresponsible but irresistible. We didn't really elect him but fell in love with him.

   He followed every old movie script to the letter. It wasn't until he was discovered selling guns backstage to the terrorists in Iran, of all people, that we woke up at the beginning of the last act, stunned by the crash.

   How could it have happened? What did the American people know and when did they know it? They knew everything from the start and did nothing about it. They like him because they're like him: well-meaning, optimistic, credulous, stubborn and a little bit dumb.

   It's not new either. We knew the Japanese wouldn't dare attack us at Pearl Harbor; that the Chinese wouldn't cross the Yalu when MacArthur went beyond the 38th parallel in Korea; that we could rout the Cubans at the Bay of Pigs; that the North Vietnamese would run away when they saw our tanks and planes; that Beirut would settle down when the Marines landed; and with our money and our guns the "freedom fighters" would triumph in Nicaragua.

   We still don't know who went South with Col. North's money, or who those "moderates" were who were supposed to swap hostages for guns in Iran, but we know governments often drift into trouble and that there's enough blame around now to cover us all, including the people.

   We have another election coming up, however, and it will break our hearts if we don't learn the lessons of these recent events.

   "We must adopt the habit," Walter Lippmann wrote over 40 years ago, "of thinking as plainly about the sovereign people as we do about the politicians they elect.

   "It will not do to think poorly of the politicians and to talk with bated breath about the voters. No more than the kings before them should the people be hedged with divinity. Like all princes and rulers, they are ill served by flattery and adulation."

   This suggests not only taking a different look at our officials but at ourselves in the 200th year of the Constitution. Our low voting record is an acknowledged disgrace, and the method of choosing and nominating candidates is little more than a television show. ˙

It will probably be even worse in 1988 when the candidates are flying around 13 states on Super Tuesday, appealing to local prejudices instead of the national interest.

We will need to know far more this time about the character and age and health of the candidates, and about the people they propose for their cabinets and staff.

This will or should mean earlier examination of the personal and political record and more direct debates between the nominees without the intrusion of reporters. In short, more attention by the people at the beginning of the election process rather than at the end.[21]

2. Now, here are excerpts from a rather long article by Patrick J. Buchanan, former director of communications for President Reagan and special assistant and speechwriter to President Nixon during his administration. The article was widely circulated and appeared in the *San Francisco Chronicle* on July 20, 1987, shortly after the conclusion of Lt. Col. Oliver North's testimony before the Congressional Iran-Contra committee:

> Noon Wednesday, suddenly, it was over; and everyone knew it.
> The coup d'état had failed. Ronald Reagan would survive. . . .
>
> In November, when it was first revealed that Ronald Reagan had authorized weapons sales to mullahs—in contravention of stated policy—the anger, the anguish, the outrage—even among the president's own—were genuine, legitimate. Today, they are synthetic, feigned, and transparently so. . . .
>
> In a single week Ollie [Lt. Col. Oliver North] not only put God and Country and the Constitution, and all the splendid values he represents, back on the side of the president and the Nicaraguan resistance; he held up a mirror to the ugly face of the inquisition.
>
> How, when Colonel North admitted to setting up secret bank accounts, to deceiving Congress, to shredding documents, can the American people consider him a national hero. . . ?
>
> The answer is simple. What the American people saw was genuine drama: A patriotic son of the Republic who, confronted with a grave moral dilemma—whether to betray his comrades and causes, or to deceive members of Congress—chose the lesser of two evils, the path of honor. It was magnificent. The American people watched daily the anguish and pain of a genuinely moral man; and contrasted that with the stuffy self-righteousness of the pharisees putting him through his ordeal. . . .
>
> Colonel North speaks the language of duty, honor, country; his is a faith deeply rooted in Christian tradition. He did not, and would not, proclaim some amoral "right to lie"; he was forced into a moral dilemma by an immoral act of Congress.

---

[21]James Reston, "America Takes the Fifth," *New York Times* (March 8, 1987). Copyright 1987 by The New York Times Co. Reprinted by permission.

With the Boland Amendment, the Congress of the United States passed a death sentence upon the embattled friends of Colonel North; and then it instructed men like Colonel North to carry it out. Instead, the colonel built a new and ingenious lifeline to keep the Contras alive; and when Congress came to close that down as well, Colonel North protected it, at risk of his own career.

He deceived Congress, to save his friends on a field of battle. That is what the American people, deeply moved, were applauding. That is why American people laughed out loud, when Colonel North volunteered that even as Justice Department lawyers were seizing documents in one room, he was shredding documents in the next.

"They were doing their jobs, and I was doing mine," Ollie said; and every American knew in his heart that Colonel North had done a brave and beautiful thing. For all this moralizing about "the end does not justify the means," the truth is the colonel's ends were noble and his means—secrecy and shredding documents—licit or not, were not inherently immoral.

There is another reason America took Colonel North into her heart. That is because they believe that the Left, the Sam Donaldsons of the world, lack the moral standing to sit in judgment on anyone—especially Colonel North.

Men who have proclaimed it a great advance for human freedom, when 4,000 unborn children are daily shredded in abortuaries of the United States, are to be laughed at when they profess moral horror over the shredding of documents. . . .

The Boland Amendment did not forbid Iranian contributions to the Contras; it did not forbid private aid to the Contras; it did not apply to the NSC [National Security Council]. It was a civil statute with no criminal penalties. And there is no hard evidence either man [Colonel North and NSC presidential advisor Admiral John Poindexter] violated that amendment. . . .

But if the letter of the Boland Amendment was not violated, its "spirit" merited contempt. For the Boland Amendment was rooted in malice; it was a calculated, cold-blooded congressional act to abandon to their communist enemies thousands of Nicaraguan patriots who had taken up arms, at the urging of the United States, to expel Moscow's Quislings from Central America.

The Boland Amendment was rooted in the same malevolence that motivated an earlier Congress to disarm and desert to its communist enemies a South Vietnamese army that had fought for seven years alongside our own. . . .

It is not Poindexter and North who belong in a court of law; but Congress that belongs in the court of public opinion explaining why, for three years, it has actively sought a Contra defeat—and its natural concomitant, a communist victory in Central America.

In 1985 and 1986, while Fidel Castro moved 3,000 combat advisers into Nicaragua, while Gorbachev pumped in a billion dollars in military hardware, the Congress did its damndest to discredit, defund and defeat the army of peasants fighting on the side of freedom and the United States. The Boland Amendment was nothing less than the American corollary to the Brezhnev Doctrine. . . .

No more no-win wars, Mr. President. Did not you tell us, sir, that this was the central lesson of Vietnam?

And should the Democratic Party in Congress, with no policy of its own for dealing with the beachhead of the Warsaw Pact on the mainland of North America, choose to pursue its dog-in-the-manger tactics and defund the Contras, the president should find the supplies, ship them openly, and challenge the Congress to impeach him. As Colonel North demonstrated, they haven't got the cohones. . . .

Any indictment of Colonel North or Admiral Poindexter would be an offense against justice that ought not to be permitted by the president, whom they served honorably, faithfully and well. And the president should so state, publicly. . . .

Never strike a king unless you kill him. That was among the first things taught us by Richard M. Nixon when I hooked up with him more than two decades ago. For the last six months, the left wing of the Democratic Party, and its auxiliaries in the press, have sought to use the Iran-Contra affair to cripple and kill the presidency of Ronald Reagan as they used Watergate to kill the presidency of Richard Nixon.

They failed, Mr. President; they are retreating in disarray; and now is the time to let the jackal pack know what it means to strike a king.

4. Constructing Cogent Essays

Learning how to analyze and learning how to construct cogent essays go hand in hand.

Get Clear About Your Thesis

Whether analyzing someone else's work or doing our own, we need to get clear about the thesis of a passage. When reading what others have written, we need to discern what the author's thesis is. When writing our own arguments, we need to get clear as to what precisely we want to prove.

It's usually best to start right out with our thesis, perhaps in an interesting opening paragraph that introduces the topic. Here is an example:

If there's one issue that divides Americans these days, it's the abortion issue. Arguments pro and con seem endless.

This tells the reader that the topic will be the abortion issue and prepares the reader for our thesis:

> Yet there are two simple reasons why abortion should be made illegal.

Now the reader knows what the thesis is and knows that there will be two basic reasons offered in its support.

Spell Out Your Reasons for the Thesis

Having informed the reader of the thesis, we need to give our reasons for accepting it. In our antiabortion essay, we might continue:

> The first reason is that abortion takes the life of a human being. We sometimes hear that a fetus is not human, not a baby. Ridiculous. Look at a three-month-old fetus, and you'll see what can't be mistaken for anything but a human baby. [And so on.]

How much detail we provide at this point depends on our intended audience and how resistant they're likely to be at this point. We don't want to hit people over the head with what they already know or believe.

Now for our second reason, anticipating a possible objection:

> Of course, it isn't always murder when we kill a human being. Police officers kill in the line of duty. So do soldiers in wartime. No one calls that murder. The same is true of those who kill in self-defense or to defend innocent people.
>
> But if we look at these cases, we find that they involve killing an aggressor or someone who has done something seriously wrong. Killing in battle is not wrong, for instance, because the point is to defend the nation against attack. In the case of abortion, however, the fetus has harmed no one. The fetus is innocent. [And so on.]

Help the Reader to Understand

Merely giving reasons for a thesis generally isn't good enough to persuade the reader to your point of view. For one thing, your reasons themselves may need to be justified by additional reasons, for instance, by appeals to relevant facts or authorities. And for another, you may need to help the reader *understand* (or be moved by) your reasons. There are many ways to do this, for instance, by *comparing* and *contrasting* the case in point with similar ones or by quoting authoritative statistics or the word of an acknowledged expert. But perhaps the best way is by giving *examples*. For example, in our little essay on abortion, we explained what we meant in saying that killing isn't always wrong by giving the examples of killing in self-defense, in battle, and by police in the line of duty. (This last sentence, in fact, is an example presented to help readers understand that they need to give examples to help readers understand.)[22]

---

[22]No doubt the most frequently used expressions in this book are *for example* and *for instance*.

Examples also are often useful in convincing readers to *accept* our claims, not just to understand them. In our abortion essay, for instance, we gave examples to convince readers that killing wrongdoers or aggressors isn't always wrong, preparing them for the contrasting case of abortion, where an *innocent* life is taken.

A Summary May be Helpful

Having presented our case, it's usually a good idea to remind readers of its main drift. For instance, in our abortion example, we might want to conclude this way:

> So abortion should be illegal, because it amounts to the *unjustified* taking of a human life. After all, we're justified in killing human beings only when they're guilty of an extremely serious wrong, but a fetus is completely innocent.

Provide Transition Expressions

A good essay obviously has to have a logical structure. But it also has to make it easy for readers to follow that structure. So we need to use transition terms to tell readers what to expect. For instance, the sentence just before this one used the word *so* to indicate that that sentence would "follow" from the previous one. In general, we want to let readers know whether we're giving them reasons, or conclusions, by using expressions like *because, due to this, hence,* and so on.

But we also want to direct readers in other ways. In particular, we want to use words like *however, but,* and *and* when appropriate. In the abortion essay, we did this quite often, for instance, in the sentence "In the case of abortion, *however,* the fetus has harmed no one." (The word *however* here has the sense of "on the other hand.") Flavoring words of this kind help a passage to flow so that readers can follow it as the author intended.

Write for Your Audience

The point of a critical essay is to convince readers to accept some thesis or other. So we want to include only those things that readers will need in order to understand and agree with us.

While it's obvious that we should write for our audience, in practice it's sometimes hard to carry this out. The reason is that it's human nature to spend lots of time explaining and illustrating those things we ourselves understand best or are most sure of, while sliding quickly past the parts that we don't quite understand ourselves or are unsure of. What we should do, of course, is almost the exact opposite. Those things we think our readers will grasp clearly and easily need to be mentioned relatively briefly, with at most one example, while harder things should be gone into in more detail and illustrated by more (and more varied) examples. (How well *we* understand a point is often our best measure of how well our readers will grasp it.)

Think Your Position Through Carefully

That's one reason why analyzing arguments and writing them go hand in hand. To write a good argumentative essay, we need to carefully analyze our own ideas and beliefs on the topic, to root out inconsistencies and dubious or fuzzy beliefs, and to arrange the various points into a coherent whole.

You'll Probably Need to Rewrite

And that's one reason why you'll no doubt need to write and rewrite several times. When writing a critical essay, most people find that their thoughts on the topic aren't as cogent or clear as they supposed. The writing process itself thus becomes part of the reasoning process.

That's why some writers deliberately construct the first draft of an essay as a learning or thinking device. They do the best job they can on the first draft and then critically analyze it as they would an opponent's essay. Their next draft then takes account of this critical evaluation, either by introducing new arguments that aren't open to these criticisms or by showing that the objections they've discovered can be overcome by further argument.

But one thing is clear. Only a few of the very best writers can construct a really good critical essay in one draft. (One writer who could do this was the philosopher Bertrand Russell.) The rest of us have to write at least two drafts, usually more, in order to get our thoughts into good order and to arrange our exposition so as to present these thoughts in a logical, understandable manner. And you won't be surprised to find out that this takes *practice, practice, practice.*

Exercise 7-8

So let's get some practice writing short critical essays. Here are several issues college students might be interested in. Select one and write a short essay (about 500–1,000 words), taking one side or another. Then write a critical analysis in reply to your own thesis (as though you were a fair opponent attacking your argument). And then rewrite your original essay to take account of your own criticisms. (You may find that you've changed your mind and now want to defend a different thesis.) Think of your audience as your fellow students, *not* your instructor. When you've done that, pick another topic (from the list that follows or from year head) and do the same thing over again (hopefully finding that you can do the job easier and better the second time around).

1. Should all students be required to take at least basic introductory courses in math and science? In a foreign language?

2. Is the lecture method a good way to teach certain college courses? Specify which kinds of courses you're talking about.

3. Should we have a peacetime draft?

4. Should marijuana, cocaine, or other drugs be legal?

5. Should the United States supply military aid to anticommunist governments and/or rebels in Central America?

6. Should we have sex education courses in high school?

7. Should we raise (lower) the legal drinking age? Should convicted drunk drivers lose their licenses?

8. How can we improve the college curriculum?

9. Are there fair ways to make American industry more competitive with foreign industry?

10. Should we require that every adult be tested for AIDS?

Summary of Chapter 7

Chapter 7 deals with the analysis and construction of extended arguments.

1. There are several guidelines to use in evaluating such passages:
   a. Find the thesis and keep it in mind as you read.
   b. Find the reasons supporting the thesis, and (sometimes) the reasons for the reasons, and so on.
   c. Skip whatever doesn't support the thesis.
   d. Add relevant information, pro or con.
   e. Come to an evaluation.

2. In everyday life, there usually isn't time to thoroughly analyze an extended passage. So it's useful to develop the knack of quick appraisal. The trick in quick appraisal is to learn how to informally and quickly do the basic things just mentioned *as you read the passage.* In particular, you have to learn how to bring relevant information to bear and to evaluate as you read.

3. When a more careful analysis is required, margin notes are useful. And when you need to be sure, the margin note and summary method is better yet. There are four basic steps in the margin note and summary method: Read the material carefully; read it again and add margin notes at the relevant spots; construct a summary from the margin notes; and evaluate the summary.

4. Learning how to analyze extended arguments and learning how to write them go hand in hand. Some hints for writing good essays of this kind are:
   a. Get clear about your thesis.
   b. Spell out the reasons for your thesis.
   c. Help readers to understand your argument (and convince them of its cogency) by providing examples, facts, and so on.
   d. (Sometimes) summarize your argument at the end.
   e. Use transition expressions, such as *but, therefore,* and *for example,* so that your writing flows, and the reader can follow it more easily.
   f. Write with your audience in mind, in particular so that you tell them all and only those things they need to know.
   g. Think your position through carefully (you may find your ideas are changed by the writing process itself).
   h. Write and rewrite until your essay says just what you want it to say.

Photo by Rita Nannini

A white-haired woman sits in an overstuffed chair and says, "All this talk of cutting Social Security is really making me nervous." She goes on to say that's why she's voting for Barney Frank. "How can I be sure Barney will do the right thing by us older people?" She smiles. "Because he's my son." It's irresistible.

This excerpt from a Harper's *magazine article on TV spot commercials[1] illustrates what has been happening to political campaigns in recent years. They are being won or lost primarily on television, and 30- and 60-second spots like the one above are perhaps the most important component of a TV campaign. Notice that the appeal is chiefly to emotions, not reason. And notice that it is irresistible. We're all suckers for Mom and apple pie. (Yes, Barney Frank won.)*

---

[1]Nicholas Lemann, "Barney Frank's Mother—And 500 Postmen." Copyright © 1983 by *Harper's* magazine. All rights reserved. Reprinted from the April 1983 issue by special permission.

8

Advertising: Selling the Product

Advertising is so obviously useful that it's surprising it has such a bad name. Ads tell us what is new, what is available, where, when, and for how much. They tell us about a product's (alleged) quality and specifications, and sometimes they even show us the product itself (on television or in pictures). All for free, except for the effort of reading or paying attention.

Yet there are legitimate gripes about advertising. Ads often exaggerate or are otherwise misleading; some even lie. Surely that's not what we want. And since some products are advertised more heavily or more effectively than others, ads tend to skew our choices in an unreasonable way. And that too is undesirable.[2]

---

[2]A third common charge against advertising is that it increases sales costs and thus increases retail prices. But this charge is false. It's true that advertising costs a great deal of money, but not true that it raises prices. That would be true only if things could be sold more cheaply by some other selling method, and quite clearly there is no such other method. It's no accident that virtually all businesses advertise—they don't know a cheaper way to sell their products. Those who argue that advertising raises prices forget that if a company doesn't advertise, it will have to increase other selling costs (for instance, sales commissions).

But let's move to the more pressing problem of how to best use advertising without getting used. One solution to that problem is to become familiar with the advertising devices and gimmicks used to con the unwary or, more politely, to appeal to our emotions, weaknesses, or prejudices. It should come as no surprise that these devices are pretty much the same as those used in most persuasive rhetoric (except that ad experts are the acknowledged masters).

1. Promise and Identification Advertisements

First of all, it's important to understand that virtually all ads are of two kinds (or combinations of the two). **Promise advertisements** promise to satisfy desires or allay fears. All you have to do is buy the product advertised (for instance, remove bad breath by using Listerine). Most promise ads, but not all, give "reasons why" the product will fulfill the promise or do it better than competitors (example: Kleenex tissues are softer).

Identification advertisements sell the product by getting their audience to identify with the product, to remember its name, and to think of it positively (for instance, "Come to Marlboro country"). (Some identification ads are designed to get you to identify with a particular company, not a special product.)

People tend to identify with their own kind (or, in a slightly different way, with the rich and powerful), and identification ads frequently take advantage of this fact. Recall the Life cereal ads that featured an appealing little kid and the slogan: "Try the cereal Mikey likes." (Grownup Mikey wasn't quite so appealing.)

Magazine ads, for example, are tailored to match their audience. The National Rifle Association's ads in *American Hunter* magazine showed a state trooper— very macho—over the line "I'm the NRA." But their ads in women's magazines featured a pediatrician and father under the same line, "I'm the NRA." Similarly, most Virginia Slims ads feature a dolled-up, foxy white lady and the slogan "You've come a long way, baby," but in magazines with primarily black readers, such as *Essence,* their ads feature a dolled-up, foxy *black* lady and the same slogan.

2. Things to Watch Out for in Advertisements

The good feature of ads is obvious: As stated before, ads give us useful information about products and companies, often in a *very* entertaining way. It's the bad features we have to watch out for.

Ads Don't Say What's Wrong with the Product

No product is perfect. Hence the completely informative ad would mention at least some drawbacks. But no one has yet seen an ad that deliberately said anything negative about a product.[3] This means that practically every ad invites the fallacy of *suppressed evidence* by concealing negative information.

Movie and theater ads routinely quote the few nice words in a negative review while omitting all the critical ones. This seems to have gone too far in the case of advertising for the Broadway play *Alone Together*. Its sponsors were convicted of violating a local regulation forbidding "out of context" quotes. The headline in the misleading ad set the tone:

The kind of play we hardly see on Broadway anymore.

—Frank Rich,
New York Times/WQXR

And here are some excerpts from that Frank Rich review to illustrate how misleading indeed this out-of-context quote was:

> *Alone Together* . . . is the kind of play we hardly see on Broadway anymore. It's a flat-out television sitcom—expanded to two hours—that assumes the theatre audience is at least as unsophisticated as a typical Nielsen household. The play is quite awful. . . . Pathetic as this play is, however, it is not to be confused with those Broadway bombs that are so ludicrous that they actually become perversely entertaining. . . . It's strictly a run-of-the-mill turkey.

Ads Use Psychological Tricks
More than Direct Appeals to Reason

We said before that promise advertisements claim the product will satisfy some need or desire or alleviate some fear, and that they usually give reasons why the product can do this for us. (Listerine will cure our bad breath because it will kill millions of germs in our mouths.) Thus, it would be reasonable to suppose that such ads appeal chiefly to the rational side of our nature, since that's what "reasons why" are all about. In fact, most ads are a blend of devices designed to appeal both to reason and, via nonrational psychological ploys, to emotions. And in most cases, the nonrational aspect predominates. This is even more true of identification than of promise ads.

---

[3]Except when employing "reverse twist," that is, trying to make a virtue out of an apparent defect. The Avis Rent-A-Car campaign—"We try harder (because we're only number two)"—is an example. So is the Listerine ad that implies bad taste is needed for, or is a sign of, greater effectiveness.

Here is ad executive Alec Benn explaining the difference between promise and identification advertising and why identification ads are so effective when done well.

How to Get People To Do What You Want with Words and Pictures

An animal learns in two ways. First, through identification: The cub sees what the mature animal does and does not do, and follows his example. He *identifies* with the other animal. Second, through promises: The trainer causes the animal to do what he wants by holding out the hope of food or [expectation of] punishment. No one has figured out any other way of influencing the behavior of an animal, even an animal as sophisticated as man.

It is easier to influence the behavior of men and women because of language. An animal must engage in random behavior in order to discover what he must do in order to gain the promised benefit. Men and women can appreciate what is required in seconds. An animal can only imitate what it sees and hears, while the wonders of language and the facility of the human mind make it possible for men and women to identify with an ideal and understand a promise.

Shakespeare, that master of audience communication, shows how to do it. Here's Henry Tudor, just before the key battle in *Richard III*, promising his troops just about all they could ever hope for:

If you do fight against your country's foes,
Your country's fat shall pay your pains the hire;
If you do fight in safeguard of your wives,
Your wives shall welcome home the conquerors;
If you do free your children from the sword,
Your children's children quit it in your age.

Look at the promises: money, love, a better life for their children! What life insurance copy Shakespeare could have written!

Advertising deals with more mundane matters, but the same emotion must be aroused: hope of a better life. The promise may be of something superior: "Get clothes whiter than white." Or something more: "Get four for the price of three." Or something cheaper: "Lowest fares to Europe."

The most successful promises aim directly at the audience's self-interest, the more physical the better: taste, comfort, easier life, health, security, the chance to save time, the chance to save or make money, pleasure, power, greater sexual attractiveness. And the promise is backed up by logic. The formula is: "To get what you want, do what I want." The technique is cerebral.

The identification technique is quite different. It need not be logical. It does not depend upon reason for success but upon instinct. It aims at the heart, not the brain.

Another example from Shakespeare may help make the technique clear. Here is Henry V to his men just before the battle of Agincourt. Note that Henry V even uses the word "imitate," and suggests identification with admirable animals and the audience's fathers and mothers. The emotional appeal is to pride—and there's hardly any logic to it at all.

> . . . But when the blast of war blows in our ears,
> Then imitate the action of the tiger;
> Stiffen the sinews, summon up the blood,
> Disguise fair nature with hard-favour'd rage;
> Then lend the eye a terrible aspect;
> Let it pry through the portage of the head
> Like the brass cannon. . . .
> On, on you noble English,
> Whose blood is fet from fathers of war-proof!—
> Fathers that, like so many Alexanders,
> Have in these parts from morn till even fought,
> And sheath'd their swords for lack of argument:—
> Dishonour not your mothers, now attest
> That those whom you call'd fathers did beget you!
> Be copy now to men of grosser blood,
> And teach them how to war!—And you, good yeomen,
> Whose limbs were made in England, show us here
> The mettle of your pasture; let us swear
> That you are worth your breeding: which I doubt not;
> For there is none of you so mean and base,
> That hath not noble lustre in your eyes.
> I see you stand like greyhounds in the slips,
> Straining upon the start. The game's afoot:
> Follow your spirit; and upon this charge
> Cry—God for Harry! England! and Saint George!

Ideals change, but the fundamental technique remains the same. Marlboro became the leading cigarette brand by causing smokers to identify with the masculine cowboy. Virginia Slims became a big seller by associating itself with the women's liberation movement—"You've come a long way, baby!" . . . The U.S. Marines modernized Henry V in billboards showing good-looking young Marines in their distinctive dress uniforms and the words: "We're looking for a few good men."

The 27 Most Common Mistakes in Advertising (New York: AMACOM, 1978). Copyright © Alec Benn. Used by permission.

Consider the very successful ad campaign for Lite Beer from Miller. The "reasons why" you should buy Lite Beer touted in that series of commercials were quite simple: Lite Beer is better tasting and has fewer calories than regular beers. But the Miller commercials didn't just inform us of these two reasons for buying their product. Miller spent many millions to tell us this simple message in a way that's psychologically more likely to be accepted by us, as all good ads do. In the Lite Beer ads, the psychological devices are *identification* and *humor*. They feature famous athletes (identification) in endless variations on the theme of ridiculous (therefore funny) confrontations between one group of athletes who say they drink Lite Beer because it tastes better and another group who say they drink Lite Beer because it's "less filling" (has fewer calories). No halfway intelligent viewer actually believes battles of this kind ever do or could occur in real life. But that, obviously, isn't the point. The primary appeal here is not to reason.

That's also why the same ads are used over and over, and why the theme of the whole ad campaign is repeated endlessly. The average TV sports fan has heard this Miller pitch hundreds of times. Miller wanted beer drinkers to hear it so often because they know that human psychology (not human rationality) must be appealed to to make beer drinkers think of Miller Lite when they step up to the bar or go out to the supermarket.

It's hard to be sure why this repetitive humorous identification really works, while telling us straight just once or twice doesn't (or doesn't as well). Scratch two psychologists and you'll get two different theories on the matter.[4]

However, one thing we can be pretty sure of is that merely knowing something generally isn't enough to make human beings *use* that information when it comes time to act in everyday life. There is a great gap between mere knowledge and *effective* knowledge. This is true in general, not just concerning advertising. (One reason public opinion in America turned against our participation in the war in Vietnam was that for the first time in our history the folks back home got to see just a little of the horror of war—brought into their living rooms in living color on television evening news. Seeing one soldier shot and killed on camera has more effect on most of us than merely being told about a hundred soldiers being killed in battle.)

I'm a salesman. Salesmen don't tell you things that will cause you not to buy a product. If you are buying a used car, the salesman won't tell you what is wrong with the car.
  —U.S. Army recruiter, Dallas, Texas, answering charges that military recruiters mislead potential recruits, in *Moneysworth* (May 1979)

Anyone thinking of enlisting in the military should realize that military recruiters are sales representatives who get paid to sell their product and that they will not necessarily tell you the fine print that sometimes makes all the difference.

---

[4]For the ad executives' view on this, see "Commercials. Can You Believe Them? . . . Why the Same Ones Again and Again? *TV Guide* (December 2, 1982).

So, if Miller just told us that Lite Beer tastes better and is less filling, without us-ing humor, repetition, identification, or some other device, they wouldn't effec-tively bridge the gap between merely hearing or understanding the message and *acting* on that understanding. To be effective, an ad has to take account of human psychology. Man is a rational animal, to some extent. But he is also an emotional cauldron.[5]

To (repetitively) illustrate the point about ads playing primarily to emotions, not reason, consider one of the classics of advertising history, built around a head-line that for a time became part of the language:

> They laughed when I sat down at the piano—
> But when I started to play! . . .

The promise of this ad was that the product would satisfy the desire to shine at par-ties. In the fine print, having put prospective customers into the proper emotional frame, the ad promised to teach piano playing quickly and with "no laborious scales—no heartless exercises—no tiresome practicing." Reason would caution the reader. After all, how is it possible to learn to play the piano without lots of practicing? But no matter; emotions sufficiently aroused will override rationa-lity—in a sufficient number of cases. This famous ad was a tremendous success.[6]

Ads Often Are Deceptive or Misleading

Among the three or four widely used deceptive or misleading devices, *false impli-cation*—stating something that is (usually) true while implying something else that is false—is perhaps the most insidious.

London Fog commercials are sometimes set in London, suggesting that London Fog raincoats and jackets are made in England. In fact, they're made in Baltimore, Maryland, U.S.A. The ads never say they're made in England, but some people are bound to think so, which is why the commercial makers went to the trouble of showing models standing in front of Big Ben.

The Armour Star frank ads that correctly stated that one pound of Armour franks and one pound of steak are equal in nourishment implied that a hot dog meal is just as nourishing as a steak meal. But did you ever try eating ten Armour franks at one sitting?

Here's an item that won one of Esquire's *1980 "Dubious Achievement Awards":*

When third grade students in a Connecticut grammar school were asked to spell the word *relief,* more than half of them answered R-O-L-A-I-D-S.

—*Esquire* (January 1981)

---

[5]Note that, in general, this book doesn't just tell you something; it also illustrates it, some-times repetitively. Miller similarly wants to "educate" you into preferring their beer.
[6]Frank Rowsome, Jr., used its opening phrase as the title of his delightful book on advertis-ing, *They Laughed When I Sat Down* (New York: Bonanza Books, 1959). Some of the other examples used in this chapter also appear in Rowsome's book.

Somewhere West of Laramie

SOMEWHERE west of Laramie there's a broncho-busting, steer-roping girl who knows what I'm talking about.

She can tell what a sassy pony, that's a cross between greased lightning and the place where it hits, can do with eleven hundred pounds of steel and action when he's going high, wide and handsome.

The truth is—the Playboy was built for her.

Built for the lass whose face is brown with the sun when the day is done of revel and romp and race.

She loves the cross of the wild and the tame.

There's a savor of links about that car—of laughter and lilt and light—a hint of old loves—and saddle and quirt. It's a brawny thing—yet a graceful thing for the sweep o' the Avenue.

Step into the Playboy when the hour grows dull with things gone dead and stale.

Then start for the land of real living with the spirit of the lass who rides, lean and rangy, into the red horizon of a Wyoming twilight.

JORDAN MOTOR CAR COMPANY, Inc. Cleveland. Ohio

Early automobile ads featured facts and figures. This 1920s ad was one of the first to tout romance rather than nuts and bolts and also was one of the first directed at women. The success of this kind of ad taught Madison Avenue a great lesson in human psychology.

Claude Hopkins (a great from advertising's past) was the first to understand and use a beautiful variation on the false implication gambit. Hopkins believed it was a waste of money to claim your product is the best, or pure, or anything so general. He tried to understand his product sufficiently to be able to provide more specific "reasons why" a person should buy that product. (This may sound as though his ads really did inform the public about the product, and Hopkins himself may have believed this. But it didn't work that way.)

One of Hopkin's early and famous ad campaigns illustrates this well. When he was put to work on Schlitz beer ads, he discovered that each Schlitz bottle was sterilized with live steam. So he built his campaign around headlines such as "Washed with Live Steam!", omitting the fact that all breweries used live steam. He knew that competitors could not then advertise that they too used live steam—that claim had been preempted for Schlitz. And he knew most readers would assume that *only* Schlitz washed their bottles with live steam. (Apparently, he was right; Schlitz's sales went from fifth to first in short order.)

Most ads claiming a certain quality for their product without explicitly asserting its uniqueness to that product are designed to make you *assume* that only their product has that quality. If you make that assumption, you reason fallaciously.

Another misleading or deceptive device frequently employed in ads is *ambiguity*. Fleishmann's margarine says on the package, "Fleishmann's—made from 100 percent corn oil." But on the side we read in the fine print that it's made from "Liquid Corn Oil, Partially Hydrogenated Corn Oil, Water, nonfat dry milk, vegetable mono and diglicerides and lecithin, artificially flavored and colored (carotene), Vitamins A & D added."

Well, did the statement mean that Fleishmann's is made from 100 percent corn oil and nothing else, or did it mean that the oil that is the main ingredient in margarine is 100 percent corn oil (instead of, say, partly soybean oil, as in many other brands)? If challenged, Fleishmann's can say they meant the latter while being confident that some consumers will take them to mean the former.

An interesting variation on the ambiguity theme is the *ambiguous comparison*. A Colgate fluoride toothpaste ad claimed that "Most Colgate kids got fewer cavities," but it failed to state fewer than who. Again, the hope was that readers would take the ad to claim that Colgate kids got fewer cavities than those using other fluoride toothpastes, such as Crest (by far the best seller at that time). But the *true* claim was that Colgate fluoride kids got fewer cavities on the average than they did before using Colgate, when, of course, some of them used a nonfluoride toothpaste, or perhaps didn't brush their teeth at all.

This is the successful Marine Corps identification advertisement Alec Benn referred to in saying that "the U.S. Marines modernized Henry V in billboards. . . ."

> Schoolchildren might examine . . . the meaning of *free gifts* offered by savings banks in return for new deposits. Strictly speaking, if a gift is not free, it is not a gift. The bank's gifts, however, are not really free: If the deposit is withdrawn before a minimum period, the gift, or an equivalent amount of money, is taken back. The free gift turns out to be a conditional gift all along.
> —Fred M. Heckinger, *Saturday Review/World* (March 9, 1974)

The use of *weasel words* is also common in advertisements. Words like *virtually, helps,* and *fights* almost always signal a claim that is smaller than it seems (as in "*helps* control dandruff with regular use").

Similarly, *evaluative terms*, like *good, better,* and *best*, are often used in sneaky ways. At the worst (itself a slightly sneaky expression), the word *best* translates into "tied for first with all the rest" or "tied for first with all major competitors." *Lowest* also is often misleading. The "*lowest* fare to Europe" may turn out to be the standard fare. And when they say, "No one sells _____ for less," the best inference is always that others sell for the same price.

Another deceptive device often used, especially in print ads, is the *fine print qualification*. Sometimes this device is used just for humor. An example is the TWA ad with a very large boldface headline:

TWA announces the lowest price
to Europe in history
$0.

Below that is a large picture of part of a globe with a TWA plane superimposed, and below *that* we're told: "Only TWA offers two free tickets to Europe as a bonus for flying with us in the U.S.A." But it turns out still further down in the ad that to qualify you'd have to fly at least 60,000 miles on TWA in the U.S.A. (that's about 20 trips across the country).

> Advertising expenditures, for example, between 1970 and 1980 soared from $19.5 billion to $53.6 billion, totaling more than $362.5 billion for the decade. Over 42,000 *new* TV commercials are developed each year, adding to the hundreds of thousands already made. Some estimates claim the average American child sees 100,000 commercials before being old enough to go to school. In 1981, a Cap'n Crunch cereal contest, unnoticed by most adults, asked kids to respond by using an 800 phone number; in four months, the Captain and his crew were overwhelmed by 24 million phone calls. Such gee-whiz statistics can only suggest the scope of advertising's impact on our society.
> —*Quarterly Review of Doublespeak* (January 1983)

Robert Glatzer called the Marlboro campaign the "campaign of the century."[7] This is a typical ad from that campaign (generally credited with vaulting Marlboros from way back in the pack to the number one brand, in America and in the world. The Marlboro campaign is an excellent example of the power of identification *advertising. (The warning note appearing in the lefthand corner was required by law and did not appear in earlier ads of the campaign.)*

[7]Robert Glatzer, *The Great Ad Campaigns from Avis to Volkswagen* (New York: Citadel Press, 1970).

Puffery Is Legal

Most ads that are deceptive or misleading fall into the category of *puffery* or *puffing,* a category that has gained legal recognition. Ivan L. Preston[8] characterizes puffery this way:

> By legal definition, puffery is advertising or other sales representations which praise the item to be sold with subjective opinions, superlatives, or exaggerations, vaguely and generally, stating no specific facts. It appears

------

[8]Ivan L. Preston, *The Great American Blowup* (Madison: University of Wisconsin Press 1975). © 1975 by the Regents of the University of Wisconsin. Reprinted by permission.

Shoot-Out in Marlboro Country

A gathering storm darkens the desert sky. Heroic movie music. The TV screen shows the stark, barren mountains of northern New Mexico, and in their shadow, a lone cowboy slowly herding his cattle home. We first see him riding in the distance behind the ambling herd. Then closer; his head is bowed beneath a sweaty, broad-brimmed oversized hat. The scene could be straight out of one of the old Marlboro commercials . . . until the cowboy comes close enough for us to see the oxygen tank strapped to his saddle. Tubes from it run up his nostrils. "New Mexico rancher John Holmes has emphysema," the crisp British voice of the narrator informs us, "brought on by years of heavy smoking."

This scene is from a TV documentary called *Death in the West.* It is one of the most powerful anti-smoking films ever made. You will never see it. . . . [It was shown once in a few areas in 1983, and again seems to have disappeared back into the closet.]

Death in the West was filmed in 1976 by director Martin Smith, reporter Peter Taylor and a crew from *This Week,* a weekly show on Britain's independent Thames Television network. The show is roughly the British equivalent of *60 Minutes.* Taylor's searing half-hour film simply intercuts three kinds of footage. The first is old Marlboro commercials—cowboys lighting up around the chuck wagon, galloping across the plains at sunset, and so forth. The second is interviews with two Philip Morris executives who claim that nobody knows if cigarettes cause cancer. The third is interviews with six real cowboys in the American West who have lung cancer or, in one case, emphysema. And after each cowboy, the film shows the victim's doctor testifying that he believes his patient's condition was caused by heavy cigarette smoking.

After opening with a commercial showing Marlboro men around a campfire, the film cuts to another campfire, where narrator Taylor is interviewing cowboy Bob Julian. "For Bob," Taylor says, "the last roundup will soon be over."

in various verbal and pictorial forms, the best known being slogans which are used repeatedly, sometimes for years, on behalf of a throng of nationally advertised products and services. Perhaps the oldest of these still actively used is P. T. Barnum's "The Greatest Show on Earth." One might call it the king of them all, which would be puffing about puffing.

He then furnishes us with a lengthy list of one-line puffs, from which the following have been selected:

"The World's Greatest Newspaper" (*Chicago Tribune*)
"King of beers" (Budweiser)
"You can be sure if it's Westinghouse"
"State Farm is all you need to know about insurance"

"I started smoking when I was a kid following these broncobusters," says Julian. "I thought that to be a man you had to have a cigarette in your mouth. It took me years to discover that all I got out of it was lung cancer. I'm going to die a young man." (He lived only a few months after the interview.)

Emphysema victim John Holmes, the man with the oxygen tank on his horse, tells what it's like to periodically gasp for breath. "It's hard to describe . . . it feels as if someone has their fingers down in my chest." Another man interviewed, Harold Lee, had only a few months to live, and you can see it in his stubbled, emaciated face.

Death in the West was shown only once, from London, to an audience of some 12 million TV viewers, in September 1976. It was high noon for Philip Morris, and the company walked in with guns blazing. Philip Morris promptly sued Thames Television and then got a court order preventing the film from being shown until its suit could be heard. . . .

Before the injunction, the American Cancer Society was eager to use the smoking program, and *60 Minutes* was negotiating to buy it from Thames TV. Officials at *60 Minutes* had seen a print of the film and were enthusiastic about using part of it on the air. "But then," explains the show's senior producer, Palmer Williams, "the people from Philip Morris—and I don't know how—heard we were interested. They came over here right away and wanted to know why. The very next day, out came this Queen's Bench Warrant or whatever the hell it was, barring Thames TV from selling the film anywhere in the world. So we couldn't get it."

Today, the film remains locked in a London vault, headed off at the pass.

Adam Hochschild, in *Mother Jones* (January 1979).
Reprinted by permission of *Mother Jones* magazine.

Compare this with the Marlboro ad on page 209.

"We try harder" (Avis)
"Toshiba—in touch with tomorrow"
"You can't get any closer" (Norelco)
"Allied Van Lines—We move families, not just furniture"
"With a name like Smucker's, it has to be good"
"Georgia, the unspoiled"
"Live better electrically" (Edison Electric Institute)
"Come to where the flavor is" (Marlboro)
"Breakfast of Champions" (Wheaties)
"Every kid in America loves Jello brand gelatin"
"Prudential has the strength of Gibraltar."

Preston then goes on to list several examples of puffery consisting entirely of names—"Wonder Bread" and "Super Shell" being two examples.

The law allows puffery because of an interesting line of reasoning, plus a good deal of fudging. It might be supposed that the law should prohibit most puffery in a general prohibition against false statements. But this would be a mistake. Truth or falsity is not the issue. *Deceptiveness* is. We don't want to forbid all false claims or even allow all true ones, for two reasons. First, a literally true claim may imply a false one. For example, a Bayer aspirin commercial pictured an announcer holding a bottle of Bayer aspirin while stating the truth that doctors recommend aspirin for pain relief, thus implying the falsehood that doctors recommend Bayer's aspirin. And, second, a literally false statement is not deceptive if hardly anyone takes it to be true. Here is Preston's example:

> The representation that you'll have a tiger in your tank when you use Esso (now Exxon) gasoline illustrates a kind of falsity which is not deceptive. There's no tiger, but regulators have never found anyone who expected a tiger. There was no disappointment and therefore no injurious deception, even though there was falsity.

For Incurable Optimists

A reader from Massachusetts sent us a newspaper ad from the state Lottery Commission, stating "There's a good chance you could win the Numbers Game today. Just ask the 12,000 people who won yesterday."

There's more: ". . . the only thing that's hard to do is lose. When this many people win, how can you lose?"

We called the Massachusetts Lottery Commission and asked about the odds. It seems that a four-digit number is picked every day. According to the Commission spokesman, if you bet on only one digit, the odds of winning are 10 to 1 and the payoff averages about 7 to 1; if you bet on all four digits, the odds are 10,000 to 1, and the payoff averages 5000 or 6000 to 1.

How can you lose? Easy.

—*Consumer Reports* (February 1987)

So regulators are supposed to work on the theory that it is *deceptive* advertising that should be forbidden, not false advertising. So far, so good. Now comes the fudging. It has been decided in general, as a result of actual cases, that most puffery is not illegal because it is not *deceptive* (although there have been a few cases of successful prosecution for puffery, perhaps the best known being against Geri-

---

Advertisements for food and labels on food packages contain more than their share of gimmicky language. Here are several examples:

Nabisco 100% Bran advertises that it is "flavored with two naturally sweet fruit juices," suggesting it is better than some other cereals that contain sugar. But they didn't say "flavored *only* with two naturally sweet fruit juices," and in fact list sugar as one of the ingredients.

Speaking of Nabisco, Nabisco Premium Crackers are advertised as

Crispier, Tastier, Premiumier

(Premiumier?)

Alpha Beta supermarkets advertise their "ultra pasteurized whipping cream" (but they don't tell us what that "ultra" is all about).

The tops on some Quaker Oats cereal boxes state:

FREE
COOKIE TIN
WITH 2 PROOFS OF
PURCHASE AND 75¢

But nothing that costs 75¢ is free, not to mention those proofs of purchase.

Keebler's *Tato Skins* say on the front of the package that they are made with REAL POTATO SKINS. Looking at the list of ingredients on the back, we find "DEHYDRATED POTATOES, POTATO STARCH, VEGETABLE SHORTENING (partially hydrogenated soybean oil, with TBHQ to preserve freshness), CORN SUGAR, NON-FAT MILK, SALT and [finally!] dehydrated POTATO PEEL," meaning that there is more salt than real potato skin in Keebler *Tato Skins*. On the back of the package, it says:

MADE WITH REAL
POTATO SKINS

The Keebler elves have created a crunchy chip for people who love baked potatoes—skins n' all. *Tato Skin*®! . . . made with real potatoes and real potato skins.

tol). But, of course, most puffery *is* deceptive—that's the point of it. If it weren't, it wouldn't be effective in getting people to buy products; it wouldn't be one of the main ingredients in so many successful ads. For instance, the Esso ad just mentioned implied that their gas is peppier, or somehow better, than other brands, which is false and deceptive.

The moral is that we can't count on the government to protect us from deceptive advertising—we have to learn to protect ourselves.

Ads Often Use Meaningless Jargon or Deceptive Humor

As language is used with less and less precision, it comes closer and closer to being meaningless noise or jargon (jargon fools us because it often sounds so sensible). Ads, of course, contain lots of examples, in some of which their general mindless-

---

Advertising is part of a modern package that is transforming human life, for good or evil. One of the evils is an increase in the number of essentially similar products available, taking away shelf space from genuinely different products, so that meaningful choice is reduced. Here are some excerpts from a well-researched, first-rate article on how beer and other products are advertised:

Market-Shelf Proliferation—Public Pays

Market segmentation, brand proliferation and advertising intensification—all part of the same marketing strategy aimed at increasing market share and profits—comprise the dominant form of competition in most consumer packaged goods categories. Price competition is passé. Manufacturers realize that if one producer cuts prices, competitors will be forced to follow, and this will hurt the profits of all without giving the initial price-cutter any lasting advantage. Producers seldom cut the price even of a failing brand, preferring to let it die and to replace it with a new full-priced brand. [This obviously is less true in hard times than in good, since price appeals are more effective in hard times.]

The FTC's seven-year-old antitrust suit against the largest cereal producers, Kellogg, General Mills, and General Foods, charges that they have used the proliferation and heavy promotion of . . . basically similar cereals to inflate prices and profits artificially. The cereal companies also are charged with discouraging new competition by making the pieces of the cereal market so small and costly to acquire that outsiders do not find entry attractive.

As some alarmed businessmen have pointed out, the FTC's test case against brand proliferation in breakfast cereals can be applied to nearly all consumer packaged goods, from cigarettes to chewing gum, from shampoo to soft drinks. In nearly every product category, the use of brand proliferation to maintain or increase market share has the effect, if not always the intent, of

ness is masked by a kernel of sense. But what does it *mean*, really, to say that a brand of detergent gets clothes "whiter than white" or "beyond white"? What does an ad ask you to do when it advises you to "recreate yourself"? These appeals use language in a jargony, almost meaningless way, a way designed not to *inform* but to play on emotions.

In addition to jargon, ads often soften the pitch by using humor (especially plays on words—puns) to mask weak or ambiguous appeals. A full-page Eastern Airlines ad centered around the headline statement: "It is now within your means to live beyond your means. At least for a weekend." Stripped of ambiguity and humor, the ad's claim fizzles down to simply: "Fly now—pay later." Or, in other words, Eastern will extend you credit—if you're a reasonable risk, of course. If they thought it was really beyond your means, Eastern obviously wouldn't extend credit.

---

pushing up prices, increasing profits for those most adept at playing the game, discouraging competition, and in some cases even reducing meaningful product variety and innovation.

Although it has yet to run afoul of the FTC for proliferation, the generally acknowledged master at churning out essentially similar brands and using them to plug market holes and preempt shelf space is Procter & Gamble. Its multiple brand entries in dozens of food, toiletry and household products make it the market share leader or contender in just about every category it's in.

"Isn't free enterprise wonderful?" a Procter & Gamble public relations man says of the multiplicity. Yes, indeed. But while any enterprising individual is free to make soap—it can be done at home—trying to sell it nationally in competition with a marketing giant that spends half a billion dollars a year on U.S. advertising seems a freedom without meaning to all but a handful of similarly huge corporations.

Manufacturing efficiency, often reduced by the shorter production runs associated with multiple brands, is less important in giving Procter & Gamble and other large packaged goods manufacturers an edge over small competitors than economies of scale in marketing.

The main reason that consumer packaged goods industries are becoming more oligopolistic is that market fragmentation and the soaring costs of new product development and promotion are deterring new entrants. Most would-be entrants simply cannot afford the huge advertising outlays required to penetrate the existing noise level and break down loyalties to entrenched brands. Nor can they borrow the capital required, because lenders know they can't recover tangible assets from an unprofitable investment in advertising the way they can from an unprofitable investment in plant and machinery.

A. Kent MacDougall, in the *Los Angeles Times* (May 27, 1979).
Copyright 1979, Los Angeles Times. Reprinted by permission.

All of us come from someplace else.

Just once, you should walk down the same street your great-grandfather walked.

Picture this if you will.

A man who's spent all his life in the United States gets on a plane, crosses a great ocean, lands.

He walks the same streets his family walked centuries ago.

He sees his name, which is rare in America, filling three pages in a phone book.

He speaks haltingly the language he wishes he had learned better as a child.

As America's airline to the world, Pan Am does a lot of things.

We help business travelers make meetings on the other side of the world. Our planes take goods to and from six continents. We take vacationers just about anywhere they want to go.

But nothing we do seems to have as much meaning as when we help somebody discover the second heritage that every American has.

PAN AM.
America's airline to the world.

See your travel agent.

Courtesy of Pan American World Airways, Inc.

Advertising tends to concentrate on marginal needs, desires, and fears at the expense of many more important ones. Indeed, a frequently heard charge against advertising is that it increases the already strong tendency of people in industrial countries to become preoccupied with the buying and consumption of goods. (Note the humorous bumper sticker "When the going gets tough, the tough go shopping.) Occasionally, however, an ad comes along that reminds us of what (for most of us) are much more important values, even though we tend to forget them in the hustle and bustle of everyday life. This Pan Am ad is one of those rare ads that tend to push us in the right direction. Yes! If we can afford it (and more of us could if we spent less on lesser needs), just once, we should walk down the same street our great-grandfather walked.

Exercise 8-1

Here are several ad snippets (usually including the main ad ploy). In each case, state: (1) whether the ad, if true, would provide a good reason for buying the product; (2) whether the ad contains questionable claims, and, if so, which claims are doubtful *and why*; (3) which, if any, of the devices employed were discussed in this (or some other) chapter (explain); and (4) which, if any, of the ads use emotive language unfairly (that is, so as to con).

1. *Rolaids television commercial, showing a Rolaids user rejecting another brand:* Rolaids active ingredient—medically recognized safe and effective.

2. *Chevron ad showing a hand clasping an American Express card:* Now You Can Express Yourself at Chevron. *Then, in smaller print:* Your American Express Card is now welcome at over 9,000 Chevron stations. . . .

*3. *Photo of young woman in bathing suit riding some sort of aquamobile through the water:* VANTAGE. Performance Counts. The thrill of real cigarette taste in a low tar.

*4. *Photo of four beautiful young women:* The most unforgettable women in the world wear REVLON.

5. Take my "Hundred Dollar Knife," yours for only $4.99.

6. The ingredient in Anacin *is* doctors' number one choice.

*7. Emeralds. $5 apiece. (This is not a misprint.)

*8. Clorets has Actizol.

9. *Robert Morley, in a British Airways ad:* "If I didn't live in Britain, I'd take these tours myself."

10. *Sign on Highland Park, Illinois, retail establishment:* 100% Pre-Driven Cars.

11. I switched from sugar to Sweet 'n Low because I care.

12. *Sign on Royal Trust Bank in Vancouver, B.C.:* Trust Royal Trust.

13. *Ad for the new Olympic Towers Apartments:* A landmark ahead of its time.

14. *Soup Starter commercial:* It's so easy, I'll feel guilty. . . . But I'll get over it.

15. Just as you can depend on the sun to rise, you can count on Metropolitan [Life Insurance Co.].

16. *Ad for Calvert Gin:* Dry, Drier, Driest, Crisp.

17. *Greyhound Bus ad:* Say Hello to America. Say Hello to a Good Buy.

18. *Mail ad:* Special collector's edition. Priceless recordings. $6.98 per album.

19. *Man speaking:* My boss was right [that I should use Sinutab]. That's why she's the boss [photo of smiling woman on screen].

20. Penthouse *ad*: Statistics show 100 percent of the readers of the biggest selling men's magazine on the newsstands [*Penthouse*, of course] . . . wear clothes.

21. Read *Time*—You'll understand.

22. When E. F. Hutton talks—people listen.

23. Nothing beats a great pair of L'Eggs.

24. Help keep America beautiful. Wear Underalls.

*25. (*In this case, here's the whole ad*—the Steinway ad on the next page.)

26. You're in the Pepsi generation.

*27. How'd you do it [get Kleenex even softer]? We've got it down to a science.

28. Some of New York's winningest players are playing at OTB [Off Track Betting—the video shows star athletes Walt Frazier and Sam Huff].

29. *Ad depicting a rich elderly gentleman talking to another one between their palatial homes:* "I was wondering if I could possibly borrow a cup of Johnny Walker Black Label."

30. Dodge trucks are ram tough.

31. *Beginning of a form letter from Teachers Insurance and Annuity Association of America (TIAA):* It simply wouldn't be true to say, "Howard Kahane [alias, Alfred Hitchcock] . . . If you own a TIAA life insurance policy you'll live longer." But it is a fact, nonetheless, that persons insured by TIAA do enjoy longer lifetimes, on the average, than persons insured by commercial insurance companies that serve the general public. Lower mortality rates are an important reason why TIAA policies cost less.

Exercise 8-2

Critically evaluate the following paraphrase of key arguments in a Vantage ad (which appeared in many magazines in 1979).[9] The question addressed in the ad is whether people should smoke cigarettes:

Whatever the arguments, people do smoke, and will continue to. The more relevant question is thus what smokers should do. Critics could rec-

---

[9]R. J. Reynolds Industries (which also makes Winstons, Camels, Salems, and several other brands) refused permission to reprint the Vantage ad verbatim on the grounds that it is the policy of R. J. Reynolds not to do anything that might be construed as encouraging smoking among the young, pointing out that they do not advertise or promote on campuses, where *Logic and Contemporary Rhetoric* is primarily used. (They also refused permission to reprint from their letter of refusal.) No other advertiser has ever refused permission to reprint an ad in any of the five editions of this book, including Philip Morris (Marlboro's) and The Tobacco Institute. (You might want to critically evaluate Reynolds's reason for refusing to grant permission.)

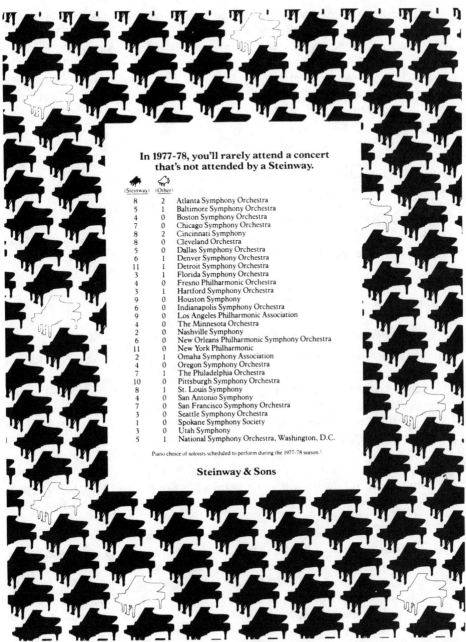

In 1977-78, you'll rarely attend a concert that's not attended by a Steinway.

(Steinway)	(Other)	
8	2	Atlanta Symphony Orchestra
5	1	Baltimore Symphony Orchestra
4	0	Boston Symphony Orchestra
7	0	Chicago Symphony Orchestra
8	2	Cincinnati Symphony
8	0	Cleveland Orchestra
5	0	Dallas Symphony Orchestra
6	1	Denver Symphony Orchestra
11	1	Detroit Symphony Orchestra
3	1	Florida Symphony Orchestra
4	0	Fresno Philharmonic Orchestra
3	1	Hartford Symphony Orchestra
9	0	Houston Symphony
6	0	Indianapolis Symphony Orchestra
9	0	Los Angeles Philharmonic Association
4	0	The Minnesota Orchestra
2	0	Nashville Symphony
6	0	New Orleans Philharmonic Symphony Orchestra
11	0	New York Philharmonic
2	1	Omaha Symphony Association
4	0	Oregon Symphony Orchestra
7	1	The Philadelphia Orchestra
10	0	Pittsburgh Symphony Orchestra
8	1	St. Louis Symphony
4	0	San Antonio Symphony
7	0	San Francisco Symphony Orchestra
3	0	Seattle Symphony Orchestra
1	0	Spokane Symphony Society
3	0	Utah Symphony
5	1	National Symphony Orchestra, Washington, D.C.

Piano choice of soloists scheduled to perform during the 1977-78 season.)

Steinway & Sons

Reprinted by permission of Steinway & Sons.

ommend that those who want to continue smoking but are worried about nicotine or tar could switch to a low-nicotine, low-tar cigarette, such as Vantage. Vantage isn't lowest in tar or nicotine, but reducing them further would very likely compromise taste. We're not going to argue about whether you should continue smoking—the fact is that you do smoke. To reduce nicotine and tar, consider Vantage Menthol cigarettes (11 mg tar, 0.7 mg nicotine per cigarette).

Exercise 8-3

One-A-Day Plus Mineral tablets advertised that their product is more complete than several other major brands of vitamin tablets costing much more, and then went on to show that One-A-Day contains this mineral not in Brand *B*, that vitamin not in Brand *C*, and so on (thus providing evidence for the claim that their product is more complete). Would you trust this ad and switch to One-A-Day Plus Minerals, or would you figure there was probably a catch to it, and if so what catch?

Exercise 8-4

Here are two more advertisements. Check them for ad ploys and the like:

1. *From the side of a Cap'n Crunch cereal box:* THE SUGAR STORY. In considering presweetened cereals, there is no substitute for the facts: a serving of Cap'n Crunch contains 12 grams of sugar. That's about two rounded teaspoonsful, enough to make Cap'n Crunch's wholesome blend of corn and oats taste great and stay crunchy in milk. Yet a serving of Cap'n Crunch contains no more sugar than many other everyday foods. . . . [A comparison is made to one cup of canned spaghetti, half a peanut butter and jelly sandwich, one frosted "pop-up" fruit tart, and a half cup of flavored gelatin.] Served with ½ cup milk, one ounce of Cap'n Crunch provides 25% of the U.S. Recommended Daily Allowances of eight essential vitamins and minerals. . . .

2. *Headline on Monsanto chemical company ad:* Mother Nature is lucky her products don't need labels. [And then, below a picture of an orange with a long, fine print list of its ingredients:] All foods, even natural ones, are made up of chemicals. But natural foods don't have to list their ingredients. So it's often assumed they're chemical free. In fact, the ordinary orange is a miniature chemical factory. And the good old potato contains arsenic among its more than 150 ingredients. This doesn't mean natural foods are dangerous. If they were, they wouldn't be on the market. The same is true for man-made foods. All man-made foods are tested for safety. And they often provide more nutrition, at lower cost, than natural foods. They even use many of the same chemical ingredients. So you see, there really isn't much difference between foods made by Mother Nature and those made by man. What's artificial is the line drawn between them. Monsanto. Without chemicals, life itself would be impossible.

Exercise 8-5

Find two or more ads for the same product in different publications that are tailored to different audiences, and explain how it's done. *Example:* The Virginia Slims ads containing a foxy white or black lady, depending on the expected audience.

3. Selling the Candidate: Political Rhetoric as PR

By now, just about everyone knows that political candidates are marketed pretty much like breakfast foods or laundry detergents.[10] And that might be all right if the appeals in breakfast food and detergent advertising were rational. But they aren't, a fact we have been taking pains to illustrate.

In recent years, radio and then television have transformed the political process. A candidate standing in front of a camera can influence more voters in one 30-second spot than candidates used to reach in a whole campaign. The result is a decline in the use of billboards, lawn signs, posters, newspaper ads, Fourth of July hoopla, and whistle-stop campaigns (but not in direct mail appeals). Television wins or loses most political campaigns.

The chief political ad device on television is the spot commercial, which generally runs from 30 to 60 seconds. It is almost impossible to say anything that is truly informative on any controversial topic in 60 seconds or less.

The first presidential campaign in which television ads played an important role was the 1952 Eisenhower-Stevenson campaign. In that campaign, General Eisenhower would read from letters received from "citizens" asking questions that Eisenhower then "answered." Here is an example:

> *Citizen:* Mr. Eisenhower, what about the high cost of living?
> *General Eisenhower:* My wife Mamie worries about the same thing. I tell her it's our job to change that on November 14th.[11]

The appeal here is to Eisenhower the father figure, who will set things right just as daddy used to. (Appeal to a father figure may well be the most effective version of *appeal to authority.*) You don't have to know *how* papa fixes things, and you didn't have to know how Eisenhower was going to reduce prices. (He didn't, of course, but that's hindsight.) All you had to know was that if you voted for him, he would be on the job after the election doing something about the high cost of living.

This Eisenhower example illustrates the fact that in presidential campaigns, at least, *identification* will win every time *if* you've got the sort of candidate people can identify with. Someone like John Kennedy, who had such tremendous charis-

---

[10]Except that laws regulating deceptive advertising don't apply to political rhetoric. The First Amendment to the Constitution prohibits restrictions on free speech.

[11]David Ogilvy, *Confessions of an Advertising Man,* p. 159. Ogilvy quotes Eisenhower as moaning between television takes, "To think an old soldier should come to this." Notice again that the ploy used is to bring up a strong desire (for lower prices) and tie the product (candidate) to the satisfaction of that desire without giving a single "reason why" the product will satisfy it.

ma, illustrates this. But Eisenhower, the great father figure, would be hard for anyone to beat. (On TV, Walter Cronkite was hard to beat for the same reason.)

Richard Nixon, on the other hand, always was handicapped by an image problem. ("Would you buy a used car from this man?") So he had to work much harder than most on his image. (In a TV interview with Theodore White, he was quoted as saying, "The main thing is to get a good picture, where you're not wiping your brow," which he then demonstrated by wiping his upper lip.)

In December 1980, the *Washington Post* gave awards to several spots that had run during 1980, including one to Ronald Reagan for the "Best Performance in a Leading Role. . . ." It gave poor old Jimmy Carter what it called the "League of Women Voter's Award for Responsible but Dull Political Advertising":

> This one is a perfect example of the shortcomings of political advertising designed to appeal to the prejudices of good-government types who hate campaign razzle-dazzle. It shows Carter, in a red-white-and-blue tie, sitting in the Oval Office speaking with very little vocal inflection and looking straight at the camera. He's talking issues just like Adlai Stevenson did in the 1950s. That's what we all think candidates should do. It's deadly dull.
>
> After watching the expressionless Carter say, "On the economy, we've taken prudent steps to control both inflation and unemployment. . . . Present trends indicate that we've been on the right track," how much of the audience stayed riveted to its sets?

A Chinese View of Advertising

Hu Yun Huan, an English language specialist from China, spent the last year teaching in a private high school in Boston. When asked about American television, he commented:

> The advertisements are pretty fantastic. Sometimes, I admire these advertisement makers. How can they imagine to make propaganda this way?
>
> In China, the process of changing ideas reminds me very much of the television advertisements. The businessman doesn't force you to buy anything. But he gives you propaganda for his product. By and by, you believe you need this kind of thing.
>
> Now, people talk about mind control in China. Actually, you are being educated to make you believe what is good and what is evil. You are not controlled any more than the businessman controls the consumer.
>
> —*New York Times* (September 6, 1981). Reprinted in the *Quarterly Review of Doublespeak* (November 1981).

The *Harper's* magazine article[12] from which the following two spots are taken succinctly explained a serious consequence of the use of TV spots, namely

> the way they encourage politicians to follow their constituencies rather than lead them. All political ads are based almost entirely on the results of polling, and they stress only those points that the pollsters tell the admen will evoke a response from the voters. So the ads tend to appeal to special-interest groups in the most chicken-hearted way.

Harper's is certainly right about the consequences of the use of TV spots. But is it chicken for politicians to want to *win*? Does the fault rest on the shoulders of the politicians or we the people who allow ourselves to be taken in?

Harper's gave its "Tylenol Triple Seal Award for the Best Repackaged Politician" to the makers of a spot for Tom Hayden of California:

> Hayden's problem was his image as a leftover 1960's student radical who had made a propitious marriage [to Jane Fonda]. In the ad, Mrs. Hayden, a pert housewife [!], bids Tom and their son farewell. Tom and son drive off to school. Weirdos carrying picket signs confront them. They walk on. "I'm not the same angry young man I was in the 1960's," says Hayden in the voiceover. "I've changed. But I still care about people."

Harper's "Common Cause Medal of Honor for Most Substantive Advertisement" of 1982 went to the makers of a spot for Jerry Springer, of Ohio:

> Here Springer faces the camera squarely and talks for thirty seconds about taxes, ending with the single most honest remark in any political ad [in 1982]: "But if there's still a deficit and you still want potholes filled and decent schools and more jobs, understand, you're talking state income tax. You can't have it both ways." Springer lost big.

Think about that ad the next time you criticize a successful politician for being gutless and telling the voters the lies they want to hear.

The one exception to the "tell them what they want to hear" rule of political rhetoric occurs when an elected official has to tell the people the truth "in the line of duty" (the extreme case being when the nation is threatened from without). In these cases, people want to close ranks against the common foe or to solve the common problem. The trouble is that politicians know it's relatively easy to get the electorate to *think* a crisis is at hand and to whip up public opinion; a classic case was Senator Joseph McCarthy in the early 1950s, and a more disputed one is the "missile gap" various politicians have been shouting about since the early 1960s. The incumbent gains even from minor or symbolic threats to public safety, as Ronald Reagan knew very well when he stepped in front of the cameras in 1983 and,

---

[12]Nicholas Lemann, Barney Frank's Mother—And 500 Postmen." Copyright © 1983 by *Harper's* magazine. All rights reserved. Reprinted from the April 1983 issue by special permission.

wiping a smile from his face, announced in grave tones his feigned outrage at the bombing of the U.S. embassy in Beirut. (Do you think Reagan had PR in mind when he invaded Grenada a few days later?)

Perhaps the most famous of all political TV commercials is the 1964 *Daisy/ Girl/Peace* one-minute spot, which was run as a paid commercial only once but received so much comment that it was rebroadcast several times as a news item.[13]

The spot starts showing a very young girl picking petals from a daisy while counting "1, 2, 3, 4, 5, 7, 6, 6, 8, 9, 9," at which point there is the voice-over of a man counting "10, 9, 8, 7, 6, 5, 4, 3, 2, 1, 0" followed by the blast on an atomic bomb on the screen and the voice-over of President Lyndon Johnson saying "These are the stakes—to make a world in which all of God's children can live— or to go into the dark. We must either love each other or we must die." Then another voice-over: "Vote President Johnson on November 3. The stakes are too high for you to stay home." The point of this spot was to portray President Johnson as a responsible peace candidate in contrast to his opponent, Senator Barry Goldwater, who by inuendo was portrayed as too willing to push the button.

Is it an accident that this best known of all political spots is also one of the most vicious, nasty, and unfair?

One of Hubert Humphrey's 1968 spots ran a close second for nastiness. It played on the fact that Nixon had chosen as his running mate a man who was almost unknown outside of his home state of Maryland, a man who happened to have the unusual name "Agnew." Democrats at the time often bucked up their sagging spirits by asking each other, "Spiro who?" So Humphrey's television advertising geniuses concocted a television spot consisting of almost a minute of laughter, with a voice saying, "Agnew for vice-president?" and at the end of the video reading, "This would be funny if it weren't so serious. . . ." All of which amounted to nothing other than a vicious *ad hominem* argument against Spiro Agnew.

The only important campaign device other than television (and radio) is use of the U.S. mails. Campaigning by mail begins the day after taking office for most elected officials and gives an incumbent a large head start over potential

---

I'm not an old hand at politics. But I am now seasoned enough to have learned that the hardest thing about any political campaign is how to win without proving that you are unworthy of winning.

—Adlai Stevenson (1956)

What one (losing) candidate learned from two runs at the presidency.

---

[13]It was erroneously stated in earlier editions of this text that the spot was not rerun because of public outcry. In fact, the original plan was to run it just once. See *A Viewer's Guide*, by David Beiler, a companion pamphlet to the fascinating videotape documentary *The Classics of Political Television Advertising* (Washington, D.C. Campaigns & Elections, 1986).

opponents (one reason why we're never likely to see Congress give up its frank-ing privilege).

Of course, members of Congress aren't supposed to send out-and-out cam-paign literature free of charge, but they are allowed to frank letters containing questionnaires and, in particular, answers to letters from constituents. A *Washing-ton Monthly* article ("Mail Fraud on Capitol Hill," by Mark Feldstein, October 1979) argued quite plausibly that at least one United States senator, Milton R. Young of North Dakota, owed his repeated reelection to his considerable ability in talking out of both sides of his mouth when answering letters from constituents. (It can't be because of accomplishments or notoriety—Milton who? Yet he was reelected regular-ly, starting in 1945, until his retirement in 1980.)

The article described his (and some other senators') responses to twin letters, one favoring and one opposing abortion. (Of course, no senator could possibly compose an individual reply to each letter received; every senator thus uses stan-dard replies, classified by issue and by position taken on an issue.) Here is the main part of Young's standard reply to antiabortion letters:

> I thought you would be pleased to know that I have strongly supported the position you take. I have been a co-sponsor of a resolution in the Senate proposing a Human Life Amendment since the Supreme Court issued its decision liberalizing abortion almost six years ago.

I participated in preparations for nearly forty of John F. Kennedy's [extremely effective] news conferences and can recall only two questions that had not been anticipated and discussed; neither was very important.

—Robert Manning, editor of *The Atlantic* magazine,
quoted in *The Atlantic* (February 1977)

Running for president is a long-term operation. If you're already president, the trick is to take advantage of the office in your campaign to win reelection. News conferences are scheduled primarily as an opportunity for the president to display presidential capabilities by being on top of whatever reporters are likely to ask—an easy task since what they ask is pretty much predictable, as Manning indicates. (Ronald Reagan is an exception, because of his tendency to disobey instructions and put his foot firmly in his mouth.) Imagery is so important in politics that a president is forced to integrate his plans for doing his job as president with his plans to get reelected. Jimmy Carter's handling of the Begin-Sadat Camp David agreement is a good example. The whole thing was planned so that the three leaders would sign on the dotted line and congratulate each other on national television programs which were watched by a very large international audience. Such exposure is free, of course, which is one reason it's so hard to beat an incumbent. (But media coverage of the Iranian hostage crisis, especially given the "incomplete success" of the rescue attempt, may have shot Carter down in 1980.)

But here's the sort of thing you got in reply to a pro-abortion letter:

> I appreciated hearing from you and receiving your views on this matter,
> . . . I agree with you that a woman should have a right to decide whether
> or not she wants an abortion.

All politicians have to do this sort of thing.

While TV is the principle ring in which political battles are fought these days, candidates still have to conduct grueling "grass roots" campaigns and thus be on almost continual public display for several months. The main point of this, of course, is to get a minute or two on TV evening news programs. This marathon campaigning doesn't leave much time for thinking about what to say. So a candidate is likely to have the same set items, which are juggled to fit each particular audience. Here, for example, is Jimmy Carter in his famous 1976 *Playboy* interview (in which he admitted he lusted in his heart after other women). The question was whether he didn't feel numb delivering the same speech over and over:

> Sometimes. But I generally have tried to change the order of the speech and emphasize different things. Sometimes I abbreviate and sometimes I elaborate. Of 20 different parts of a speech, I might take seven or eight and change them around. It depends on the audience—black people, Jewish people, chicanos—and that gives me the ability to make speeches that aren't boring to myself.

True. But it also gave him the chance to tell each group what it wanted to hear that other groups might not have wanted to hear.

Another Carter answer was revealing in what it said about reporters who cover presidential campaigns:

> The local media are interested, all right, but the national news media have absolutely no interest in issues *at all*. . . . The traveling press have a zero interest in any issue unless it's a matter of making a mistake. What they're looking for is a 47-second argument between me and another candidate or something like that. There's nobody in the back of this [campaign] plane who would ask an issue question unless he thought he could trick me into some crazy statement.

Reporters want confrontation and controversy because that's what gets viewer or reader attention. Carter, naïve or idealistic as he was, wanted to talk about the issues, but was rarely able to. So did Gary Hart in 1987.

Speaking of issues, they, too, can be advertised successfully by the standard Madison Avenue techniques. Here is Richard E. Smith, U.S. Corps of Engineers area engineer for the Tennessee-Tombigbee Waterway boondoggle, on the corp's "public posture on costs": "I would recommend we hold the federal cost under $1 billion. Say $975,000,000. Considering the size of the estimate, $975 million is no less accurate than $1 billion and it has less emotional impact." Does this remind you of how businesses will price an item at $49.50 instead of $50 even? (At least businesses don't jack up the price as you're about to hand over the money. In the case of the federal government, the price—called an "estimate"—is usually raised several times.)

Political image building is not restricted to candidates for office. J. Edgar Hoover, the first director of the FBI, was a master image builder, both for himself and for his baby, the FBI. The FBI's "Ten Most Wanted" list is one of the great image ploys of all time (no puffery here). In order to gain maximum publicity for the bureau, the list has had to mirror the interests of the times. Thus, in the 1950s, it ran to bank robbers and auto thieves, leaving organized mobsters and such types alone. As the 1960s wore on, left-wing radicals like Angela Davis, Bernadine Dorn, and H. Rap Brown were featured. But by the late 1970s, that was passé, and we had accused sex killers like Ted Bundy and alleged porno kings like Michael G. Davis, along with an occasional big-time mobster. The Ten Most Wanted list was never an important part of the bureau's crime-fighting equipment, but until recently it was great media hype.

Political rhetoric is not much different from other advertising when you get right down to it. The point is to manipulate the public to buy the product. For instance, vagueness and ambiguity are used, just as elsewhere—leading Jerry Brown to remark during his 1976 California gubernatorial campaign, "In this business, a little vagueness goes a long way."

This is true in particular of the vague generalities and mom-and-apple pie clichés—used even more frequently in political rhetoric than in soap commercials. Mike Royko (in his column of August 21, 1976) marveled at this string of clichés from just the first paragraph of a Republican convention speech by then vice-presidential candidate Robert Dole: "Proud of the confidence. . . . Gratified by your trust. . . . Humbled by this new opportunity. . . . Determined to work with all my heart. . . ." Dole then topped himself with these dazzlers: "The eyes of the world are. . . . Weathered the storm of. . . . The future gleamed brightly for. . . . A long and noble chapter in. . . . Those principles upon which America was founded are. . . ."

While political debates between opposing candidates are hardly a new idea (think of the famous debates between Abraham Lincoln and Stephen Douglas),

---

About seven years ago Dialcom began working with Rep. David Emery (R-Maine), a former electronics engineer, to develop software that would allow a congressional staff to answer and file letters more quickly. Now, two-thirds of the House members pay Dialcom $1,000 a month for access to a system that allows staffers to compose letters by drawing from a bank of prewritten paragraphs relating to most political subjects in which their bosses have an interest.

The next step: computer terminals on every desk that would permit a staffer to type in a constituent's name and see a history of the constituent's correspondence. Which means a member of Congress about to talk with Joe Voter could instantly know Mr. Voter's pet peeves and prejudices.

—*Washington Post* magazine (June 6, 1982)

Psychologists are looking into political campaigns very carefully these days. So far, however, they have not succeeded in fully understanding voter psychology, and in fact are still a good deal behind the advertising geniuses in their ability to predict advertising success or failure. But they are making rapid progress. Here are some excerpts from a Time *magazine article (November 12, 1984) about the 1984 presidential contest between President Reagan and Walter Mondale:*

One woman recently told a pollster, "I liked how decisive President Reagan was during that crisis. I forget which one." According to some political scientists and psychologists, comments like this are not just slip-ups among political innocents but glimpses into the process by which Americans elect their Presidents: facts, issues and party affiliation are becoming less important than voters' emotions. Observes Yale Psychologist Robert Abelson: "Feelings are three or four times as important as issues or party identification. . . ."

Abelson believes there are four crucial emotions: if a candidate can push the hope and pride buttons and avoid touching the anger and fear buttons, he will probably win. "Politics is theater," he says. "We just don't know yet exactly where the public gets its impressions—from facial expressions, style of delivery, incidents that signify decisiveness." Indeed, some researchers have found that voters develop strong opinions about candidates simply by watching them on television without hearing what they are saying. . . .

One implication of the new research is that a presidential candidate will induce the right emotions if he acts decisively, regardless of what action he takes. President Reagan helped himself considerably by ordering the inva-

the Nixon-Kennedy TV debates of 1960 set an example that now looks to become a part of all presidential campaigns. (The fact that an enormously popular sitting president, Ronald Reagan, debated candidate Walter Mondale in the 1984 campaign pretty much assured that these debates will become an institution.)

No doubt this is all to the good—one more chance for voters to hear the candidates on the issues. The trouble, of course, is that viewer responses to these TV debates don't reflect who "win" the debates but rather whose personality comes across better on TV. The 1984 debates are a good example because, on any objective scale, Walter Mondale easily won; unfortunately, the viewing audience didn't see it that way and rejected Mondale's (later justified) true claim that Reagan didn't have much of an idea of what he was talking about.[14]

---

[14]The media, following the lead of nose-to-ground politicians, tended to go along with the mass of voters, in particular, going soft on "correcting data" that would have confirmed Reagan's ignorance on important matters. See Chapter 9 for more on why the media tends

sion of Grenada and breaking the air-traffic controllers' strike. Reagan's score on leadership is so high, says one source who has seen some of the data, that it swamps all other factors. This made it difficult for Mondale to impress voters with his charges that the President makes mistakes and is ignorant of the facts. "The public knows Reagan isn't knowledgeable, and it doesn't care," said the source.

Abelson thinks Mondale's toughest challenge was to establish himself as a leader, not by arguing issues but by taking some decisive step to display leadership. "Any dramatic act would have helped," says Abelson. "It sounds silly, but he could have walked into a bar and picked a fight with a drunken lumberjack. If he had got mad at how his campaign was going and shook up his staff—any show of strength or decisiveness, even with a superficial relation to the issues, would have helped."

. . . A team of researchers at Dartmouth reports that facial expressions of candidates may be more important than any of the issues they discuss. Says Denis Sullivan, a political scientist who worked on the study: "The evidence is that people are very quick to make attributions of character from facial expressions on the basis of very little evidence. . . ."

Another finding is that with angry expressions a candidate is unlikely to alienate his supporters, but with happy or neutral ones he reaches out to opponents and moderates. "The upshot of this," says Sullivan, "is that you should talk about the evil empire outside of prime time, and use prime time to say, 'We are really good guys and have good things in mind for you.' "

—"Not by Issues Alone," *Time,* (November 12, 1984).
Copyright 1984 Time, Inc. All rights reserved.
Reprinted by permission.

Of course, Reagan was a likely winner no matter what happened in the debates. But in the Nixon-Kennedy debates in 1960, the situation was much different. The election was extremely close,[15] and the debates may well have made the difference. Those who watched the debates on TV tended to think Kennedy won because he exhibited "vigor," youth, and that great charisma that is the mark of the Kennedy politicians. Nixon lost because he looked overcautious and a bit sneaky (five o'clock shadow and all that, and Nixon's TV makeup was incorrectly applied). But reading the transcripts of the debates gives one another impression altogether. It isn't at all clear that there was a winner; both candidates did pretty well. However, *reason* is not the point; image is everything. So Kennedy really did win the debates in 1960, just as Reagan did in 1980 and 1984.

---

to go along with public opinion and the various power blocks, even when it is sure that public opinion is wrong.
[15] There are still those, including this writer, who believe that the election was stolen from Nixon by vote counting chicanery in Illinois and Texas.

Two college professors, John F. Cragon and Donald C. Shields, applied marketing research techniques to political issues and wrote a mock political speech conforming to what they had learned. The speech contains "no notion of a coherent policy. It is just telling people what they want to hear. The rhetoric does not flow from any thought-out foreign policy. These are just winning phrases." Typical are the following:

"America requires a President who is experienced in diplomacy and capable of managing world stability. The international scene demands a chief executive who carries out a coherent and consistent foreign policy that can be understood and respected by allies and adversaries alike."

"Today's international scene is one in which the major powers have reached military parity. What we must do is manage and stabilize our relationships with each other and maintain the balance of power. In a nuclear age we cannot escape the responsibility to build a safe future through wise diplomacy."

"The U.S. will continue to meet its responsibilities to its allies. However, to maintain world order, we will continue to seek and negotiate stable relationships with all nations."

"The U.S. is not a crippled giant. We are still a great economic and military power. In a showdown with communism, it will be American power that will determine the destiny of free men and women."

"The U.S. needs a President with a moral vision of promoting the welfare of mankind. America requires a leader who treats other nations with mutual respect; who promotes and encourages increased human rights and fundamental freedoms; who responds consistently in a calm, cool and reasoned manner."

"Detente means a state of affairs marked by the absence of significant tensions that could lead the U.S. to a nuclear confrontation. Detente does not mean that all differences will be resolved or that Russia no longer will attempt to expand her influence. It does mean that peaceful co-existence is the only rational alternative."

—Bob Greene, *Chicago Tribune*, (October 23, 1980). Reprinted in the *Quarterly Review of Doublespeak* (July 1981).
Used by permission of Donald C. Shields.

So they were shocked when several political candidates approached them to write speeches for them just like the mindless, computer-generated, market-tested speech they'd invented.

Summary of Chapter 8

1. Advertising is useful because it tells us about products we may want to buy. There are two basic kinds of ads. *Promise* ads promise to satisfy desires or reduce fears and usually give us "reasons why" the product will do that. *Identification* ads sell the product by getting us to identify with it (or with a company). Of course, most ads contain a combination of both promise and identification devices.

2. But advertising has its drawbacks. We have to be a bit wary:
   a. *Ads don't tell us what's wrong with the product,* thus tempting us to commit the fallacy of *suppressed evidence.*
      Example: Ads for over-the-counter nonprescription drugs that rarely tell us about possible side effects.
   b. *Ads use psychological tricks more than direct appeals to reason.*
      Example: The Lite Beer TV commercials that use identification, humor, and repetition, while giving us the quickly stale "reasons why" over and over again.
   c. *Ads are often deceptive or misleading,* in particular by making *false implications* while literally stating the truth.
      Example: The London Fog commercials that imply their raincoats are made in England.
      Note that all sorts of other devices, such as *weasel words* and *fine print qualifications* are also used.

   d. *Ads commonly use puffery.* (Note that puffery is legal.)
      Example: The *Chicago Tribune's* motto: "World's greatest newspaper."
   e. *Ads often use meaningless jargon or deceptive humor.*
      Example: Tide getting clothes "whiter than white."
   f. *Ads tempt us to reason fallaciously.*
      Example: Testimonials inviting the fallacy of *appeal to authority.*
   g. *Ads tend to twist our values* toward those values that an easily advertised product might satisfy.
      Example: Making us more concerned with buying just the right detergent or cold symptom suppressor than with the real necessities of life.

3. It's also important to realize that political candidates and policies are sold via advertising in much the same way as other "products." Identification, in fact image making in general, is the most frequently used device.
   Political campaigns nowadays are fought chiefly on television (although the mails are also important, especially to raise money). The quality of their TV spots, plus their ability to get coverage on TV news programs, wins or loses the race for most candidates. (TV debates are becoming more important.)
   Example: The Barney Frank commercial featuring his mother.

DOES THE GOVERNMENT SUPPORT THE TOBACCO FARMER?

NO, THE TOBACCO FARMER SUPPORTS THE GOVERNMENT.

Some people want to hear only one side of an argument.

That's not you, obviously—or you wouldn't be reading this.

You've heard the side of the anti-smokers—that the government is, in some way, "supporting" or "subsidizing" the tobacco farmer.

Here is the other side of that argument. And if you're not a tobacco farmer, you'll probably be surprised, maybe even pleased, to hear it.

Because the truth is the other way around: It's the tobacco farmer who's supporting the government.

There *is* a government program called the tobacco price support program. It began in 1933, and for the past 45 years it has been the single most successful farm program the government has ever had. It costs next to nothing, and it pays enormous dividends to all taxpayers.

The heart of it is a simple businesslike arrangement. The government offers the tobacco farmer what *he* needs: a guaranteed price for his crop. If commercial buyers do not meet this price, the farmer receives a government loan and surrenders his crop. And the government gets, in return, what the *government* needs: the farmer's agreement not to plant any more than the government tells him he can.

The government's interest, and the taxpayer's, is in preventing economic chaos. Without the weapon of the loan agreement, the government would be powerless to limit the production of tobacco. The results would be as predictable as any disaster can be: overplanting of the crop by big farmers with extra land and by

newcomers, a fall in the price of tobacco, a drop in the income of small farmers to the point where many would be squeezed off the land and onto welfare rolls, sharp decreases in tax collections in the 22 states that grow tobacco, widespread disruptions in the banking and commercial systems and, if you want to follow the scenario out to its grim conclusion, very likely a regional recession.

The value of the program to the government, and to the taxpayer, is thus very great. And the cost is unbelievably low. Over the entire 45 years of its operation, the total cost of the government guarantee has been less than $1¼ million a year, or roughly what the government spends otherwise every 79 seconds. This is because the program has been able to sell, at a profit, almost all the tobacco it has taken as loan collateral.

From the farmer's viewpoint, the tobacco support program might as easily, and more justly, be called a *government* support program, since it does more to support the government than it does to support him.

One fact above all others tells you the true story. For all his labors in planting, growing and harvesting his crop, the farmer receives $2.3 billion. And from the products of his labor, the government (federal, state and local) collects $6 billion in taxes.

It's enough to make even an anti-smoker, at least a fair-minded one, agree that, on balance, it's the tobacco farmer who's supporting the government. And doing it superbly.

THE TOBACCO INSTITUTE
1776 K St. N.W. Washington, D.C. 20006

Warning: The Surgeon General Has Determined That Cigarette Smoking Is Dangerous to Your Health.

Exercise 8-6

Evaluate the Tobacco Institute advertisement on the opposite page, following the instructions given for evaluating extended passages in Chapter 7. Also point out any ad ploys discussed in this chapter.

Exercise 8-7

Repeat the experiment described by Mark Feldstein in his *Washington Monthly* article (p. 225), choosing a different topic than abortion. That is, write two letters to one of your senators or representatives in Washington, one letter taking a short, strong stand on some issue, the other letter taking an equally strong but different stand (opposite, if possible) on the same issue. Compare the two replies you get and draw conclusions. (Send each letter from a different address or at different times and use different names because some members of Congress are keeping track on computers.)

Exercise 8-8

Representative Barney Frank was still in Congress as this fifth edition was going to press in 1987. (He represented the 4th Congressional district in Massachusetts.) What has been his record on Social Security? Did he keep the implied promise of his TV spot (page 198)? (This will no doubt take a bit of research.)

Exercise 8-9

Do some research and find out what candidate Ronald Reagan promised the American public he'd do in the next four years if elected in 1980, and then compare that with what in your opinion President Reagan actually accomplished in those four years. Support your research and opinions with evidence or reasons; don't pontificate or bullsling. (This is quite a difficult exercise.)

Drawing by David Levine. Copyright© 1975 NYREV, Inc.
Reprinted by permission from *The New York Review of Books*.

David Levine is one of America's foremost caricaturists. In this drawing, he pictures the television viewing audience as contented sheep being fleeced. Do you agree?

When covering the Capitol, the first thing to remember is that every government is run by liars.

      —I. F. Stone

In all TV the defeat of evil is the consequence of superior craft and power and what becomes clear is that right is on the side of the cleverest, the most powerful, and the fastest gun.

      —Jules Henry

Freedom of the press is guaranteed only to those who own one.

      —A. J. Liebling

Has any reader found perfect accuracy in the newspaper account of any event of which he himself had inside knowledge?

      —Edward Verrall Lucas

The headline of the Daily News today reads BRUNETTE STABBED TO DEATH. Underneath in lower case letters "6000 Killed in Iranian Earthquake." . . . I wonder what color hair they had.

      —Abbie Hoffman

I really look with commiseration over the great body of my fellow citizens who, reading newspapers, live and die in the belief that they have known something of what has been passing in the world in their time.

      —President Harry Truman

If you want your name spelled wrong, die.

      —Al Blanchard

9

Managing the News

Reasoning about political and social issues requires factual knowledge. That's why the success of a democratic form of government depends on a *well-informed* electorate. Unfortunately, the American mass news media (newspapers, television, mass magazines, the radio) do not adequately or accurately inform their readers and listeners. In particular, they fail to inform them of the great gulf between the way our society is supposed to work (the ideal—the "official story") and the way it actually works.

  Yet we all have to rely on the mass media for news. Those who understand how and why things get reported as they do will be better able to evaluate that reporting, better able to read between the lines, separate wheat from chaff, and not be taken in by questionable reasoning or poor coverage. They'll also understand why the mass media have to be supplemented by selectively chosen non-mass media sources.

1. The Mass Media and Money

The one overriding fact to bear in mind in trying to understand the mass media is that CBS, the *Los Angeles Times, Newsweek* magazine, and all the rest are *businesses,* intended to return a profit. They have two sets of "buyers"—their audiences (readers, viewers, listeners) and their advertisers. When they displease, annoy, or threaten either of these groups too seriously, they're likely to fail, or at least seriously reduce profits. *There is always more money in catering to both groups.*

We should expect, then, if our world view tells us businesses are run to maximize profits,[1] that media executives will shape the news so as to please their buyers. And this is just about what we find to be true.

News Selection Reflects the Interests, Opinions, and Prejudices of Its Audiences

Viewer and reader interests, opinions, and prejudices must be taken into account in reporting the news. Newspaper readers and television viewers are not captive audiences (as they were, say, in Nazi Germany and Fascist Italy, where outdoor loudspeakers blared the official line to the public). They can flick the switch or turn the page. The result is *provincialism*—news reporting that tends to reflect the interests and foibles of its audience, as world travelers often are amused (or dis-

---

It is dangerous to let the public behind the scenes. They are easily disillusioned and then they are angry with you, for it was the illusion they loved.

—W. Somerset Maugham

If the media succeed with their spectacles and grand simplifications, it is because their audiences define happiness as the state of being well and artfully deceived.

—Lewis H. Lapham (*Harper's* editor)

[On the other hand] The journalist usually has a few hours to write and the perspective of last week. Why then expect the poor fellow to revise the history of the world?

—Lewis H. Lapham

---

[1] Fortunately, small-circulation political publications tend to be exceptions. While theoretically *in business,* they rarely make a profit or pay a dividend. People "invest" in such enterprises to champion a point of view or gain an outlet for their own opinions, not to make money.

mayed) to discover. (That was the import of the Abbie Hoffman remark quoted at the beginning of the chapter.)[2]

The media cater to their audiences in all sorts of ways. For instance, they play up stories about alleged UFO citings (flying saucers and that sort of thing), often with an implication that there might actually be something to that nonsense. An example is the *U.S. News and World Report* article (February 20, 1978) titled "Is There Something to UFO's After All?" which gave the impression that reasonable people might differ on this topic. Here is a snippet giving the flavor of the whole (one-page) article:

> How many of these sightings are given much credence by UFO experts?
>
> Most can be explained. Among the objects that have been misidentified as UFO's are stars, planets, meteors, advertising planes, helicopters, balloons and even a street light.
>
> What about the others?
>
> Opinions differ sharply. Persons who advocate more research on UFO's contend that the unexplained sightings are an indication of life from other worlds visiting earth. Disbelievers argue that the phenomena either have logical explanations or are fabricated reports.

The reason for *U.S. News*'s "balanced" account of the UFO business is quite simple—large numbers of their readers would like to believe flying saucers really exist.

Jules Feiffer. Copyright 1978. Distributed by Field Newspaper Syndicate. Reprinted by permission.

Most of the U.S. media audience is white, in particular the portion with the most money to spend. The news in most papers thus gets slanted to their interests and prejudices.

---

[2]News reporting also reflects the prejudices and interests of media employees, top management, and owners. Run of the mill employees, including most reporters, tend to have the same biases as the rest of us. But owners and top brass generally see things from the point of view of the rich and powerful (with whom they associate).

A large majority of the 1,500 or so daily newspapers left in the United States carry regular horoscope columns in which oracular advice (extremely general and likely to "fit" almost anyone and any situation—"Be careful with financial matters today") is dished out to the faithful. Yet astrology has no scientific validity whatever, and the basic objections to it were raised centuries ago, a fact newspapers rarely tell their audiences. So long as astrology columns attract readers, newspapers will print them.

Similarly, so long as lots of readers are offended by certain four-letter words, the media will do their best to pretend these words don't exist, which is fair enough, given that there isn't any reason to gratuitously offend audiences. But then you should realize that your favorite ball players, or politicians, probably didn't say "shucks," "darn," or "baloney."

The need for the media to cater to their audiences also is (partly) responsible for the general *lack of proportion* in media coverage. While it's true to some extent that an event becomes as important as the media decide to make it, it's even more true that they play stories up or down depending on audience interest. This is nicely illustrated by the way the media played up the 1982–1983 Israeli "incursion" into Lebanon, while playing down the much larger and bloodier war between Iran and Iraq.[3] Or compare the vast coverage of the Iranian hostage "crisis" with the Iran-Iraq war.

The mass media also cater to their audience by means of *sensationalism,* in particular by picturing certain kinds of nasty extremes as common or even the rule. For example, *Time* magazine's cover story for April 11, 1983—"Fighting Cocaine's Grip—Millions of Users, Billions of Dollars"—started out with this extreme case, which actually fit only a handful of users:

Crashing on Cocaine

Burnt-out cases proliferate, as drug-traffic cops wage a no-win war

Phil and Rita's life shimmered like an advertisement. Indeed, to an outsider it seemed less a life than a perfect life style: tree-lined California

---

In a media-dominated world, children who insist upon the actuality of the Bermuda Triangle, the reality of pyramid power, or the accuracy of astrological projections are quick to refer to having seen it on TV, having read it in a book, or having seen it in the newspaper. This presents a problem for skeptical adults. When the media uses such terms as "Bermuda Triangle" freely, they are, in effect, creating an air of legitimacy. Logically, children conclude that there must be some truth to the matter if they see it in their local paper.

—Ray Hyman, book review in *Skeptical Inquirer* (Winter 1980–1981)

---

[3]Another reason for this great difference in coverage was the availability of motion pictures for TV news programs. For more on this and related points, see "Is TV News Too Tough—or Too Easy—on Israel?" in *TV Guide,* September 19–25, 1987.

suburban street, tasteful $150,000 home (with piano), two sunny young-
sters. Phil, 37, was a $30,000-a-year microchip sales engineer in Silicon
Valley. Rita, 34, was a $20,000-a-year bookkeeper. Like their smart,
attractive Northern California friends, Phil and Rita played tennis and
ate interesting foods and knew about wine and, starting four years ago,
sniffed coke.

And more coke. And then more. That is why several times last year
Phil stood quivering and feverish in the living room, his loaded pistol
pointed toward imaginary enemies he *knew* were lurking in the garage.
Rita, emaciated like her husband, had her own bogeymen—strangers with
X-ray vision outside the draped bedroom window—and she hid from
them in the closet. The couple's paranoia was fleetingly sliced away, of
course, as soon as they got high: they "free-based," breathing a distilled
cocaine vapor, Phil alone all night with his glass water pipe and thimble
of coke, Rita in another room with hers. In the mornings, Phil and Rita
got back together, down on all fours, scratching and picking at the carpet
for any stray grains of coke.

[Below was drawn an X ray of a man's head being blown apart (presumably by coke).]

But no doubt the most serious media distortions of truth forced on them by
public opinion concern the portrayal of well-liked elected officials. It is very risky
indeed to convey unpopular truths about, say, a popular president of the United
States in news stories where they might have serious effect. The true nature of Ronald Reagan's sleezy rhetoric was known to reporters starting in his days as governor of California; yet it was not until the Irangate scandal that the mass media
could consistently do more than hint at it. (They were permitted to do this on editorial pages, provided they pulled their punches.) Television and newspaper coverage of President Reagan and his administration changed dramatically after the
Iran-Nicaragua mess came out into the open[4] and Reagan's power had been
reduced. (Of course, even after the scandal broke, Reagan was treated with a certain respect not justified by what he had said or did about this matter, but simply
because he was, after all, still president of the United States.)

News Is Simplified for the Mass Audience

Another of the standard ways in which the news is distorted is *simplification*. On
the whole, media audiences are not sophisticated. They cannot, or at least will not,

---

Don't be afraid to make a mistake. Your readers may like it.
—William Randolf Hearst (news mogul)

Remember, son, many a good story has been ruined by over-verification.
—James Gordon Bennett (news mogul)

---

[4]See, for instance, William Boot, "Iranscam: When the Cheering Stopped," *Columbia
Journalism Review* (March/April 1987).

pay attention to complicated material (we saw the result of this in political spot commercials). The trouble is that almost all social and political issues are complicated, so that simplified accounts of events or issues must in general be distorted accounts.

Take the ongoing question of an alleged "missile gap" between the United States and the Soviet Union. By some point in the 1950s, both nations had developed gigantic nuclear missiles capable of traveling thousands of miles to their targets. Within a very few years, all sorts of politicians found it expedient (particularly at election time) to shout from the housetops about how the Russians were getting ahead of us in "nuclear capability." John Kennedy was one of the first to use this ploy, and every president since then has played with this gambit at one time or another. The media have dutifully reported their allegations, but without a convenient exposition of the complex arguments on both sides of the issue that would enable the average person to come to a rational conclusion. There have been occasional exceptions, but they have had little effect on the mass of voters. (Note, however, that there are other forces tending to oversimplify reporting on this and other issues. Some are discussed in the next few sections of this chapter.)

Organized Groups Apply Effective Pressure

The power of one person is small compared to that of an organized group. All but one advertiser withdrew its support from CBS's documentary about World War I, *The Guns of August,* after a letter-writing campaign organized by the National Rifle Association. Similarly, General Motors dropped out of the NBC mini-series *Jesus of Nazareth* in 1977 after criticism by Protestant church leaders. Even the PTA was powerful enough to pressure Sears, Roebuck into dropping sponsorship of *Charlie's Angels* (too much sex) and *Three's Company.* And no newspaper in Utah was foolish enough to run the 1979 Pulitzer Prize-winning exposé of Mormon Church power in that state.

News Selection Reflects the Interests of Advertisers

The interests of advertisers are almost as important as viewer interests in distorting the news. It could hardly be otherwise given that most media revenue, and thus profit, comes from advertisers. This is true even of newspapers, which charge for their product. Indeed, most successful big city newspapers get more than three-quarters of their revenue from advertisers. (Cable television is an exception to this, since a large part of their revenue comes from viewers.)

New York Times columnist Tom Wicker illustrated this in his book *On Press* by explaining how the power structure in Winston-Salem, North Carolina, influenced local news coverage. He concluded (not surprisingly, in a town named "Winston-Salem") that "the cigarette-cancer connection got short shrift in [the *Winston-Salem Journal*] newsroom."[5]

---

[5]Tom Wicker, *On Press* (New York: Viking Press, 1978).

News Selection Reflects the Power of Government

Government has the right and often the power to regulate business activity. It can thus harass a news source that displeases it by being strict (as it usually isn't) about the rules it sets up and the licenses it requires. Even the threat of government action has a "chilling" effect on the media as a whole, as it did in April 1987, when the Federal Communications Commission threatened to ask the Justice Department to consider criminal prosecution of station KPFK, a nonprofit Los Angeles FM station, for airing an allegedly obscene play about AIDS and gay love.

Each issue of the Columbia Journalism Review *awards "Darts and Laurels" for unusually bad or good reporting, respectively. Here are three examples:*

Laurel: to *The Philadelphia Inquirer* and reporters Frank Greve and Ellen Warren, for a two-part report (December 16, 17) detailing charges that a secret U.S. Army helicopter unit had been sent repeatedly into hostile territory in Central America to aid pro-American forces. Based on spine-tingling interviews with the widows, parents, and friends of sixteen members of the task force killed in what the government describes as "noncombat" accidents in 1983, the *Inquirer* pieces prompted immediate calls in Congress for further probes into what could prove to be a violation of the War Powers Act.

Dart: to the *Chicago Tribune,* for a curious omission in its front-page story of August 29 headlined 40 MAJOR FIRMS PAID NO INCOME TAX IN '84. Based on a study issued by the Citizens for Tax Justice titled "Corporate Taxpayers and Corporate Freeloaders," the article was accompanied by a chart which purported to compare the profits and tax rates of "the 28 largest companies" in Illinois but which, on close inspection, actually revealed the names of only twenty-seven such firms. As noted by radio commentator John Madigan on Chicago's WBBM, the missing company was Commonwealth Edison, whose chairman, like his predecessor, sits on the Tribune Company's board. (Had that particular company's name not been—as managing editor Richard Ciccone put it—"inadvertently" dropped, readers would have learned that, on 1981–84 profits of $3.6 billion, the utility had paid a federal tax of a mere .2 percent.)

Laurel: to WCCO-TV, Minneapolis, for a constructive piece of consumer news, a genre that's generally fallen into disrepair. On November 26–27, the station aired a "For Your Money" segment comparing prices at local do-it-yourself building-supply stores that showed Budget Power, one of WCCO's major advertisers, to be among the most expensive of the lot. As a result of the report, Budget Power pulled all its advertising from WCCO, adding a $140,000 loss to an already strained bottom line.

—Columbia Journalism Review. © March/April 1985;
© March/April 1987. Reprinted by permission.

Last year, 300,000 Americans were arrested for smoking an herb that Queen Victoria used regularly for menstrual cramps.

It's a fact.

The herb, of course, is *cannabis sativa*. Otherwise known as marijuana, pot, grass, hemp, boo, mary-jane, ganja—the nicknames are legion.

So are the people who smoke it.

By all reckoning, it's fast becoming the new national pastime. Twenty-six million smokers, by some accounts—lots more by others. Whatever the estimate, a staggeringly high percentage of the population become potential criminals simply by being in possession of it. And the numbers are increasing.

For years, we've been told that marijuana leads to madness, sex-crimes, hard-drug usage and even occasional warts.

Pure Victorian poppycock.

In 1894, The Indian Hemp Commission reported marijuana to be relatively harmless. A fact that has been substantiated time and again in study after study.

Including, most recently, by the President's own Commission. This report stands as an indictment of the pot laws themselves.

And that's why more and more legislators are turning on to the fact that the present marijuana laws are as archaic as dear old Victoria's code of morality. And that they must be changed. Recently, the state of Oregon did, in fact, de-criminalize marijuana. Successfully.

Other states are beginning to move in that direction. They must be encouraged.

NORML has been and is educating the legislators, working in the courts and with the lawmakers to change the laws. We're doing our best but still, we need help. Yours.

Used with permission of NORML.

Ad Censorship. *NORML marijuana ad rejected by* Time *and* Newsweek, *accepted by* Playboy. Time *and* Newsweek *readers tend to strongly oppose dope smoking.*

Government officials also manipulate the news by playing favorites among reporters, leaking only to those sources who play ball in return. Since leaks are such a large source of media news, reporters have to think twice before crossing their government informants.

Henry Kissinger was famous for his use of selective leaks to keep the media in line. So was J. Edgar Hoover. Even Jack Anderson, who (along with his assistants) does as much real digging for news as anyone, is alleged at one time to have agreed to write only "nice things" about J. Edgar Hoover in exchange for access to FBI files.

But then the media often lack the information that might incline them to buck the official government story. The 1976 swine flu program is a good example. There was no swine flu epidemic and little reason to think there would be. But government experts did think there would be, or rather they were convinced it was prudent to think so just in case there was one (heads often roll when something like that is missed—from the bureaucratic point of view, it's better to err on the side of safety). So the media by and large played it that way—perhaps (let's be charitable) because they assumed that the government knew what it was talking about. It was primarily readers of non-mass circulation magazines and papers like the *Village*

Inside Hollywood: Hollywood superstars are breathing easier now that congressional investigators have backed off a filmland drug probe. But there's more to the headline controversy: Narcotics experts confided that they had big names set to testify but that a lot of California biggies have backed off now that Ronald Reagan is in the White House. No one wants to be caught embarrassing the White House's tinseltown friends.

—The Investigator (September 1981)

Nothing a government does is as important as how it chooses to spend the taxpayers' money. Yet budgetary matters, particularly on the local level, are usually decided by bureaucrats and elected officials with little public involvement.

Not so in Clinton, Connecticut, thanks in part to the *Clinton Enquirer.* Each spring this small magazine prints its community's annual budget. The *Enquirer* doesn't stop with the largest figures: it prints everything from how much dog food the dogcatcher uses to the salaries individual teachers and policemen receive. By encouraging people to familiarize themselves with the details of how government operates in their own community, the *Enquirer* has set a highly useful example for other papers.

This daring practice won Jeanne and George Allardice the Washington Monthly's *April 1982 Journalism Award.*

Voice (see, for instance, the December 6, 1976, issue) who were aware all along that the whole thing was a phony scare.

The United States Constitution guarantees freedom of the press as one of several freedoms needed to make representative government function. Nevertheless, governments do censor the media on occasion. Of course, the most common type of censorship is of alleged pornography (*Hustler* magazine's publisher, Larry Flint, got seven years for publishing material judged to be obscene). But on occasion, they also censor political material (for instance, books critical of the CIA) and occasionally harass the media in other ways (for example, by forcing them to reveal the names of confidential sources). *U.S.A. Today* reported, for instance, on September 21, 1983, that Air Force Secretary Verne Orr had "advised" several defense contractors not to advertise in news media that criticize defense policies. And the government has used provisions of the McCarran-Walter Immigration Act to deny visas to many foreign political and cultural figures, including all six of the El Salvadorean presidential candidates in their 1982 election and (in 1987) Austrian Chancellor Kurt Waldheim, accused of Nazi activities during World War II.

Governments also put a chill on freedom of the press through court decisions in libel suits. *Fact* magazine went bankrupt when it lost a libel suit brought by Senator Barry Goldwater. And similar suits (such as those brought by actress Carol Burnett and writer Lillian Hellman) have made many newspapers leery of making unfavorable comments even about public figures.

Much Foreign Reporting Is Suspect

While it's true that government censorship happens on occasion in the United States, government officials here rarely threaten reporters with physical violence

Jules Feiffer. Copyright 1978. Distributed by Field Newspaper Syndicate. Reprinted by permission.

An attempt via humor to explain the insidiousness of government power over the press.

or death. Yet this happens quite often in some other countries, making the "news" from those countries extremely unreliable, even when it appears in the (usually) most reliable publications.

Here are excerpts from two *TV Guide* articles (October 23, 1982, and March 6, 1982) on foreign intimidation of American reporters and how it influences news coverage:[6]

> Four Dutch television journalists are killed and mutilated by government troops while on their way to a rendezvous with guerrilla forces in El Salvador. In the month before their deaths, 31 percent of the stories broadcast from El Salvador by the three American TV networks dealt with guerrilla activities. In the month after the killings, that percentage dropped to 3 percent. *Intimidation.*
>
> An American television correspondent is about to satellite a story from Libya. A man armed with a Kalashnikov automatic rifle says that if she does not alter her script, the story will not be transmitted. She changes the script. *Intimidation.*
>
> [During the 1982–83 Israeli invasion of Lebanon,] a number of broadcast correspondents left Beirut because they were threatened with death by Palestinian or Syrian groups. The BBC's Tim Llewellyn, for one, was

---

Here is an excerpt from a Village Voice *interview with a reporter who had been to El Salvador and seen the news reporting from that war-torn land firsthand:*

Alan Riding [of the *New York Times*] represented the only case in which a North American journalist did his work very competently. He used to visit places, travel places, and he had sources. But in the beginning of January 1980 the extreme right threatened his life. Since then he left El Salvador and he hasn't been back. So he reports from Mexico. . . .

Bernard Diederich of *Time* and the others. . . . They get to the airport, they go to the Camino Real hotel where all the newspaper people stay and they don't go out. Maybe they go to the Presidential House, to the headquarters of the armed forces or to the American embassy. We say they cover the war from the hotel. One cannot have an ample vision of what is going on in the country. Most American correspondents don't understand what is going on in El Salvador, that there is a class struggle. They see it as painted by the State Department, as a struggle of the superpowers.

—*Village Voice* (April 8, 1981)

---

[6]See also Xan Smiley, "Misunderstanding Africa," *Atlantic* (September 1982), for an account of why lots of reporting from black Africa is mangled by government interference and intimidation. And for an account of the more subtle intimidation American reporters face at home, see *TV Guide* (October 30, 1982).

evacuated because of threats against his life. It is rumored, but not confirmed, that ABC's Jerry King left Beirut for the same reason.

Of course, another country that makes it hard for reporters to get any information worthy of the name is the Soviet Union. (The same is true of Soviet Eastern European satellites.) Until recently, the Russians even killed stories about commercial airline crashes. In fact, at first they killed the story about the Korean airlines commercial jet, flight 007, that they themselves had shot down, and they later gave a ridiculously false account of what had happened.

But with the *glasnost* (openness: public airing or disclosure) policy of Premier Mikhail Gorbachev, things have improved a bit in the Soviet Union[7] (but not as yet in Eastern European satellite countries). How permanent these changes will be and whether they will be carried further remains to be seen.

It is important to remember that many other countries (chiefly those with authoritarian or dictatorial regimes, like Zaire) also consider news to be more or less a device to further the interests of government. The American tradition of freedom of the press is not universal; in fact, it is quite the exception.

The powers that be in the United States take whatever advantage they can of the fact that reporters have trouble finding out what is happening in some foreign countries. For example, when "elections" were held in El Salvador in 1982, the United States government put out self-serving accounts of what had transpired and the media printed them, perhaps because few other sources were available without risky digging among the peasants.[8]

News-Gathering Methods Are Designed to Save Money

If a newspaper or television station is a business, with a bottom line that determines eventual success or failure, owners have to make sure that the bottom line is not written in red ink. Since it has to operate as economically as it can, just like other businesses, the news business cannot regularly spend more money on a story than is returned in reader or listener interest.

Regular News "Beats" Have Been Established

There are two principal ways in which the news is gathered, both designed to be efficient and to save money. One is through established news "beats." The two major wire services, the three big TV networks, and a few top newspapers routinely assign reporters to cover a few institutions that regularly generate news. For instance, they have reporters covering the United States Congress and the Supreme Court (on days decisions are to be handed down).

Most News Is Given to Reporters, Not Ferreted Out

The other important way the media gather the news is by having it given to them by government officials or by others who have power (or money—but money implies

---

[7]See, for instance, the cover story in the July 27, 1987, issue of *Time* magazine.
[8]Part of this is explained in Joel Millman, "Reagan's Reporters: How the Press Distorts the News from Central America," *The Progressive* (October 1984).

Here are a few excerpts from a Consumer Reports *(March 1986) article on the use of handouts by the media.*

Last year, Procter & Gamble Co. launched a special promotion for *Spic and Span.* Cubic zirconia—fake diamonds—were inserted in more than two million boxes of the powdered cleaner. But 500 boxes contained real diamonds, worth about $600 each. You could tell which type of stone was in your package by taking it to a participating jeweler for a free evaluation.

The promotion got plenty of exposure on television. That might not seem surprising, since Procter & Gamble is the nation's largest television advertiser, spending more than half a billion dollars a year on network and local television.

But in this case, the air time didn't cost the company a cent. Hill & Knowlton, the large public-relations firm that represents Procter and Gamble, sent a package of materials to some 200 TV stations. It featured a 90-second videotape designed to be inserted directly into local news broadcasts. There was also supporting footage, prominently featuring the *Spic and Span* assembly line.

The story line ostensibly was that cubic zirconia are difficult to distinguish from diamonds without special test equipment, and that sales of the low-priced diamond mimics were growing fast. But blended in were plenty of snippets about the Procter & Gamble promotion.

Hill & Knowlton says that its materials were used by stations in at least 27 cities nationwide, including San Francisco (KPIX), Dallas (WFAA), Boston (WBZ), and New York City (WCBS).

For Hill & Knowlton, the *Spic and Span* campaign proved a resounding success. But consumers have no reason to rejoice over such campaigns. By blurring the distinction between news and advertising, such activities imperil an important function of the media: providing consumers with accurate, unbiased information about the marketplace. . . .

On the newspaper side, such "canned news" is most often seen in special sections, such as those devoted to real estate, automobiles, travel, and food. The company that wants to promote its products will frequently hire a distribution service that devotes itself entirely to canned news. One such firm, Chicago-based Associated Release Service Inc., each month distributes between 40 and 100 articles to more than 3000 newspapers. "We send out original quality proofs that are already typeset," says Ted Hathorn, Associated's president. "If they like the material, they can put it right into their page layout. . . ."

A skilled PR person will bury the commercial plug so that the reader won't easily guess the source of the story. As one example, Associated recently distributed a nine-paragraph article headlined "Heartburn—A Peril in the Night." Not until the story's eighth paragraph does the name of Associated's client pop up: "Another option is an over-the-counter antacid that works even when the nighttime heartburn sufferer is lying down. Gaviscon, a unique foaming antacid, is physician-recommended and has been proven effective in relieving nighttime heartburn for many years. . . ."

Who uses this sort of stuff? When Sun Color Service, another distribution agency, polled newspapers on the subject, only 25 percent said they didn't want to receive its releases. Dorothy Rabb, a Sun Color executive, says that "the large papers, with 200,000 circulation and up, for the most part do their own articles. Most of our material is accepted by papers with less than 80,000 circulation. . . . "

On days with lots of news space to fill because of heavy ad volume, a newspaper can brim with canned news. Last Thanksgiving, for instance, the Wyoming Tribune-Eagle, the newspaper of Cheyenne, the state capital, carried 15 canned news articles—13 of them mentioning specific brand names and two plugging generic products. The paper advised its readers to use *Blistex,* a lip ointment, "on the mistletoe circuit," to fill their Christmas stockings with *Hazel Bishop Moisture Gloss Stick,* and to install "the watchful eye" of the *Sony WatchCam* security system, which "helps to make certain it's just Santa stirring in the house and out."

Isn't it deceptive to use this canned copy alongside legitimate news articles? "I've asked a number of times to label the copy advertising," says Tribune-Eagle editor Don Hurlburt, who notes that the Wyoming paper's canned articles are selected by the advertising department. "My voice has fallen on deaf ears. I don't like it; I don't like the way they do it, but it's not my decision to make."

A Tribune-Eagle advertising executive, who asked not to be identified, insists that the canned news is justified. "Products that are usable by the public are news," he contends. "It's the economics of the retail business that keeps all of us going."

power). Since only those with power or money can call press conferences or issue press releases and attract attention from the mass media, the news is bound to reflect established powerful interests more than those of the rest of us.

Even a good deal of beat reporting results mainly in handouts. For instance, most of the news generated by reporters covering the coveted White House beat is given to them by White House officials. Similarly, most news from the local crime beats is told to reporters by district attorneys or local police officials.

The important thing to notice about all this is that *very few news stories result from true investigative reporting!*[9] It's much easier and quicker to interview heads of government agencies than to find out for yourself what's going on in these agencies.

---

[9]Those that do tend to get buried back on page 49, and thus get read by fewer people. Recently, many newspapers that do little or no investigative or background reporting themselves have been reprinting more items from magazines and other newspapers (although so far they too tend to get buried in the back pages).

It might be supposed that the media would routinely check up on stories given them by the high and mighty or by alleged experts. And they often do. Unfortunately, they often don't. This is illustrated nicely by the following snippet:

> In New York some years ago, special prosecutor Maurice Nadjari leaked to reporters of the more influential papers certain grand-jury proceedings. And they printed what they got. One unfortunate judge wound up on the front page of the *New York Times* as a suspect in a bribery case because of a Nadjari leak to reporters from a grand-jury session. A year later, when the judge was wholly exonerated, the *Times* gave him an inch of type deep inside the paper. . . .
>
> If the *Times* reporter who swallowed the Nadjari leak had bothered to do the most minimal checking, he would have found out that there was no way the hapless judge could have been involved in any bribery connected with the case at issue because he had never had the case before him. The special prosecutor had believed the court calendar, which did list this particular judge as hearing that case. But the assignment had been changed.[10]

While reporter bias is occasionally the reason for such inaccurate reporting (see below), the main reason is simply that it takes a great deal of time and money to verify information. (The only newspaper or magazine this writer knows about that tries to verify *all* alleged facts it prints is the *New Yorker* magazine. Not that this writer is in a position to cast stones at all the rest on that score.)

English majors who have an interest in journalism should give themselves a treat and verify something important about the newspaper business by going to the library and reading the September 28, 1981, *Wall Street Journal.* One of its front page articles describes how a journalism teacher, Joseph Skaggs, got United Press International (UPI), the *Chicago Tribune,* the *Dallas Times-Herald,* and lots of other newspapers (but not the *Wall Street Journal!*) to carry a phony story about "Joseph Gregor" and his organization "Metamorphosis" and how they were improving their health by chewing "cockroach pills." Skaggs's intent, of course, was to show how the media will fall for just about anything, and won't bother to verify a story, *if* you handle them in the right way. (One bit from that story: UPI's managing editor saw no reason to correct the story when the hoax was revealed because "The story was accurate at the time." Wonderful doubletalk. What he no doubt meant was that UPI reporters accurately relayed what the hoax perpetrators told them.)

2. Theories and Practices

People don't often stand back and look at what they're doing from a wider context; they don't often theorize about their activities. Media workers on the whole theorize more than most workers. But their theories are frequently self-serving.

---

[10]Nat Hentoff, *Inquiry* (January 11, 1982). He was responding to criticisms of the movie *Absence of Malice,* which itself was very critical of media coverage.

In the following interview excerpts, Congressman Les Aspin of Wisconsin explains his unusual success in getting the media attention necessary for reelection and for the political power needed to be effective in Washington:

A: If a congressman were to go out on the steps of the Capitol and set himself on fire, he'd probably get on the evening news, but otherwise it's really hard. If a congressman does something really bizarre—takes an absurd position or gets involved in Abscam—he'll get his name in the paper, but that doesn't help him. If a congressman is going to get on the wires, or in the *New York Times* or *Washington Post,* he's got to do something very different, put out something that wasn't there before—either more information, or a different point of view. So you have to anticipate a little bit. You can't take what's in the headlines today and do a report on that because by the time the reporting is finished, the story will have moved on. You've got to be able to anticipate where the story's going two weeks ahead. . . .

Q: Describe what you do with a press release.

A: You've got to release it on a slow news day—Monday. The press release has to go out Thursday by 2 o'clock, with a Monday a.m. embargo. I remembered sitting with Hubert Humphrey on the floor of the Congress before a State of the Union message, and he said, "Say, I was just wondering how you get so much press. How do you get your staff to work on the weekends?" And I said, "What do you mean, work on the weekends?" "Well, you always get those stories to come out on Monday." I said, "No, no, no, you don't understand. The staff doesn't like to work on the weekends. Reporters sure don't like to work on the weekends. You've got to get the press release out on a Thursday afternoon, so the reporters get it Friday morning, and can write their Monday story and go away for the weekend. . . .

Q: Does anybody in the Pentagon do this kind of selective placing of stories, say on the MX? Is anybody over there doing the same thing?

A: Oh, yeah. They're planting stories. The whole operation there is a very different thing. They don't want their names on the stories. . . .

Q: What press release of yours got the most attention?

A: . . . The ones that got the most attention were the funny ones. The classic was the one we did that riled up all beagle owners. The Army was conducting poison gas tests on beagle puppies. We were mad at Eddie Hebert at the time, so we thought the way to really do him in was to send out a press release saying that Hebert [the chairman of the House Armed Services Committee] was the guy in Congress who could stop the gassing of beagle puppies. Gee, I went down there in Hebert's office and they were wig deep in bags of mail. . . .

—*Washington Journalism Review* (June 1981). Reprinted with permission.

The Unusual Is News, the Everyday Is Not

Theory says that news is what's *new*—the unusual, not the commonplace. Yet what happens every day is generally more important than the unusual occurrence. Prison uprisings get big play, but the poor treatment prisoners receive every day, which leads to the uprisings, goes relatively unreported. Big court cases such as the Watergate trials receive much attention, but thousands of everyday cases in which justice is flouted tend to be ignored. (A whole disgraceful area of courtroom practice, plea bargaining, was pretty much ignored in the media until former Vice-President Spiro Agnew "copped a plea.")

News Reporting Is Supposed to Be Objective, Not Subjective

Those who work on the news often say that facts are objective, conclusions or value judgments subjective, and that media workers are supposed to be objective. Even J. Edgar Hoover subscribed to this view, although he didn't practice it. His motto was that the FBI does not draw conclusions, it only reports the facts.

But this theory of objective reporting is mistaken. Reports of facts generally depend on someone's judgment that they are facts. A reporter must *reason to the facts* just as one reasons to anything else.

Similarly, the idea that newspapers should not make value judgments is incorrect. When we read of the death of a famous movie star on page one of our morning newspaper but nothing about the death of an eminent philosopher, it becomes obvious that newspapers have to make value judgments to determine what is important and what is not. The same is true when a hurricane on the Gulf Coast, which kills two dozen people, gets more space than reports of the My Lai massacre in Vietnam, or when the George Foreman–Muhammad Ali fight in Zaire gets more space than mass starvation in Africa. In other words, *editing*, one of the chief tasks of any newspaper, requires value judgments about the relative importance of events.

So the media's theory about objective reporting is not correct. Of course, real life practice differs significantly from this theory anyway.[11]

News Is Supposed To Be Separated from Analysis or In-Depth Reports

The theory of objectivity requires that facts be reported separately from conclusions or evaluations (which are thought of as "subjective"). But the separation of news from analysis further aggravates a defect already in evidence in most media reporting, namely their failure to tie what happens to some *explanation* of why it

---

[11]For what it's worth, this writer's opinion on the matter is that in everyday practice, the theory of objectivity requires only that reporters stay within the social consensus when they make judgments or draw conclusions. This means that the real point of the theory of objectivity is to discourage the reporting of radical, nonestablishment, or nonconsensual views—to placate the media audience and media advertisers.

Here is columnist Richard Cohen nicely skewering Time, Newsweek, *and such, and their "latest trend" articles that exaggerate every little blip on the American scene.*

First came newsmagazine cover stories about terrorism abroad, and then came the perfectly logical follow-up story that Americans were going to stay home this past summer, choosing to spend their money—and their lives— where they both still had some value. It was, we were told, a new trend.

But then came the news that domestic travel was down by something like 10 percent. That meant that a considerable number of people had not gone to Europe and had not taken their vacations in America and were, therefore, simply unaccounted for. And so, being hopelessly addicted to newsmagazines, I naturally concluded that these missing people were engaged in still *other* newsmagazine trends.

I decided that some of the people must be staying home doing drugs, another trend. Maybe some were snorting coke and others were doing crack while even more were doing absolutely nothing, preparing for a drug test on the job.

Maybe a small percentage of the unaccounted-for were politicians like Sen. Alfonse D'Amato, out on the streets buying drugs to show that you could go out on the street and buy drugs. In an election year, the number of people engaged in the politically opportunistic purchase of drugs could reach into the millions, keeping in business pushers who heretofore had sold only to reporters for newsmagazines.

It could be, though, that millions of people were simply staying home not having babies—the latest trend. Or maybe they were all at Ralph Lauren's new store on Madison Avenue, spending the billions they had made as inside traders. Maybe they had taken a *People* magazine cover story to heart and canceled a vacation to "do" infidelity. The magazine reported that everyone who was not already doing crack or shopping at the new Ralph Lauren store was having an affair.

Even adding the cheaters could not account for all the people who did not go to either Europe or the Grand Canyon. This is because other cover stories have told us that no one is having sex for fear of herpes or because of the new celibacy (remember that?) or because of the new morality and the return to commitment. Some people, for sure, were not smoking or not drinking or returning to religion, although why they needed it, given their life styles, is beyond me. Still others had taken up tap dancing or were trying to figure out if Andrew Wyeth really had an affair with Helga and, if so, why?

Of course, I know all these things from reading the newsmagazines. I take their word that these are genuine trends even though I know no one who indulges in them. Like a teen-ager sitting at home on a Saturday night, I have the uneasy feeling that everyone else is doing something (is the "new celibacy" *doing* something?) and I have not the faintest clue what it is. Monday morning is when I find out, just the way I did in high school. But now, instead of overhearing my classmates, I read the newsmagazines.

I have learned that Richard Nixon is back (where? how?) and that fathers are playing with kids. This is because they are not reading (which explains why Nixon is back), not going to the movies, not watching television and not playing video games anymore. They are, instead, reading pornography, walking around shopping malls for exercise, traveling to Nashville to diet, enlisting in neo-Fascist organizations, becoming Republicans, starting their own businesses, sexually abusing their children, taking poison pills (they deserve it) or—can these be the same people?—learning how to cry (start with my plumbing bill).

Most of us are getting older. Some of us, inexplicably, are getting younger. Everyone is moving west and south except the people we know. None of us can afford a house, and all of us live in condominium communities that ban children and pets—although the latter are absolutely essential for a full and rounded life while the former, for some reason, are not. We eat an average of 126.8 pounds of sugar a year, have cosmetic surgery, ignore our aged parents and use the money we save to send our aged parents videotapes of what we now look like.

God is dead, says the *Times*. No, she's not, counters *Ms*. There's a new nationalism, a new isolationism, a new interventionism, and surrogate mothers are being sexually harassed while at work. Kids are no longer sexually promiscuous except when they are, and yuppies have more money to spend, only, of course, they don't and, anyway, they ought to because they are childless and were all raised by single mothers in condominiums where they were all abused by crack-crazed inside traders. And that's only in the out years.

All women are having abortions or are marching against them—with the exception, of course, of those who spent a lifetime ignoring their need for calcium and cannot walk at all. They are divorcing the surrogate father of their child by another man, working, not working, seeking their G spot (it's in the West and the South) and answering surveys from newsmagazines.

Everyone is watching Eddie Murphy movies, Bill Cosby television shows, Bruce Springsteen concerts, showing the flag, being a single parent, being a spy, wanting to be Sam Shepard, worshiping the sun, rejoicing in the return of women to rock music, taking over media companies and, it seems, being afraid to venture out of the house. Who can blame them?

Nixon's back.

—Richard Cohen, "Making Trends Meet,"
The Washington Post Magazine (September 28, 1986).
© 1986 Washington Post Writers Group. Reprinted by permission.

happened and why it's important. So those who stick to the mass media aren't likely to *understand* what happens or be able to *anticipate* the flow of events.

Most of the better "in-depth" or "analysis" reporting on television is done by the Public Broadcasting Service (PBS). But they too often fall into the same traps as do other media workers. A documentary widely shown on PBS in 1979 attempted to get behind the façade and show us how the U.S. House of Representatives really works (a marvelous idea). But it merely followed House Majority Leader "Tip" O'Neill around for a whole (supposedly) typical day of work. The impression given was that we were getting an inside glimpse of powerful people at work; we looked over their shoulders and heard what they told each other in the halls and behind closed doors.

To no avail. The members videotaped were aware of that fact and tailored their conversations accordingly. While it seemed that we were getting the real lowdown, we got instead lots of remarks like: "We've got to move that bill by the seventh," which revealed nothing about the true behind-the-scenes wheeling and dealing (still quaintly called "logrolling" in public school textbooks, where it's described without mentioning mundane things like payoffs by lobbyists, campaign contributions, betrayals, or veiled threats).

Reading Between the Lines

Given that advertisers, the government, and other powerful groups are so influential in determining how the news is reported, the question naturally arises as to what viewers and readers can do about it. One answer is to learn how to read between the lines. Here is an excerpt from Harper's *magazine (October 1983) explaining how to do that with respect to auto magazines:*

[*Car and Driver*] will rarely blast a major new [American auto] industry offering in its first few paragraphs of a lead review [because of pressure from Detroit advertisers]. The experienced reader knows this and quickly skips to the "armpit" of the article, ¾ of the way through, where the reviewer feels free to draw long knives. Using this well developed instinct, for example, veteran *CD* readers would have skimmed over the initial pages of predictable praise for the new Ford Tempo's "contemporary appearance" to find the buried complaint about Ford's "biases toward traditional American-sedan performance." (Translation: the steering is vague and the suspension mushy.) In preparation for this article, I [the writer of the article]drove some two dozen new cars, and in no case did my own impressions seriously contradict those I had previously gleaned from *Car and Driver* using this simple interpretive technique.

The same technique used by the Harper's *writer in this case can be used in all sorts of cases. Find the bias that the various forces may push onto a news item, discount what is required by that bias, and see whether, as in* Car and Driver *articles, lots of nuggets aren't left over.*

The Opinions of the "Right" Authorities Take Precedence

The reporters and editors who gather and assemble the news are not usually experts in the fields they cover. They couldn't be, given that they must deal with practically all the social and political questions of the day. It seems plausible, then, that they should seek out expert opinion on these matters. The trouble is that experts can be found on all sides of a really controversial issue. In everyday practice, *which* experts are consulted is determined by the other factors that influence the news.

In the first place, experts whose views are very unpopular with either the media's audience or their advertisers, or with media bigwigs themselves, will tend to be passed over or played down. Take the question of the safety of nuclear power. A great many top-notch physicists (and organizations, such as the Union of Concerned Scientists) have been shouting as loudly as they can for some time now that the current state of the art makes nuclear power plants inherently unsafe. But until the serious accident at Three Mile Island, Pennsylvania, in 1979, their voices were drowned out in the media, to the point where one supposed expert—Department of Energy boss James Schlesinger (what did he know about atomic physics or how nuclear plants produce power?)—received more coverage than all the protesting scientists combined. No, it was those scientists who stated that nuclear power was safe who were given the space—along with politicians like Schlesinger, of course. (When, if ever, did you first hear about the much more serious Russian nuclear disaster that occurred way back in 1957?) It wasn't until after the 1986 Chernobyl disaster that the antinuclear power factions finally were heard loud and clear, at least occasionally.

Further, the fact that time is money means that the media will often as not take the first expert they can find—which most of the time means an expert in the employ of the rich or powerful, the same experts who are constantly being foisted on reporters via press conferences and other public relations operations.

Good Citizenship Requires Self-Censorship

Though unusual, self-censorship is not rare. Major newspapers and the TV networks tend to engage in self-censorship more often than other media sources, no doubt because they have access to more sensitive information. Perhaps the most famous example of this kind occurred during the Kennedy administration, when the *New York Times* decided not to print the Bay of Pigs story.[12]

The September 23, 1979, issue of the *Washington Post* magazine featured a cover story, "Hoover: Life with a Tyrant," which disclosed lots of the nastiness, dirtiness, unfairness, and illegality of J. Edgar Hoover's long reign as FBI chief. But where was the *Post* (or any mass media outlet) when Hoover had power and was perpetrating all these crimes? (It wasn't until June 3, 1982, that ABC got around to telling its viewers about this.)

---

[12]President Kennedy is alleged later to have had the "chutzpah" to take the *Times* to task for this censorship on grounds that publication of the story by the *Times* might have resulted in calling off that ill-fated venture!

The problem of self-censorship is made particularly difficult by the countertug of the right to privacy. A person in the public eye is still, after all, entitled to a private life. And yet it is difficult to know what bears on a person's public life (and thus can be exposed) and what does not (and thus ought to be censored). It was well known to news people, for instance, that as a congressman, senator, and president, John F. Kennedy was quite a lady's man. The media, on the whole, chose not to report this feature of Kennedy's private life and were generally applauded for their restraint (after all, stories on Kennedy's sex life would have found an eager audience).

The shock of Dec. 7 [1941] can be well imagined. When the last Japanese plane roared off, five American battleships had been sunk and three damaged, three cruisers and three destroyers badly hit, 200 planes destroyed, and 2344 men killed. For the loss of only 29 planes, Japan had virtually crippled the U.S. Pacific Fleet at a single blow.

The American service chiefs immediately decided that news of a disaster of such magnitude would prove unacceptable to the American people, and steps were taken to ensure that they did not learn about it. So effective were these measures that the truth about Pearl Harbor was still being concealed even after the war ended. The cover-up began with an "iron curtain" of censorship that cut off the United Press office in Honolulu from San Francisco in the middle of its first excited telephone report.

So drastic was the suppression of news that nothing further, except for official communiques, came out of Pearl Harbor for another four days. These claimed that only one "old" battleship and a destroyer had been sunk and other ships damaged, and that heavy casualties had been inflicted on the Japanese. It cannot be argued that these lies were necessary to conceal from the Japanese the extent of the disaster they had inflicted on the U.S. Pacific Fleet. The Japanese knew exactly how much damage they had done, and reports in Tokyo newspapers accurately stating the American losses meant that the Americans knew that the Japanese knew. The American censorship was to prevent the American public from learning the gravity of the blow.

After flying to Hawaii on a tour of inspection, the Secretary of the Navy, Colonel Frank Knox, held a press conference in New York at which, with President Roosevelt's approval, he gave the impression he was revealing the full extent of the American losses at Pearl Harbor. Colonel Knox told correspondents that one United States battleship, the Arizona, had been lost and the battleship Oklahoma had capsized but could be righted.

This must have made strange reading for anyone actually at Pearl Harbor, who had only to lift his eye from his newspaper to see five United States battleships—the Arizona, the Oklahoma, the California, the Nevada, and the West Virginia—resting on the bottom.

In wartime, truth is the first casualty, censorship the first expedient.

From *The First Casualty,* copyright © 1975 by Phillip Knightley.
Reprinted by permission of Harcourt Brace Jovanovich, Inc.

And yet, self-censorship of similar stories concerning Kennedy's brother, Ted Kennedy, may well have been a mistake, given what happened at Chappaquiddick. Knowledge of a person's sex life *may,* after all, be relevant to character and thus to suitability for public office. (Nevertheless, reporters who kept quiet about brother Robert Kennedy's affair with Marilyn Monroe surely deserved some credit.)

Of course, sometimes the media have private dirt forced on them and must print it whether they want to or not, a good example being the business about TV evangelist Jim Bakker's affair with his secretary. And anyway, standards on reporting about the private lives of famous politicians seem to be changing. Witness how the media jumped on then presidential candidate Gary Hart in May 1987 for alleged sexual indiscretions. And contrast this with, say, the way the media a generation earlier had ignored the well-known (to them) philanderings of long-time Tennessee Senator Estes Kefauver.

3. Devices Used to Slant the News

So far we have been considering *why* the media slant the news and how that affects the selection of stories. Now let's look at a few of the devices used to slant stories (primarily in newspapers and magazines).

Stories Can Be Played Up or Down

If you like something in a story, you can play it up. If you don't, you can play it down. You bury it by putting it toward the end (relatively few readers get past the first few paragraphs) or by mentioning it in passing. You play it up by doing just the opposite. On TV, stories are buried by running them toward the end of the program when eyes have begun to glaze and by cutting them to run less than a minute.

The *Canton* (Ohio) *Repository* may have set some sort of record on this in its July 28, 1974, issue. Under the front page headline "Wowee. . . . What a Weekend," the *Repository* devoted most of the page to an account of the first National Football League exhibition game of the season, plus a description of ceremonies surrounding the induction of four new members into Canton's Football Hall of Fame. Relegated to a bottom corner of page one was the decision of the House Judiciary Committee to recommend impeachment of President Nixon, a key event in one of the biggest ongoing news stories in American history.

Misleading or Sensational Headlines Can Be Used

Many more people read the headlines on a story than read the story itself. So even if a story is accurate, a misleading or sensational headline, generally not written by whoever wrote the news report itself, distorts the news for many readers. Here are a few examples reported in *The New Republic* (September 7, 1987):

Poll shows voters think women
capable as men to be president
—*Knoxville News-Sentinel,* August 13

Woman president? Voters not enthusiastic

—*Knoxville Journal,* August 12
(Thanks to Jean Ash, Knoxville, Tennessee)

OSHA'S newfound zeal puzzles industry, labor

—*Minneapolis Star and Tribune,* August 2

Is OSHA Falling Down on the Job?

—*New York Times,* same day
(Thanks to Bert M.Gross, Minneapolis, Minnesota)

Sensational news reporting of the kind common in Britain and some other countries (for instance, African countries like Nigeria and Kenya) has never caught on in the United States. But there is one U.S. newspaper, the *New York Post,*[13] that specializes in sensational shlock. Here are some examples of *Post* front page headlines, all from one week (collected by Rudy Maxa for his *Washington Post* column of November 29, 1981):

IRS Sex Ring Busted:
He spanked thousands of coeds, police say

Death of a Hitman
Preppie Porn King Slain:
Smith College girl shot in head in Chelsea sex pad

Nun Rape Bombshell

Follow-up Stories Can Be Omitted

Follow-up stories rarely make headlines, primarily for two reasons. The first is that they are relatively difficult to obtain. It takes much less time and effort to report a prison uprising than to investigate day-to-day prison conditions. The second is that the public (and media) conception of "news" is what is *new,* and therefore different. Follow-up is reporting on "old news," which isn't really news. But isn't it news if, say, a president of the United States fails to keep his word, or a bill passed by Congress fails to get implemented? (A recent important exception was the widespread page one reporting on Bob Woodward's book exposing the chica-

---

Newspapers start when the owners are poor and take the side of the people, and so they build up a large circulation, and presently, as a result, advertising. That makes them rich, and they begin most naturally to associate with other rich men—they play golf with one and drink whiskey with another, and their son marries the daughter of a third. They forget about the people.

—Joseph Medill Patterson

The late newspaper mogul was in a position to know.

---

[13]Owned by news magnate Rupert Murdoch.

nery of William J. Casey while director of the CIA. See, for instance, the *Washington Post* from September 26 through October 1, 1987.)

The media covered Ronald Reagan's campaigns from his start in California through his terms in the White House. Stacked away in their files are mountains of items on Reagan campaign rhetoric and performance showing that what he did bore little relationship to his campaign promises. Worse, it shows clearly that Reagan rarely uttered a remark that demonstrated sophistication or detailed knowledge about any topic. Plenty of reporters felt from the start that this movie star was unfit for high office. Yet it was rare for a news outlet to follow through on the news and point out the disparity between Reagan's words and his actions, or to show how often what he said was simply false—until Irangate made him fair game.

Emotive Language Can Be Used

Since we devoted a large part of Chapter 6 to the emotive side of language, let's give just one example at this point from the media. *A National Enquirer* article (September 7, 1982), headlined "A *Juicy* Way to *Waste* Your Tax Dollars," started out: "*Fruitcakes* at the National Science Foundation . . ." (italics added). Now if, say, *U.S.A. Today* had started one of their articles: "Fruitcakes at the *National Enquirer. . . .*"

Ignorance Is Cloaked in an Aura of Authority

Television and newspaper reporters and editors are not generally experts on the topics they have to cover. How could they be when reporters may cover one thing one day and something much different the next. And they can't spend much time on background digging (because it's too expensive). But it would be hard to guess at this ignorance when reading the polished stories the media turn out. On the contrary, reporters quote facts and figures (and the words of the high and mighty) in a way that makes them seem on top of their subjects.

However, closer investigation reveals cracks in the veneer of expertise. Here is an excerpt from *TV Guide*[14] illustrating that point:

> **Arbitrary but plausible explanations.** In 1984 it was obvious to all three networks very early that Ronald Reagan was winning a landslide victory. The obvious question was "Why?" When network commentators attempted to explain, two things were striking. The first was how much their explanations differed. The second was how little evidence commentators gave for their explanations.
>
> For example, on NBC, John Chancellor alone offered three equally plausible reasons for Reagan's win, but gave viewers no basis to choose one over the other. His first crack at understanding the landslide used NBC exit-poll data. "It's the mood of the electorate," he declared, showing graphics indicating that on leadership qualities and the economy

---

[14]Richard Joslyn and Mark Howard Ross, "Election Night on TV: The Calls are Good—The Analysis Isn't," (November 1, 1986).

Political columnists who last long enough generally become "experts" just because they're well known. Here is Alexander Cockburn on these "experts" and their reporting of the 1980 political campaign:

"Bigfoot" was used to describe any senior officer of the press permitted by status and function to leaven fact with advertised opinion. . . . [T]he reaction provoked among the troops was analogous to that of a general visiting the trenches in the first world war. Among the smoke of press releases, . . . he would make a dignified tour of inspection, briefly confer with the candidate and senior officers on the spot, inscribe a few paragraphs of sagacious observation in his notebook, and return to the soft life in Washington.

When finally published, the Bigfoot's observations would be read by the troops left behind him with spite and derision. How could the Bigfoot know that the sentiments of the candidate he recorded in Pittsburgh as novel and refreshing insights had been daily staples of the stump for the previous six months . . . ?

Cockburn then went on to discuss one of the champion bigfoots, Walter Lippmann (often referred to in his day as the "dean of American journalists"), pointing out Lippmann's abysmal batting average. Here are a few examples:

"Democracy," [Lippmann] opined [in 1930], "cannot last long; it must, and inevitably will, give way to a more settled social order." . . .

In 1933, just after books were burned in the streets of Berlin, he solemnly wrote that repression of the Jews, "by satisfying the lust of the Nazis who feel they must conquer somebody and the cupidity of those Nazis who want jobs, is a kind of lightning rod which protects Europe." A week later he was praising Hitler for "a genuinely statesmanlike address" that expressed "the authentic voice of a genuinely civilized people." . . .

[In 1938], concerned with "distracted" Europe's overpopulation problem, he suggested that a million "surplus" Jews be sent to Africa. . . .

Knowledgeable of the corridors of power, he told Eric Sevareid and a CBS audience in [1965] that war hawks are "not found in the interior and at the top of the White House." In the same year, too, he endorsed the U.S.-backed coup in the Dominican Republic.

Then, somewhat late, he discovered that LBJ was a hawk, and that the war in Vietnam was a bad idea. Of the president he said sadly, in the distressed tones of a betrayed pundit, "He misled me." [But] disillusion did not lead to wisdom. In 1968 he reported that there was a "new Nixon, a maturer and mellower man."

Reagan outscored Mondale, and that most people felt that a war with the Soviets in the near future was unlikely.

By the middle of the evening, however, Chancellor identified a second key factor, suggesting that what was crucial was a national desire for political stability, meaning a two-term President. "There's been," he declared, "a hunger in this country for a President who will stay in there for more than four years." By the end of the evening, Chancellor came to bat a third time: "When disposable income goes up in a Presidential year," he began, "the party in power wins. It usually goes up about four per cent. This year it went up six and the party in power won."

Meanwhile, on CBS, speaking particularly about the President's sweep of the South, Bill Moyers delivered his highly publicized remarks suggesting that the strong Reagan vote was racial in motivation. Dan Rather countered that the President's support for patriotism and family values also appealed to Southerners. Later in the evening CBS viewers could variously have heard Rather attribute the election to Reagan's personal popularity; Bob Schieffer say it was the state of the economy; and Bruce Morton say it was his ability to use TV and the stability of his political convictions. Moyers, at one point, listed prosperity, strength, delivering on what he had promised, getting his programs through Congress, restoring faith that the country could be governed, his conservative philosophy, his consistency[!] and his uplifting personal spirit.

4. Television: Tail Wags Dog

Although still a relative baby, television, the newest of the mass media, is by far the most important. Television gives us the closest thing we have to a way of bringing a whole nation together. It is the town meeting, town crier, certifier, authenticator, grapevine of modern industrial life. That's why political campaigns are fought on it, the news is broadcast on it, and (more and more) a nation's mood and tone are set by it.

But before going into details about this new communications medium, perhaps we should stop for a moment and reflect on the wonder of it all. Television gives us the privilege of sitting in our living rooms and being magically transported down

---

The medium of television has so taken over the country that it has become our *only* mass medium. The number of people who read a best-selling book, the subscribers to the most successful magazines, the listeners to even the most powerful radio stations, and the readers of the most popular newspapers, the pre-TV film crowds, are all statistical gnats when compared to the viewers of a network series canceled for lack of an audience.

—Jeffrey Schrank, *Snap, Crackle, and Popular Taste*
(New York: Delacorte Press, 1977)

the Nile, through steaming African jungle, or parched Australian desert. It gives us the opportunity to see the famous figures of our time almost as though in the flesh, from the Pope to Jane Fonda, from Lech Walesa to Ronald Reagan. And so it gives us a much better chance to judge the character of our leaders than by just looking at pictures or still photos. (That most viewers judge poorly anyway reflects on them, not television.)

It's important also to see the political power this media "baby" possesses. All of the media have political power, because the power to expose the bad and publicize the good yields power automatically. But television's power to expose and publicize is vastly greater, more immediate, and more graphic than the other media, and so its political power is awesomely, indeed frighteningly, greater. (The Polish government's control of television was one of its two main weapons in defeating Solidarity in 1981 and 1982.[15] The other, of course, was military power.)

The point here is that the power of TV, especially national TV, to expose chicanery is bound to have an effect on the behavior of government officials (as it did during the Vietnam War, when TV brought the war into everyone's living room).

To illustrate this TV power further, consider what Americans know about Nazi Germany's extermination camps, compared to what they know about Soviet slave labor camps. Russia, of course, is pictured on TV as a very nasty dictatorship, which it is, but very few of us know that many more people have died in Soviet labor camps than were murdered by the Nazis in their World War II extermination camps. In the 1980s, millions of Americans have learned about or been reminded of the "Holocaust"—the killing of almost 6 million Jews by the Nazis—when the plight of European Jews in World War II was portrayed graphically on TV. Few of us know of the Russian camps. But just one TV epic similar to "The Holocaust" could make the barbaric Russian camps and the millions worked to death in them common knowledge in America (as it is in Russia—via the grapevine, *not* Russian TV!), so that the name *Kolyma* would be as familiar to us as is *Auschwitz* or *Treblinka*.

TV Entertainment Gives a Juvenile Impression of Life

Going from horror to the ridiculous, most television entertainment programs give us a hopelessly juvenile impression of human nature and human society. Hollywood endings are almost the universal rule—the good guys win in the end, or the foolish misunderstandings that sustained half an hour of comedy are cleared up, and everyone is happy (except for a few villains).

Even *All in the Family,* praised widely for its exposure of bigotry (in particular racial bigotry), bore little resemblance to the genuine article. It's hard to imagine Archie Bunker killing anyone, even indirectly. He *talked* against blacks but never *ever* raised his fist against them, or anyone else. He was a friendly bumbler. Real-life bigots are another matter. They frequently do things that *kill,* as did U.S. State

---

[15]See, for instance, "Polish Government vs. the Workers: Why TV Is the Prized Weapon," *TV Guide* (November 7, 1981).

Department bigots during the Nazi period who refused entry into the United States to thousands of Jews trying to escape from Hitler's horror.[16]

In his book *The View from Sunset Boulevard,* Benjamin Stein discusses the "cleaned-up" world of television entertainment programs:

> Today's television is purer, in terms of backdrop and story endings, than the lines of a Mercedes convertible. Every day's shows bring fresh examples. A while ago, I saw an episode of "Charlie's Angels" about massage parlors that were really houses of prostitution. The three beautiful "angels" of the show were compelled to pretend they worked at massage parlors in seamy areas. Anyone who has ever passed by a massage parlor knows that they are invariably dirty, shabby places, with pitiful and degraded denizens. On "Charlie's Angels," the Paradise Massage Parlor compared favorably in terms of cleanliness with the surgical theater at Massachusetts General Hospital. The girls were immaculate and well-groomed, soft of speech and clear of eye and skin.

But Television Tends to Break Down Ethnic Prejudices

Still, the television picture isn't all dark. In helping to shape our world views, television has done much to reduce prejudice against blacks, women, and other groups, one of the great improvements in life that has taken place in post–World War II America.

The record-breaking docudrama "Roots" let Americans know how hard and unfair everyday life has been for blacks through most of our history by showing relatively simple things, like the difficulties Alex Haley and his family had in finding a motel room, and also more serious things, like the humiliating treatment blacks received in the segregated (until after World War II) United States Army. Many white Americans learned about the extent of these lapses from the American ideal of equality and freedom for the first time—they didn't read about them in their school textbooks.[17]

Television news reporting also helped to break down prejudices. It was an important event when the first woman, Barbara Walters, and the first black person, Max Robinson, read the evening news to us on national TV.

Television is chewing gum for the eyes.
—Frank Lloyd Wright

But then, how many TV viewers ever heard of Frank Lloyd Wright?

---

[16]Arthur D. Morse, *While Six Million Died* (New York: Random House, 1969), has the grisly details.

[17]Not that television docudramas are all that accurate. Historians railed against the inaccuracies and distortions of "Roots"—forgetting how accurate it was compared to what most people are generally exposed to. For more on the negative side of the docudrama drama, see "Docudramas Unmasked," *TV Guide* (March 4, 1979).

Blondie. Reprinted with special permission of King Features Syndicate, Inc.

Comic strips such as Doonesbury *are so obviously political that their influence on social and political attitudes is widely recognized. Less noticed is that virtually every comic strip conveys some message or other in addition to overt humor. Even* Dennis the Menace *has a message about what normally robust little kids are like. This* Blondie *cartoon strip is a throwback to 25 to 30 years ago when the stereotype of the empty-headed housewife getting over some insignificant hurt by buying a new hat was the rule rather than, as today, the exception.*

But TV shapes our ideas in more subtle ways also. Take the way several scenes were handled in a *Colombo* TV movie. Trying to solve a murder case, Colombo had to wait in a long line at a government office to find out the answer to a question that took just a minute or two. Then he was instructed to go down the hall to wait in another line. Then he went back to the first office with the document in hand, but the clerk was now out to lunch, and Colombo had to wait. The point was obvious, and made much better than by just saying it: Bureaucracies are a pain in the neck and usually aren't run for *our* convenience. Very true, and very important.

TV Presents the News More Effectively for a Mass Audience

When we think of the mass media, it's important to remember that at least one-third of American adults are functionally illiterate.[18] For them, and lots of others, a picture really is worth a thousand words, and a sound motion picture is worth more than any number of printed words. So for the mass of people, television is the best news source of all the media.

Capturing and informing a mass audience requires extremely tight editing (matched in print only by advertisements). The average attention span is short and comprehension limited. TV does a better job than the other media in editing the news so that it can be understood by most Americans.[19]

Looking backward, it is easy to see now that while CBS News excelled at big set-piece journalism of the 1960s and 1970s—space, the political conventions, the Kennedy assassinations, the civil rights march on Washington—the news organization floundered when it came to enterprise or investigative reporting. The Pentagon papers, My Lai, the Tonkin Gulf fakery, Michigan State University's CIA connection, auto safety, the perils of DDT, and Watergate itself were all stories that we who worked at CBS in those years were frustrated to find had shown up first in such magazines and newspapers as *The Nation, Ramparts, The New Yorker, I. F. Stone's Weekly, The New York Times* or *The Washington Post*.

—Desmond Smith, veteran ABC and CBS news reporter, quoted in *The Nation* (September 16, 1978)

Have things changed since then?

---

[18] See Jonathan Kozol, *Illiterate America* (New York: Anchor Press/Doubleday, 1985).

[19] For a maverick view on this topic, see James David Barber, "Not the *New York Times:* What Network News Should Be," *Washington Monthly* (September 1979). Barber argues that the "trouble with television news is that it is . . . too intellectual, too balanced. It passes right over the heads of the great 'lower' half of the American electorate who need it most. If [it] stopped thinking in terms of . . . the *Encyclopaedia Britannica* or the *New York Times,* it could realize its enormous, unexploited potential for reaching and enlightening voters who now do not know what it is talking about."

However, even the illiterate can save time, as can we all, by replacing the half-hour spent watching the evening news on TV with five minutes listening to national news on radio.

TV Documentaries Are a Mixed Bag

A careful television viewer can get a remarkable amount of accurate background from TV documentaries, as well as from programs like ABC's "Nightline" and CBS's sometimes excellent "60 Minutes" (the only news or information program that has ever topped the Nielsen ratings).

On the other hand, some of the documentaries on network television are absolutely awful, pandering to the worst irrationalities of their audience. Some examples are the ones on the Bermuda Triangle (trying to make a case for the silly idea that something funny is going on down there in the Atlantic Ocean) and on Eric von Daniken's even sillier ideas about astronauts having visited the Earth in ancient times, being responsible for humans having had the knowledge to build the Maya pyramids and move the Easter Island stone figures. (In fairness, the networks also have run occasional rebuttals, shredding this nonsense with scientific evidence and accurate facts—after protests from the scientific community.)

Until somewhere around 1985, CBS was easily the best of the three major television networks in its presentation of the news. Some of its news specials were excellent. For instance, on August 1, 1983, it ran a story on the recent increase of hunger in America, showing us people who had worked hard all their lives but now could not afford to buy themselves and their families enough food to keep healthy. This was exactly the kind of reporting of an ongoing problem that might have great impact if done more than occasionally. But since becoming the victim of a successful takeover, CBS has greatly reduced its news budget. Serious, in-depth reporting has been cut to the bone.

On the other hand, cable television has begun to increase at least the quantity of television news coverage. The Cable News Network (CNN) now presents 24 hours of news every day, and while a good deal of this news is secondhand, canned news is still better than no news.

Cathy by Cathy Guisewite. Copyright 1981 Universal Press Syndicate. All rights reserved. Used by permission of Universal Press Syndicate.

PBS and NPR are Superior to Commercial TV

Perhaps the brightest spot on television is PBS, the Public Broadcasting Service. In a typical week, PBS carries about (depending on who's counting) ten informative and interesting evening documentaries. (National Public Radio [NPR] provides the best news coverage on the radio.) One of the best series on TV is "Nova." Most "Nova" programs are well organized and easy to watch, and except for an occasional klinker, they're also pretty accurate. An example is the "Nova" cosmology documentary, which explained the big bang theory of the universe and the discovery of low-frequency background radiation that confirmed it. Another superb "Nova" program, "The Miracle of Life," featured stunning motion pictures of living cells in action, from fertilization of the egg to the development of a human being. And no account of PBS would be complete without mentioning "Masterpiece Theatre," which for many years now has been giving viewers an alternative to the silly sitcoms that dominate network prime time television. But the audience for even the best things on PBS is small compared to that for a typical sitcom on commercial TV.

Unfortunately, not all is sweetness and light on public television. We have to remember that PBS and the Corporation for Public Broadcasting (CPB), created to provide financial support, are government agencies and thus subject to direct government censorship. When CPB staff members came up with the neat idea of exchanging Soviet and American television programs so viewers could gain a better understanding of life and propaganda in Russia, CPB directors killed the idea. Said Richard Brookhiser, once a speech writer for Vice-President Bush and in 1985 a member of the CPB board, "I mean the Bolshoi is fine. You know, ballet is ballet. . . . Nature programs. . . . little things grazing in the Tundra. Fine. . . . but if we are going to be opening doors to wonderful Soviet ideas on their own history or something, this is just disastrous.[20]

5. The Non-Mass Media to the Rescue

We've just gone on at great length about the limitations of the mass media. Two basic reasons for these limitations stand out. The first is that the media select the

> *Here is a little item from the* Harper's *Index (Harper's, April 1987) shedding some light on one reason serious political magazines have such small circulations:*
>
> Rank of *Cosmopolitan, Glamour,* and *Vogue* among the best-selling magazines in college bookstores: 1, 2, 3
>
> *Makes you wonder what, if anything, high school grads are reading.*

---

[20]For more on this, see S. L. Harrison, "CPB: Prime Time Pablum: How Politics and Corporate Influence Keep Public TV Harmless," *Washington Monthly* (January 1986).

From *Penthouse*. Reprinted by permission of Edward Sorel.

Truth at the Movies. *Motion pictures have an important influence on cultural standards and worldviews (although not as important as before television.) This Sorel cartoon makes the point that their portrayal of the FBI hasn't been exactly accurate (nor has TV's—think of the series* The FBI*), and suggests that fat-cat movie moguls know there's more money in going along with public opinion and power than in bucking it.*

news to appeal to a mass audience, and the interests of that audience run to spectacle, to individual events, and to short-term, on-going crises (like the Iranian hostage crisis—Americans spent an incredible amount of time listening to the details on that one). The media thus aren't sensibly selective in what they report and generally miss the underlying trends.

The second reason is that the mass media tend to give us secondhand opinions gleaned from the powerful and the rich, not those of more serious thinkers. Politicians are in the business of getting elected and running a government, not theorizing about what's going on. And to be crude, but accurate, Walter Cronkite, Dan Rather, and company (there are a few exceptions) are in the business of news entertainment. They aren't great theorizers and rarely penetrate behind the day-to-day individual events to give us a focused big picture. (The best in recent years has been Ted Koppell on *Nightline,* way above any of the "pretty people" on the evening news.)

When young people come to realize the limitations of the mass media, they often become disillusioned or cynical. If you can't trust good old CBS, *Time* magazine, or the *Lawrence Daily Journal World,* who can you trust?

Fortunately, this cynicism is hasty (and often a reaction to an overly rosy world view that needs amending, anyway). In fact, more solid information and sensible opinion is available in the United States today than anywhere else in the history of the world. Books of all kinds are full of it (double entendre not intended). Of course, the "it" varies from book to book—you have to pick and choose. And the rest of the non-mass media, in particular magazines, provide a rich and (for many) more succinct and convenient mother lode. Trading in ABC, *U.S. News and World Report, The New Britain Herald,* or the *Chicago Tribune* for *Harper's, PBS,* the *Washington Monthly,* or the *Wall Street Journal* is bound to give you a better picture of what's going on. (Or if you're industrious and willing to dig on page 49, try the *New York Times, Los Angeles Times,* or *Washington Post.* And remember that the difference between these compendious newspapers and your local paper may not be all that great. Your local rag *may* have lots of goodies in it—stashed away toward the back—but then again it may not.) Even *Time* and *Newsweek* have improved considerably in recent years.

Selectivity Is the Key

The point is that it isn't exactly a matter of mass versus non-mass media. It's a matter of learning how to be *selective*—learning to separate pearls from schlock. The non-mass media contain lots more pearls per square inch and are, on the whole, much more sophisticated.

Take books. On the whole, popular books on social-political matters of interest can be expected to be rather shallow—long on "human interest" but not very penetrating. Even the excellent and very important popular book *The Final Days,* by *Washington Post* reporters Bob Woodward and Carl Bernstein (Avon paperback, 1977) isn't all that authoritative. While it can be trusted concerning the basic facts of Nixon's final days in office, its portrayal of most of the characters in the drama is close to being naïve. In particular, Woodward and Bernstein write as though the public stances of these sophisticated politicians were their true responses to the Watergate revelations. When Senator Hugh Scott expressed public dismay, or Senator Barry Goldwater mouthed platitudes, the authors take them at their word. Here are a few examples to illustrate:

> Few of the President's men were as shocked by the transcripts as the senior academic-intellectual members of the Nixon administration: Arthur F. Burns, the Chairman of the Federal Reserve Board; Daniel Patrick Moynihan, ambassador to India and formerly advisor on domestic policy; George P. Schultz, formerly the President's economic counselor. They read the [Watergate] transcripts in different parts of the world. They heard a Richard Nixon they had never been exposed to before. [page 175]
>
> [Gerald Ford's] belief in Nixon's innocence remained steadfast: Watergate was a political vendetta conducted by Nixon's old enemies in the press and the liberal wing of the Democratic Party. The impeachment drive was not motivated by considerations of law or justice or principle. . . . The Vice President was showing signs of uneasiness. He hadn't planned to become President, and he wouldn't plan for it now. He had wanted to be nothing more than Speaker of the House, and he had accepted the Vice-Presidential nomination largely because it seemed a fitting way to end his political career. Now events were spinning out of control. Though the reality of the situation pressed itself on his logical mind, emotionally he succeeded in pushing it away. [Page 184]

That makes President Ford different from just about any other American you'll ever encounter. Which of us didn't dream as a kid of becoming PRESIDENT OF THE UNITED STATES? Of course, the vice-president couldn't lick his chops in public, but isn't it likely he did in private? Anyway, how did Woodward and Bernstein find out that "emotionally he succeeded in pushing" thoughts of the "reality of the situation" away? Even a mildly sophisticated world view concerning human nature contradicts the portrayal of these battle-hardened politicians as kindergarten characters the way Woodward and Bernstein sometimes pictured them.

Of course, books that aren't likely to have a mass audience aren't likely to be widely advertised. A good way to find out about smaller circulation books with more serious and sophisticated content is to read the book reviews (or book excerpts) in non-mass media magazines (such as *Atlantic, New York Review of Books, Washington Monthly, Skeptical Inquirer,* and so on).

For example, if you're interested in the U.S.-U.S.S.R. arms race (and if you're not, you should be), you might have read the review of two books—*The Soviet Estimate: U.S. Intelligence Analysis* and *Russian Military Strength* and *Russian Roulette: The Superpower Game*—in the October 1982 issue of *Inquiry* magazine (and, if they sounded interesting, you might have gone out and bought them). Or you might have read the *Harper's* (March 1983) excerpt from *The Threat: Inside the Soviet Military Machine.* Or lots of others.

Of course, for those who don't have the time or inclination to read *whole books* (for gosh sakes!), and also for those who do, the non-mass magazines are the thing to read if you really want to find out what's going on in the world and improve your world view and background knowledge. That means weaning yourself from news on the tube, or better, cutting down on "Dallas," "Dynasty," "The Cosby Show," and fluff of that kind. Do it.

Summary of Chapter 9

1. The news media are businesses. So they have to satisfy advertisers, their audience, and the government.

   They cater to their audience in two ways that affect the news: They simplify the news to make it more easily understood, and they slant coverage to reflect audience prejudices and interests (in particular, those of organized pressure groups).

   They cater to advertisers primarily by suppressing news that reflects badly on advertisers and their products (for instance, suppressing news of the cigarette-cancer connection in Winston-Salem). And to a lesser extent, they cater to government power so as to avoid harassment (for example, over licenses) and in return for favors (for instance, to obtain leaks and other handouts).

   Being businesses, media use news-gathering methods that are designed to save money. (They usually want to get the truth, but not at any cost.) So most news is gathered from regular news beats or from handouts (or both—much news beat news consists of handouts). It thus reflects the opinions and interests of the rich and powerful who can gear up to give them handouts much more easily than the rest of us. (In addition, it should be noted that much foreign news is suspect because of the ways that foreign governments intimidate reporters—including threatening their lives. The American principle of a free press is the exception in the world.)

2. Media theorizers tend to draw the wrong conclusions about what makes for good journalism. The usual (usually) is not considered news because it isn't *new*, however important it (cumulatively) may be. Reporters are supposed to be objective, not subjective, and to separate analysis or in-depth reports from objective straight news stories. The opinions of recognized authorities are supposed to take precedence (in practice, this tends to mean authorities who agree with powerful political factions). In addition, theory requires the media to be good citizens and to censor news that might be bad for society.

3. The media use several standard devices that slant the news (inadvertently or otherwise). They play up stories they like and play down those they don't. They use misleading, sensational, or slanted headlines, omit follow-up stories (even corrections), and use emotive language to con. (It should be noted that they tend to cloak their ignorance of the subjects on which they report in an aura of authority.)

4. Television is the newest and by far the most important of the mass media. It's the chief way in which the whole nation comes together. Its power to ex-

pose, or inflate, is so great that important political events are arranged so as to have the greatest possible impact on tube watchers.

But television has its drawbacks as a source of information. TV entertainment programs give a juvenile impression of life and how people really act. And news programs on the tube suffer from all the defects of the other mass media (simplifying the news for an unsophisticated audience, using handouts to save money, bowing to government power, not following up on stories, and so on).

However, television also has been a strong force breaking down ethnic prejudice, and it does present the news in a way that is more easily understood by the masses. In addition, TV gives us the privilege of occasionally seeing stunning documentaries (for instance, *Nova*'s "The Miracle of Life").

5. On the whole, the non-mass media are better, more sophisticated sources of information, not so much for finding out which particular events occur on a given day, but rather for learning about the underlying forces that shape these individual events, so that we can come to understand what is happening during our lifetimes. (Several of the mass media newspapers also contain a good deal of solid information, although it tends to get buried amid the usual news stories. Perhaps the best of these are the *Los Angeles Times,* the *Washington Post,* the *New York Times,* and the *Wall Street Journal.*)

The point is that we have to be *selective* in what we read and listen to. And we might even consider reading whole books once in a while.

Exercise 9-1

1. Evaluate the coverage of a particular event or issue of national importance covered in your local newspaper with respect to: (a) objectivity; (b) original vs. secondhand reporting of the news; (c) use of headlines; (d) "establishment" viewpoint; and (e) other matters discussed in this chapter.

2. Do the same for a recent issue of *Time* or *Newsweek*.

3. Do the same for an ABC, NBC, or CBS evening news program.

4. Listen to several episodes of some television series and determine what world view is illustrated (for example, *Marcus Welby, M.D.* presented a world in which doctors are conscientious, professional, and successful in treating patients, a world in which all who need medical attention get it).

5. Check the front page of a single issue of your local newspaper and determine as best you can the sources of their stories. (In the case of things like wire stories, try to determine their sources.) How many of these stories are based on a single handout or speech, how many are compiled from several such sources, and how many resulted from reporters finding out for themselves what's going on?

6. How do you think the news would be different if the federal government controlled and managed it? Try to be specific, and back up your answer with reasons.

7. Compare the way in which the three major news magazines (*Time, Newsweek,* and *U.S. News and World Report*) report an important news event (such as American involvement in some foreign country, unemployment, government attempts to enforce drug laws, and so on).

8. Compare articles on the same topic in three magazines, one liberal (for instance, *The New Republic, Washington Monthly,* or *Harper's*), one conservative (say the *National Review, Wall Street Journal,* or *Conservative Digest*), and one libertarian (for example, *Inquiry,* the *Libertarian Review, Reason,* or *Policy Report*). Is their bias evident? What about quality?

9. How are the elderly and teenagers portrayed on television, both in news stories and especially in popular entertainment programs? Back up your conclusions with details.

10. For the energetic: Dig through back issues of some mass media publication (guided perhaps by the *Reader's Guide to Periodical Literature*), and evaluate their coverage of some important, long-term national issue (such as nuclear disarmament, unemployment, America's reduced industrial strength, and so on).

11. Also for the energetic: Write your own news story about a personal event that in truth makes you look bad. Write it as though it were to appear in your local paper, including headlines and everything else. Now rewrite the story so as to make your part appear in the best light possible without actually lying. Compare the two.

Evolutionary Controversies

The controversy between the phyletic gradualism and punctuated equilibrium viewpoints is by no means the first such controversy in evolutionary theory. Like many other scientific fields, evolutionary theory has had its share of controversy and disagreement. Even Darwin and Wallace, who together formulated the theory of natural selection, came to disagree about the actual role of natural selection in the evolutionary process.

Wallace favored a very strict application of the concepts of natural selection. He and others thought that each and every characteristic of every organism was a product of natural selection. Darwin, however, was convinced that natural selection was the main factor, but not the only factor, involved in evolutionary change. He viewed an organism as an integrated whole and thought that while natural selection might result in adaptive changes in one part, other parts might change in ways that had neither positive nor negative effects on the odds of reproductive success, which is the final test of adaptation according to the theory of natural selection.

Historically, a key part of evolutionary theory has been the idea of long periods of accumulating gradual change, usually associated with geographic isolation, and the eventual emergence of new and reproductively isolated species. The concept of punctuated equilibrium challenges this idea. It proposes instead that evolution of any particular line is characterized by long periods of relative stability punctuated by periods of abrupt change, change that occurs in periods of time that are relatively short compared to the enormity of the geologic time scale.

Disagreements such as the one that exists among evolutionary theorists regarding phyletic gradualism and punctuated equilibrium are not unusual in science. Unfortunately, however, people who do not think that life on earth has an evolutionary history cite such controversies as indicating some fundamental weakness in the theory of organic evolution, or that scientists are coming to doubt that an evolutionary process has occurred. These people have a mistaken view of science and the way scientists work. Such controversies are inherent in the nature of science and characterize most, if not all, fields of scientific endeavor. This vigorous debate is by no means a weakness in the theory of organic evolution. Rather it is a strength, an expected characteristic of an active field of scientific endeavor. Scientific progress is made through careful examination that leads to acceptance or rejection of competing conceptual schemes. The theory of organic evolution remains one of the central unifying themes of modern biology, and it provides one of the basic conceptual frameworks for interpreting biological phenomena.

Views of the history of life on earth, possibly more than any other set of scientific concepts, engender emotional responses and controversy of another sort. The great majority of scientists conclude that available evidence indicates a very long history of life on earth that is measured in thousands of millions of years and characterized by evolutionary descent. But some individuals believe that the history of life on earth is much shorter, possibly as short as 10,000 years, and that it is characterized by a series of divine creation events. Their view of life is essentially compatible with literal interpretation of the biblical creation story of the Judeo-Christian religious tradition.

Many scientists, however, do not find the idea of a long evolutionary process incompatible with their religious faith and experience. They do not feel that their faith is compromised because they interpret a creation story in terms of modern scientific understanding. They recognize that the biblical creation story was written in a form compatible with the experience of people living several thousand years ago. Possibly their view of faith and life can best be summarized with the words that Charles Darwin used following his summary of the theory of natural selection at the very end of the first edition of *On the Origin of Species:* "There is a grandeur in this view of life, with its several powers, having been originally breathed by the Creator into a few forms or into one; and that, whilst this planet has gone cycling on according to the fixed law of gravity, from so simple a beginning endless forms most beautiful and wonderful have been, and are being evolved."

Leland G. Johnson, *Biology,* 2nd ed. © 1983, 1987
(Dubuque, Iowa: Wm. C. Brown Publishers).
All rights reserved. Reprinted by permission of the publisher.

Above is a page from an exceptionally good high school biology text explaining to students how "creation scientists" fail to understand science and why most religious biologists have no problem reconciling their faith with their acceptance of evolution and natural selection as proven facts. (See pp. 278–279 for more on this topic.)

The easiest way to change history is to become a historian.

—Anonymous

Probably all education is but two things: first, parrying of the ignorant child's impetuous assault on the truth; and second, gentle, imperceptible initiation of the humiliated children into the lie.

—Franz Kafka

The less people know about how sausages and laws are made, the better they'll sleep at night.

—Bismarck

And the crowd was stilled. One elderly man, wondering at the silence, turned to the child and asked him to repeat what he had just said. Wide eyed, the child raised his voice and said once again, "Why, the Emperor has no clothes. He is naked."

—The Emperor's New Clothes

To limit the press is to insult a nation; to prohibit reading of certain books is to declare the inhabitants to be either fools or slaves.

—Claud Arrien Helvetius

[Studying] history has no purpose but to teach wise disillusionment.

—Noel Annan

10

Textbooks: Managing World Views

First, the bad news. The textbooks on United States history, social studies (civics), and world history that you read back in public school weren't just dull, dull, dull. They also suppressed evidence, pulled their punches, lacked a sense of proportion, and in general gave you a distorted view of history, your country, and the world.

Now for the good news. While public school textbooks still tend to be dull, otherwise they've been getting better and better. In particular, the minor revolution started in about 1960 (because of changing American attitudes toward blacks and other minority groups) has reached maturity, producing texts that slant history and how our system works much less than they used to. It would not be a case of puffery to say that some of the recent public school history and social studies texts are the best of their kind in history, anywhere.

1. Textbooks and Indoctrination

The first thing we have to remember is that the ultimate purpose of public schools is to educate the young to fit into adult society. That means, first, giving them the knowledge they'll need to be productive citizens and, second, inculcating in them the values, attitudes, and practices that will make them good citizens. Education thus inevitably involves a certain amount of indoctrination.

Applying these thoughts to public school textbooks yields some tentative conclusions as to their likely content. The first is that noncontroversial topics, like mathematics, will be presented in a more or less straightforward way, with indoctrination at a minimum. Society wants just about everybody to be able to read and to do arithmetic.

The second tentative conclusion is that history and civics texts are bound to distort their material. The history of any nation has its dark spots as well as bright, and no system works the way it's supposed to. Social studies texts thus deal with extremely sensitive political and social issues. (Also, even the best scholars disagree on these topics, so it's hard to present a true account of them.) Public school history and civics texts therefore inevitably have to distort their subject matters so as to make "Our Great Nation" appear better than it really is. (No society wants to raise disaffected citizens.) Controversial and embarrassing points have to be papered over somehow or other. Exactly how and to what extent this is done depends on social and political factors that change from time to time. Today, these factors are more favorable for providing students with greater accuracy and less indoctrination than ever before in our history. (However, biology texts are under attack, and a small amount of backsliding has occurred, as we shall see.)

2. Textbooks Are a Commodity

We also have to remember that textbooks are a commodity very much like newspapers and magazines. So we should expect that the various parties involved in their production, sale, and use will have power over their content. It turns out, however,

---

The first requirement of any society is that its adult membership should realize and represent the fact that it is they who constitute its life and being. And the first function of the rites of puberty, accordingly, must be to establish in the individual a system of sentiments that will be appropriate to the society in which he is to live and on which that society itself must depend for its existence.

—Joseph Campbell, *Myths Men Live By*

Throughout history, . . . people have had to be taught to be stupid. For to permit the mind to expand to its outermost capabilities results in a challenge to traditional ways. . . . A certain amount of intellectual sabotage must be introduced into all educational systems. Hence all educational systems must train people to be unintelligent within the limits of the culture's ability to survive.

—Jules Henry, *On Sham, Vulnerability, and Other Forms of Self-Destruction*

that the relative power of each faction is a bit different than in the case of the mass media.

There are six groups who have an interest in textbooks: authors, publishers, state regulators, local buyers, teachers (and principals), and students. All exercise power in some way or other. But those who actually buy a product in a relatively open market have the largest share of say as to what the product will be like.

In the United States, local school boards are the ones who ultimately spend the cash that feeds the textbook industry. So in a sense local boards have the most power in determining textbook content. But they're constrained in their choices. First, state regulating agencies limit the books local boards can select from. Second, local boards almost inevitably delegate authority for textbook selection to local teachers (and principals), retaining only indirect control. And third, personal scruples and professional standards keep textbook authors from straying too far from the straight and narrow. (Remember too that local boards are elected by local citizens whose taxes buy public school textbooks.)

Oh, yes, students also have an indirect say in textbook style and (to a lesser extent) content. Unliked books tend to be less effective, and that's bound to influence selection somewhat. But student power is smaller than that of any other of the concerned groups. That's why the term *indoctrination* isn't far off the mark. In the case of the mass media, the ultimate user of the commodity wields the greatest power, as should be evident from the discussion in the last chapter. In the case of public school textbooks, the ultimate user has the least say. (But then, most

---

The House of Representatives of the State of Texas, in a 1961 Resolution, desires ". . . that the American history courses in the public schools emphasize in the textbooks our glowing and throbbing history of hearts and souls inspired by wonderful American principles and traditions."

—Jack Nelson and Gene Roberts, Jr., in *The Censors and the Schools*

Philosophy of History–Social Science Education in California

The central purpose of history–social science education is to prepare students to be humane, rational, understanding, and participating citizens in a diverse society and in an increasingly interdependent world—students who will preserve and continue to advance progress toward a just society. (From the 1981 History Social Science Framework for California Public Schools Kindergarten Through Grade Twelve, the basic document governing California schools.)

Notice that the purpose of history and civics texts is not to tell you the history of the nation or how things really work, except incidentally as these serve other purposes. (Texas and California statewide selecting agencies have more influence on public school textbooks than all the other state agencies combined.)

mass media audiences consist of "responsible" adults, while public school textbook audiences consist of "children.")[1]

3. Textbooks Are Censored

It's very difficult to distinguish censorship from the ordinary pressures on textbook content. But however it's defined, we have to realize that government agencies do in fact force changes in the content of public school textbooks (and also of nonprint material.) This is particularly true of the state agencies in Texas and California, since no publisher wants to be shut out of the two most lucrative markets.

Prior to 1960, minority groups, in particular blacks, tended to be invisible in public school textbooks, as they were also in the mass media. But now no major publisher will publish a United States history or civics textbook that does not give lots of space to minorities. They won't, for one reason, because such a book wouldn't satisfy the California state board's criteria and so would be a victim of California censorship. Prejudice against minority groups has decreased considerably since the 1950s, and textbooks reflect that fact.

The Controversy Over Biology Texts

In recent years, Christian fundamentalists have also tried to censor public school biology texts that teach the theory of evolution (and natural selection) as fact. Although they dislike having principles of evolution taught in biology classes at all, they do not demand that they no longer be taught. Rather, they insist that if evolution is taught, it be labeled a mere unproven hypothesis, with their own biblical view, "creation science," given equal time. So far their chief success has been in the state of Texas.

We showed in earlier editions of this text how a very few biology texts that were distributed nationwide had to make some changes so as to satisfy the Texas State Textbook Committee that selects all the textbooks used in Texas public schools. But in the last few years, the situation has changed just a bit. In effect, the market now is divided into texts that fudge on the issue, used in Texas and in a few other schools around the country, and those that rather firmly hold the line. Most texts fall into the second category, including every book permitted to be used in California, the other state with great power to influence what textbooks are like in the United States today.

Most of the texts in this second category refer to evolution as a fact proved by scientific evidence and don't even mention creation science or religious objections to the teaching of evolution as fact. A few do mention fundamentalist objections but insist that creation science is not a science, and in some cases, firmly state that

---

[1]In recent years, power has shifted away from local school boards to state agencies that set uniform state requirements for textbooks. This move has been influenced, surprisingly, by federal government actions, such as the 1967 ruling that all schools meet statewide requirements to get federal aid. See, for instance, Eugenia Froedge Toma, "Bureaucrats and Education," *Policy Report* (June 1982).

When a federal judge in Alabama ordered 50 textbooks removed from Alabama schools in late 1986, the controversy between Christian fundamentalists and most of the rest of society heated up considerably. At issue was the question whether teaching what fundamentalists call the "religion of secular humanism," which they say puts human beings and their values above God and His values is or is not constitutional. Soon after the ruling, a higher court ordered a stay of execution of the lower court order, setting off another round in the ongoing battle over the content of books used in public schools. Here are short excerpts from two of the books objected to by fundamentalists:

Values are personal and subjective. They vary from person to person. You will be able to understand and get along with other people better if you keep an open mind about the value judgments they make. . . .

The number of *one-parent families* in the United States is growing. In this family structure, an adult lives with one or more children. The adult may be widowed, separated, divorced or never married.

A few adults plan this family structure. They do not want to marry, but they want to experience parenthood. So they adopt one or more children. The large majority of one-parent families are not planned. They are the result of circumstances. This does not mean, however, that they are inferior. The one-parent family can perform the family functions. . . .

The increased number of divorces is accompanied by a change in public attitude. In the past, divorced persons were considered failures and social misfits. Today, society does not look down on divorced persons. Divorce is viewed as a misfortune that can happen to anyone. Divorce is considered an acceptable way of solving a problem.

—*Homemaking: Skills for Everyday Living* (Goodheart-Willcox, 1981)

One of the most important leaders of the equal rights movement was a young minister named Martin Luther King Jr. Dr. King said there was only one way to work for equal rights. That way was nonviolence. Nonviolence meant that protest must be peaceful.

The equal rights movement suffered a great loss in 1968. Martin Luther King Jr. was shot and killed. But the supporters of the movement continued to work for the ideals and methods in which he had believed.

King is buried in Atlanta, Georgia. Carved on his tombstone are famous words from one of his speeches: "Free at last, free at last, thank God Almighty, I'm free at last."

—*America: Past and Present* (Houghton-Mifflin, 1980)

Most college textbook publishers also produce public school texts, but Wadsworth, the publisher of Logic *and* Contemporary Rhetoric, *rarely does so. Consequently, Wadsworth editors were rather surprised, and a bit amused, when they discovered the changes that the Texas State Textbook Committee required before accepting the Wadsworth high school text,* The Mass Media in Modern Society. *Here are the chief changes they were required to make:*

Censored Passage

Playboy, first issued in 1953, zoomed to a million circulation by 1960, with subscribers bearing a large share of the cost. Since then, circulation has climbed to more than five million.

Acceptable Replacement

Prevention, America's leading health magazine first appeared in 1950, rapidly established a place for itself in the marketplace. Today, its circulation is about 2,500,000.

Censored Passage

Cosmopolitan (circulation 2,848,399), after some years of shifting content, has emerged as the feminine *Playboy,* dealing frankly with permissiveness and the issues of the single woman in today's society.

Acceptable Replacement

Redbook (circulation 4,368,523) maintains its traditional content including health and fashion advice, recipes, crafts, and fiction but has moved to shorter stories, more photos, ads, and art, and brighter graphics.

Censored Passage

Playgirl, started in 1973, has reached over 700,000.

Acceptable Replacement

And *Self,* a woman's fitness magazine founded in 1978, has soared to over a million in circulation.

What do you think? Is this silly, or is it serious?

But enough of trashing Texas. Let's move to Massachusetts and Harvard University. In 1968, James D. Watson, who won a Nobel Prize as the co-discoverer of the structure of DNA, the single most important discovery in biology in the twentieth century, wrote a book, The Double Helix, *about the events leading up to the discovery, revealing the competitiveness, foibles, and weaknesses of those involved in the race to be first. (Scientists are human too.) The president of Harvard University, where Watson had been teaching since 1956, ordered Harvard University Press not to publish the book, which when published by another house became a best-seller. Censorship is ubiquitous.*

belief in evolution is not inconsistent with religious beliefs. (See the first page of this chapter for an example.)

It is difficult to be sure why fundamentalists are losing everywhere except in Texas. But one reason has to be the pressure exerted by an aroused scientific community, worried that a generation of scientific illiterates will be raised in the United States. Eminent scientists have testified in several court cases that creation science is not a science and have convinced courts to hold that this is the case.

Nontextbooks Also Are Censored

Censorship occurs more overtly in the case of nontexts used in classrooms or shelved in school libraries. The censor in most of these cases is the local school board.

Almost any book may be censored. The principal reasons for censoring a book are obscenity, favorable portrayal of an immoral life-style, and racial or ethnic bias. A Tennessee county school board removed the old standby *Drums Along the Mohawk* from the assigned list of books in local schools because it contained words they judged to be obscene (such as *hell* and *damn*). Shakespeare's *The Merchant of Venice* is censored occasionally because Jewish groups object to its portrayal of Shylock.

But perhaps silliest of all, one of the most frequently censored books is *The Adventures of Huckleberry Finn*. It has two groups on its back: blacks offended by its portrayal of blacks and others offended by Huck's throwing off of conventional morality, glorifying "immoral conduct." (Irony of ironies, one of the schools censoring *Huck Finn* at one time or another turns out to be Mark Twain Intermediate School in Fairfax County, Virginia.)

It would be provincial to conclude that book censorship in public schools is an American phenomenon. On the contrary, school censorship in the United States is less frequent and much less severe than in most, perhaps all, other countries.

In the early 1980s, for instance, Japanese textbook censorship raised quite a storm, even involving then Japanese Prime Minister Zenko Suzuki. Until a few years ago, Japanese texts portrayed Japan's aggression before and during World War II in a modestly accurate way (no doubt under the prodding of Allied occupation officers after the war). But then changes in textbook content, allegedly engineered by Japanese hawks, produced new history texts in which, for instance, Japan's invasion of China was called an "advance," and the 1919 rebellion in Korea against Japanese rulers was referred to as a "riot."[2] The hawks had one textbook changed because it stated that there have been significant changes in the way Article Nine of the Japanese constitution is being interpreted. The textbook's statement was a rather gentle way of pointing out the truth that this important article in

---

[2]Public outcry in Far Eastern countries overrun by Japan during its "expansionist" period forced the Japanese government to promise reinstatement of the censored material. For more on this, see *The Nation* (December 19, 1981).

their constitution has been violated in recent years. (Article Nine requires that military forces "never be maintained" by Japan. In one recent year, Japan spent $11.5 billion on its "peacekeeping" force—which sounds like pretty good evidence that Article Nine *is* being grossly violated.)

Even paintings of the catastrophes following our dropping of atomic bombs on Hiroshima and Nagasaki were censored by the Japanese Ministry of Education. They forced elimination of pictures of crowds of people being burned alive, screaming, collapsing, and dying, saying that "Extremely tragic subjects will be removed from textbooks." Nothing even remotely like that sort of national government interference in textbook content ever occurs in the United States.

In the United States today, banning books outside of public schools is much less common than censorship within educational walls. But it does occur, and obviously limits what students as well as adults can read. Favorite targets are books with sexual content and those affecting national security. (For more on the history of book censorship, see *Banned Books,* by Anne Lyon Haight, revised by Chandler B. Grannis.) However, in the history of censorship, all sorts of things have been banned or censored. For instance, in 1933, the U.S. customs office confiscated copies of "obscene photo books" it described as "Ceiling Sistene Chapel Filles Michael Angelo." In 1961, Canadian customs officials confiscated as obscene the

---

The number of books and magazines censored out of public school classrooms and libraries runs into the thousands every year. (In the world as a whole, the all time champ is probably the Bible.) Here are a few other examples:[3]

The Sun Also Rises (Ernest Hemingway)
The Catcher in the Rye (J. D. Salinger)
The Grapes of Wrath (John Steinbeck)
Andersonville (McKinley Kantor)
Look Homeward Angel (Thomas Wolfe)
1984 (George Orwell)
Brave New World (Aldous Huxley)
The Invisible Man (Ralph Ellison)
Native Son (Richard Wright)
Slaughterhouse Five (Kurt Vonnegut, Jr.)
Marjorie Morningstar (Herman Wouk)
Ms. magazine
The Naked Ape (Desmond Morris)
The American Heritage Dictionary (banned because it included "gutter words" like *ball, nut, and tail*, and included certain uses of the term *bed* as a transitive verb)

---

[3]The American Library Association's *Newsletter on Intellectual Freedom* contains a list in each issue of "Titles Now Troublesome," which means books somebody or other is censoring.

offiicial report of the trial in England in which D. H. Lawrence's *Lady Chatterley's Lover* was held to be *not* obscene. Not long after that, Ralph Ginsberg went to jail in the U.S. because the *advertising* for his magazine *Eros* was judged to be obscene. Way back in 1526, the first English translation of the *New Testament* was banned and copies burned; in Spain, a similar fate awaited the first translation into Spanish. In more recent times, several states have banned *Fanny Hill* as obscene; material dealing with our defeat at Pearl Harbor was censored during World War II; and just in the past few years, the U.S. federal government has forced censorship of several books dealing with the CIA and its clandestine operations.

4. Textbooks Distort History

Public school history texts are more accurate today than they've ever been before. But they still distort history, in particular the history of the United States.

United States History Is Sanitized

History texts "clean up" our past in order not to reduce student pride in America. Our leaders are pictured as better than human, all dressed up and minus their warts.[4] Take the way in which President Theodore Roosevelt, affectionately called *Teddy* in many texts (the teddy bear was named after him), is spruced up for textbook readers. In textbooks, Roosevelt is pictured as energetic, hard driving, exuberant, brave, a trustbuster, conservationist, big-game hunter, reformer, and progressive who was against big business and for the workers, although (in some recent texts) a bit of an imperialist who made the Panama Canal possible as an American enterprise—a great man well deserving of his place on Mt. Rushmore.

And perhaps he was. But no textbooks say much about another side of good old Teddy. They don't describe him as a bloodthirsty bigot who, though unusually brave, reveled in the slaughter he personally dealt out and witnessed during the Spanish-American War; a man who expressed pleasure that 30 men had been shot to death in the Civil War draft riots—"an admiral object lesson to the remainder"; a person who justified slaughtering Indians, on the grounds that their lives were only "a few degrees less meaningful, squalid, and ferocious than that of the wild beasts," and said that "no triumph of peace is quite so great as the supreme triumph of war." Not exactly a teddy bear, this Teddy Roosevelt.

America's Role in History Is Distorted

Public school textbooks can't use puffery the way ads do. But they use other devices to accomplish a similar end—in particular, the simple *omission* of historical events and the distortion of those they mention by careful control of *emphasis*. Both of these are very hard for uninformed or unsophisticated readers to detect.

---

[4]There are a very few obvious exceptions—villains who can't be dolled up to look virginal. Richard Nixon is the best example. But then, how do you picture the only president driven from office as a saint?

Take the way that America's role in World War II is exaggerated, omitting all but a few of the details of the Russian role and playing down those that are mentioned. Although reliable statistics on World War II are sometimes difficult to find, common estimates place the total killed in that war at between 40 and 50 million and the Soviet Union's dead at 15 to 20 million, almost half of the total. The United States lost 322,000 soldiers (almost no civilians), about 88 percent of them in the European theater of war. The Germans were defeated by a combination of British, American, and Soviet military action, but the Russian effort was incompa-

Drawing by David Levine. Copyright © 1969 NYREV, Inc.
Reprinted by permission from *The New York Review of Books*.

Hamburger Hill

David Levine's drawing of Hamburger Hill (a hill in Vietnam on which many soldiers lost their lives) pictures two American presidents as jolly mass murderers. Would the Texas State Textbook Committee give its approval to a book containing this caricature?

rably greater than that of Britain and America combined. From June 1941, when Germany invaded Russia, to the end of the war in Europe, the largest and most powerful element of the German Army fought on the Russian front against the Soviet Army. The overwhelming majority of German military losses, in equipment and men, were inflicted on them by Russian forces on the Eastern front, not by British and American forces in Africa or Western Europe. There were many times more Russian *civilian* deaths than all the American deaths in all the wars in our history.

But public school textbooks don't play it that way. They emphasize our role in Europe in World War II and play down the Soviet role. One reason for this is to make our own country look better than other countries. Another is to prejudice readers against communism, Communist governments and countries, and in particular the Soviet Union. (The Cold War had to be fought in textbooks as well as elsewhere, and it was. It still is.)

The worst distortions of our history occur in grade school texts, as might be expected. These texts have room for only a very few facts, and indeed tend to give relatively few details about any wars. And certainly there is no reason to tell grade school students more than a tiny bit about the gory details in our past. But this does mean that students are exposed to the worst account of our history when just starting out.

Junior high school texts give many more details, including a few of the ones that are less glorious than we might wish. In the last edition of this text, we showed how a typical eighth grade United States history text deals with the Russian ordeal in World War II. So let's now see how one of the best senior high school American history texts deals with this topic, remembering that such a text has plenty of room

---

Public school history texts generally tell the nice things about America's heros while neglecting the not so nice. To get the whole picture, undistorted, you need to consult other sources, one of the best being the magazine American Heritage. *Here is a snippet from their May/June 1987 issue revealing a not so nice feature of founding father George Washington:*

"Shall we have a King?" John Jay asked George Washington in 1787, when the new nation, still pinned together by the Articles of Confederation, seemed likely to fly apart. More than any other man, Washington would make sure that the answer to that plaintive query was a resounding no. But his own sense of the Presidency was itself fairly kingly; guests at his Philadelphia levees were not to speak to him unless spoken to, nor would he shake their hands—to ensure that no one dared try to press *his* flesh, he rested one hand upon the hilt of his dress sword and held a specially made false hat in the other.

It was Washington, too, who determined that his successors should live in a "palace" in the new federal capital . . . and initially favored . . . a residence five times the size of the one that we now know.

to say a great deal on any topic it chooses to. The text in question is *A History of the United States,*[5] and one of its authors is Daniel J. Boorstin, a Pulitzer Prize-winning historian.

This book has 26 pages on World War II itself, plus several more on events leading up to the war. It describes the invasion of Poland that started the war, early German victories, the fall of France, Britain being bombed and standing alone against Hitler, and so on, as all texts do. This takes several pages. We also are treated to an unusual section on Billy Mitchell and U.S. air power of about one and a half pages in length.

When the chronological story reaches June 1941, the Russians enter into the picture, and we get the first of the five short paragraphs in the text that present the bulk of what this book says of Russian fighting and suffering (there is only one other reference to the Soviet Union, to be mentioned later):

> Eight days later Hitler made his great blunder. In his crazy belief that all battlefields were alike, and that blitzkrieg could conquer all, on June 22, 1941, only a year after conquering France, he suddenly invaded Russia. If he had studied history, he might have learned that more than a hundred years before, Napoleon had lost his empire in the same desperate gamble. Vast, frigid Russia embraced and paralyzed invaders. At first it seemed that Hitler might conquer Russia as quickly as France. But when the Germans were deep in Russia—only fifteen miles from Moscow—the Russian winter arrived. The fingers of Nazi soldiers became numb. Frozen oil crippled the motors of tanks. The Nazis had to stop to await the return of warm weather.

Note that this text says it was the Russian winter, not Soviet soldiers, that stopped Hitler, whereas in fact, it was both. (There also are minor errors of fact.)

Here is a snippet from an American Heritage *magazine (October/November 1985) article on how white Americans and their government treated Indians back in the nineteenth century:*

[To get the Seminole removed from Florida, U.S. government] officials wrote up a fraudulent treaty stating that the Seminole were willing to move west, obtained signatures of chiefs who did not represent the entire tribe, and disregarded the clauses in the treaty that obstructed their aims. [Seminole resistance was crushed] when Indian leader [Osceola] met with Army officials under a flag of truce—and was imprisoned. He died in jail the next year.

If you didn't recognize this as part of our history, perhaps one reason is that you definitely did not read anything like this in your high school history textbooks.

---

[5]Daniel J. Boorstin, Brooks Mather Kelley, and Ruth Frankel Boorstin, *A History of the United States,* 3rd ed. (Lexington, Mass.: Ginn, 1986).

Russians then become invisible for ten pages, during which lots of fighting on other fronts is described, and we are treated, among other things, to what was happening on the American "home front." We then get this paragraph:

> Meanwhile the Russians were pressing the Allies to open a "Second Front" in Europe with a new invasion of the continent into lands held by the Axis powers. This would divert the enemy from their attacks on Russia.

And soon after this appears the first paragraph indicating that Russian soldiers were defeating Germans on the battlefield:

> In November 1942, the Russians had gone on the counteroffensive. After some of the bloodiest fighting of the war, they broke the seige of Stalingrad and surrounded an entire German army. After the army was captured in February 1943, the Russians swept rapidly westward. Meanwhile in January the seige of Leningrad had ended. The tide was beginning to turn.

It is eight pages later before Russia again enters the picture, during which readers are given a half-page of details concerning the battle of Guadalcanal, a third of a page on the fall of Tunisia, and a page and a half on D-Day, including a picture of Ike with paratroopers:

> Meanwhile [!] from the East, huge Soviet armies were hastening toward the German border. A great Russian offensive had speedily swept 460 miles across the Ukraine and Poland to the gates of Warsaw. There, unfortunately, the Russians stopped. This gave the Germans time to crush a heroic revolt of the Polish underground in the city.

Note how Soviet victories are diminished by coupling them with an account of the trick the Russians played on Polish patriots (although it isn't made clear just how nasty and politically motivated the Russian pause had been—the Russians wanted potential opponents of their planned communist regime in Poland to be wiped out by the Germans, as they were):

> When the Russians moved toward the South, Romania and Bulgaria surrendered quickly. On October 20 [1944] the Russians reached Belgrade. In December at Budapest, the Germans dug in and put up stubborn resistance.

And that is it for the Russians in World War II, except that they are mentioned in the five-paragraph, excellent discussion of the American decision not to take Berlin but to leave that to the Russians, a decision the authors found appalling.

The distortion in this account of World War II is enormous. One person, and a minor bit player at that, General Billy Mitchell, is given more attention than the entire war on the Soviet front. The relatively minor battle on Guadalcanal, involving a few thousand troops, receives almost as much attention as the four years of fighting on the Russian front that decided the war in Europe, where battles in which well over a million German and somewhere between 7 and 10 million Soviet soldiers lost their lives, not to mention well over 10 million civilians who died or the extreme suffering of tens of millions of other Russian civilians. Nothing re-

One of the great improvements in public school texts since about 1960 has been the treatment of minority groups, in particular, blacks and women. This improvement mirrors the change in attitudes that has been taking place in America since World War II. In previous editions of this text, we showed how American history was doctored so as to mask the essential fact that white Europeans who had no claim to even a foot of the North American continent defeated its legitimate owners (the Native American Indians) and stole the whole continent from them. To mask this fact, or at least to blunt it, textbooks had to make Indians as invisible as possible, except for the "good" Indians (Pocahontas, the Thanksgiving Indians, Indian guides) and for the few cases where land may actually have been bought instead of just taken by force (Manhattan Island). Today's textbooks don't exactly shout grand theft on every page, but they do give some specifics concerning the suffering of the Indians (the "Trail of Tears") and some idea that the Indians didn't willingly give up their land to the Europeans.

In previous editions, we also showed how history and civics texts in the 1960s had to change their treatment of blacks so as to keep up with public opinion and the increased power of blacks. For instance, we showed cases in which the only significant differences between old and new editions were in photos—replacing pictures of whites with those of blacks—and in mentioning more blacks—Frederick Douglass, Harriet Tubman, W.E.B. DuBois— than just the few standard or token blacks, like Booker T. Washington, who had always been mentioned.

Let's look at one particularly obvious (some would say hilarious) example of this from earlier editions, to illustrate the cleansing process established texts underwent during that period (and thus to illustrate indirectly the way

motely like the suffering that occurred in Russia during World War II has ever been inflicted on citizens of the United States. (Note that world history texts do no better with respect to World War II, and most distort even more than the Boorstin text, which, as we remarked before, is one of the best senior high school American history texts.)

The point of relating these facts here is certainly not to diminish America's effort in World War II, or to take anything away from the wonderful bravery and fighting skill of American soldiers (the author of this text had relatives who fought in the Second World War). Rather, it is to provide a graphic example of how history is rewritten in public school textbooks (illustrating along the way the truth in the saying given at the beginning of this chapter that the easiest way to make history is to become a historian).

Before ending our discussion of history textbooks, perhaps we should say a few words about another area in which these texts distort our past, and indeed the present, in a way that has distressed many people, particularly religious fundamentalists. In United States history texts, religion is mentioned many times when the colonial period is being discussed. The point is made that many people came to these

in which political power translates into changes in textbooks). The text Building Citizenship[6] *had the following snippet on President Theodore Roosevelt in its 1961 edition:*

> Some people found fault with Theodore Roosevelt because they said he acted as if he had discovered the Ten Commandments. Quite likely, however, many more people became interested in applying the Ten Commandments to present-day life because they admired something in "T.R."

This is changed in the 1966 edition (same page, same exact spot on the page) to read:

> Some people find fault with [brace yourself] Martin Luther King because he acts as if he had discovered the Ten Commandments. Quite likely, however, many more people have become interested in applying the Ten Commandments to present-day life because they admire Dr. King's fight against racial discrimination.

This was one of very few changes introduced in the 1966 edition. Most of the others were changes in photos to include blacks, who had been invisible, or in tiny paragraphs like the one in question. In this context, the purpose of the switch from "T.R." to "M.L.K." becomes obvious—say something about a black leader that will fit a particular spot so the new edition can be published as quickly and cheaply as possible and the book can catch up to public opinion. (None of this had to do with anything so crass as making textbooks come closer to the truth.)

shores to get away from religious persecution and to be able to practice their religion in their own way. The Puritans are mentioned, as is Roger Williams and the rest of the familiar cast of characters. But by the nineteenth century, the fact that the majority of Americans have been Christians tends to get lost. The only references to religion concern a very few events, such as the Mormons' great trek west and the election of the first Catholic president, John F. Kennedy. The recent increase in the number or at least political strength of Christian fundamentalists is not mentioned in any text this writer has ever seen. Again, no student would be able to tell from reading these textbooks that the majority of people in this country have been Christians, indeed Protestants. The word *Protestant* is rarely ever mentioned in history texts, except occasionally with reference to Connecticut Protestants of the colonial period.

---

[6]This text was in use for a long time. The original author was Ray Osgood Hughes (Boston: Allyn & Bacon, 1921); it had been revised by C.H.W. Pullen and by James H. McCrocklin, the latter being responsible for both of the versions considered here.

5. Textbooks Minimize the Gulf Between Theory and Practice

In the constant struggle for power and wealth that goes on in America (and no doubt everywhere else), national ideals and standards get violated. Thus, a great gulf is going to exist between the theory as to how our system is supposed to work and actual everyday practice. It is extremely important that we know about this gulf so we can get a better idea of what is in store for us under various possible circumstances. We ought to know what our chances are of getting justice if we have to go to court, or how far we can trust our leaders to obey the laws of the land or tell us the truth about what they are up to.

For instance, one of our official myths[7] is that no one is above the law—that a Rockefeller can't break into someone else's property with impunity any more than you can. Civics texts have to stress the positive and play down the negative, so they don't tell students that this particular official myth really *is* a myth—that the rich sometimes are above the law in ways we common folk never are, and that a Rockefeller can (because one actually did) at least sometimes break into someone else's property and get away with it. Here, for instance, is a *Washington Post*[8] tidbit you're not likely to run across in any public school texts, although it reveals a great deal about privilege differences between rich and poor:

Rules Are Made to be Broken, for Some People

> Late one night in Kansas City, [Nelson] Rockefeller couldn't find his Water Pik. "He had dental work that debris would catch in sometimes," recalls Hugh Morrow, the former Rockefeller spokesman. "So with the aid of the local police, [aide] Joe [Canzeri] broke into a drugstore, got the Water Pik and left the money on the counter—including the local sales tax. . . ."
>
> During the 1968 New York City garbage strike, Rockefeller was once in all-night negotiations with the union. By 5 A.M. the group was tired and hungry. Canzeri broke a kitchen lock at the nearby Gotham Hotel, then made bacon, scrambled eggs, coffee and toast for the group of 30.

Until recently, the way the American system works was discussed primarily in civics texts. In earlier editions of this book, we went to great pains to show how these civics texts gave the impression that theory and practice coincide more than they in fact do. We showed this with respect to court systems, labor unions, the working of government agencies such as the FBI, and so on.

But civics texts are on the way out, replaced by "social science" texts that tend to concentrate on other matters and are indeed a bit more accurate in most of what they tell students, even if they still retain the goody-goody tone of the old civics books. Typical texts tell about "our nation and the world," America's neighbors," and so on.

However, to the extent that they attempt to describe how things actually work in the United States, they are as misleading as the old civics texts, or more accurately,

---

[7]Recall Mark Twain's colossal lies of silent assertion mentioned in Chapter 5.
[8]December 1, 1981. Reprinted in *Policy Report* (January 1982).

as the civics texts published after, say, 1975, since most civics texts in use prior to about that time were very much inferior to any texts on the market today.

6. Textbook Style Is Deadly Dull

Textbooks also fail to truly educate young people because they tend to be devoid of literary style. Since they're supposed to be objective, emotively neutral locutions are the rule, especially where anything controversial is mentioned. Facts and details roll on, one after the other, with all of the life squeezed out of them. Atrocities are mentioned the way one might discuss the weather or a math problem. The idea is not to get students upset or disaffected, say by letting them find out the true horror of "Indian removal" as carried out by the white man. Injustices that are mentioned are discussed either in a way that minimizes them or to point out how they are being corrected.

After a few pages of such writing, eyes begin to glaze over, and true understanding goes out the window. At best, most students will start reading for "facts" they may need to regurgitate on exams. So they may hardly notice when something they really need to know about is discussed. Reading between the lines is discouraged by boredom and is made harder by the upbeat or even-handed style in which controversial topics are discussed.

Here, for instance, is how one of the last civics texts, *Civics for Americans,*[9] *talks about courtroom justice:*

Equal Justice for All

Our legal system is based on an important ideal—**equal justice** for all under the law. The goal of the legal system is to treat every person the same.

Perhaps some readers still may be wondering whether all that much progress has occurred in recent years. So here's a little excerpt from a really bad textbook that was in circulation until about the early 1970s, to give you an idea of how much things have improved:

As you ride up beside the Negroes in the field they stop working long enough to look up, tip their hats and say, "Good morning, Master John." You like the friendly way they speak and smile; they show bright rows of white teeth. "How's it coming, Sam?" your father asks one of the old Negroes. "Fine, Marse Tom, jes fine. We got more cotton than we can pick." Then Sam chuckles to himself and goes back to picking as fast as he can.

—Mentioned in the TRB column of the *New Republic* (July 25, 1970) and best left anonymous here.

If that sort of writing doesn't make every *current textbook look good, nothing will.*

---

[9]John J. Patrick and Richard C. Remy, *Civics for Americans* (Chicago: Scott, Foresman, 1980).

Public school textbooks don't have to be as dull and uninformative as they are. The proof is that a very few texts are not. To illustrate, here is a page from an exceptionally good high school text, Understanding Mass Media.[15]

Economic Control

Magazines, newspapers, television, and radio stations, book publishers—all, with a few rare exceptions—share one common goal; to make money. This fact controls to some extent the content of what these media produce.

With the exception of book publishing, all these media receive most of their income from advertising. The question thus arises: Does advertising in any way influence the content of mass media?

One illustration of economic influence is the true case of the Car-Puter Company's attempt to buy ads in major newspapers and magazines. Car-Puter is a company that supplies customers with a computer read-out of dealer costs on any new car they may want to buy, including options. The company also supplies the name of a local automobile dealer who, through a special arrangement, will sell the customer the car for about $150 over dealer cost. The company charges the consumer $5 for this service, which is legitimate and helpful to consumers. However, when Car-Puter attempted to run a small ad, they were refused by most newspapers as well as by some magazines.

The ads were refused without a detailed explanation. The newspapers claimed they had a right to turn down any advertising—and they do. But the reason for the refusal most certainly is related to the fact that automotive ads are an important source of income for newspapers and magazines. Car-Puter Company would not be approved of by other auto advertisers.

As another example, sponsors of television programs are not likely to buy time for programs that attack business. Sponsors carefully monitor network TV shows. A group called "Stop Immorality on Television" asked major TV sponsors about their "moral stance" on the programs they sponsored. Gillette replied that "we try to see that our advertising runs in programs which are suitable for general family viewing.

Under the Constitution, every person accused of breaking the law has the right to a public trial. Every accused person has the right to a lawyer. If an accused person cannot afford a lawyer, the courts will appoint one and will pay the lawyer's fee. Every person is considered innocent until proven guilty. And a person has the right to ask for a review of his or her case if, in that person's view, the courts have made a mistake.

The idea of equal justice is a difficult goal to reach. Judges and juries are not free from the prejudices of their communities. Poor people do not have the money to spend on legal help that wealthy citizens or large companies do. Nonetheless, Americans believe in the ideal. There are

---

[10]Jeffrey Schrank, *Understanding Mass Media*, 2nd ed. (Skokie, Ill.: National Textbook Company, 1986). Schrank did have to pull punches a bit, but he still manages to tell students lots of things they need to know.

Under this policy we have declined to participate as sponsors in programs such as *The Smothers Brothers* and *Laugh-In.* " Eastman Kodak commented that they preview all scripts before the airing of a program: "If we find a script is offensive, we will withdraw our commercials from the program."

Although advertisers have no formal censorship power, they can exert great influence on the kinds of programs that networks will offer the viewers. A TV network would think twice before showing a documentary exposing the faults of the over-the-counter drug industry, because so much of its advertising revenue comes from pain-killers and headache remedies.

A question often asked at networks is "Will the show gain sponsors?" The importance of this question can easily limit consideration of another question: "What is in the best interests of the public?"

Newspapers and magazines vary widely in the amount of control they allow advertisers to exert. Some keep "news" and ads completely separate and will report the problems and failings of local food chains or auto dealers even though these provide the paper with thousands of dollars yearly in advertising revenue. Some newspapers, however, still have a policy of not "biting the hand that feeds them." If the health department closes or issues a warning to a local food store or restaurant, such papers will ignore the story for fear of "hurting" the advertiser's reputation. A story about a shady car dealer or home builder might go unreported if that company is a large advertiser in the newspaper.

Such control is less frequent now than it used to be, but it still exists, especially among smaller newspapers struggling to stay in business.

Record companies put pressure on radio stations to play their records. Every time a radio station plays a record, the "exposure" is as good as or better than an ad for the record. The more radio stations play any given song or record, the more it sells. Record companies can give away free records but are not supposed to give money to stations as an inducement to play the records. There have been many instances, though, of record companies slipping a little extra money ("payola") to disk jockeys to gain air time for a song. As with newspapers, this practice is less common among the largest stations and offers a greater temptation to small stations.

some countries in the world where prejudice is legal and where there are different laws for different groups of people. In the United States, all people are equal before the law. If injustice occurs, citizens have the right to speak out and correct it.

Even those students who are paying attention are unlikely to get much of an idea from this about the gulf between the theory of equal justice and the reality of everyday practice. So they're not going to learn about their chances of being treated fairly if they sue or are brought into court when they become adults. But if we don't tell students that, what good are all the details about the theory of jury selection or which courts handle what? (The text follows this snippet with almost two pages of forgettable details, including, for instance, a paragraph called "Disputes between States or People from Different States," which tells us things even most lawyers might have to look up, for example, that "Such suits must involve a sum of at least $10,000 to be handled in Federal Court.")

7. Textbooks Fail to Give Students Genuine Understanding

From what has been said so far, it should be clear that textbooks fail to give students true understanding of the history and function of their society. They fail, to put it in a nutshell, because the various relevant pressures force them to fail. Since our society is far from perfect and our history somewhat tarnished, textbooks have to pull their punches, reveal injustice primarily as it is being corrected, and in general puff up our society as much as they can in order to mold young people into loyal citizens.

Of course, it could hardly be otherwise, and in fact it's the same or worse in every other country. Read a Soviet text on the 1956 Hungarian uprising, which they call "the events of 1956," or consider how the Nazi period tends to be neglected in German public schools, and you'll gain new respect for the American educational system. The point is not to knock the United States, but rather to see that a society's textbooks are going to be slanted in favor of that society. All have the same goal: to make their youth into good citizens. Whether or not this is best for a nation as a whole, it does make it hard on those students who would like to know the true history of their countries or the way their system actually works. So far, public school textbooks are not going to tell them right out. But perceptive, selective readers can learn a great deal from slanted texts—in particular, naked facts, like dates—so that all is not lost by any means. A careful reader can get a good deal of information even from Russian textbooks, compared to which ours are treasure troves of information. But anyone who wants a sophisticated knowledge of these matters has to go to the other sources.

If the test of true education is understanding, and not mere digestion of facts, the best test of understanding is the ability to foresee events, or at least not be unduly surprised at their occurrence. If American public school textbooks had helped students to achieve a true understanding of their own system and how it really works, would the Watergate scandal have been such a shock to them? Would they have accepted our government's denial that we had interfered in the internal affairs of Chile (and then later accepted the clearly untrue explanation of *why* we had in fact interfered)? Would they have been so surprised by the overthrow of the Shah of Iran and the odiousness of this regime of one of our "allies"? (Of course, textbook indoctrination is only one reason so many Americans were taken in by their leaders on these issues.)

It should be clear now that the author of this college text doesn't like the idea that public school textbooks and education use large doses of indoctrination in lieu of useful truth. He realizes, of course, that indoctrination can't be entirely eliminated, but he believes that it can be reduced to some extent and that students can be taught to guard against it.

This text was written in a completely different spirit from that of indoctrination. A student who accepts its contents uncritically has missed its main point, which is that in controversial social and political matters, free men and women must be their own experts, or at least must be able to judge for themselves the opinions of those who call themselves experts. A free society does, after all, depend on a correctly informed and thinking electorate, not an indoctrinated one.

8. Postscript on College Texts

The question naturally arises about college textbooks. Do they distort American history and practice, as do public school texts? If the forces at work are the same in both cases, we should expect the results will be roughly the same (taking into account the greater maturity of college students). If they aren't, we should expect the finished products to be different. What do our world views tell us about this question?

The first thing to notice is that the sellers of college texts have exactly the same motives as those who sell public school texts. In fact, many publishers in one field also publish in the other. The second key point is that most college texts are adopted by the teachers who will use them in their own classes (or, in the case of large classes with several sections, by group faculty decisions), not by school boards or state agencies. (Students then buy them but can't choose which one to buy.)

The reason for this important difference is the history (and current funding) of higher education in America, as compared to primary and secondary education. Primary and secondary school traditions are largely "homegrown" and intended for a mass audience. Public school teachers have always had their rights to academic freedom infringed by local schools boards, or, more accurately, never had such rights. But American colleges and universities evolved on the model of their European counterparts (chiefly in Germany and Britain), which were intended for an elite clientele. Professors, at least, were granted a great deal of academic freedom. (Of course, this was not true during the Nazi period in Germany!) The result of transplanting this tradition into the United States, the freest Western society, has been academic freedom for almost all college faculty members; thus, college teachers themselves select the texts they and their students will use. It follows, then, as night follows day, that college textbook publishers will try to produce books that please college faculty members, their potential buyers.

And that's the main reason why college texts, wherever they may rest on an absolute scale, are unlike their public school counterparts. College teachers want widely differing things from their textbooks, creating a split market in which all sorts of views (and to a lesser extent qualities) find a constituency. College texts even tend to be less dull than lower level counterparts, a happy note on which to end this particular college textbook.

Summary of Chapter 10

1. Every society needs to indoctrinate its young. Public school textbooks are just one device used in this educational process.

2. But textbooks are a commodity. So in the United States, they are tailored by publishers to reflect buyer preferences, which means the preferences of

local school boards and state agencies responding to local citizens (in particular, organized citizens). We should expect, then, that texts will reflect the views of local citizens. And they do.

3. What public school students read is censored in two ways. First, the truth is bent or omitted to conform to local or state pressures. Those texts that fail to conform are not permitted to be used.
Example: No text that slights minority groups is likely to be used in California schools. And second, certain nontextbooks are not permitted space on library shelves or allowed to be used in classrooms.
Example: The removal of *Drums Along the Mohawk* from reading lists because it contains words like *hell* and *damn*.

4. Public school texts distort the history of our country by omitting as much as possible that is bad in it and playing down the rest, and by generally puffing up our role in history.
Examples: Portraying just the good side of Teddy Roosevelt; puffing up our role in World War II at the expense of the Russians.

5. Textbooks tend to cover up the gulf between theory—the way our system is supposed to work—and practice—the way things really work—as a way of papering over injustice and evil in our society.
Example: Telling students how our court system is supposed to work but not how it actually works.

6. Textbook style is bland or dull. Emotive language is kept to a minimum and is rarely used to get students excited about injustice or other ills in our system. Evils tend to get slipped in only as they are being corrected or so as to have minimal effect.
Example: Snowing students with lots of dull and soon-forgotten facts about our court system.

7. The upshot of all this is that students are given lots of dull facts but little understanding, either of their country's history or of how their political-social system works. Everything comes out goody-goody, which means that education in public schools tends to contain a large dose of indoctrination.

8. But college texts are different. (*Vive la différence.*)

Exercise 10-1

In college, the subject matter dealt with in high school civics or social studies classes becomes the province of political science, history, and (to some extent) other social science courses. Along with these changes in titles, there is a broadening of subject matter and a change in motive (indoctrination with the "American way" surely is not attempted in the typical college-level social science course or text). But some college texts still display a few of the defects we have been discussing, including an "objectivism" that hides a controversial point of view, a distortion of the difference between theory and practice (often by ignoring practice that doesn't conform to theory), and an unconscious bias against certain groups (for example, women). College history texts also often display these defects.

Examine one of your history, political science, or other relevant social science texts (or get one from the library) for evidence of bias, distortion, suppressed evidence, or "textbook objectivity," and write a page or two on your findings. Be sure to *argue* (present evidence) for your conclusions, trying, of course, to avoid fallacious argument.

*Exercise for the Entire Text

This text, as all others, is based on certain presuppositions (only some of them made explicit) and no doubt contains fallacious reasoning, in spite of the author's best efforts to reason cogently. So, as the final exercise, write a brief critique of this textbook with respect to: (1) its major presuppositions (that is, the world view of the author as exhibited in the text), (2) possible fallacious arguments, (3) biased selection of material, and (4) rhetorical devices used to convince the reader to accept the author's opinion on this or that. (Be sure to *argue* for your findings.)

Dennis the Menace. © 1984 North America Syndicate, Inc.
Reprinted by permission of Hank Ketcham.

"It'll stop, Joey. It always has before."

A youthful inductionist at work.

A simple person believes every word he hears; a clever one understands the need for proof.
—*Proverbs* 14:15

He who knows only his side of the case knows little.
—John Stuart Mill

The object of reasoning is to find out, from the consideration of what we already know, something else which we do not know.
—Charles Sanders Peirce

Appendix: More on Cogent Reasoning

Recall from Chapter 1 that good (cogent) reasoning, as opposed to bad (fallacious) reasoning, must satisfy three conditions. It must (1) contain warranted (justified) premises; (2) include all relevant information; and (3) be valid (correct), which means roughly that the reasons offered in support of the conclusion must truly support that conclusion.

It should be quite clear what is required by the first two of these criteria for cogent reasoning. We should not accept arguments containing premises that we are not able to justify believing or arguments that suppress relevant information. But what sort of connection must there be between premises and conclusion to make an argument valid? While theoreticians disagree on how best to categorize valid or correct reasoning, two sorts of correct argument have been worked out, one (deductive validity) very well indeed, the other (inductive validity) modestly well.

1. Deductive Validity

As stated in Chapter 1, if the premises of a deductively valid argument are true, then its conclusion must be true also (roughly, because its conclusion already is contained in its premises, although usually only implicitly).

Different arguments may have the same **form,** or **structure.** Here are two deductively valid arguments that share the same form:

(1) 1. If the president acts forcefully, he'll gain points in the polls.
     2. He will act forcefully.
∴ 3. He'll gain points in the polls.

(2) 1. If the national debt is paid off with inflated money, then borrowers will benefit, and lenders will be harmed.
2. The national debt will be paid off with inflated money.
∴ 3. Borrowers will benefit, and lenders be harmed.

And here is the form or structure they share:

1. If [some proposition] then [a second proposition].
2. [The first proposition].
∴ 3. [The second proposition].

Or, using *A* and *B* to stand for the two propositions:

1. If *A* then *B*.
2. *A*
∴ 3. *B*

This form has been traditionally called **modus ponens.**

Now here is another commonly used and intuitively valid form, called **modus tollens:**

Form: 1. If *A* then *B*.
                 2. Not *B*.
              ∴ 3. Not *A*.

Example: 1. If he ran for office successfully, then he wasn't fit to hold that office.[1]
                 2. But he was fit to hold that office.
              ∴ 3. He didn't run successfully.

Here is the valid argument form called **disjunctive syllogism:**

Form: 1. *A* or *B*
                 2. Not *A*.
              ∴ 3. *B*.

Example: 1. Either Mondale won in 1984 or Reagan did.
                 2. But Mondale sure didn't win. (Not, Mondale won.)
              ∴ 3. Reagan did.

And here is the valid form called **hyopthetical syllogism:**

Form: 1. If *A* then *B*.
                 2. If *B* then *C*.
              ∴ 3. If *A* then *C*.

Example: 1. If we have a free market in oil and gas, then these commodities will become cheap and plentiful.

---

[1] A takeoff on Adlai Stevenson's famous remark that the hardest thing to do is win election to office without proving unfit to hold that office.

      2. If oil and gas become cheap and plentiful, then the energy problem will be solved.
∴ 3. If there is a free market in oil and gas, we can forget about the energy crisis (the problem will be solved).

Finally, here are several argument forms of a slightly different nature[2] (all but the first and last are called **syllogisms**):[3]

Form:
      1. No *F*s are *G*s.
∴ 2. It's false that some *F*s are *G*s.

Example:
      1. No police officers accept bribes.
∴ 2. It's false that some police officers accept bribes.

Form:
      1. All *F*s are *G*s.
      2. All *G*s are *H*s.
∴ 3. All *F*s are *H*s.

Example:
      1. All TV evangelists have high moral standards.
      2. All who have high moral standards live up to those standards.
∴ 3. All TV evangelists live up to high moral standards.

Form:
      1. All *F*s are *G*s.
      2. This is an *F*.
      3. This is a *G*.

Example:
      1. Elected officials always tell the truth. (All elected officials are truth tellers.)
      2. Ted Kennedy is an elected official.
∴ 3. Ted Kennedy always tells the truth.

Form:
      1. All *F*s are *G*s.
      2. No *G*s are *H*s.
∴ 3. No *F*s are *H*s.

Example:
      1. All males are chauvinist pigs.
      2. No chauvinist pigs are likeable.
∴ 3. No males are likeable.

Form:
      1. No *F*s are *G*s.
      2. Some *H*s are *F*s.
∴ 3. Some *H*s are not *G*s.

Example:
      1. No Russians can be trusted.
      2. Some newborn babies are Russians.
∴ 3. There must be some newborn babies that can't be trusted.

---

[2] See Howard Kahane, *Logic and Philosophy*, 5th ed. (Belmont, Calif.: Wadsworth, 1986) for more on this difference.
[3] In spite of their names, *disjunctive syllogism* and *hypothetical syllogism* are not syllogisms.

Form: 1. All *F*s are *G*s.
          ∴ 2. If this is an *F,* then this is a *G.*

Example: 1. All salamis are tasty.
          ∴ 2. If this is a salami, then it tastes good.

In everyday life, arguments tend to come bunched together in extended passages that are usually designed to justify one grand conclusion or theme. Here is a very simple example containing just three related arguments (with structure exhibited to the left):

1. If *A* then *B.*   1. If the politicians have their way, we'll increase our nuclear arsenal faster than the Russians.

2. If *B* then *C.*   2. But if we do (increase our stockpile faster), there will be no nuclear disarmament.

∴ 3. If *A* then *C.*   3. So if the politicians have their way, there won't be any nuclear disarmament.

4. If *C* then *D.*   4. But then (if there is no nuclear disarmament), an all-out nuclear war will be inevitable, sooner or later.

∴ 5. If *A* then *D.*   5. All of which proves that if the politicians have their way, we'll all end up fighting a nuclear war sooner or later.

6. Not *D.*   6. But it's ridiculous to think we'll actually have an all-out nuclear holocaust (that is, it's false that we'll have an all-out nuclear war).

∴ 7. Not *A.*   7. So the politicians aren't going to have their own way this time.

Beetle Bailey cartoon reprinted by permission of King Features Syndicate.

Humorous use of disjunctive syllogism. General Halftrack's reasoning is this: Either the box is too small or we're not running this camp right. It's false that we're not running this camp right—that is, we are running it right. So the box is too small—build a bigger one. Halftrack omits as understood the premise that the camp is being run right.

Deductive Invalidity

Any argument that doesn't have a deductively valid form is said to be *deductively invalid*. The number of deductively invalid argument forms is legion, but a few are so common they've been given names. Here are two (to give the flavor):

Fallacy of **denying the antecedent:**

Form:	1. If *A* then *B*.
	2. Not *A*.
	∴ 3. Not *B*.
Example:	1. If abortion is murder, then it's wrong.
	2. But abortion isn't murder.
	∴ 3. Abortion isn't wrong.

The conclusion doesn't follow (abortion may still be wrong for other reasons).

Fallacy of **asserting the consequent:**

Form:	1. If *A* then *B*.
	2. *B*.
	∴ 3. *A*.
Example:	1. If Carter is still president, then a liar is now president.
	2. A liar is now president.
	∴ 3. Carter is still president.

The conclusion doesn't follow because, for one thing, some other liar may now be president.

Exercise A-1

Invent deductively valid arguments having the forms of *modus ponens, modus tollens, disjunctive syllogism,* and *hypothetical syllogism.* Then invent arguments having the forms of the fallacies *denying the antecedent* and *asserting the consequent,* and show that they are deductively invalid.

2. Inductive Validity (Correctness)

The basic idea behind valid or correct induction is that of learning from experience. We notice many sorts of *patterns, resemblances,* and other kinds of *regularities* in our experiences, some quite simple (sugar sweetening coffee), some very complicated (objects moving according to Newton's gravitation law). A valid induction merely projects regularities noticed in our experiences so far (our *sample*) onto future experiences (all or part of the *population* from which it was drawn). Various kinds of inductions have been described in the literature.

Induction by Enumeration

One of the simplest forms of induction is called **induction by enumeration,** or (its everyday name) **generalization.** We use this form when we reason from the fact that all *A*s observed so far have been *B*s to the conclusion that all *A*s whatsoever are *B*s. For instance, a check of 15 secondary school civics tests from major publishing houses indicating that all of them play down the gap between American ideals and actual practice would be good evidence for the conclusion that all such texts stray from the truth in this way.

It should be clear that the conclusion of an inductively valid argument is not already contained in its premises, even implicitly, unlike the case with respect to deductively valid arguments. This, in fact, constitutes the great virtue of good inductions—their conclusions take us beyond their premises and thus may give us genuinely new beliefs, not merely what is psychologically new, as in the case of valid deductions.

But this also means that, unlike valid deductions, even the best inductions involve an element of risk. For even if the premises of such an argument are true and its reasoning perfectly good, its conclusion may not be true. The "inductive leap" from premises to conclusion may lead us astray simply because the pattern stated in the premises turns out not to be nature's general pattern after all, but perhaps only a special case or an accidental connection brought about by as yet unrecognized factors. In some cases, it is obvious, given our background beliefs, that an observed pattern is almost certain to be accidental. Finding that the stock market rose and fell in concert with the Olympic elk population during a five-year period would not convince many people to conclude that the two will continue to fluctuate together because all sorts of background beliefs contradict this idea. But when there is no such overpowering background evidence, it is usually perfectly sensible to conclude by induction that an observed regularity will hold universally. For example, at one time, scientists concluded by induction that asbestos does not conduct electricity under any conditions, based on lots of observations and experiments. This induction was perfectly valid and not contradicted by any background beliefs; yet it turned out to be false at extremely cold temperatures. Of course, this is a small price to pay for using such a powerful tool as induction in figuring out what Mother Nature is up to.

Reasoning by Analogy

In addition to induction by enumeration, there are several closely related forms of induction by **analogy**. In one version, we reason from the similarity of two things in several respects to their similarity in another. Thus, if we know that two people have similar tastes in books, art, food, music, and TV programs and find out that one likes Kurasawa flicks, we're justified in concluding that the other probably does also.

In another version of reasoning by analogy, we reason from the fact that all items of a certain kind, *A,* in our sample have some property, *B,* to the conclusion that some as yet unexamined *A* has property *B*. We use this form of analogy, for instance, when we reason from evidence that all 50 members of Congress checked up on used franked mail in their reelection campaigns to the conclusion that a certain other member is going to campaign via franked mail in the next election (and thus have an advantage over all challengers).

Reasoning by analogy is clearly safer than induction by enumeration, since analogies have much weaker conclusions (given the same evidence). We inferred previously that one particular member of Congress would abuse his right to free official mail, which clearly is a weaker (and thus safer) prediction than that all members of Congress will abuse this privilege.

Statistical Induction

When drawing a sample from a population, we often find that not all As we examine are Bs, so we cannot draw a valid induction by enumeration connecting As to Bs. But having found that a certain percentage of As in our sample have the property B, we can conclude that the same percentage of As in the population as a whole have the property B. An induction of this kind is said to be a **statistical induction.**

Political polls are based on sophisticated theories of valid statistical induction. For instance, from the fact that well over 50 percent of those potential voters polled prior to the 1984 elections favored President Reagan over Walter Mondale, it was concluded by statistical induction that this was true of the voting population as a whole (and it was).

Obviously, some inductions are better than others, in particular, because they are based on better samples. While opinions concerning the general theory of good samples differ, a few things are pretty much agreed on.

Greater sample size yields greater probability.   It is generally held that the larger the sample, other things being equal, the greater the probability of an induction based on that sample.[4] A presidential poll based on a well-chosen sample of 2,500 American adults clearly yields a more probable conclusion than a similar poll of only 250 people. The point is that more of the same sort of evidence doesn't change the conclusion of an induction; it changes the degree of probability of that conclusion, and thus changes the strength of belief a rational person should have in that conclusion.

More representative samples yield higher probabilities.   The quality of a sample is even more important than its size. (Indeed, the higher its quality, the smaller a sample need be). When sampling apples in a barrel, for instance, it won't do to just sample a few from the top (the classic case); after all, rotten apples tend to congregate at the bottom of barrels. Samples that neglect possible rotten apples at the bottom of metaphoric barrels are said to be *biased.* Obviously, we want our samples to be as unbiased, as *representative,* as possible of the population from which they are drawn.

One definite counterexample invalidates an induction.   Is a particular birth control pill completely effective? Can we conclude on the basis of an enumerative

---

[4]However, a few writers deny this. See, for instance, Thomas Leddy, "Is There a Fallacy of Small Sample?" *Informal Logic* (Winter 1986).

induction that all who take the pill do not get pregnant? If we know even one definite case in which a woman took the pills as directed and then became pregnant, no valid enumerative induction can be drawn. (We still, of course, could make a statistical induction connecting the pill and a woman's *chances* of getting pregnant.)

However, it's often hard to be sure that what looks like a counterexample really is. Suppose a woman taking a certain birth control pill becomes pregnant. Does this disprove the manufacturer's claim that the pill in question is 100 percent effective? Should it count as a genuine counterexample? Yes, if there is good evidence that the woman in question really did take her pills in the prescribed way and didn't, say, accidentally skip a day. Otherwise, no. The trouble is that in everyday life the needed evidence may be hard to come by. (For instance, it's easy to forget to take a pill and not realize this later.) The moral is that it's risky to reject a theory or idea because of one or two counterexamples unless we're very sure that at least one is the genuine article.

Higher Level Induction

Induction of a broader, more general, or higher level can be used to evaluate (correct or support) lower level inductions. For centuries, Europeans noted that every swan they'd ever seen was white. Using induction by enumeration, many concluded that all swans are white. But some ornithologists, observing that bird species tend to vary in color in different locations, reasoned by means of a broader, **higher level induction** to the conclusion that swans might vary in color also. They reasoned (roughly) in this way: Most bird species observed so far vary in color. Therefore, probably, swans vary in color also (a conclusion that turned out to be correct, since some Australian swans are black).

Higher level inductions of this kind are used all the time in daily life. For example, we use higher level induction when we conclude that an automobile will break down eventually and need repairs even though it has run perfectly so far. Our higher level induction goes roughly like this: All mechanical devices with moving parts eventually wear out and need repairs. So, *very* probably (because our evidence is so overwhelming), this particular mechanical device with moving parts (it happens to be an automobile) will wear out eventually and have to be repaired.[5]

---

[5]This use of higher level evidence to support or refute a lower level conclusion is a familiar one in science. Physicists, for instance, used evidence about the tides and about objects falling toward the earth as evidence for Isaac Newton's very general law of universal gravitation. (Each observed case in which the tides or objects falling toward the earth conform to Newton's law constitutes an instance of the enumerative induction whose conclusion is Newton's law.) This law in turn implies Kepler's laws, which describe the orbits of planets around the sun as ellipses of a certain kind. So evidence about the motion of the tides and the velocity of objects falling toward the earth confirms Kepler's laws by confirming Newton's higher level law, of which Kepler's laws are a special case. (More precisely, Newton showed that Kepler's laws are very close approximations to the truth.) The relevance of watches wearing out to automobile durability is thus no more mysterious than the relevance of the tides to Kepler's laws about planetary motion.

Causal Connections

When we reason inductively, we are often looking for explanations or **causes.** For example, early investigators of the connection between cigarette smoking and lung cancer, emphysema, and heart disease wanted to determine by means of statistical inductions whether smoking *causes* these death-dealing diseases. They found that smokers get these diseases much more often than nonsmokers, and heavy smokers more than light. That is, they discovered a statistical connection between smoking cigarettes and contracting these diseases. Finding no higher level evidence to the

Joseph Farris cartoon. Reproduced by special permission of *Playboy* Magazine: Copyright © 1982 by *Playboy.*

"How can we know that no one can win a nuclear war unless we try it and see?"

Most readers of Playboy *magazine no doubt smiled when they read the caption under the above cartoon. But few would have been able to explain the nature of the folly in the respondent's reasoning. He seems to assume that the only way to establish or justify factual beliefs is by low-level induction by enumeration (or perhaps by statistical induction)—trying out several nuclear wars to see whether any nation can win them. He overlooks the use of higher level induction (plus deductive reasoning) by means of which many of us conclude that the destruction caused by an all-out nuclear war would leave neither side a winner.*

contrary, they concluded that cigarette smoking does indeed *cause* these life-threatening illnesses, although the fact that many smoke and do not get sick weakens this conclusion (and suggests that part of the cause of these diseases must be some other factor).

But finding a statistical connection does not always mean that we can claim a causal connection. This is true even if the statistical connection is 100 percent, and even if we're convinced that the 100 percent connection will continue indefinitely. It all depends on what other beliefs we have that are relevant.

To take a famous example, before Newton, some scientists believed that the earth would circle the sun forever, revolving on its axis every 24 hours. They thus believed in a constant connection, a one-to-one correlation, between occurrences of night and of day. That is, they believed that every time one occurred it would be followed by the other. But they did not believe night *causes* day, nor day night, for they knew that *if* the earth stopped rotating on its axis (of course, they believed this would never be the case), then night would not follow day, nor day night. Thus, for them, night could not be the cause of day, nor day the cause of night.

By way of contrast, we assume that the constant connection between, say, putting sugar into coffee and the coffee tasting sweet *is* a causal connection, because (unlike the day/night case) we have no higher level theories that show how this constant connection might be broken. In other words, we feel justified in assuming that the 100 percent statistical connection between sugar and sweet-tasting coffee is a causal connection because doing so does not conflict with higher level (and thus better confirmed) inductive conclusions.

A Misconception About Deduction and Induction

There is a widespread but erroneous idea about the difference between deductive and inductive validity. This is the idea that in deductively valid reasoning we go from the general to the particular, while in inductively valid reasoning we move from the particular to the general. But there is little to be said for this idea. For instance, the deductively valid argument

1. All Republican politicians are to the right of Teddy Kennedy.
∴ 2. All who are not to the right of Teddy Kennedy are not Republican politicians.

moves from the general to the equally general, while the inductively valid argument

1. Richard Nixon made promises in 1960 and 1968 he didn't intend to keep.
∴ 2. Richard Nixon made promises in 1972 he didn't intend to keep.

moves from the particular to the equally particular. And the inductively valid argument

1. So far, all Republican party presidential candidates have been male.
∴ 2. The next Republican party presidential candidate will be male.

moves from the general to the particular, not the other way around.

So there isn't much truth to the old idea that deductive reasoning moves from the general to the particular while inductive reasoning moves from the particular to the general. More accurately, when we reason deductively, we reason to conclusions already contained (implicitly or explicitly) in our premises; when we reason inductively, we move to conclusions by extending patterns or resemblances observed in our experiences to predict our future experiences.

Exercise A-2

1. Here is a deductively valid argument that goes from the general to the particular: "Presidential candidates all have their private lives interfered with by the media during the campaign. So if Mario Cuomo runs for president, his private life will be interfered with by the media." And here is an inductively valid argument that moves from the particular to the general: "Every professor hired by the University of Maryland so far has spoken English passably well. So it's very likely that the next professor they hire will do so also." In the light of examples such as these, what is wrong with saying that deductively valid arguments move from the general to the particular, or to the less general, and inductive ones move from the particular, or less general, to the more general? Prove your case with examples, original if possible.

2. Carefully explain the difference between induction by enumeration and induction by analogy. Provide examples, original if possible, to illustrate your answer.

3. On what sort of inductions are polls, such as the Gallup Poll, based? Carefully explain what makes some of these polls more reliable than others, again using examples to make your point.

4. What sort of induction is a higher level induction? Provide an example not in the text, and show how it illustrates the nature of higher level induction.

5. Since we believe that day will always be followed by night, and night by day, at least for millions and millions of years, what is wrong with saying that day causes night and night, day? Carefully defend your answer.

3. The Dilemma

Several of the many deductively valid argument patterns play a special role in everyday arguments, particularly in the political realm. One is the **dilemma**. Here is an example commonly heard during the Irangate scandal that was designed to attack President Reagan (put into logical form):

1. President Reagan either knew of the Irangate attempted trade of arms for hostages or he did not.
2. If he did know, then he's guilty of breaking the law.
3. If he didn't know, then he's guilty of careless ignorance concerning his duties.
4. He's guilty either of knowingly breaking the law or of carelessly being ignorant concerning his duties.

The logical structure of a typical dilemma is this:

Structure	Reagan Example
1. *A* or *B*.	1. Reagan knew or he did not know.
2. If *A* then *C*.	2. If he knew, he's guilty of a crime.
3. If *B* then *D*.	3. If he didn't know, he's guilty of ignorance.
4. *B* or *D*.	4. He's guilty either of a crime or of ignorance.

An argument having this form has traditionally been called a *dilemma* when it presents two alternatives that are both bad for someone or some position. In the example just given, the dilemma presents two alternatives and argues that both are bad for Ronald Reagan. In the history of the subject, Reagan supporters could be said to have been "impaled on the horns of the dilemma."

To defeat, or rebut, a dilemma, the parties being gored by it must either successfully argue that there is a third possibility, so that the first premise is not warranted, or challenge the second or the third premise. Someone who argues that there is a third alternative is said to "go between the horns" of the dilemma, and those who argue that one or both alternatives do not lead to the negative results are said to "grasp the dilemma by the horns."

In the Reagan example, the dilemma cannot be defeated by going between its horns because there is no possible third alternative in addition to the two given. Either the president knew or he did not know; the two alternatives are *exhaustive.* (In this case, they also are *mutually exclusive,* which means that the two alternatives cannot both be true—Reagan could not both know and not know.)

But a Reagan supporter might have tried to defeat this dilemma by grasping one of its horns. For example, some Reagan partisans actually did argue that, although the president did not know of the deal, this did not show careless ignorance on his part; after all, no one can be up on everything in running such a large organization. One slipup isn't all that bad seen in this light. And so on. Whether such a rebuttal overturns a dilemma successfully in the minds of listeners is, of course, another matter.

Finally, it should be noted that, although uncommon, we also can have *trilemmas,* and so on. Here is a trilemma designed to prove that we are never responsible for what we do:

1. All our actions are caused either by hereditary or by environmental factors, or by both acting together.
2. If caused by heredity, we aren't responsible, since we can't choose when or where we will be born or raised.
3. But if caused by the environment, we aren't responsible either, since we can't choose when or where we will be born or raised.
4. Obviously, then, we also aren't responsible for actions caused by both heredity and environment.
5. So we are never responsible for any of our actions.[6]

---

[6]This is roughly how some *hard determinists* argue on the question of free will versus determinism.

Exercise A-3

Construct the most plausible dilemma you can think of on any topic mentioned in this text. Then do your best to defeat your dilemma by grasping one of its horns or by going between the horns.

4. Contradictions, Tautologies, and Contingent Statements

Declarative statements divide nicely into three interesting types: *tautologies,*[7] *contradictions,* and *contingent statements.* The first two are of great importance for mathematics, logic, and philosophy, but are rather scarce in their pure form in everyday life (and thank goodness for that).

A **contradiction** both makes a claim and denies that very claim. Obviously, then, all contradictions are false. An example is the contradictory remark that President Reagan knew of the Iran arms sales and didn't know about them, clearly a false claim.[8]

It should be obvious that it is the *structure* of a contradiction that makes it false. The above contradiction about the Iran arms sale is not false because of the facts in the matter, since it is false if he knew and false if he didn't know. No matter what the facts in the matter, the statement that he both knew and didn't know couldn't possibly be true; whatever the facts of the matter, they couldn't make a statement having that structure be true. That's why we can know that a contradiction has to be false even though we don't know the facts in the matter, as we may not know whether Reagan knew of the Iran arms sale.

Now consider this very similar sounding but in fact quite different sort of statement: "The president knew of the arms sale or he did not know." Unlike the contradiction just mentioned, which has the structure "This *and* not-this," this statement has the structure "This *or* not-this." Just a moment's reflection should make it obvious that such a statement must be true and that all statements having this structure must be true. Indeed, logicians have given this structure the honorific title of *law of the excluded middle.*

A statement whose structure makes it true is said to be a **tautology.** All statements that are instances of the law of the excluded middle are thus tautologies.

---

[7] Where this term is construed a good deal more broadly than it is by most logicians.
[8] Here is a little dilemma that proves this contradiction is false:
1. Reagan either knew about the arms sale or he didn't.
2. If he did, then the statement that he both did and didn't is false, because it asserts (in part) that he didn't know.
3. If he didn't, the statement is false, because it says (in part) that he did.
∴4. The statement that he both did and didn't is false.

And here is another famous structure, called the *principle of noncontradiction*: "Not (this and not-this)," for instance, "It's not true both that Reagan knew and didn't know."

Now consider the still different kind of assertion that President Reagan did indeed know about the Iran arms sales. To evaluate this statement, we need to know a great many facts about Reagan and the arms sale. Whether we judge the assertion that he knew as true or as false is *contingent* on what we discover when we investigate the matter. So an assertion of this kind is said to be a **contingent statement** because its truth or falsity is contingent on facts about the world, and not just on the assertion's structure.

Well, we aren't going to find many public speakers or writers going around uttering explicit contradictions. "I'll balance the budget, but I won't balance the budget" is a statement no candidate is ever likely to make. Rather, in daily life, contradictions tend to get embedded in complicated programs or masked in synonyms and euphemisms. So it is useful to stretch the notion of a contradiction, or of what it is to be *inconsistent,* to cover these cases, as in fact is done in everyday life. As an example, Ronald Reagan's pledges in 1980 and 1984 to spend a lot on defense and yet not raise taxes while at the same time balancing the budget were widely regarded as contradictory because they were contradicted by the realities of political life. (That is the point of the cartoon on p. 64.)

Unlike explicit contradictions, tautologies in the strict sense do play a role in everyday discourse, although not a very large one. They are most commonly used, perhaps, to evade a hard question while seeming to answer it or to hedge on a controversial issue. Thus, when asked about import quotas on foreign products, a politician might waffle by saying, "We may or may not impose quotas if domestic sales decline further," thus remaining uncommitted while appearing to say something.

This and other ways to evade issues or beg questions were discussed somewhat in Chapter 3. But perhaps now we should mention that the concept of a tautology has been broadened in daily life to include statements that come close to being empty of content or are completely uninteresting and obvious. Here is an example from Chapter 6 that might be called a tautology in this extended sense: "Although the effects of mental attitudes on bodily disease should not be exaggerated, neither should they be minimized."

The point of all this is that we should always demand evidence or reasons for accepting contingent statements and not be swayed by impressive sounding but empty statements or by politicians who pronounce policies that on close inspection turn out to be contradictory or tautological.

Exercise A-4

Which of the following are tautologies, which contradictions, and which contingent statements? Defend your answers. (Be careful. Some of these are sneaky.)

1. Either Geraldine Ferraro ran for president in 1984 or lots of newspapers were mistaken.

2. Geraldine Ferraro didn't campaign in 1984 both for president and vice-president.

3. Snow is always white, except, of course, when it isn't.

4. The media always report accurately.

*5. No politicians ever keep any of their campaign promises.

6. He who laughs last laughs best.

7. I've been told time and time again that drinking impairs driving ability, but I don't believe it for one minute.

8. Either you're in favor of the ERA or you're against it.

*9. All trespassers will be shot, or they won't.

10. If you don't play the Maryland lottery, you can't win it.

5. Indirect or Reductio Ad Absurdum Proofs

Another way sometimes used to argue a point is called an **indirect proof,** or a **reductio ad absurdum proof** (to use its classical name). The point of such a proof is to assume for a moment the opposite, or negation, of what we want to prove and then show that this assumption leads to an absurd conclusion and thus must be false, so that its negation, the thing we want to prove, must be true. Here is an example (put into 1, 2, 3 form):

1. Assume for the moment that America's balance of payment problems arose in the early 1980s exclusively because the high value of the dollar compared to other currencies made imports cheaper for us while making our exports more expensive for others.

2. If this were the reason, other countries whose currencies were tied to the dollar (for example, Taiwan) should have suffered with respect to balancing imports with exports. (A currency tied to the dollar rises in value when the dollar rises and lowers when the dollar value is lowered.)

3. But we all know that several of these countries had no balance of payment problems whatever, again Taiwan being an example.

4. Therefore, the troubles America got into in the early 1980s when we imported a great deal more than we exported and became the world's biggest debtor nation could not have been caused simply by the high value of the dollar at that time.

This was in fact an indirect argument used with some success by several well-known economists.

6. Calculating Probabilities and Fair Odds

Billions of dollars are legally wagered on games of chance each year in the United States, and hundreds of millions, perhaps billions, are *lost* at the track, gambling casinos, and so on, not to mention state lotteries. The amount wagered illegally is greater still, but obviously is hard to estimate. Yet most gamblers don't even know how to calculate fair odds for the events on which they bet, one reason almost all of them lose in the long run.

Legitimate odds depend on the *likelihood, probability,* or *chances* that a given outcome will occur. For example, when you flip a coin, the chances are roughly *one out of two,* or ½, that the coin will land heads up because there are two possibilities, and both are (with a perfectly symmetrical coin) equally likely. **Fair odds** on heads thus should be even money—one to one—and someone who bets a dollar and wins should win a dollar.

Most games of chance are designed so as to present players with a specific number of equally likely alternatives or combinations of alternatives on which they must wager. To find the **probability** of an outcome in such cases, simply divide the number of favorable outcomes by the total number of possible outcomes, favorable or unfavorable.

Suppose we want to calculate the chances of getting a 7 on the next toss of an honest (symmetrical) pair of dice. There are exactly 36 possible outcomes on each toss of a pair of dice, of which exactly 6 add up to 7. In other words, there are exactly 6 equally possible ways to get 7 out of 36 equally possible outcomes altogether, namely, the 6 combinations 1 and 6, 2 and 5, 3 and 4, 4 and 3, 5 and 2, and 6 and 1. So the probability of getting 7 on a given toss equals $\frac{6}{36}$, or $\frac{1}{6}$. This means that out of 6 tosses of the dice, the average wagerer on 7 will win one time and lose the other five times. So fair odds on 7 equal 5 to 1, and someone who bets, say, $1 on 7 and wins should win $5. (At a casino, where a wagerer is actually required to place a dollar bet on the table, a winner would be paid back $6 on a $1 bet, namely, the $5 won plus the $1 bet. That is, a winner would be paid this much *if* the casino paid fair odds. Of course, every casino in the world *always* pays less than fair odds. Gambling establishments are not in business to let patrons win!)

State lotteries probably give gamblers the worst odds of any popular games of chance, since they pay back in winnings only from one-half to about two-thirds of what is wagered.[9] (The percentage varies from state to state.) Even the horses give wagerers a better break. Typically, the track and state take somewhere around 15 percent as their cut before the rest is divided among winners. So a horseplayer has to be at least 15 percent better than the average in order just to break even (the reason for the saying that horseplayers are all broke). Poker players have a bit better chance, since the house typically takes only 5 percent off the top.

---

[9]This is the reason that playing a state lottery amounts to paying a voluntary state tax. Thomas Jefferson, among other illustrious figures, favored lotteries over the normal kinds of taxes for that very reason. Ordinary taxes are compulsory; lottery "taxes" are completely voluntary. Good point.

The best odds on games of chance that required no skill are usually found at the dice tables.[10] This means that players get more "action" per dollar at the dice tables than when playing a state lottery or even the slot machines that advertise a 97 percent payback. But whichever of these games involving sheer luck we play, and no matter where we play, the law of averages dictates that almost everyone will lose in the long run, no matter how close the odds are to being fair. Even the tiniest edge in the odds virtually guarantees that the house will win in the long run.[11]

The Probability Calculus

The correct way to calculate fair odds on games of chance was figured out during the seventeenth century, largely for the benefit of rich gamblers. (Another reason was to aid the newly formed insurance industry in determining fair premiums on insurance policies.) The point of a **probability calculus** is to provide a method for determining fair odds in more complicated cases when the probabilities for simpler cases are known (as they are for symmetrical games of chance such as dice and blackjack).

Some pairs of events are such that the occurrence of one of them has an *effect* on the occurrence of the other. For example, drawing an ace from a deck of cards (without putting it back into the deck) has an effect on the chances of drawing an ace on the next draw.

But other pairs of events are such that the occurrence of one has no effect on the other. For example, drawing an ace from a deck of cards has *no* effect on the chances of getting an ace on the next draw *if* the ace has been put back into the deck for the second draw. (The cards don't "know" that an ace was picked on the first draw.) If two events are unrelated to each other, so that the occurrence of one has no effect on the occurrence of the other, they are said to be **independent** events.

In addition, some pairs of events cannot possibly both occur. For example, we can't get both a 7 and a 9 on a single toss of the dice. If the occurrence of one event precludes the occurrence of the other, they are said to be **mutually exclusive** events.

Restricted Conjunction Rule

This rule is used to determine the probability that both of two *independent* events will occur. It tells us simply to multiply the probability of one event occurring times the probability of the other. So to calculate the odds of getting 7 on two given tosses of honest dice, we simply multiply the probability of 7 on the first toss,

---

[10]Better odds, in fact odds favorable to the gambler and unfavorable for the house, can be obtained at blackjack (twenty-one) by using a mildly complicated card counting system, but casinos quickly spot card counters and refuse to let them play. Again, the point of running a gambling casino is *not* to let patrons win.

[11]Another reason the house wins in the long run virtually every time is that the party with the largest reserves has the best chance of withstanding runs of bad luck without being wiped out, and the house almost always has far larger reserves than any of the gamblers playing against it.

namely $\frac{1}{6}$,[12] times the probability of 7 on the second, also $\frac{1}{6}$. The probability of getting two 7s on any two given tosses therefore is $\frac{1}{6}$ times $\frac{1}{6}$, or $\frac{1}{36}$. This means that we can expect to get two 7s in two given tosses only one time on an average in 36 tries, losing the other 35 times. A winning bet at a casino on this combination should therefore return $36 for every $1 wagered ($35 won plus $1 wagered). Needless to say, every casino pays less than this so as to guarantee that the house wins in the long run. The rule we have just followed is called the **restricted conjunction rule.** It tells us that when two events are independent of each other, the chances that both will occur equal the chances of the first occurring times the chances of the second occurring.

General Conjunction Rule

But suppose the two outcomes in question are not independent of one another. Then the *restricted conjunction rule* does not apply. The reason is illustrated in calculating the probability of randomly drawing two cards out of a deck and having both of them be spades. If the first card drawn is put back into the deck before the second one is drawn, so that the same card can be drawn twice, then we can indeed use the *restricted conjunction rule.* Doing so, we will find that the probability is 1 in 16 ($\frac{13}{52}$ times $\frac{13}{52}$, or $\frac{1}{16}$).

However, if the first card drawn is not put back before the second is selected, then the probability of drawing two spades in a row is less than $\frac{1}{16}$ because, if a spade was drawn on the first draw, then, on the second draw, only 12 spades remain in the deck out of the 51 cards still in it. So the chances of getting that second spade are 12 in 51, or $\frac{12}{51}$, not $\frac{13}{52}$. And then it follows that the probability of getting two spades in a row equals $\frac{1}{4}$ times $\frac{12}{51}$, or $\frac{1}{17}$. Fair odds on this should thus be 16 to 1, and a winning $1 bet on two spades out of two draws should therefore pay back $17 ($16 won and $1 wagered).

The principle we have just used is called the **general conjunction rule,** and it tells us that the probability of two events occurring equals the probability that the first will occur times the probability that the second will occur *given that the first occurs.* In the spade example, this means the probability of drawing a spade on the first pick times the probability a second spade will be drawn given that a spade was selected on the first draw and not replaced, and this equals $\frac{1}{4}$ times $\frac{12}{51}$,[13] or $\frac{1}{17}$.

Restricted Disjunction Rule

Now suppose we want to calculate the probability of getting either a spade *or* a heart on a given draw from a standard deck. Since these events are *mutually exclusive* (we can't pick a card that is both a spade and a heart), we can use the **restricted disjunction rule,** which tells us to calculate the probability of drawing one or the other of two mutually exclusive outcomes simply by adding the probability of get-

---

[12]Recall that we previously showed why it is $\frac{1}{6}$.
[13]Because when the first spade is removed from the deck, 12 of the remaining 51 cards are spades.

ting one to that for getting the other. In this case, since ¼ of the cards are spades and ¼ hearts (no card being both), the likelihood of selecting either a spade or a heart on a given draw equals ¼ plus ¼, or ½. So a $1 wager on spade-or-heart should pay winners $2 ($1 won plus $1 risked).

General Disjunction Rule

Now let's consider cases where two events are not mutually exclusive. What, for instance, is the probability of getting at least one heads in two given tosses of a symmetrical coin? To start with, we know that the chances of getting heads on any single toss equal ½, since there are only two possibilities, and they are equally probable. But we can't calculate the probability of getting at least one heads out of two tosses simply by adding the probability of getting heads on the first toss to the probability of getting heads on the second. For one thing, that yields an answer we know has to be wrong (the probability can't be ½ plus ½ equals 1 because we know two heads in a row can easily occur). And we know, in fact, that the correct probability in this case has to be ¾, since there are exactly four equally possible outcomes (namely, heads-heads, heads-tails, tails-heads, and tails-tails), and three of the four win for those betting that at least one toss will land heads up. Knowing this, we should calculate fair odds in this case to be three to four, and a $3 winning bet should be paid back $4 (the $3 bet plus the $1 won).

The incorrect calculation of the probabilities in this case as equal to one was off the mark because it failed to take account of the fact that *both* of the two tosses might land heads up. In adding together the probabilities for the two tosses turning up heads, we thus would count some tosses twice. Subtracting these cases from one will get us the right answer. And so the **general disjunction rule** tells us that the probability of at least one of two outcomes occurring equals the probability of the first plus the probability of the second *minus* the probability that both will occur.

Let's now put the four rules for calculating the probabilities, or fair odds, which we've just presented, into a shorter and perhaps more easily remembered form. In doing so, we'll use the small letter *a* to stand for the first event or outcome and *b* for the second, and let the capital letter *P* be shorthand for the term *probability*.

Restricted conjunction rule

If *a* and *b* are independent events, then $P(a \& b) = P(a) \times P(b)$.

General conjunction rule

$P(a \& b) = P(a) \times P(b, \text{given } a)$.

Restricted disjunction rule

If *a* and *b* are mutually exclusive, then $P(a \text{ or } b) = P(a) + P(b)$.

General disjunction rule

$P(a \text{ or } b) = P(a) + P(b) - P(a \& b)$.

It should be obvious, incidentally, that the probability of a contradiction equals zero, since no possible outcome will make a contradiction true. And the probability of a tautology equals one, because every possible outcome is compatible with a tautology. No matter what happens or how things are, all tautologies will be true and all contradictions false.

Exercise A-5

*1. What is the probability of getting either 2 or 12 on a given toss of an honest pair of dice?

2. How about one or the other in two tosses?

3. What is the probability of getting a red jack, queen, or king with an ordinary deck of cards on one random draw?

*4. If a state lottery paid fair odds, how much should a $2 wager pay a winner who picked the correct five-digit number?

5. What about drawing a pair, any pair, in a poker hand (five cards)?

6. How about the probability of getting a straight (five cards in a row), given that you already have two, three, four, and five in your hand, and you are to be given one more card from the deck?

Exercise A-6

Here is a "system" proposed in a book on gambling.[14] (A tiny part of the system has been omitted.) Explain why it doesn't work (hard question).

There is only one way to show a profit. *Bet light on your losses and heavy on your wins.* (Italics added.)

Bet minimums when you're losing.

You recoup losses by betting house money against the house, not your own. When you win with a minimum bet, let the winnings ride and manage to come up with a few more wins. . . .

Bet heavy when you're winning.

Following a win with your minimum bet, bet the original minimum plus the amount you won. On a third win, drag [keep?] the minimum and bet the rest. You now have a one-minimum-bet profit on the round, regardless of what happens. . . . As soon as you lose, go back to the minimum bet. . . .

Always make your heavy bets with the other fellow's money, not your own.

The worst you can do betting house money against the house on a bet is break even on that particular wager. Actually, you've lost money on the round—but it was money that you got from the other fellow, not part of your original venture money. . . .

---

[14]Clement McQuaid, ed. *Gambler's Digest: The World's Greatest Gambling Book,* 2nd ed. (Northfield, Ill.: DBI Books, 1981).

Don't limit your winnings.

Always ride out a winning streak, pushing your skill to the hilt. . . .

Quit on a losing streak, not a winning streak.

While the law of mathematical probability averages out, it doesn't operate in a set pattern. Wins and losses go in streaks more often than they alternate. If you've had a good winning streak and a loss follows it, bet minimums long enough to see whether or not another winning streak is coming up. If it isn't, quit while you're still ahead.

Summary of the Appendix

1. *Deductive validity.* An argument is deductively valid if the content of its conclusion is either explicitly or implicitly contained in its premises. Different deductively valid arguments may share the same *form. Example:* "It's snowing and cold, so it's cold" and "Ronald Reagan is tall and handsome; therefore he's handsome" share the same form.

   There are many deductively valid argument forms, including, for example, *modus ponens,* which has the form "If *A* then *B*, and *A*; therefore *B*," and the syllogism having the form "No *F*s are *G*s, and some *H*s are *F*s, and thus some *H*s are not *G*s."

   Of course, not all forms are deductively valid, a famous example being this one: "If *A* then *B*, and not-*A*, so not-*B*," called the fallacy of *denying the antecedent*.

2. *Inductive validity.* Valid or correct inductions are based on the idea of learning from experience. Having figured out patterns or regularities in our experiences so far, ways in which kinds of things resemble each other, induction allows us to project those patterns or resemblances onto future experiences.

   In *induction by enumeration,* or *generalization,* we reason from the fact that all observed items of a certain kind have a given property to the conclusion that all items of that kind whatsoever have it. *Example:* Noting that sugar has always sweetened coffee so far, we conclude that it always will.

   Using *induction by analogy,* we reason from the similarity of two or more things in certain respects to their similarity in some other respect, or from the observation that all things of a certain kind observed so far have had some particular property to the conclusion that some other thing of that kind will have that property. *Example:* Reasoning from the fact that all takeout fast food pizza we've eaten so far has been mediocre to the conclusion that the next pizza of this kind will also be mediocre.

   We use *statistical induction* when we reason from the fact that a certain percentage of a sample has a given property to the conclusion that some other part (or all) of the population has that property. *Example:* reasoning from the observation that 55 percent of those polled in May 1987 felt that President Reagan had lied about Irangate to the conclusion that 55 percent of the population as a whole believed this. Note that all other things being equal, the larger a sample, the more probable the conclusion, and likewise the more *representative* the sample, the more probable the conclusion.

When we bring higher level background information to bear in evaluating an induction, we reason by *higher level induction. Example:* Concluding that our automobile won't run forever without repairs even though it has so far, since we know that all mechanical objects break down or wear out sooner or later.

One reason for using induction is to find *causal connections. Example:* Having found a certain kind of statistical connection between smoking cigarettes and lung cancer, we conclude that smoking cigarettes may *cause* that dread disease, or at least be part of the cause.

But we have to be careful that reasoning of this kind is not overruled by higher level inductions. *Example:* Although the bells in a particular Manchester church have always tolled right after those in a church in London, we don't conclude that the one caused the other, because on the basis of higher level inductions, we know how we could stop this as yet constant connection between the two (for example, by tearing down the church in London).

Note that the old idea that valid deductions move from general premises to particular conclusions while it is just the reverse in the case of valid inductions is completely false. *Examples:* The valid deduction that since it is cold and wet outside, it must be cold moves from the particular to the equally particular; the induction that so far all presidential candidates have been male and so the next Democratic party candidate will also be male moves from the general to the particular.

3. *The Dilemma.* Dilemmas are typically three-premise arguments like this one: "President Reagan knew about the lawbreaking or he didn't. If he knew, he's guilty of a crime, but if he didn't, he's guilty of ignorance. So he's guilty either of a crime or of ignorance." Note that to rebut a dilemma, you have to either "go between the horns," which means showing that there is a third alternative, or "grasp the dilemma by the horns," which means showing that its second or third premise is questionable. *Example:* We can grasp the dilemma just mentioned by one of its horns if we can show, say, that Reagan was not necessarily guilty of ignorance since a president simply has too much information to keep track of.

4. *Tautologies, Contradictions, and Contingent Statements.* A *tautology* is a statement that is logically or necessarily true or is so devoid of content as to be practically empty. *Example:* "President Reagan knew or he didn't know." A *contradiction* is a statement that is necessarily false (because it contradicts itself). *Example:* "The president both knew and didn't know." All other statements are said to be *contingent. Example:* "Reagan didn't know about the transfer of funds."

5. *Indirect or Reductio Ad Absurdum Proofs.* We reason by way of an *indirect* or *reductio ad absurdum* proof when we assume the opposite of what we wish to prove and then derive a conclusion claimed to be absurd. *Exam-*

ple: "Suppose for the moment that we assume Reagan actually knew about what was going on. Then he would have been seriously derelict in his duty as president of the United States. But we all know that he is an honorable man, and honorable men don't break the law in this way. So clearly Reagan didn't know about the lawbreaking."

6. *Calculating Probabilities and Fair Odds.* When each possible alternative is equally likely, the *probability* of any particular outcome or combination of outcomes equals the number of alternatives favorable to that outcome divided by the total number of alternatives. *Example:* There are four alternative results when tossing a coin twice (namely, heads-heads, heads-tails, tails-heads, and tails-tails). Of these, two are favorable to the outcome of one heads and one tails (namely, heads-tails, and tails-heads). So the probability of getting one heads and one tails equals $\frac{2}{4}$, or $\frac{1}{2}$. Since there are two outcomes that are *un*favorable to getting one heads and one tails (namely, heads-heads and tails-tails), *fair odds* on getting one heads and one tails in two tosses with a symmetrical coin should be one to one, or even money, and a $1 bet should reward winners with $1. (In gambling casinos, where the $1 bet has to be placed on the table, the house would give winners $2— the $1 won and the $1 wagered. That is, they would do this if they paid fair odds, which gambling houses never do.)

The *probability calculus* was invented to enable us to calculate all sorts of complicated cases. The *restricted conjunction rule* tells us that the probability both of two *independent* events (events that do not have an effect on each other) will occur equals the probability of one times the probability of the other. *Example:* The probability of getting a spade on one card draw and a heart on the next equals $\frac{1}{4} \times \frac{1}{4} = \frac{1}{16}$. The *general conjunction rule* tells us that the probability both of two events will occur equals the probability of one times the probability of the other, given that the first occurs. *Example:* The probability of getting two spades in two draws given that we don't replace the first card drawn before drawing the second equals $\frac{1}{4} \times \frac{12}{51} = \frac{1}{17}$. The *restricted disjunction rule* tells us that the probability of one or the other of two *mutually exclusive* events (events that both cannot occur) equals the probability of one plus the probability of the other. *Example:* The probability of getting either a spade or a heart equals $\frac{1}{4} + \frac{1}{4} = \frac{1}{2}$. The *general disjunction rule* tells us that the probability of one or the other of any two events occurring equals the probability of one plus the probability of the other minus the probability that they both will occur. *Example:* The probability of getting at least one heads in two tosses of a coin equals $\frac{1}{2} + \frac{1}{2} - \frac{1}{4} = \frac{3}{4}$. Finally, the probability of a contradiction equals zero, and that of a tautology equals one.

Answers to
Starred Exercise Items

These answers certainly are not presented as revealed truth. They represent one person's thoughts on the matter, which it is hoped will prove useful to the reader.

Chapter 1, Exercise 1-1

1. *Premise:* At the present rate of consumption, the oil will be used up in 20–25 years.
   Premise: We're sure not going to reduce consumption in the near future.
   Conclusion: We'd better start developing solar power, windmills, and other "alternative energy sources" pretty soon.

3. No argument. Just a list of things the student doesn't like.

10. *Premise:* Animals that live in the sea are called fish.
    Premise: Whales live in the sea.
    Conclusion: Whales are fish. (This conclusion is then used as a premise of another argument.)
    Premise: Whales are fish.
    Premise: My textbook says whales are mammals.
    Conclusion: My textbook is wrong.

Chapter 2, Exercise 2-1

1. *Popularity.* On this planet, all sorts of things, some quite monstrous, have become popular. *Example:* Daughter to mother (Berlin, Germany, 1932): "Nazism is the coming thing."

7. *Traditional Wisdom.* But for some, given their world views, it isn't fallacious. Suppose Smith believes that God transmits his wishes by means of long-term traditions. Then, the fact that long Catholic tradition excludes women from certain roles would be a good reason for continuing to do so, since the tradition would be a sign of God's will. The point is that for most of us, including most Catholics, accepting this argument is fallacious.

15. *Equivocation.* Roche meant political repression—for instance, of limiting freedom of speech or movement. Freud was talking about psychological repression—for instance, of the desire to sleep with one's mother.

22. Reverse *Appeal to Authority.* If even the *Devil* believes there's a God, well, by God, there must be a God!

26. *Equivocation.* To imagine our own death is to visualize what it would be like to experience it. In this sense we can and do imagine our own death. Freud changes the meaning of the word *imagine* so that to imagine it we would have to *not* visualize it, which of course is impossible.

28. *Irrelevant Reason.* Suppose the police mistakenly charge you with murder. In defending yourself, you don't have to prove that someone else, Smith, did it; you just have to prove *you* didn't do it—say, by providing an air-tight alibi. Why, then, should Warren Commission critics have to prove who did murder John Kennedy, if they can show Lee Harvey Oswald couldn't have done it alone?

Chapter 3, Exercise 3-1

2. *Begged Question.* She wanted to know why the mechanism that produces saliva wasn't working and was told that it wasn't working.

6. No fallacy; certainly not *inconsistency.* Aristotle intended to point out to his friends that in this harsh world, friendship, alas, has its limits—that even good friends can be counted on only so far. This sour view has its exceptions, but on the whole is true.

11. *Inconsistency.* He doesn't want to forbid people from eating pork, but just from the ability to buy it. Since the vast majority of people in Israel can't raise their own pigs (they live in cities, where raising animals of this kind is inconvenient, if not forbidden), forbidding the sale of pork has almost the same effect as forbidding the eating of pork.

15. *Inconsistency* (between words and actions). While allowing a 15-minute tape to be shown wasn't *exactly* crossing a picket line, it's in the same spirit. The point of Hope's not crossing a picket line was to show solidarity with ordinary laborers—in this case, by depriving those inside of the benefit of Hope's entertainment. (People who sneak out of obligations in this way are derisively called "legalists.")

16. *Begged Question.* The question was whether reporters should be an exception to the rule. To point out that it would be an exception thus begs the question.

26. *False Dilemma.* The Creator might have intended sexual intercourse to have both of these consequences, reproduction and pleasure, or perhaps some other function.

Chapter 4, Exercise 4-1

3. *Questionable Analogy.* Depending on the kind of accident, knowing how to drive *is* a help, as every driver knows, even though not absolutely essential (say, in judging a case of alleged negligent driving). The line also suppresses a bit of evidence— namely, that judges who drive are easily obtained to try auto accident cases, but judges who have been raped (or mugged, or murdered) are in very short supply.

7. *Questionable Cause.* An even greater percentage of heroin addicts first drank milk, coffee, tea, and booze, and smoked cigarettes. (And, as the greeting card noted, they all are habitual breathers). To support a causal connection, we need evidence showing that all or most pot smokers go on to heroin, but in fact we have all sorts of statistics proving that the vast majority who smoke dope never even try, much less get hooked on, heroin.

16. Here is a student's answer to this question: Fallacy: *Questionable Analogy.*

    Valid reasoning by analogy leads from a similarity between two things in several respects to their similarity in another respect. If the initial similarities are reasonable, then the similarities in the latter respect are reasonable.

    Weinberger's comparison lacks the initial similarities between the circumstances. Ordering the military to seal the border against drug traffickers does not violate the laws of nature as does ordering the tides back. The former is a practical impossibility whereas the latter is a physical impossibility. The latter is foolish; the former is just not feasible. They are both absurd but for very different reasons. The analogy is not valid.

    Do you agree with this analysis?

18. *Questionable Classification.* Homosexuals burned the books. But so did males, human beings, people between the ages of 16 and 60, and so on. The *relevant* classification of those against whom Ms. Bryant has brought evidence is *Bible burners,* since most homosexuals would no more burn Bibles than anyone else.

24. *Questionable Analogy,* or *Begged Question.* Singer's point was that it is wrong not to consider the interests of other sentient animals equally with those of human beings, just as he and most others think it wrong to favor one sex or race over another. His analogy between speciesism and racism or sexism is questionable because it begs the question of why an equality principle should apply to other sentient creatures. (In all fairness to Singer, he does address this question in other places in his book, roughly speaking, basing his case on the wrongness of inflicting gratuitous pain on sentient beings, an idea many philosophers, including this writer, find uncompelling in the absense of further argument.)

Exercise 4-2

1. *Questionable Cause.* It's plausible for a candidate to campaign harder where support is weak rather than where it is strong. The relevant figures to prove he should have stayed at home would have to show, say, that his popularity dropped in a given area after Taft campaigned there—figures not provided, one suspects, because they don't exist.

3. *Faulty Comparison.* Britain is wealthier than it ever was. It is, however, poorer relative to other northern European countries. (Their economies have been growing much faster.) The comparison relevant to whether Britain can still afford to be preoccupied with distribution is between the wealth she had then (when she could afford that preoccupation) and now, not between what she has now and what other nations have, since the latter is irrelevant to the consumption of goods in Britain.

7. *Suppressed Evidence* and *Hasty Conclusion.* (1) Many other factors are believed to have been at work reducing mortality, for instance, improved diet and more exercise. (2) There are known side effects of the pill. (This indicates that the pill was a health hazard, but *we'd* be guilty of *hasty conclusion* if we concluded from this that the pill was a *major* health hazard.) (3) There were other health hazards at the time. If increased female longevity proved the pill was not a major health hazard, it would equally prove no other health hazard was major. But there seem to have been several other major health hazards, for instance, cigarette smoking. (4) By the same reasoning, we could conclude that cigarettes were not a major health hazard even for males, since male longevity also increased. Since cigarettes certainly were a major health hazard for males, the original reasoning must be fallacious.

8. *Suppressed Evidence.* (1) Superstition is more accurately defined as belief without good evidence, or in the face of contrary evidence. (So the article changed the meaning of the term *superstition*.) (2) Some of the greatest scientists may have been superstitious—Newton being an example (the line between superstition and mysticism is not sharp). But the part of their beliefs that became part of science was not superstitious—Newton again being a good example. (3) In addition, a great deal of what scientists once accepted, *on good evidence,* they now reject, or have modified or sharpened, because of better evidence (for instance, the rejected aether theory and the modified Newtonian theory of the nineteenth century). But

rejecting or modifying a well-supported theory because of better evidence for a more accurate theory is the heart of science, and is definitely not superstition.

11. *Hasty Conclusion.* The statistic quoted certainly is evidence for the conclusion. But it isn't sufficient. It still could be that similar family environment is the principal reason why alcoholism tends to run in families *Example:* the higher incidence of alcoholism among present-generation Jews in America as compared with the incidence among their genetically similar grandparents.

14. *Questionable Cause* and *Suppressed Evidence.* This is one of those cases where background information and world views are crucial. Each of these presidents died under different circumstances—Kennedy was shot, Roosevelt had a stroke after 12 health-destroying years in office. Further, we have vast amounts of higher-level evidence and theories to the effect that mere passage of time cannot cause anything so complicated as the death of an incumbent president.

Chapter 6, Exercise 6-1

4. (Simplifying translation): We shall use the expression "social problem solving" to refer to cases where an actual or expected result will (possibly) solve a problem. (Put that way, it doesn't sould like much.)

11. What the good admiral meant was that Navy teams had gone around the country trying to find ways to get naval installations to spend more money. (It was close to the end of the fiscal year and the Navy had not used up its appropriation for that year.)

Chapter 7, Exercise 7-1

4. *Thesis:* None of the historical or anecdotal parts of the Bible are the word of God.

Reason: What I've seen (or know?) needs no revelation.
Conclusion: Revelation is that which reveals what we didn't know (haven't seen) before.

Reason: Revelation is that which reveals what we didn't know (haven't seen?) before.
Conclusion: Revelation can't tell us about earthly things men could witness.

Reason: Revelation can't tell us about earthly things men could witness.
Conclusion: None of the historical or anecdotal parts of the Bible count as revelation. (Paine assumed an equation between revelation and the word of God.)

Exercise 7-4

2. Here is Stephen T. Yelverton's letter, with margin notes:

In a recent editorial entitled "Smoke," The Post asks why the federal government should be sponsoring a program that supports a product such as tobacco, a major health hazard and thus a contributing factor in health-care costs.

Question: Why have a program supporting growing of health-hazard tobacco?

The answer is simply that the federal tobacco program has absolutely nothing to do with whether people smoke, or even whether tobacco is grown. What this program does is to limit the amount of tobacco grown and to determine what price the tobacco manufacturers should pay the growers for their product.

Answer: The program is irrelevant to quantity of tobacco grown or smoked. It limits amount of tobacco grown and determines price.

Without the federal tobacco program, tobacco would still be grown. But under a free-market system, more tobacco would be grown, most likely by corporate agribusiness rather than by small family farmers, as is now the case. This would happen because the productions allotment aspect of the program has served as a barrier to the entry of large corporate farms into tobacco production.

Without the program, more tobacco would be grown.

Because the program blocks growing by large corps.

Does The Post really believe that the anti-smoking cause would be better served by allowing more tobacco to be grown and tobacco production to be taken over by big business?

(Not important for his conclusion.)

The federal tobacco program should be retained, even if one disagrees with its purposes, also because the economy of the tobacco-producing regions of the country is dependent on it. This program has been in existence for over 50 years. Farm values and thus local property tax revenues are directly linked to the existence of the program.

The economy of the tobacco-producing area depends on the program: Farm values and local property taxes are based on it.

Does The Post really believe that it is enlightened or rational public policy to disrupt the economy of the tobacco-producing regions of the country?

Repeal would disrupt the region's economy.

Counting past years and the immediate future, tobacco growers will have contributed more than $100 billion in excise tax revenues to our county. In contrast, over the 50-year history of the federal tobacco program, the total cost to the taxpayers has been only $50 million.

Tobacco excise taxes have raised over $100 billion; the program has cost taxpayers only $50 million.

In view of the enormous excise tax revenue contributions that tobacco growers have made to our country and will continue to make, is it too much for them to ask that a federal program, which they find beneficial and which has absolutely nothing to do with whether people smoke, is continued?

So it isn't too much for federal government to benefit tobacco growers.

Yelverton's thesis is that the tobacco-support program should be continued. He offers essentially three reasons for accepting his thesis, plus one rebuttal:

1. Without the program, more tobacco would be grown, because the program blocks large corporations from growing tobacco.
2. The economy of tobacco-growing regions has come to depend on the program, and repeal would be disruptive to the local economy.
3. Tobacco excise taxes have raised over $100 billion while the program has cost only $50 million. So it isn't too much of growers to ask for.
4. In rebuttal to common claims, the program does not increase the amount of tobacco grown or smoked.

To this reviewer, the first point seems at best only marginally correct. In the long run, doesn't demand determine how much tobacco is grown? Competition from large growers might reduce the price of tobacco somewhat, but would that have much effect on how much tobacco is smoked? This writer doesn't think so. How much is grown depends on the amount smoked. Since such a large part of the price of a pack of cigarettes results from taxes and other nongrowing costs (advertising, delivery, and so on), and smokers are not *that* influenced by small changes in price, reductions in the cost of the basic tobacco would not have a great effect on the amount of tobacco smoked. (But the point is not central to Yelverton's argument.)

What is central is his claim that the program itself does not increase either the amount of tobacco grown or the amount smoked. And this claim seems quite plausible.

But his point about all that money raised in excise taxes on tobacco, while true, is irrelevant. The tax on tobacco would be collected whether the program is retained or repealed.

Which brings us to the crux of the matter, namely the disruption of local economies by repeal of the program. The harms he cites are basically two: to local property-tax revenues and to the small tobacco farmers themselves. The first of these does not seem correct, because the large corporation growers he believes would supplant the current small farmers would have to pay local property taxes, just as do the small farmers.

So it comes down to the the current small growers themselves—the value of their land and their ability to compete with large growers. And Yelverton is probably right that repeal would lower the value of tobacco-growing land, at least to some extent, because a decrease in the price of raw tobacco would make the land less profitable to farm, and probably right that repeal would harm their ability to stay in business. This means that the underlying question is whether the federal government should take sides in the economic competition between the current small growers, by continuing the subsidy, and the large corporation who he believes would prevail in an open market. Those who believe in general in a free market in which the government does not ordinarily interfere will answer *no* whereas those who want to keep small farmers in business no matter what the economics are will answer *yes*.

There is one other issue involved in many disputes about subsidies of this kind, illustrated by the case of the subsidy given to most homeowners by the Schedule A federal income tax interest exemption. Suppose that Smith buys a house for a price determined in part by the attractiveness of the interest exemption and then the Congress does away with this exemption (as they discussed doing but didn't in 1985–1986, because of public outcries). Smith then would lose because the value of his house would decline, which many people have said would be unfair to Smith. The issue is exactly the same one that lurks in the background in the tobacco-subsidy case. To be consistent, one must take the same side in both cases, or else show what is different about one than the other. (In fact, these issues usually get settled primarily on the basis of power politics, not rights or wrongs of the matter.)

Exercise 7-5

Here is one person's evaluation of the excerpts from Adolf Hitler's *Mein Kampf* (from the chapter called "Nation and Race"). The chapter starts out this way:

> There are some truths which are so obvious that for this very reason they are not seen or at least not recognized by ordinary people. They sometimes pass by such truisms as though blind and are most astonished when someone suddenly discovers what everyone really ought to know. Columbus's eggs lie around by the hundreds of thousands, but Columbuses are met with less frequently.

So far, all we have is flavoring material, but no substance.

> Thus men without exception wander about in the garden of Nature; they imagine that they know practically everything and yet with few exceptions pass blindly by one of the most patent principles of Nature's rule: the inner segregation of the species of all living beings on this earth.

Now, it's time to mark the page, or make a mental note. Is the thesis going to be the natural segregation of species? If not, is this going to be used later to support some other thesis? The title of the chapter, "Nation and Race," suggests the thesis may be that various human racial groups should not interbreed. (Those with background information about Hitler would be likely to reach the same tentative conclusion.) Let's see.

> Even the most superficial observation shows that Nature's restricted form of propagation and increase is an almost rigid basic law of all the innumerable forms of expression of her vital urge. Every animal mates only with a member of the same species. The titmouse seeks the titmouse, the finch the finch, the stork the stork, the field mouse the field mouse, the dormouse the dormouse, the wolf the she-wolf, etc. . . .

Here we have evidence for the "thesis" (in quotes, because we can't yet be sure it is his thesis) that animals mate only with members of their own species. While not strictly true (closely related animals such as lions and tigers have been mated in captivity), experience shows it is generally true.

> Any crossing of two beings not at exactly the same level produces a medium between the level of the two parents. This means: the offspring will probably stand higher than the racially lower parent, but not as high as the higher one. Consequently, it will later succumb in the struggle against the higher level.

Here is the first substantive statement that seems grossly wrong, in that it seems to contradict any reasonable interpretation of the theory of evolution. For instance, there is reason to say that mating a large dog and a small one will produce medium-sized offspring on the average, but labeling one dog "higher" and the other "lower" seems to be an unwarranted value judgment. Is a Great Dane "higher" than a dachshund?

Notice also that at this point Hitler has to be talking about breeding *within* a species, because he's just argued that breeding doesn't occur between species. So he implies that some races or breeds within a species are "higher" than others. Will he provide evidence for this, showing, say, that German dachshunds are higher or lower than French poodles? Or that Aryans are higher than Latins, Slavs, or Jews? And will he use the idea of higher and lower races (within species) to support the thesis that human races shouldn't interbreed? If so, the acceptability of his reasons supporting his claim that some racial types are "higher" than others may be crucial.

> Such mating is contrary to the will of Nature for a higher breeding of all life. The precondition for this does not lie in associating superior and inferior, but in the total victory of the former. The stronger must dominate and not blend with the weaker, thus sacrificing his own greatness. Only the born weakling can view this as cruel, but he after all is only a weak and limited man; for if this law did not prevail, any conceivable higher development of organic living beings would be unthinkable.

Hitler saw animals evolving from a lower to a higher state, something most of us would deny, although we might agree that there is a tendency to evolve from the simpler to the more complex, as a fly is much more complex than an amoeba. But suppose we allow that more complicated animals are "higher" than less complicated ones. Then it will be true that higher animals don't breed with lower, since only genetically very similar animals breed successfully (like a Great Dane with a dachshund or a lion with a tiger). In this sense, the "will of nature" is against the interbreeding of "higher" with "lower" animals. Of course, it also is against the interbreeding of higher but genetically diverse animals, for instance a lion and a goat.

> The consequence of this urge toward racial purity, universally valid in Nature, is not only the sharp outward delimitation of the various races, but their uniform

character in themselves. The fox is always a fox, the goose a goose, the tiger a tiger, etc., and the difference can lie at most in the varying measure of force, strength, intelligence, dexterity, endurance, etc., of the individual specimens. But you will never find a fox who in his inner attitude might, for example, show humanitarian tendencies toward geese, as similarly there is no cat with a friendly inclination toward mice.

Therefore, here, too, the struggle among themselves arises less from inner aversion than from hunger and love. In both cases, Nature looks on calmly, with satisfaction, in fact. In the struggle for daily bread all those who are weak and sickly or less determined succumb, while the struggle of the males for the female grants the right or opportunity to propagate only to the healthiest. And the struggle is always a means for improving a species' health and power of resistance and, therefore, a cause of its higher development. . . .

Putting aside Hitler's anthropomorphisms (he seems to think of "nature" as a living person) and all sorts of minor errors, we can see what he's getting at. This is his way of saying that species evolve from lesser to greater complexity by competing for food and mates within a species, which certainly is in accord with the main thrust of the theory of evolution (there are exceptions, but they're not important here).

No more than Nature desires the mating of weaker with stronger individuals, even less does she desire the blending of a higher with a lower race, since, if she did, her whole work of higher breeding, over perhaps hundreds of thousands of years, might be ruined with one blow.

Now he is talking about races, not species. So he seems to be saying that just as members of a higher species can't interbreed with those of a lower one, so members of a higher race shouldn't mate with those of a lower. Will he *argue* for this idea that one race is "higher" than another? (Remember, we were willing to allow that some species are higher than others only if he meant by this that they are more complex. But all human races are equally complicated.) And will he justify his move from what he claims *is* the case (that higher species don't interbreed with lower) to what he says *should* be the case (that higher races should not interbreed with lower)?

Historical experience offers countless proofs of this. It shows with terrifying clarity that in every mingling of Aryan blood with that of lower peoples the result was the end of the cultured people. North America, whose population consists in by far the largest part of Germanic elements who mixed but little with the lower colored peoples, shows a different humanity and culture from Central and South America, where the predominantly Latin immigrants often mixed with the aborigines on a large scale. By this one example, we can clearly and distinctly recognize the effect of racial mixture. The Germanic inhabitant of the American continent, who has remained racially pure and unmixed, rose to be master of the continent; he will remain the master as long as he does not fall a victim to defilement of the blood.

This is the second justification Hitler gives in this part of *Mein Kampf* for his ideas on racial superiority. (Elsewhere, he gives similar, equally bad, arguments to support this belief.) The trouble with this argument is that the North American "Aryans" (he thought of the English as Aryan cousins) have been happily interbreeding with Latin Italians, Hispanics, Slavic Russians, and all sorts of other non-Aryan groups, even occasionally including Jews, Orientals, and blacks, yet still are masters of North America. And worse still for Hitler's argument, those foolish Latinos who did interbreed with the natives became and still are the masters of Central and South America.

Anyway, immense amounts of history contradict Hitler's thesis about the superiority of the Aryans. To mention just one point, the most powerful civilizations up to about A.D.

1400 were Chinese, Indian, Egyptian, and so on, never German. So on Hitler's criteria these "races" were superior, or higher. Yet there is no significant genetic difference between, say, Chinese people in A.D. 1000 and today, or between Germans in A.D. 1000 and today. (Hitler also overlooked, probably because he didn't know, or want to know, the fact that his beloved German "race" itself evolved from countless cases of interbreeding with surrounding groups,[1] as virtually all large human populations have.

But the main problems with his argument are two. First, he just assumes that Aryans (Germanic peoples) are a race and are superior to other races. They aren't a race, and, of course, Hitler never provided sensible reasons for thinking they are superior to other peoples. (It is a doctrine of many, perhaps most, peoples that they are superior to others—a classic example, ironic in this context, being the "Chosen" people of the Bible.)

The other great defect in his argument is his implied move from what is more or less true of species—that in general they *cannot* interbreed—to what he claims is true of races—that they *should not* interbreed. Because members of different races can and often do interbreed whereas those of different species cannot, there is no relevant analogy here, and his talk of species is therefore irrelevant. To put the point another way, that different species cannot interbreed is not a good reason for believing different races should not interbreed, given that in fact they can. (This writer's guess is that Hitler did not understand the concept of a law of nature, being misled by the term "law" to see laws of nature more like human laws than in fact they are. This anthropomorphic view of natural laws fits with his similar ideas about Nature and its "will.")

So there isn't much to Hitler's arguments. That they played a part in generating the most destructive war in human history illustrates again the great harm that can lurk in ignorance. Hitler was undoubtedly a smart man, but he also was an ignorant one. In particular, his ignorance of the true principles of evolution and natural selection, coupled no doubt with his neuroticism, made him fair game for charlatans peddling erzatz twaddle about higher and lower races and the like.

Chapter 8, Exercise 8-1

3. *Identification.*

4. *Identification.* Plus implied *promise* that you too can look beautiful if you use Revlon.

7. *Misleading Statement.* When you think of emeralds, you think of gemstones. But these emeralds are not of gem quality. The point is that you should realize *no one* would sell gem-quality emeralds for $5. If you saw an ad for a 1988 Cadillac for, say, $500, wouldn't you assume it had been wrecked, or some such? (Just to be sure, the author of this text answered the ad and received a tiny nongem emerald that a jeweler declared virtually worthless.)

8. *Meaningless Jargon.* "Actizol" is just one of those phony names, like "Platformate," for a widely used ordinary ingredient.

25. Definitely not a fallacious appeal to authority. Concert pianists tend to be extremely fussy about pianos, and while the sheer availability of Steinways tends to increase their use, there can be no doubt that concert pianists prefer Steinway overwhelmingly *and* are more likely to know piano quality than thee and me.

27. *Begged Question.* Saying they've got it down to a science doesn't tell us how they did it. By the way, is the new Kleenex any softer than the old?

---

[1]An oddity of the Nazi period is the fact that Hitler himself did not fit the blond hair–blue eyes Aryan image.

Exercise for the Entire Text

I'll never tell.

Exercise A-4

5. *Contingent.* Its truth or falsity depends on whether politicians do or don't keep campaign promises. If even one does, the statement is false; if none do, it is true.

9. *Tautological.* It is true whether or not all trespassers happen to be shot.

Exercise A-5

1. Since it isn't possible to get both 2 and 12 on a given toss, we can use the restricted disjunction rule. And given that the probability of getting a 2 $= \frac{1}{36}$ and of a 12 $= \frac{1}{36}$, the probability of 2 or 12 $= \frac{1}{36} + \frac{1}{36} = \frac{2}{36} = \frac{1}{18}$.

4. There are 100,000 five-digit numbers, each one equally likely to be picked. Thus, the odds on any given number are 100,000 to 1. So a winning $2 bet should pay $200,000 plus the $2 wagered. (None do.)

Bibliography

Language

Atkinson, Max. *Our Master's Voice: The Language and Body Language of Politics* (New York: Methuen, 1984).

Burns, Roger, and Vogt, George. *Your Government Inaction: Or in God We'd Better Trust . . .* (New York: St. Martin's Press, 1981). (A collection of examples of bureaucratese "from desks and cabinets throughout government.")

Carroll, Lewis. *Alice's Adventures in Wonderland* (New York: New American Library, 1960). Reprint.

Enright, D.J. *Fair of Speech* (New York: Oxford University Press, 1985).

Frank, Francine, and Anshen, Frank. *Languages and the Sexes* (Albany, N.Y.: SUNY Press, 1983).

Green, Jonathan. *Newspeak: A Dictionary of Jargon* (Boston: Routledge, 1984).

*"Guidelines for Equal Treatment of the Sexes in McGraw-Hill Book Company Publications." (Eleven page in-house statement of policy that has been generally adopted in the publishing business).

Hall, Edward T. *The Silent Language* (New York: Doubleday, 1973).

*Jones, Gregory M. "Confessions of a Reg Writer." *Quarterly Review of Doublespeak* (July 1981).

*Hilgartner, Stephen; Bell, Richard; and O'Connor, Rory. *Nukespeak: Nuclear Language, Visions and Mindset* (San Francisco: Sierra Club Books, 1982).

LaFalce, Rep. John J. "The Packaging of Public Policy: Government by Euphemism and Slogan." *Vital Speeches of the Day* (February 1, 1982).

Lutz, William. "Notes Toward a Description of Doublespeak." *Quarterly Review of Doublespeak,* (January 1987).

Orwell, George. *Nineteen Eighty-Four* (New York: New American Library, 1949). (Shows how language control helps control thoughts, and thus behavior.)

*_____ "Politics and the English Language." Reprinted in *A Collection of Works by George Orwell* (New York: Harcourt Brace Jovanovich, 1946).

Cogent Reasoning

Carroll, Lewis. *Symbolic Logic and the Game of Logic* (New York: Dover, 1958).

*Kahane, Howard. *Logic and Philosophy,* 5th ed. (Belmont, Calif.: Wadsworth, 1986). (A mostly formal logic text.)

Lemmon, E. J. *Beginning Logic* (revised by G.N.D. Barry). (Indianapolis, Ind.: Hackett, 1978). (A strictly formal logic text.)

Impediments to Cogent Reasoning

Gardner, Martin. *Science: Good, Bad, and Bogus* (Buffalo, N.Y.: Prometheus, 1981). (Debunking of pseudoscience.)

_____. *Fads and Fallacies in the Name of Science* (New York: Dover, 1957). (The classic debunking of pseudoscience.)

---

*Asterisks indicate items mentioned in the text.

*Goleman, Daniel. *Vital Lies, Simple Truths* (New York: Simon & Schuster, 1985). (The best understandable explanation of recent scientific ideas about self-deception, its biological functions, and the unconscious.)

*MacKay, Charles. *Memoirs of Extraordinary Popular Delusions and the Madness of Crowds* (New York: Harmony Books, 1980). (Reprint of 1841 edition, with foreword by Andrew Tobias.)

Nickell, Joe. *Inquest on the Shroud of Turin* (Buffalo, N.Y.: Prometheus, 1982). (An example of sanity on a foolishness-provoking topic.)

Nisbet, Robert. *Prejudices* (Cambridge, Mass.: Harvard University Press, 1986).

Paul, Richard. "Teaching Critical Thinking in the 'Strong' Sense: A Focus on Self-Deception, World Views, and a Dialectical Mode of Analysis." *Informal Logic* (May 1982).

Peirce, Charles Sanders. "The Fixation of Belief." *Popular Science Monthly* (1877) (A classic article by America's premier philosopher.)

*Rice, Berkeley. "O Tempora, O Cult." *Psychology Today* (March 1979).

*Twain, Mark. *Mark Twain on the Damned Human Race,* ed. by Janet Smith (New York: Hill & Wang, 1962). (The great American humorist on all sorts of human foibles.)

Fallacious Reasoning

Bentham, Jeremy. *The Handbook of Political Fallacies* (New York: Harper Torchbooks, 1962). (A classic nineteenth-century tract.)

Broad, C. D. "Some Fallacies in Political Thinking." *Philosophy 29* (April 1950). (Interesting article by important twentieth-century philosopher.)

Cerf, Christopher, and Navasky, Victor. *The Experts Speak: The Definitive Compendium of Authoritative Misinformation* (New York: Pantheon, 1984).

Chase, Stuart. *Guides to Straight Thinking* (New York: Harper & Row, 1962).

*Green, Mark, and McCall, Gail. *There He Goes Again: Ronald Reagan's Reign of Error* (New York: Pantheon, 1983). (A disheartening compendium of Ronald Reagan's contradictions, falsehoods, and erroneous public remarks.)

Hamblin, C. L. *Fallacies* (Newport News, Va.: Vale Press, 1986). (A reprint with new preface of the definitive history of fallacy theory.)

Huff, Darrell. *How to Lie with Statistics* (New York: Norton, 1954).

*Kahane, Howard. "The Nature and Classification of Fallacies." In *Informal Logic: The First International Symposium,* ed. by J. Anthony Blair and Ralph H. Johnson. (Inverness, Calif.: Edgepress, 1980).

Kinsley, Michael. "The Art of Polling." *The New Republic* (June 20, 1981).

*Miller, James Nathan. "Ronald Reagan and the Techniques of Deception." *Atlantic Magazine* (February 1984). (Nice illustration of how statistics can be misused for political advantage.)

Morgan, Chris, and Langford, David. *Facts and Fallacies: A Book of Definitive Mistakes and Misguided Predictions* (Exeter, England: Webb & Bower, 1981). (One of several excellent books illustrating expert feet of clay.)

Morgenstern, Oscar. "Qui Numerare Incipit Errare Incipit." *Fortune* (October, 1963). (Still one of the best explanations of how government statistics on business and such can be and are manipulated for political purposes.)

Smith, H. B. *How the Mind Falls into Error* (Darby Books, 1980). (Reprint of the 1923 edition.)

Thouless, Robert H. *Straight and Crooked Thinking* (New York: Simon & Schuster, 1932).

Wheeler, Michael. *Lies, Damn Lies, and Statistics: The Manipulation of Public Opinion in America* (New York: Dell Laurel Edition, 1977).

Analyzing and Constructing Extended Arguments

Cavender, Nancy, and Weiss, Len. *Thinking/Writing* (Belmont, Calif.: Wadsworth, 1987).

Cavender, Nancy, and Kahane, Howard. *A Critical Thinking Reader/Rhetoric* (Belmont, Calif.: Wadsworth, 1988).

Flew, Antony. *Thinking Straight* (Buffalo, N.Y.: Prometheus, 1977).

Lanham, Richard. *Revising Prose* (New York: Scribner, 1979). (A good guide to clear writing.)

St. Aubyn, Giles. *The Art of Argument* (Buchanan, N.Y.: Emerson Books, 1962). (A beautifully written little book on argument.)

Weston, Anthony. *A Rulebook for Arguments* (Indianapolis, Ind.: Hackett, 1987).

Advertising

Baker, Samm Sinclair. *The Permissible Lie* (Cleveland: World Publishing, 1968).

*Beiler, David. *The Classics of Political Television Advertising: A Viewer's Guide* (Washington, D.C.: Campaigns and Elections, 1986). (Companion guide to 60-minute video cassette containing some of the great TV campaign spots. Great fun and educational too.)

*Benn, Alec. *The 27 Most Common Mistakes in Advertising* (New York: AMACOM, 1978).

Diamond, Edwin, and Bates, Stephen. *The Spot: The Rise of Political Advertising on Television* (Cambridge, Mass. MIT Press, 1984).

*Feldstein, Mark. "Mail Fraud on Capitol Hill." *Washington Monthly* (October, 1979).

*Glatzer, Robert. *The New Advertising: The Great Campaigns from Avis to Volkswagen* (New York: Citadel Press, 1970).

*Gunther, Max. "Commercials. Can you Believe Them?" *TV Guide* (December 2, 1982).

*Hopkins, Claude. *Scientific Advertising* (New York: Crown, 1966). (One of the classics on advertising.)

*Lemann, Nicholas. "The Storcks." *Washington Post Magazine* (December 7, 1980).

*_____. "Barney Frank's Mother and 500 Postmen." *Harper's* (April 1983).

*A. Kent MacDougall. "Market-Shelf Proliferation—Public Pays." *Los Angeles Times* (May 27, 1979).

McGinnis, Joe. *The Selling of the President 1968* (New York: Trident Press, 1969). (Still the best account of a presidential campaign.)

Newsom, Doug, and Scott, Alan. *This is PR: The Realities of Public Relations* (Belmont, Calif.: Wadsworth, 1981).

*Ogilvie, David. *Confessions of an Advertising Man* (New York: Atheneum, 1963).

*Preston, Ivan. *The Great American Blowup: Puffery in Advertising and Selling* (Madison: University of Wisconsin Press, 1975).

*Rowsome, Frank, Jr. *They Laughed When I Sat Down* (New York: Bonanza Books, 1959). (Perhaps still the most interesting book on the history of advertising.)

Managing the News

*Barber, James David. "Not the New York Times: What Network News Should Be." *Washington Monthly* (September 1979).

*Boot, William. "Iranscam: When the cheering stopped." *Columbia Journalism Review* (March/April 1987).

Brand, Stewart; Kelly, Kevin; and Kinney, Jay. "Digital Retouching: The End of Truth in Photography." *This World* (November 24, 1985).

Breslin, Jimmy. "Guilty Makes Larger Headlines than Innocent." Syndicated column, June 19, 1980.

"Broadcasting and the First Amendment." *Cato Policy Report* (May/June 1984).

"Censors at Work." *The Progressive* (April 1984).

*Cockburn, Alexander. "The Pundit's Art." *Harper's* (December 1980).

*Cohen, Richard. "Making Trends Meet." *Washington Post Magazine* (September 28, 1986). (How *Time* and *Newsweek* exaggerate and invent trends and fashions.)

Cross, Donna Woolfolk, *Mediaspeak: How Television Makes up Your Mind* (New York: Signet Mentor, 1983).

English, Deirdre. "Brokaw: Seen but Not Heard?" *Mother Jones* (July 1983).

*Harrison, S. L. "CPB: Prime Time Pablum: How Politics and Corporate Influence Keep Public TV Harmless." *Washington Monthly* (January 1986).

Hertsgaard, Mark. "Foul-Ups, Bleeps, and Blunders." *The Village Voice* (October 30, 1984).

Hickey, Neil. "Henry Kissinger and TV: 'Did I Sometimes Use the Press? Yes.', " *TV Guide* (April 2, 1983).

Hitchens, Christopher. "Blabscam: TV's Rigged Political Talk Shows." *Harper's* (March 1986).

Hitt, Jack. "Warning: CIA Censors at Work." *Columbia Journalism Review* (July/August 1984).

Kalter, Jeanmarie. "Exposing Media Myths: TV Doesn't Affect You as Much as You Think." *TV Guide* (May 30–June 5, 1987).

King, Larry L. "How Good Are TV's News Analysts?" *TV Guide* (January 25, 1986).

*Knightly, Phillip. *The First Casualty* (New York: Harcourt Brace Jovanovich, 1975).

Lapham, Lewis H. "Gilding the News." *Harper's* (July 1981).

*Levine, Richard M. "Polish Government Versus the Workers: Why TV Is the Prized Weapon." *TV Guide* (November 7, 1981).

*Millman, Joel. "How the Press Distorts the News from Central America." *The Progressive* (October, 1984).

Panem, Sandra, and Vilcek, Jan. "Interferon and the Cure of Cancer." *Atlantic Monthly* (December 1982). (Documents poor media coverage of a science story).

Parenti, Michael. *Inventing Reality: The Politics of the Mass Media* (New York: St. Martin's, 1986).

Shevchenko, Arkady N. "Danger: The Networks Are Misreading the Russians." *TV Guide* (August 9, 1986).

*Smiley, Xan. "Misunderstanding Africa." *Atlantic Monthly* (September 1982). (How government intimidation and interference mangles news from Africa.)

Toffler, Alvin. *The Third Wave* (New York: Morrow, 1980). (Interesting ideas on the import of the media.)

Ullman, John, and Honeyman, Steve. *The Reporter's Handbook: An Investigator's Guide to Documents and Techniques* (New York: St. Martins, 1985).

Weisman, John. "Stories You Won't See on the Nightly News." *TV Guide* (March 1, 1980).

*_____. "Intimidation." *TV Guide* (October 23–30, 1982). (How brutal treatment of foreign correspondents results in slanted news.)

Westin, Av. "Inside the Evening News: How TV Really Works." *New York* (October 18, 1982).

*Wicker, Tom. *On Press* (New York: Viking Press, 1978). (How local power can influence the news.)

Textbooks: Managing World Views

American Indian Historical Society. *Textbooks and the American Indian* (San Francisco: Indian Historical Press, 1970).

Barzun, Jacques. "The Wasteland of American Education." *New York Review of Books* (November 5, 1981).

*Black, Hillel. *The American Schoolbook* (New York: Morrow, 1967).

Carlson, Peter. "A Chilling Case of Censorship." *Washington Post Magazine* (January 4, 1987).

Cohen, Muriel. "Critics Say Textbooks Dull, Call for Higher Standards." *Boston Globe* (December 1, 1985; paired with "Textbook Publishing is Profitable but Controlled").

*Elson, Ruth M. *Guardians of Tradition: American Schoolbooks of the 19th Century* (Lincoln: University of Nebraska Press, 1964).

Epstein, Noel. "Stop Giving a Bad Name to Schoolbook 'Censorship.' " *Washington Post* (March 14, 1982).

Fitzgerald, Frances. *America Revised* (New York: Random House, 1980). (A very famous, highly regarded, but in this writer's view misguided, critique of public school texts.)

"Governments Flunk History. . . Rewriting the Textbooks." *Inquiry* (October, 1982).

*"History/Social Science Framework for California Public Schools, Kindergarten Through Grade Twelve." (The basic document governing California schools.)

*Kirk, Donald. "Japan Rearms Its School Books." *Nation* (December 19, 1981).

"Mind Control Through Textbooks." *Phi Delta Cappa* (October 1982).

*Nelson, Jack, and Roberts, Gene. *The Censors and the Schools* (Boston: Little, Brown, 1963). (The best book on the topic up to 1963.)

*Schrank, Jeffrey. *Understanding Mass Media,* 2nd ed. (Skokie, Ill.: National Textbook Co., 1986.) (One of the best public school social science texts.)

Zinn, Howard. *A People's History of the United States* (New York: Harper & Row, 1980). (Perhaps the easiest to understand antidote to the history learned via public school history texts.)

List of Publications

One of the themes of this text is that good reasoning requires good information sources. Here is a selected list of (primarily) non-mass media periodicals (mostly on social/political issues or science) with one person's brief comments:

American Heritage.   The most interesting history magazine, giving fascinating details on American history. Good antidote to dull public school history texts.

Amnesty Action.   Publication of Amnesty International reporting on government torture around the world; makes one appreciate living in a democratic society.

Atlantic Monthly.   Very good general-issue magazine, with some fiction.

Columbia Journalism Review.   Perhaps the best journalism publication.

Commentary.   Neoconservative, establishment, overrated.

Consumer Reports.   Publication of Consumers Union, an unbiased, nonprofit organization; very good source of information about consumer products.

The Economist.   Quite good British news weekly concentrating on business news.

Foreign Affairs.   Establishment quarterly very influential in government; overrated.

Harper's.   Very good general-issue monthly; the *Harper's Index* has become very popular.

Harvard Medical School Health Letter.   Reasonably reliable medical information.

Inquiry.   Libertarian publication.

Mother Jones.   Successor to *Ramparts;* radical left viewpoint, with good exposes.

Ms.   Magazine of the women's movement.

The Nation.   Long-established left-wing magazine; sometimes very good.

National Geographic.   The most successful special topic monthly.

National Review.   Bill Buckley's rag; the most interesting conservative magazine.

Natural History.   Publication of the American Museum of Natural History.
*The New Republic.   Long-established liberal magazine undergoing metamorphosis.
*Newsletter on Intellectual Freedom.   American Library Association newsletter; contains lists of censored books.
*Newsweek.   Perhaps the best of the mass-circulation news weeklies.
*New Yorker.   Very long, sometimes very good article in each issue, along with good cartoons and information on events in New York.
*New York Review of Books.   Very good left-wing publication with sometimes excellent reviews and letters to the editor combat.
Nucleus.   Quarterly report of the Union of Concerned Scientists.
Policy Report.   Detailed, stuffy libertarian publication of the Cato Institute.
The Progressive.   Interesting left-wing publication.
*Psychology Today.   The best of a bad lot of popular psychology magazines.
*Quarterly Review of Doublespeak. Excellent on current uses of doublespeak, euphemisms, and other linguistic devices used to con.
Reason.   Perhaps the most interesting of the libertarian (pro free enterprise, con big government) publications.
Science News.   Very good weekly on what's new in science.
Scientific American.   Excellent science monthly; difficult going for lay readers.
*Skeptical Inquirer.   The best periodical on pseudoscience.
*Soviet Life.   Slick, picture-filled propaganda monthly by Soviet government, which makes the oppressive dictatorship in Russia seem like a wonderful place to live.
Technology Review.   Good publication of the Massachusetts Institute of Technology.
*Time.   Much improved mass-circulation news weekly.
*TV Guide.   The best and most readable magazine on TV; ironically, the largest selling magazine in the United States.
*The Village Voice.   Left wing; very good political exposès, Feiffer cartoons, lots on events in New York.
*The Washington Monthly.   This writer's favorite magazine on how our system works and might be improved; neoliberal.
The Wilson Quarterly.   Excellent summaries of articles in other magazines, plus readable and intelligent articles on many subjects.

Indexes

Index of Topics

Index of Magazines and Newspapers

Index of Names